A Guidebook to Historic W

A Guidebook to

Historic
Western Pennsylvania

GEORGE SWETNAM
and
HELENE SMITH

University of Pittsburgh Press

First printing 1976
Second printing 1977

Copyright © 1976, University of Pittsburgh Press
All rights reserved
Feffer and Simons, Inc., London
Manufactured in the United States of America

Library of Congress Cataloging in Publication Data

Swetnam, George.
  A guidebook to historic western Pennsylvania.

  Bibliography: p. 263
  Includes index.
  1. Pennsylvania—Description and travel—
1951–   —Guide-books.   2. Historic sites—Penn-
sylvania—Guide-books.   I. Smith, Helen Catherine
Snyder, joint author.   II. Title.
F147.3.S98   917.48'04'4   75-33421
ISBN 0-8229-3316-0
ISBN 0-8229-5271-8 pbk.

The county maps were drawn by Barbara A. Roby.
The photographs of sites were taken by the authors.

The publication of this book is supported
by grants from the William K. Fitch Fund and
the Vira I. Heinz Fund of The Pittsburgh Foundation
and from The Hunt Foundation.

Contents

About the Authors

George Swetnam was a staff writer for the *Pittsburgh Press* for thirty years. He has written several books on western Pennsylvania history, and his articles and stories have appeared in many publications. Helene Smith, a free-lance artist and writer, is co-author with Dr. Swetnam of a children's book, *Hannah's Town,* and two historical dramas, one presented for the Westmoreland County Bicentennial in 1973, the other for the Blairsville Sesquicentennial in 1975. They have visited over fifteen hundred locations in western Pennsylvania and have driven more than fifteen thousand miles, researching and photographing the sites.

Acknowledgments

Many people have helped us in preparing this book, and to them we would like to express our particular appreciation.

Our greatest debt must go to our spouses, Ruth Swetnam and Wayne Smith, who accompanied us on trips to many sites and who were patient throughout the many steps of writing and publishing this book.

In a guidebook to historic places there are an astronomical number of facts, and the chance for errors to slip by is great. The following authorities helped to eliminate these errors by checking over the material for specific counties: Allegheny County, Robert C. Alberts, Joseph G. Smith, and Helen M. Wilson, all of The Historical Society of Western Pennsylvania. Armstrong County, K. D. Colbert of the Armstrong County Historical and Museum Society. Beaver County, Frank F. Carver of the Beaver Area Heritage Foundation. Bedford County, William Jordan of the Bedford County Heritage Commission. Blair County, Fred E. Long of the Blair County Historical Society. Butler County, June M. Cannard of the Butler County Courthouse and John Wise and his staff at the *Butler Eagle*. Cambria County, Betty Moyer of the Johnstown Flood Museum and Betty Mulhollen of the Cambria County Historical Society. Cameron County, Edna H. Bowser of the Cameron County Historical Society. Clarion County, Edna Jean Black of the Pennsylvania Record Press. Clearfield County, Joseph A. Dague, Jr., of the Clearfield County Historical Society and George A. Scott of *The Progress*. Crawford County, Robert D. Ilisevich of the Crawford County Historical Society and James B. Stevenson of the *Titusville Herald*. Elk County, Mary C. McMahon and Alice L. Wessman, both of the Elk County Historical Society. Erie County, Helen Andrews and Clare Swisher, both of the Erie County Historical Society. Fayette County, I. N. Hagan and Eleanor Roland of the Connellsville Area Historical Society. Forest County, Ronald Childs of the Sarah Stewart Bovard Memorial Library. Greene County, Josephine Denny of the Greene County Historical Society. Indiana County, Frances S. Helman and Clarence Stephenson, both of the Indiana County Historical and Genealogical Society. Jefferson County, James H. Sterrett of Geneva College. Lawrence County, Bart Richards of the Lawrence County Historical Society. McKean County, Marian Bromeley of the Bradford Landmark Society, Joseph M. Cleary of Bradford Publications, Inc., and Merle E. Dickinson of the McKean County Historical Society. Mercer County, the *Sharon Herald* and Orvis Anderson of the Mercer County Historical Society. Venango County, James B. Stevenson of the *Titusville Herald*. Warren County, Ernest C. Miller and Chase Putnam, both of the Warren County Historical Association, and James B. Stevenson of the *Titusville Herald*. Washington County, Washington-Greene County Tourist Promotion Agency, West Middletown Historical Center. Westmoreland County, Calvin E. Pollins of the Westmoreland County Historical Society.

Particular thanks go to Marie Zini and the staff of the Pennsylvania Room, Carnegie Library of Pittsburgh, and to Sara L. Rowley and her staff at Hillman Library, University of Pittsburgh.

Others who have helped in various ways include Arthur L. Altman, Ray Austin, Mae Beringer, Joe Borkowski, Eileen Clark, Patricia Cochran, John Coleman, Anna Connors, Jo Cornish, Wendy Cox, Peggy Fields, John B. Gibson, William Graff, Frank

ACKNOWLEDGMENTS

Hood, Thomas C. Imler, Jean Kaufman, Karl Koch, Alvin Laidley, George Melvin, June Millison, Lester R. Mohr, Thomas Moore, Frank Piper, Joseph A. Plunkett, Michael Robbe, Peg Robinson, Lucille Senko, Paul Shaffer, Dorothy Sloan, Helen Cestello Smith, John B. Snyder, Mary Snyder, Arthur Stewart, Charmaine Stickel, Helen Stuebgen, Patricia Truschel, V. E. Whisker, A. D. White, Margaret White, Edward G. Williams, and Richard Wright. There were scores of people in all twenty-six counties who helped with information pertaining to their own and nearby historic properties.

And finally but far from least we want to thank Frederick A. Hetzel, Director of the University of Pittsburgh Press, and Louise Craft, Editor, for their patience and assistance.

Introduction

In days to come, when your children ask you what these stones mean, you shall tell them.

Joshua 4:7

It has long been recognized that succeeding generations, as well as newcomers and visitors to any area, have a proper—even laudable—curiosity about unusual or outstanding landscape features that they discover and about where to find those attractions they have heard of. This is the third historical guidebook to western Pennsylvania—an area remarkably full of history and wonders—to be published by the University of Pittsburgh Press. The first, compiled largely from correspondence during the great survey of the area's cultural history (sponsored by the Historical Society of Western Pennsylvania in the 1930s), was *Guidebook to Historic Places in Western Pennsylvania,* published in 1938. The second, a far more carefully prepared and comprehensive work, was *A Traveler's Guide to Historic Western Pennsylvania* by Lois Mulkearn and Edwin V. Pugh in 1954. Both books have been out of print for many years.

The necessity for a succession of guidebooks to the area is evident upon even brief consideration. A great many changes have occurred since Mulkearn and Pugh produced their work. Roads, road numbers, and travel patterns have changed, so that in numerous instances old directions for reaching a place no longer apply. Changes render former descriptions inaccurate; new facts are discovered; and unfortunately many historic structures have disappeared during the past twenty-two years, falling victim to the elements, fire, floods, and the wrecking-ball and bulldozer. Often not a trace remains. Events give interest to new places. In addition, any survey is sure to miss some locations of real worth.

This third guidebook differs from its predecessors in a number of respects. The most obvious is the omission of Potter County, thus covering twenty-six instead of the former twenty-seven counties. The reason for this change is apparent on laying a ruler over the map of Pennsylvania along the meridian of Potter's western, then along its eastern edge. The western meridian bisects Cameron County but runs along or very near the eastern edges of the other easternmost western Pennsylvania counties: McKean, Elk, Clearfield, Blair, and Bedford. The center of Potter County is appreciably nearer the eastern than the western border of the state. And a line along the meridian of Potter's eastern boundary would include all of Fulton and Huntingdon Counties, and well over half of Clinton, Centre, Mifflin, and Franklin Counties. Regretfully, but constrained by consistency, we have used the western line as our limit.

Another difference has been a sharply decreased emphasis on aboriginal, colonial, and early Federal history, in line with our conviction that history is a living and ongoing study, not simply concerned with something that happened a long time ago. While we believe we have done justice to the earlier periods and for good reason have limited the space allotted to recent matters, we feel that history is continuous and undividable, except for practical necessities.

A third difference is the greatly increased number of sites included. The first guidebook had a total of about 600, which covered nonexistent forts, stone iron furnace ruins, towns in general, and locations where events occurred, with a separate addition of travelways. Mulkearn and Pugh included 637 sites, almost half of them names and history, where nothing remained to be seen. The present book contains more than twice that number, all showing enough still remaining that the writers felt rewarded for visiting them. We omitted lists of forts and blockhouses. These are described in detail in *Report of the Commission to Locate the Site of the Frontier Forts of Pennsylvania* edited by Thomas L. Montgomery (see Bibliography). However, we did include the travelways and Indian paths in the capsule histories that introduce each county; and following the entries for each county is a list of all the Pennsylvania Historical and Museum Commission markers for the convenience of those who pass them on the highway so fast that they cannot read what site is indicated by the sign. The text of each is available in *Guide to the Historical Markers of Pennsylvania* by Henry A. Haas, available from the Pennsylvania Historical and Museum Commission, Harrisburg.

But by far the most important difference between this book and its predecessors is the outcome of our feeling that a guidebook is neither a history text nor a handbook of places and dates. Essentially a guidebook should present the reader with places where there is *something to be seen,* give a part of their story, and provide information on *how to get there.* For this reason we have omitted many sites of important events where no physical remains exist. It is discouraging to drive thirty-five miles to a spot where all you can see is a guardrail in the middle of the Pennsylvania Turnpike. The historian who is deeply concerned with every possible aspect of the event will be too well versed in his specialty to need our help in finding its exact location; most others would feel the trip only a waste of time.

No doubt critical readers will be surprised at the inclusion of certain sites and the omission of others. This is their right, as was recognized in the old proverb, "There is no arguing about tastes." We have included those places which we feel are most likely to interest the greatest number and widest variety of readers and history buffs. To a certain extent, the appeal of sites may depend on their rarity as well as their importance in other respects. In or near Pittsburgh, for instance, a log house is unusual; in Bedford County, where over five hundred log homes are still in daily use, it draws only a yawn. A mansion in the more sparsely populated counties will quickly attract attention and questions; on millionaire's row in East Liberty in Allegheny County it might not be noticed. An early stone house is a landmark in some areas; Washington County is full of them.

We have omitted many worthwhile sites in order to avoid duplication, as well as to conserve space. Only a few of the area's 184 early stone blast furnaces are included for this reason: the field has been thoroughly and accurately covered in *Guide to Old Stone Blast Furnaces in Western Pennsylvania* by Myron Sharp and William H. Thomas, available at a low price from the Historical Society of Western Pennsylvania. Material on covered bridges may be obtained from the Theodore Burr Covered Bridge Society. Many houses of principally architectural interest, especially in Allegheny County, have been passed over so as not to duplicate *The Architectural Heritage of Early Western Pennsylvania* by Charles Morse Stotz (see Bibliography) and *Landmark Architecture of Allegheny County, Pennsylvania* by James D. Van Trump and Arthur P.

Ziegler, Jr., available from the Pittsburgh History and Landmarks Foundation.

The order of the sites has proved a considerable problem, especially in the older, more populous and historically rich counties. Although it has appeared inadvisable to attempt a continuous tour arrangement, we have tried, in general, to keep places close together in the chapter if they are so geographically. However, necessary choices as to whether to turn right or left have sometimes resulted in sites not far apart in space being many pages away from one another. We hope the reader will bear in mind that the place-to-place course which may seem logical to him would have created additional problems for us.

In fixing locations we have tried to be as exact and accurate as possible. But at least half of the more than fifteen thousand miles required for the trips was covered in a foreign car whose odometer registered only miles—no fractions. The frequently used abbreviation *l.r.* stands for legislative route, a five-digit designation often found on small white signs at intersections. We have used *t.* in similar situations with even less important roads, to indicate township roads. These signs, usually with three-digit numbers, are commonly indicated in the same fashion as legislative routes. In some counties legislative and township routes are infrequently marked; in a few, not at all. When this is the case we have tried to use commonly known local designations, as minor route numbers are not well known even when marked. Locations are often hard to designate briefly, but local residents are usually helpful, if properly approached.

Hours and admission charges of museums and other public buildings are subject to change. The reader might be wise to call or write before going to considerable difficulty in visiting them. Fewer than 10 percent of the sites include any charge for the visitor.

Since more than half the houses listed are private residences, we have marked them so only when requested by the owners or occupants. These have been included because at least the outside may be seen. All houses should be assumed to be private unless obviously public. Please do not think that because a house is listed in this guide, everyone has a right to go charging into it.

Each chapter is introduced with a short history of the county. All county areas and populations in these capsule histories are taken from the *Rand-McNally Commercial Atlas and Marketing Guide* (1973) and the 1970 census.

Those who search carefully may find some errors in this book. While we have visited every site and photographed all but a few that were not suited to pictures, we have included many about which hard documentary proof either does not exist or could not be located by a reasonable amount of searching. In such cases, we have used the best information available, combining evidence of physical facts with local tradition when the former appeared to corroborate the latter. At a tavern where one of us was asking for information on ownership of a landmark, a smart aleck butted in with, "If you want to be authentic, you ought to go to the courthouse and look up the records." We did not bother to remind him that in some counties, including the one we were in, many early records had been destroyed; or that for about 1,300 sites, such searches—for which lawyers usually charge a minimum of $500 each—would require either years of time or a budget of more than half a million dollars.

At times we have rejected previously published statements because they could not be made to agree with other known facts. The printed page is not sacrosanct. Early writers could twist facts or make mistakes as readily as later informants. We trust that our judgments in our researching and interviewing have been sound.

It had originally been planned that Mrs. Smith would do only historical research and Dr. Swetnam the writing, but it did not work out that way. Mrs. Smith wrote all the capsule histories of the counties and was principally responsible for Erie, Mercer, and Westmoreland Counties. Dr. Swetnam was chiefly responsible for Cameron, Clarion, Clearfield, Elk, Forest, Jefferson, McKean, and Warren. Work on the other fifteen counties was done jointly or divided in various proportions. But each of us read, edited, and corrected the other's copy so thoroughly that it would be madness to attempt giving credit or fixing blame individually. The final form of the material is a result of cooperation between the authors and the editor and sometimes reflects compromises made by both.

Many a reader, no doubt, will note omissions startling enough to make him say—as we have said of others—"How could they have missed that?" One of the hardest parts of the preparation was deciding where to draw the line between what to include and what to leave out. In a way, that is good. We do not want to rob the reader of the delight of discovering things for himself. Just keep your eyes open; there's plenty to find.

A Guidebook to Historic Western Pennsylvania

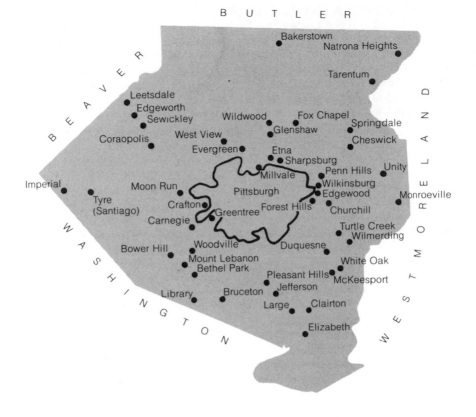

Allegheny County

Capsule History

Allegheny County took its name from the river, which in turn derived its title from the Allegewi, an early Indian tribe of the area which was vanquished by the Iroquois before the French exploration. The county, erected out of Westmoreland and Washington Counties on September 24, 1788, embraced all of what was then the northwestern portion of Pennsylvania. It was soon increased by additional territory from Washington County and in 1792 by Pennsylvania's purchase of the Erie Triangle from New York. In 1800 it was reduced by the formation of the northwestern counties. Today its area is a modest 728 square miles, with a population of 1,605,133—second only to Philadelphia County.

A number of Indian trails traversed Allegheny County, most of them converging at Shannopinstown, now Lawrenceville. The four most important were the Raystown,

Kiskiminetas, Venango-Shannopin, and Nemacolin's Paths. The *Raystown Path,* largely followed by John Forbes from Bedford, had two branches: one entered the county near Pitcairn, continued along the Old Greensburg Pike, going through Forest Hills to Wilkinsburg, and entered the Golden Triangle on Penn Avenue; a second ran through Monroeville and followed the curving ridge through East Liberty and Bloomfield. The *Kiskiminetas Path* crossed the Allegheny River just above Tarentum and followed the right bank past the Point. The *Venango-Shannopin Path* crossed the Allegheny near its mouth and passed through Manchester, West View, Perrysville, Wexford, and Warrendale, thence heading toward Evans City. *Nemacolin's Path,* principally followed by the Braddock Expedition, traced Long Run into McKeesport, crossed the Monongahela below that place and again at the mouth of Turtle Creek, and passed through Braddock (site of Braddock's defeat in 1755), joining the Raystown Path at Forest Hills.

Other Indian trails included the *Catfish Path,* which ran from the Point through the West End, Carnegie, and Bridgeville, thence southwest to the Washington County line; two *Kuskusky* paths, one from below Tarentum paralleling Bull Creek to the Butler County line, and the other leaving the Venango-Shannopin trail at the headwaters of Girty's Run and running north of Pa. 856 to the northeast corner of the county; the *Sewickley Old Town Path,* which ran south from Logan's Ferry through New Texas and Trafford to the Westmoreland County line; and the *Great Path* from Pittsburgh to Detroit, which followed the right bank of the Allegheny and Ohio Rivers in this county.

At the time of British settlement three Indian towns existed in Allegheny County. Shannopinstown was in the Lawrenceville area below the Washington Crossing Bridge, which memorializes the narrow escape of George Washington and Christopher Gist when their raft upset on December 29, 1753. A Delaware Indian town, home of Chief Shingas, was located at McKees Rocks. In 1752 Queen Allaquippa, the old Delaware ruler, and her following were living directly across the Ohio from that point, but she later had her village on the Youghiogheny River, near McKeesport. Chartiers Town was at the site of Tarentum until 1745, when it was abandoned by the Shawnee Indians, who moved to the Wabash River to be nearer the French.

George Croghan, "king of the traders," had a home and trading post in the upper end of Lawrenceville from before 1750 until it was burned during the Revolution. In 1749 he purchased from the Indians two immense areas including most of present-day Pittsburgh, and these were confirmed in the first treaty of Fort Stanwix in 1768. But the Crown refused to approve the purchase, and the rights were worthless when he transferred them to his creditor, Bernard Gratz, in 1775. John Fraser, a blacksmith driven out of the area farther north by the French, lived at the mouth of Turtle Creek in 1753.

The Point, now Pittsburgh's Golden Triangle, was a wooded area when George Washington recommended it as a site for a fort. A company sent out by the Ohio Company of Virginia began Fort Saint (or Prince) George there early in 1754, but were driven off by the French, who rebuilt it as Fort Duquesne. They held it until 1758, defeating a British force under Brig. Gen. Edward Braddock near the mouth of Turtle Creek on July 9, 1755, but blew up the fort in November 1758, at the approach of Maj. Gen. John Forbes. Upon taking over the land, Forbes immediately named the area for William Pitt, British secretary of state, and ordered the construction of both a temporary fort and the tremendous Fort Pitt, largest British fortification in America, which was built of brick and earth in 1759–60. It withstood a siege during Pontiac's

Rebellion in 1763, and Col. John Campbell laid out four blocks of a town during the following year.

During the border dispute with Virginia, Dr. John Connolly took over Fort Pitt in 1774, renaming it Fort Dunmore, for the governor of Virginia; and at the beginning of the Revolution it was occupied by Virginia troops under Col. John Neville. The dispute was settled by the two states in 1780 and was marked by the completion of the Mason and Dixon line two years later. In 1784 Col. George Woods laid out the town as far as Grant Street.

After the Revolution, Fort Pitt was dismantled and sold. It was replaced in 1792 by Fort Fayette, bounded by Penn Avenue, the Allegheny River, and Ninth and Tenth Streets, which was torn down just before the opening of the War of 1812 and in turn replaced by the Allegheny Arsenal in Lawrenceville.

Boat-building on the Allegheny and Monongahela Rivers became the county's first industry. Barges, keelboats, and ocean-going ships were constructed in the area, and in 1811 Nicholas Roosevelt built the *New Orleans*—first steamboat on western waters—on the Monongahela about half a mile above the Point.

Iron-making quickly became the principal industry, especially during and after the War of 1812. Since pig iron was available from nearby areas, no considerable amount of iron was smelted within the county until after the general adoption of coke as a fuel in 1859. The county had two stone blast furnaces. Glass was also a very important industry throughout the nineteenth century. In 1795 James O'Hara and Isaac Craig were the first glass manufacturers in western Pennsylvania.

Pittsburgh suffered a disastrous fire in April of 1845 and severe damage from floods—especially in 1907 and 1936—until the building of a system of flood-control dams.

Improved roads and (beginning in 1828) the Pennsylvania Canal promoted Pittsburgh's growth into the second major city of the state. Plentiful supplies of coal, limestone, and ore, and the genius of Andrew Carnegie made it the steel capital of the world. Also contributing to the city's progress was the arrival of the railroad in 1852.

Always smoky from its factories and the soft coal used for heating, Pittsburgh earned the title "hell with the lid off"; and from 1873 to 1909 when the Flinn-Magee political ring was in control, it became a city familiar with political corruption and social problems. Labor troubles such as the great railroad riots of 1877, the Homestead steel strike of 1892, and the Pressed Steel Car strike of 1910 made it even worse. Social conditions began to improve after the smashing of the ring and the Russell Sage Foundation's great Pittsburgh Survey 1907–08 (published 1907–14), whose disclosures helped bring about reform. State construction of Point State Park and a fire which destroyed the old Wabash Railroad warehouses in 1946 opened the way for the Pittsburgh "renaissance" and the construction of Gateway Center, which wiped out the traces of much of the city's early history.

On December 24, 1891, the United States Board of Geographic Names ordered the removal of the final *h* from all towns ending with *burgh,* specifically pointing out Pittsburgh. After a long fight, the original spelling was restored on July 19, 1911, and changed on post office canceling machines by October 1 of that year.

Landmarks

Pittsburgh—The Golden Triangle

1. The Blockhouse (brick), also called Bouquet's Redoubt, was one of two built in 1764 after Pontiac's Rebellion had shown the vulnerability of Fort Pitt's earthen breastworks facing the rivers. The last above-ground vestige of the fort, this five-sided structure miraculously survived a century of neglect, during which it was the residence of Isaac Craig, assistant deputy quartermaster general of the army, and of various others, the last of whom was a woman who ran a candy store in a slum area, surrounded by lumber yards and tenements. In 1894 Mrs. Mary Schenley (who had inherited it from her grandfather, James O'Hara) gave it to the Daughters of the American Revolution, along with a 90-by-100-foot plot of ground. *Hours:* Tuesday–Saturday, 9 A.M.–5 P.M. Sunday, 2–5 P.M. Closed Monday. *Location:* Point State Park.

2. Fort Pitt Museum (brick) is a reproduction of the Monongahela bastion of Fort Pitt, a mammoth star fort. The other bastions were the Ohio, Music (whose base, excavated, may be seen in the park), Grenadier, and Flag. Over sixty exhibits of the French and Indian War and of Pittsburgh's early history are on display at the museum. The Royal American Regiment presents eighteenth-century music and drills free every Sunday, 2:30 P.M., mid-June through Labor Day. This unit represents the original His Majesty's Sixtieth Regiment of Foot, which served under Col. Henry Bouquet in Gen. John Forbes's campaign against Fort Duquesne in 1758. The redoubt and museum are administered by the Pennsylvania Historical and Museum Commission. *Hours:* Tuesday–Saturday, 10 A.M.–4:30 P.M. Sunday, 12–4:30 P.M. Closed Monday. *Admission charge.* Free to schools, scouts, and senior citizens. *Location:* Point State Park.

3. Gateway 4 Building (steel and glass), located on the site of the 1905 Wabash Railroad Station, is felt by many to be the most beautiful of all the buildings erected as a result of the Pittsburgh renaissance. The Three Rivers Arts Festival, band concerts, and other functions are held on the courtyards beside it and other Gateway Center buildings. *Location:* Stanwix Street and Commonwealth Place.

4. World-Wide Clock, designed about 1960 by a local Bell Telephone employee, shows the time, as it revolves, of many principal cities all around the world. *Location:* Under portico of Bell Telephone Building, Stanwix Street and Boulevard of the Allies.

5. Pittsburgh Chronicle Building (brick), of uncertain age, is the remains of an edifice in which Alexander Berkman shot Henry Clay Frick in an attempt on his life during the Homestead steel strike of 1892. *Location:* Graeme and Market Streets and Fifth Avenue.

6. Jenkins Arcade (brick) is an eight-story structure which took its name and site from a former wholesale grocery warehouse. First occupied in 1911, it is almost the last of the old arcades that were extremely popular around the turn of the century. *Location:* Fifth and Liberty Avenues.

Note: The Union Trust Building (stone Gothic), bounded by Grant Street, Fifth and Oliver Avenues, and William Penn Way, was planned for the same purpose about the same time, but now houses only a few shops.

7. The Diamond, land set aside for public use by the Penns when Pittsburgh was laid out, is one of the city's most historic spots. Intended for a public market, it was also occupied by the county's first brick courthouse and later a city hall, where the Associate Reformed Presbyterian and Associate Presbyterian Churches merged in 1858 to form the United Presbyterian Church. During the Civil War it was used to feed and care for tired and ailing soldiers passing through the city. Its last structure, dating from 1916, was a market house which stood for about forty years. *Location:* Crossing of Market Street and Forbes Avenue (originally called Diamond Alley and then, after being widened early in this century, Diamond Street).

8. Heinz Hall for the Performing Arts (brick) was built in 1927 as the Penn Theater. It was bought by the Heinz family in 1967, restored, and reopened in 1971 to serve as the headquarters for the Pittsburgh Ballet, the Opera, Civic Light Opera, and the Symphony, and to provide space for other cultural activities. *Location:* 600 Penn Avenue.

9. Elks Club (terra cotta on brick) was the former Moose Club where the nation of Czechoslovakia was founded. In 1918, Tomáš G. Masaryk, a Slovak nationalist leader and professor at Charles University in Prague, met here with other Slovak and Czech leaders to sign the Pittsburgh Agreement, which provided for the equal union of Slovaks and Czechs in forming a new country. *Location:* 628 Penn Avenue.

10. Buhl Building (terra cotta on steel frame), a small, charming office building which dates from 1913, was purchased half-built and completed by Henry Buhl, Jr., merchant and philanthropist, whose Buhl Foundation also sponsored historical research and publication as well as the Buhl Planetarium, Chatham Village (both q.v.), and other worthwhile projects. *Location:* 204 Fifth Avenue.

11. Point Park College was formed in 1960 (first as a junior college) from the Business Training College, which had resulted from a 1954 merger of two century-old business schools, Duff's and Iron City.
   a. Woodwell Hardware Store (brick) was built about 1870 by Joseph Woodwell, sculptor, artist, merchant, and patron of the arts. When the Boulevard of the Allies was widened in 1921 the Eichleay Company moved this eight-story structure north forty feet and raised it twelve inches, without ever shutting it down or cutting off services to its occupants. It is now Lawrence Hall. *Location:* Wood Street and Boulevard of the Allies.
   b. Keystone Athletic Club (reinforced brick and stone) was erected just before the 1929 crash as a fashionable athletic club. It soon fell on hard times and became, in turn, the Keystone Hotel, Sheraton Hotel, and Sherwyn Hotel, and is now a Point Park College dormitory, with a dance auditorium and other features. *Location:* Wood Street and Boulevard of the Allies across from Lawrence Hall.

12. Arbuckle Coffee Building (brick) was built about 1865 by John Arbuckle, a North Side coffee merchant, who, by inventing and using automatic weighing and packaging machines and by coating coffee beans with gelatine to prevent aging, became the world's coffee king; he even successfully challenged the Havemeyer sugar trust. In sculptured relief on the exterior wall of the building are busts of Washington, Lincoln, an Indian-head-penny Indian, and a woman often presumed to be Mary Croghan Schenley, but who may be Jane Grey Cannon Swisshelm. *Location:* Behind Duquesne Club between Wood Street, Strawberry Alley, and Liberty Avenue.

13. Trinity Episcopal Cathedral (stone), designed by Gordon W. Lloyd in 1871–72 of Gothic style, became the Cathedral of the Diocese in 1928, with Alexander Mann the first bishop. The church has a graceful tower and a pulpit designed by Bertram G. Goodhue in 1922. Adjacent to the church is a cemetery containing graves of very early Pittsburghers and others, including Chief Red Pole, who died in 1797 after visiting George Washington in Philadelphia. The Trinity congregation was formed in 1787 and became a parish in 1805. Land was given to it by the Penns in 1787, but its first church (which was round and of stone) was built at Wood, Sixth, and Liberty Streets. The second church was erected at the present location in 1824–25. *Location:* 330 Sixth Avenue.

14. Half Building (brick) received its name from the days when streets were widened and buildings were sometimes torn down, sometimes moved, and now and then cut in half. This hot-dog stand is one of the few surviving examples of the last. *Location:* Northwest corner of Forbes Avenue and Wood Street.

15. Cast-Iron Fronts, a once-popular type of commerical building, are not much in evidence today. Eight of them, built between 1840 and 1870, may still be seen downtown. One, housing a paint store, is at 101–03 Wood Street. A more ornate example may be seen on Fifth Avenue at McMaster Way, adjacent to the dime store. On Liberty Avenue are twin iron fronts at 805–07 and 927–29; other examples are at 951–53 Liberty and 308 Seventh Avenue.

16. Granite Building (stone), erected in 1885 as a bank, now serves as an office building. The architecture is Romanesque, showing the influence of the courthouse (q.v.) by Richardson of the same period. *Location:* Northeast corner of Sixth Avenue and Wood Street.

17. Duquesne Club (brownstone) was founded in 1873, incorporated in 1881, and, when the present building was completed, was moved to this site in 1889. Additions to this Romanesque structure were made in 1902 and in 1930–31. It was severely damaged by fire in 1966. *Location:* 325 Sixth Avenue.

18. First Presbyterian Church (sandstone) was chartered in 1788, with its first building erected in 1789 on a Penn land grant. The present Gothic structure was designed by Theophilus Chandler and completed in 1905. The central roof-support beams (84 feet long

7

by 2 feet square) are said to be the longest timbers ever brought into Pittsburgh. A "Geneva pulpit," from which open-air services are conducted, is on the Sixth Avenue facade. *Location:* 320 Sixth Avenue.

19. Hamilton Building (stone) was the first skyscraper built in Pittsburgh. Samuel Hamilton, who had opened a piano business in 1869, built the first structure in 1885. After it burned in 1887 he rebuilt and fireproofed it, completing it in 1889. It had nine stories (ten including the tower), 116 rooms, and the largest window glasses in America. It had a seventh-floor balcony 135 feet up and an observation deck at 185 feet. The height to the top of the flagpole was 216 feet. Now, much altered, it is a savings and loan office. *Location:* 335 Fifth Avenue.

20. Grant Building (limestone, brick, and Belgian granite), having forty stories above and five below for parking, as well as a tunnel connecting with the courthouse, was designed by Henry Hornbostel. Opened in 1928, it was named for James Grant, whose advance guard in the attack on Fort Duquesne in 1758 was routed by the French. What was once the world's largest neon air beacon, blinking the city's name in international Morse code, is visible for 150 miles on a clear night. The third floor was for many years occupied by KDKA, one of the pioneer broadcasting stations of the world. (See *Conrad's Radio Station.*) A public observation deck is on the thirty-seventh floor. *Location:* 330 Grant Street.

21. Frick Building (reinforced stone) was designed in neoclassic style by D. E. Burnham & Company of Chicago and built in 1902 by Henry Clay Frick, coke magnate and former steel partner of Andrew Carnegie. The annex was added in 1906. The main lobby of this building contains a stained-glass window, *Fortune and Her Wheel* by John La Farge, and two bronze lions by A. P. Proctor. When Frick constructed this large building he was competing with Carnegie, who had built a smaller one next to the site. *Location:* Southwest corner of Fifth Avenue and Grant Street.

22. Harvard-Yale-Princeton Club (brick), built in 1894 in Georgian style, is one of the last vestiges of residential downtown Pittsburgh. Half of the building, remodeled in 1930–31 by Edward B. Lee, now operates as a club; the rest serves as offices. It was to have been torn down for the construction of the Alcoa Building, along with the old Nixon Theater, but was saved by strong protest. *Location:* William Penn Way near Seventh Avenue.

23. Alcoa Building (aluminum over steel), built in 1953, is the first skyscraper to be sheathed in aluminum. It has a charming lobby on Sixth Avenue. *Location:* 425 Sixth Avenue.

24. German Evangelical Protestant Church (reinforced stone) was erected in 1927 and is one of the few churches remaining in downtown Pittsburgh. It occupies land granted from the Penn heirs in 1787, and the congregation is the outgrowth of the oldest religious group in the city, formed in 1782 by Rev. John William Weber. This building, now the United Church of Christ, was designed by Henry Hornbostel. It has a remarkable group of windows portraying religious and Pennsylvania history, and its cast-aluminum spire is fantastic. *Location:* 620 Smithfield Street.

25. Pennsylvania Railroad Station and Rotunda (brick and terra cotta) was built in 1898–1903 on the site of the first Union Station of 1865, which was destroyed by fire during the railroad riots of 1877. This twelve-story building with its domed rotunda having four centered arches is one of the most outstanding railroad structures ever erected. The Pennsylvania Canal terminal at Pittsburgh was the site of this station. A branch of the canal ran through a tunnel (hence the name of nearby Tunnel Street) to locks on the Monongahela near the Try Street Terminal. (This tunnel should not be confused with the one in the same area used by the Panhandle Division of the Pennsylvania Railroad.) *Location:* 1100 Liberty Avenue at Grant Street.

26. First Lutheran Church (stone), of Gothic architecture, was organized in 1837 and erected its first structure in 1839–40. The present church, designed in the form of a Greek cross, was built in 1886 and consecrated in 1888. The north transept windows were designed by Frederick Wilson of the Tiffany Studios as a memorial to the Black family. Rev. William A. Passavant was the founder and one of the main forces behind the erection of this church. *Location:* 615 Grant Street.

27. United States Steel Building, 841 feet high with sixty-four stories, was once the world's second largest high-rise office building. Erected in 1967–69, it was designed to form a weathered protective steel layer. The roof was built with a heliport, though it is not now used as such. Water-filled columns provide a built-in fire protection device. *Location:* Bounded by Grant Street, Bigelow Boulevard, and Seventh Avenue.

28. Robert Morris College (brick) was until 1963 a business school. Its Moon Township campus was added in 1964, with the Edgar J. Kaufmann country home as a nucleus. Since 1963 the college has sponsored the annual Pittsburgh Folk Festival, an important civic event founded in 1956 by Duquesne University and held at the Civic Arena (q.v.) late in May. *Locations:* Downtown campus, 610 Fifth Avenue; Moon Township campus, Narrows Run Road.

29. County Courthouse was first located on Market Street. A frame structure, it was replaced by a second courthouse, of brick, which was completed in 1799 in the Diamond on the west side of Market Street and used until 1841. The third was built in 1842 by Coltart and Dilworth at a cost of $200,000 and was "the most monumental building erected in western Pennsylvania before 1860." Designed by John Chislett, this building was destroyed by fire in 1882.

The present and fourth structure, designed by Henry Hobson Richardson who died before its completion, was constructed of Worcester granite in 1884–88 on the site where a British detachment under Maj. James Grant met defeat during the Forbes expedition against Fort Duquesne in 1758. The Norman-Romanesque structure has three main entrance arches and a turreted tower. Built before the "hump" (a mound known as Grant's Hill) was cut in 1912, its first story was originally under ground. The present stone jail, built the same year, replaced the former stone one which was at the site now occupied by the Kossman Building at the foot of Forbes Avenue. It is connected to the courthouse by a "Bridge of Sighs" over Ross Street. The courthouse was expanded in 1909. *Location:* Bounded by Fifth and Forbes Avenues, Grant and Ross Streets, with jail in rear.

30. City-County Building (reinforced stone), one of Henry Hornbostel's finest works, was built in 1915–17 with an arched loggia, an interior hall with gilded metal columns, and ornate detail in the supreme court room. *Location:* 414 Grant Street near courthouse.

31. Burkes Building (brick with stone facade) was built in 1836 of Greek Revival design by John Chislett and is one of the first office buildings constructed in Pittsburgh. This structure, built on property the Burkes purchased from the Irwin family, served at one time as a bank. *Location:* 211 Fourth Avenue.

32. Dollar Savings Bank (brownstone) was built by Isaac H. Hobbs & Sons of classical design in 1868–71, with two wings added in 1906. Established in 1855, this banking company was Pittsburgh's first institution devoted to mutual banking, which operates solely for the benefit of depositors. *Location:* Fourth Avenue at Smithfield Street.

33. Chinatown in the early days was located in Herron Hill; when this uptown area became crowded about the turn of the century, most of the city's Chinese moved to the area around Second and Third Avenues. A few Chinese families and organizations still remain there, their homes easily distinguished by the tile pagoda-type roofs. Most of these houses were built before 1925. *Location:* Between Second and Third Avenues above Grant Street.

34. Smithfield Street Bridge, spanning the Monongahela River, was constructed with the double sine curve truss in 1883 and enlarged to two lanes in 1889. The upstream truss was widened in 1911. About twenty-five years ago its major framework was replaced with aluminum, to lighten its self-load. Designed by Gustave Lindenthal, it is the oldest bridge in Pittsburgh. *Location:* Smithfield Street.

Pittsburgh—Lawrenceville

1. Allegheny Arsenal was established in 1814–16 on the space now between Thirty-ninth and Fortieth Streets, from Penn Avenue to the Allegheny River. Plans were drawn by Benjamin H. Latrobe to be used by a protégé, Thomas Pope, but they were not closely followed. Col. Abraham R. Wooley was the arsenal's first commandant. Among later ones was Maj. Thomas J. Rodman, who produced the world's largest bore cannon, shooting a twenty-inch round ball. During the Civil War the arsenal produced more munitions than any other for the Union, despite an explosion on September 17, 1862, which killed more than seventy people, mostly women, boys, and girls. After about 1869 it was used only as a storage and distribution depot. Forty years later the part above Butler Street was given to Pittsburgh as a park and the rest sold in 1926. Among the few remaining structures, fast disappearing, are the stone officers' house (now a warehouse) and some storage buildings, across Butler Street from Arsenal Park, and the stone powder magazine, partly underground in the park. Researchers for the Pittsburgh History and Landmarks Foundation report that existing houses in the area at 257 Fortieth Street, 513 Carnegie Street, 5300 McCandless Avenue, 186 Home Street, and 4745 Modoc Alley, all brick and dating from 1830 to 1850 were more or less modeled on the arsenal architecture. *Location:* Arsenal Park, Fortieth and Butler Streets.

2. Marine Hospital (brick) opened in 1851 at Woods Run as a federal project to serve sick and injured boatmen on the rivers. It was closed in 1873. The second building, constructed in 1907–09, is now used by the Allegheny County Department of Health. *Location:* Northwest corner of Fortieth Street and Penn Avenue.

3. Locust Grove Seminary (brick), built as a home by industrialist Alba Fisk around 1840, became the Locust Grove Episcopal Female Seminary (a boarding and day school for girls) in 1853, with William H. Clarke as rector. Apparently in financial difficulties, it was purchased for one dollar in 1856 by ironmaster J. H. Shoenberger. After the school closed, he transferred it to the (Episcopal) Church Home Association in 1862, and it is still operated as a home for the aged and sick. *Location:* Northeast corner of Fortieth Street and Penn Avenue.

4. Holmes House (brick) was built about 1845 by Nathaniel Holmes, head of a prominent industrial and banking family, for his summer mansion. In 1885 it was endowed as the Protestant Home for Incurables by his daughter, "Pittsburgh Jane," and her cousin "Baltimore Jane" Holmes (because of her birthplace) who worked together to set up almost half of Pittsburgh's charitable institutions of the nineteenth century. Its name was changed in 1966 to the less bloodcurdling and more liberal Holmes House. *Location:* 5500 Butler Street.

5. Pittsburgh Reduction Company had its beginnings in this building, marked by an aluminum tablet, where Alfred E. Hunt, Charles M. Hall, and Arthur V. Davis produced the first commercial ingot of aluminum on Thanksgiving Day, 1888. The firm later became the Aluminum Company of America. *Location:* 3200 block of Smallman Street.

6. Saint Stanislaus Kostka Roman Catholic Church (brick and brownstone) was built in 1891–92 of Romanesque style. The congregation was organized in 1875, the first of Pittsburgh's Polish Roman Catholic parishes. The first meetinghouse was located in a former Presbyterian church at Penn Avenue and Seventeenth Street. The present structure features a large rose window, double towers, and frescoes painted by Polish immigrants. *Location:* Twenty-first and Smallman Streets.

7. Public Baths (brick) were made available to Pittsburghers in this building constructed with funds provided by steelman Henry Phipps in 1898. People used to stand in line for a turn at bathing and doing laundry. The name was changed in 1928 to the Lawrenceville Neighborhood House, and it closed near the end of 1961. *Location:* Thirty-fifth and Butler Streets.

Note: Another similar institution, Soho Public Baths, was located at 2610 Fifth Avenue, and is now occupied by an advertising firm.

8. Western Pennsylvania Medical College (brick), the first medical school established here, opened in 1886 near the old Western Pennsylvania Hospital. In 1902 it became the School of Medicine of the Western University of Pennsylvania (now University of Pittsburgh). In 1920 the property was sold to the Immaculate Heart of Mary Church, where it is used for school and lyceum purposes. *Location:* Brereton Avenue and Thirtieth Street.

9. Reineman Hospital (frame) was established in 1893 by Adam Reineman, a jeweler, who set it up as Pittsburgh's first maternity hospital, an adjunct of the above medical school. It operated until 1911 and is now an apartment house. *Location:* 3400 block of Melwood Avenue near Finland Street.

10. Emma Kaufman Clinic (brick) was founded in 1896 by Isaac Kaufman as a free clinic, dispensary, and temporary hospital. It presently serves as the Polish Falcons Home. *Location:* Brereton Avenue next to old Medical College.

11. Branch Library (brick), Lawrenceville, was the first branch of the Carnegie Library of Pittsburgh (see *Carnegie Institute*). Its first

15. Allegheny Cemetery Gatehouse

librarian was H. Elizabeth Cory. Built in 1898 at a cost of $41,200, this was the first library in America to have a separate room for children. *Location:* 1898 Fisk Street.

12. Cinderella (ash cement) was a house erected during a bricklayers' strike in July 1903, when John Fink determined to test the use of ashes in construction. Setting up forms like those for concrete, he filled them with a mixture of ashes, cement, and water, well tamped down. The house, integrally built, is still in excellent condition, with a speckled appearance. The plan proved cheaper than brick construction, but never became popular. The Cinderella originally had a bakeshop in the cellar and apartments above. It remains an apartment house. *Location:* Corner of Thirty-seventh Street and Penn Avenue.

13. Saint Mary's Academy (brick) is a late Greek Revival building of about 1850 intended for an academy in conjunction with Saint Mary's Roman Catholic Church. Its porch features charming cast-iron decorations, as does a convent next door, built in 1867. *Location:* 300 Forty-sixth Street.

14. Wainwright Brewery (brick) includes a number of buildings that date from 1866 to 1873. The firm was founded in 1818 by Joseph Wainwright. In 1899 it formed the nu-cleus of the "beer trust" which took in every brewery but one in or near the city. It became, and still remains, the Pittsburgh Brewing Company. *Location:* 3340 Liberty Avenue.

15. Allegheny Cemetery, first and most outstanding public one in the area, was founded in 1844 by a group of well-known citizens, and was modeled after Mount Auburn Cemetery in Boston. The group bought 257 acres of land for $118,500 and engaged John Chislett as superintendent. He laid out the grounds and designed the Butler Street gateway, a stone Gothic Revival structure, in 1848; it was enlarged twenty years later with a chapel and offices. The Penn Avenue gates were added in the 1880s. The first burial, in September 1845, was that of Mrs. James A. Briggs of Cleveland, daughter of George A. Bayard, who had sold the ground for the cemetery. *Location:* 4734 Butler Street.

Pittsburgh—Uptown, Oakland, Hazelwood

1. Civic Arena, built in 1961, is a $22-million structure with a stainless-steel retractable dome three times the size of that of Saint Peter's in Rome. It is used for sports and theatrical events, for conventions, and for the Pittsburgh Folk Festival. *Location:* Uptown, Washington Place, Center and Bedford Avenues.

11

2. Bethel African Methodist Episcopal Church (brick), founded in February 1827, is the oldest black church west of the Allegheny Mountains. Its first house of worship was on the northwest corner of Water (Fort Pitt Boulevard) and Smithfield Streets, later the site of the famed Monongahela House. For over a century its churches were at Wylie Avenue and Elm Street, where one of its pastors was Benjamin T. Tanner, father of the artist Henry Ossawa Tanner. *Location:* Uptown, 2720 Webster Avenue.

3. Duquesne University, established by the Dominican Order in 1878 as the College of Arts and Letters at Wylie Avenue and Fernando Street, was acquired three years later by the Order of the Holy Ghost. Moved to its present location it was renamed Pittsburgh Catholic College of the Holy Ghost until 1911, when it was recognized as Duquesne University of the Holy Ghost. The administration building, oldest structure on the campus, was erected in 1883–84 and dedicated in 1885. In 1975 this brick structure was badly damaged by fire. *Location:* Uptown, 801 Bluff Street between Colbert and Shingiss Streets.

4. Mercy Hospital was first opened by the Catholic Sisters of Mercy, January 1, 1847, in a house on Penn Avenue, downtown. Land for this institution, the oldest of its kind in Pittsburgh, was bought on Boyd's Hill. The first building there, erected in 1848, partly exists in the later complex. New wings were added, notably in 1882, and in 1903–18 the southwing buildings were constructed. The nurses' home was built in 1925–26, and in 1938 the southeast wing was added. *Location:* Uptown, Soho and on the Bluff, corner of Stevenson and Locust Streets. Hospital is bounded by Pride and Forbes Streets and Boulevard of the Allies.

5. Saint Peter's Episcopal Church (stone), a Gothic Revival structure designed by John Notman, was built in 1851–52. It originally was situated on the corner of Forbes Avenue and Grant Street, on part of the present site of the Frick Building. When Henry Clay Frick bought the property in 1900, he gave the church to the congregation, which moved it stone by stone to its present site. At this location the building has served as a chapel and social center for the juvenile court home next to it. *Location:* Oakland, corner of Forbes and Craft Avenues.

6. Carlow College was founded by the Sisters of Mercy in 1929 and at that time was called Mount Mercy College. In 1969 it became known by its present name in honor of a town in Ireland. *Location:* Oakland, 3333 Fifth Avenue.

7. University of Pittsburgh dates back to the Pittsburgh Academy of 1787. It has expanded over the years to become a state-related and nationally known institution of learning. The University Art Gallery in the Frick Fine Arts Building contains national and international collections. *Gallery hours:* Tuesday–Saturday, 1–5 P.M. Sunday, 2–5 P.M. Closed Monday.

a. Cathedral of Learning (stone), a Gothic structure forty-two stories high, was designed by Charles Z. Klauder and built in 1926–37, the only skyscraper university building in the United States and one of the greatest of its style in the country. Housed within it are the Commons Room, 87 classrooms—eighteen of which are nationality rooms representing those groups who helped build Pittsburgh—184 laboratories, 23 lecture rooms, 19 libraries, 80 conference rooms, and 60 offices, among others.

Two rooms from Picnic, the manor, razed in 1949, of Mary E. Croghan Schenley, daughter of William Croghan, Jr. (brother-in-law of George Rogers Clark) and Mary O'Hara (daughter of Gen. James O'Hara), have been restored on the first floor. According to Charles M. Stotz, these rooms are "the outstanding achievement of the Greek Revival style in Western Pennsylvania." They are now the Oval Room and the Ballroom. Tours by prearrangement. *Location:* Oakland, bounded by Forbes, Fifth, and Bellefield Avenues, and Bigelow Boulevard.

b. Stephen Foster Memorial (stone), containing an auditorium that seats almost 700, is dedicated to Stephen Collins Foster, a native of Pittsburgh and composer of some of America's best loved songs, including "Old Folks at Home" and "My Old Kentucky Home." The west wing houses the Foster Hall collection, containing more than 10,000 items relating to the musician. Foster's home site was at 3600 Penn Avenue. A statue in memory of him is located across from the memorial. *Hours:* Monday–Friday, 9 A.M.–5 P.M. Location: Oakland, facing Forbes Avenue on Cathedral of Learning plot.

c. Heinz Memorial Chapel (limestone), built in 1938, is an outstanding example of medieval French Gothic architecture, designed by Charles Z. Klauder. The carving on the Indiana limestone was the work of Joseph Gottoni, and the stained-glass windows were made by Charles J. Connick of Boston. This interfaith chapel, used for a variety of services, weddings, and organ presentations, was a gift in memory of Mr. and Mrs. H. J. Heinz from their children and grandchildren. *Hours:* Monday–Friday, 8 A.M.–5 P.M. Saturday, 9 A.M.–4 P.M. *Location:* Oakland, east lawn of Cathedral of Learning.

d. Schenley Hotel (reinforced brick) opened in 1898. This building was Pittsburgh's first large, steel-framed skyscraper hotel. In 1956 the classical ten-story structure became part of the University of Pittsburgh and at present contains the Student Union. The famous singer Eleanora Duse died at the Schenley when it was a hotel. In 1914, the Veterans of Foreign Wars organization was formed here. *Location:* Oakland, Fifth and Forbes Avenues at Bigelow Boulevard.

8. Saint Nicholas Greek Orthodox Cathedral (stone), a classical building with six fluted columns, was built in 1904 as the First Congregational Church, a connection shown by the many examples of the wreath motif evident in the interior. It became Greek Orthodox in 1921 and contains much fine mosaic work and numerous icons of interest. *Location:* Oakland, Forbes Avenue and South Dithridge Street.

9. Carnegie Institute (gray sandstone) in Italian Renaissance style was built in 1892–95 for $1 million, with funds donated by Andrew Carnegie for a free library. In 1907 an addition costing $5 million was dedicated; it included the museum of art, museum of natural history, and a music hall. That year the Pittsburgh Orchestra performed there under the direction of Frederick Archer. Victor Herbert had preceded him in 1899 in that post. The museum includes thousands of exhibits among which is the world's most complete fossilized dinosaur skeleton.

On the stone piers of the roof are large bronze figures symbolizing art and science by J. Massey Rhind. Longfellow, Alden, and Harlow of Pittsburgh designed the library, and Alden and Harlow drew the later plans which extended the building. In 1975 the Sarah Scaife Gallery of the Museum of Art was dedicated. Heinz Galleries and other galleries from endowments set up by Andrew W. Mellon will open in the future. The International Poetry Forum is housed at the institute and holds periodical readings. *Museum hours:* Tuesday–Saturday, 10 A.M.–5 P.M. Sunday, 1–6 P.M. Closed Monday. *Donation.* *Library hours:* Monday–Saturday, 9 A.M.–9 P.M. Sunday, 2–5 P.M. Summer (June–August): Sat-

11. Neil House

urday, 9 A.M.–5 P.M. Closed Sundays. *Free.* *Location:* Oakland, 4400 Forbes Avenue.

10. Phipps Conservatory is one of the largest indoor botanical gardens in the United States. It was given to the city in 1893 by Henry C. Phipps, steel magnate and partner of Andrew Carnegie. In 1896, Phipps added three other houses to the original nine display buildings, and in 1900 the city erected nine growing houses. The structures contain a palm court, a cactus room, an aquatic room, a Charleston garden, a cloistered sixteenth-century garden, a fern room, and an orchid room. Displays are readied year round with special ones usually at Easter, Thanksgiving, and during the Christmas season. *Hours:* Daily, 9 A.M.–5 P.M. *Admission charge* during annual shows. *Location:* Bigelow Boulevard in Schenley Park.

11. Neil House (log) was built between 1787 and 1795 by Robert Neil. It collapsed in 1968 and was restored by the Pittsburgh History and Landmarks Foundation. The one-room structure, with a loft reached by a ladder, has a large fieldstone chimney on one end. *Hours:* By appointment. *Location:* Oakland, Schenley Park, on Serpentine Drive near Darlington Road.

12. Carnegie-Mellon University had its beginning on November 15, 1900, when Andrew Carnegie offered buildings and a $1 million endowment (increased to about $50 million in support over forty-six years) for a trade school for poor men. By 1912 trends had changed, and it became Carnegie Institute of Technology. About this time, Andrew and Richard B. Mellon supported the organization of a scientific research program called Mellon Institute. A marriage of convenience between the two produced Carnegie-Mellon University in 1967.

a. Mellon Institute (stone), a huge structure with sixty-two monolithic Ionic columns, was built in 1931–37. On January 1, 1907, Robert Kennedy Duncan established the first Industrial Fellowship at the University of Kansas, and in 1911 Andrew W. and Richard B. Mellon financed a similar program at the University of Pittsburgh. It was incorporated as the Mellon Institute of Industrial Research in 1927, and the name was shortened to Mellon Institute in 1962. *Location:* Oakland, 4400 Fifth Avenue.

b. Margaret Morrison College (marble) was named for Carnegie's mother and intended as a women's department, later phased out by coeducation. Now a general liberal arts hall, this rather flossy classical structure was built in 1906–07. *Location:* Oakland, Margaret Morrison Street on main campus.

c. Hunt Library (glass) is a magnificent library building. Its top floor houses the world's largest private botanical book collection, gathered by Rachel McMasters Miller Hunt, an internationally known author, exhibitor, and lecturer on horticulture until her death in 1963. The priceless collection and building were the gift of the Hunt family in 1961. A decade later it became the Hunt Institute for Botanical Documentation. *Location:* Oakland, near Fine Arts Building on main campus.

13. Episcopal Church of the Ascension (stone), an English Gothic structure with distinctive red doors, was built in 1896–98. William Halsey Wood was its architect, and the wood-carving was done by Lamb Studios of Tenafly, N.J. The tower was modeled after the late Gothic tower of Wrexam Church in Wales. *Location:* Oakland, Ellsworth and North Neville Avenues.

14. Samson Funeral Home (brick), founded in 1859, was the first of its kind in the Pittsburgh area that did not also offer furniture for sale. Its founder, Hudson Samson, and his wife Susan G. came from Oswego, N.Y., and established a funeral home at 433 Sixth Street in Pittsburgh. In 1922 the building was sold to the Philadelphia Company and the business moved to the present site. Two old brick homes next to one another, the King-Jennings (left side) and the Livingston (right side), were later connected with a middle section, and in 1950 a common entranceway was built. Famous funerals at this establishment have included those of Lillian Russell and A. W. Mellon. *Location:* Oakland, 537 Neville Street.

15. Saint Paul's Roman Catholic Cathedral (stone) is a Gothic structure built in 1903–06 with double spires and designed by Egan and Prindeville. The original building, known as Saint Paul's Church and located at Grant Street and Fifth Avenue, was built in 1828–34 and destroyed by fire in 1851. When the Diocese of Pittsburgh was formed August 7, 1843, Saint Paul's became its cathedral. The second church, constructed in 1851–53 on the same site, was said to be the largest brick structure in America at that time. In 1901 H. C. Frick bought the property for his Union Trust Building at a cost of $1,325,000—the largest single transaction in the history of Pittsburgh realty up until that time. While the third and present structure was being erected, services were held in the Church of the Epiphany. The cathedral was consecrated October 24, 1906, free of debt upon completion. The organ that was donated by Andrew Carnegie for the second building and later moved to the present one was replaced by a world-famous German Beckerath organ in 1962, generally regarded as one of the finest instruments in the Americas. *Location:* Oakland, Fifth Avenue at Craig Street.

16. Bellefield Presbyterian Church (stone) is a dark, frowning structure where old-line Presbyterians met to march to the Syria Mosque for the 1958 merger which formed the new United Presbyterian Church, U.S.A. Made unnecessary by that union, the building is now used by Oakland's University and City Ministries and occasionally for dramatic shows.

Across Bellefield is a stone building that was once the manse of the Bellefield Presbyterian Church. It was built in 1891 as a gift to its pastor, W. F. Holland (a noted lepidopterist), from his wife, the former Carrie J. Moorhead. From a manse it became the former studio of WQED, the first successful educational television station, launched in 1954, and the first station to telecast instruction to elementary schools. The building now houses the University of Pittsburgh's Music Department. *Location:* Oakland, Fifth and Bellefield Avenues.

19. Historical Society of Western Pennsylvania Building

17. First Baptist Church (stone) was erected about 1911 when the congregation's former home was taken for construction of the City-County Building. A fine Gothic Revival structure, it has a remarkable bronze spire and good wood-carving in the chancel. *Location:* Oakland, Bellefield Avenue and Bayard Street.

18. Western Pennsylvania School for Blind Children (brick) was built in 1892, five years after it was established, with funds supplied largely by two cousins, both named Jane Holmes. (see *Holmes House*). Civic planners had hoped to locate it in a secluded area and were dismayed when Mrs. Mary Schenley gave it one of the most desirable lots in Schenley Farms. But she refused to reconsider and the school was built at the designated site. *Location:* Oakland, Bayard Street, between Bellefield Avenue and Bigelow Boulevard.

19. The Historical Society of Western Pennsylvania Building (brick) was erected in 1912, although the society has been active for nearly a century. Its exhibits consist of early Americana, together with an archive of old manuscripts, diaries, and letters. On the top floor of the building is a library containing more than seventeen thousand books and pamphlets devoted to western Pennsylvania. The structure is also the meeting place for the Western Pennsylvania Genealogical Society. *Hours:* Tuesday–Friday, 9:30 A.M.–4:30 P.M. Saturday, 9:30 A.M.–12:30 P.M. Tours arranged. *Location:* Oakland, 4338 Bigelow Boulevard.

20. Twentieth Century Club (limestone) was formed in 1894 and had its first head-

quarters in the old James Laughlin house on Duquesne Way. It was relocated to the present building in Schenley Farms, a structure built in 1910 and remodeled completely in 1929, with its exterior changed from brick to limestone. *Location:* Oakland, 4201 Bigelow Boulevard at Parkman Avenue.

21. Soldiers and Sailors Memorial Hall (stone) was built in 1907–11 as a memorial to Civil War veterans, as a part of the cultural build-up of Oakland. It is modeled after the Mausoleum at Halicarnassus, one of the seven wonders of the ancient world. Architect Henry Hornbostel felt that it needed a fine vista, but this was refused by county officials, who assigned it a rather unimportant lot, facing east. The structure was almost complete before they discovered he had built it facing south, and Hornbostel got his vista. It contains a museum—now of all America's wars—a dining hall, and a large public auditorium. *Hours:* Monday–Friday, 9 A.M.–4 P.M. Saturday, Sunday, and Holidays, 1–4 P.M. *Location:* Oakland, Fifth Avenue at Bigelow Boulevard.

22. Woods House (stone and frame) was erected by George Woods before 1800, and had a frame addition built about 1850. This structure, the Neil House (q.v.) in Schenley Park, and the Fort Pitt Blockhouse (q.v.) are perhaps the only eighteenth-century buildings that still survive in Pittsburgh. *Location:* Hazelwood, 4604 Monongahela Street.

Pittsburgh—East End

1. Shadyside, originally the Thomas Aiken farm and named for the county's only charcoal iron furnace built here by George Anschutz in 1793, has many interesting houses. Only a sampling is given here.

a. Hunt Residence (anodized aluminum and bauxite ore) contains all that remains of the home of Roy A. Hunt, former president of the Aluminum Company of America, who died in 1966. His father, Capt. Alfred E. Hunt, was an early pioneer in aluminum-making and the founder of the family fortune. This ultra-modern town house was built around the original Hunt Library by Alfred M. Hunt, one of the heirs to the Alcoa fortune and governor of the Ligonier Rolling Rock Club. At one time the Hunt family kept seven thousand volumes and fifteen hundred prints and paintings in this specially built two-story wing of their home. *Location:* 4875 Ellsworth Avenue at Devonshire Street.

2. Hunt House

b. Moreland-Hoffstot House (terra cotta and stucco), of French Renaissance style, was built about 1914. *Location:* 5157 Fifth Avenue.

c. Gwinner-Harter House (brick), of Victorian second Empire style, was built in 1870–80. *Location:* 5061 Fifth Avenue.

d. Burgwin House (brick) was built about 1845. *Location:* 5219 Fifth Avenue.

e. Spinelli House (batten board) was built about 1870. *Location:* 5302 Westminster Place.

f. Hillman House (brick) was built in 1878 by James Rees, local manufacturer of steamboats and engines. *Location:* 5045 Fifth Avenue.

g. Abbott and Marshall Houses (frame) were built about 1860. *Location:* 918–20 Saint James Street.

2. Hunt House (brick) was the home of Capt. and Mrs. Alfred E. Hunt at the time he was involved in launching what was soon to become the Aluminum Company of America. The building at present houses a commercial business. *Location:* East Liberty, 272 Shady Avenue.

3. Shadyside Presbyterian Church (stone) with a large central dome of Romanesque design was erected in 1889–90, replacing an earlier building of 1874–75. For years many considered it the wealthiest and most socially acceptable Protestant church in the city. In 1892 the chapel on Westminster Place was completed; in 1937–38 the interior of the church was remodeled; and in 1952–53 a new parish hall was constructed. The congregation of this church was formed in 1860. *Location:* Shadyside, Amberson Avenue at Westminster Place.

4. Sacred Heart Roman Catholic Church (stone), of English Gothic style notable for its interior beamed roof, was constructed over a period of years between 1924 and 1953. The designer, Carlton Strong, did not live to see it finished. *Location:* Shadyside, Walnut Street at Shady Avenue.

5. Rodef Shalom Temple (brick and terra cotta) was chartered in 1856. At the turn of the century it was located in the building later occupied by the Second Presbyterian Church on Eighth Avenue. The present square-domed structure was erected in 1906–07, with the additions of a school in 1938 and a social hall in 1956. *Location:* Shadyside, Fifth and Morewood Avenues.

6. Chatham College was organized in 1869 by the Shadyside Presbyterian Church as the Pennsylvania College for Women, receiving its present name in 1955. Some of its more interesting buildings were originally residences of well-to-do Pittsburghers. *Location:* Shadyside, between Fifth and Wilkins Avenues.

a. Mellon Home (brick and stone) of Tudor style was built in 1897 by the Laughlin family (of Jones & Laughlin Steel). In 1917 Andrew Mellon bought the property, renovating and enlarging the building. When he became secretary of the treasury in 1921, his son Paul moved here, deeding the property to the college in 1940. *Location:* Woodland Road.

b. Greystone (now Benedum Hall) was the estate of Thomas Marshall Howe, who had built a house on the hill before the Civil War. In 1911 M. L. Benedum bought the seven-acre estate, demolished the home called Greystone, and built another one by the same name, using some of the original stone. The Claude Worthington Benedum Foundation gave the house to the college in 1960. Howe also built the spring bearing his name below this house, where South Highland Avenue runs into Fifth Avenue. Donated for public use, it was a favorite drinking fountain for years but is now dry. *Location:* East Woodland Road.

7. Clayton (Frick House) (brick) was the home of Henry Clay Frick and is presently owned by his daughter, Helen Clay Frick. Built about 1870, it was bought by Frick in 1882 and extensively remodeled in 1893. (See also Henry Clay Frick Birthplace, Westmoreland County.) Frick's carriages of the horse-and-buggy era are still preserved here.

Not open to the public. *Location:* Point Breeze, Penn and South Homewood Avenues.

Note: The Frick Art Museum nearby at 7227 Reynolds Street contains many expert copies of old masters as well as originals. *Hours:* Wednesday–Friday, 10 A.M.–4 P.M. Saturday, 10 A.M.–5 P.M. Sunday, 1–5 P.M. Tours by appointment.

8. Motor Square Garden, a brick building with a large dome, was built as a market house in 1898–1900. It was converted to a sports arena in 1915 and became the site of the first heavyweight boxing event broadcast over a commercial radio station (KDKA)—a ten-round, no-decision fight between Johnny Ray and Johnny Dundee, announced by Florent Gibson. At present the building is an automobile showroom. *Location:* East Liberty, Center Avenue at Baum Boulevard and South Beatty Street.

9. Calvary Episcopal Church is a limestone building erected in 1906–07, replacing the second church at the corner of Penn Avenue and Station Street. The parish was organized in 1855, with William H. Paddock the earliest rector. At this church the first church service ever broadcast was transmitted on January 2, 1921, through radio wireless by KDKA. Encouraged by the rector, Dr. Edwin J. Van Etten, these broadcast services continued for nineteen years.

The designer of many of the windows, as well as the building, was Ralph Adams Cram. Outstanding stained-glass windows depicting western Pennsylvania history were made by William Willet of Pittsburgh. Beautiful fifteenth-century-style wood-carving done by Kirchmeyer of Cambridge, Mass., adorns the interior. *Location:* East Liberty, 315 Shady Avenue at Walnut Street.

10. Selma Burke Art Center, founded and named in honor of a distinguished contemporary black sculptor, presents exhibitions with emphasis on black culture and art. *Hours:* Tuesday–Saturday, 11 A.M.–7 P.M. *Location:* East Liberty, 6118 Penn Circle.

11. East Liberty Presbyterian Church (stone), fifth home of the congregation, is an immense structure that was a family memorial gift from Mr. and Mrs. Richard B. Mellon. Built in 1931–35, it was the last great effort of Ralph Adams Cram, and it features much fine wood- and stone-carving and stained glass. *Location:* East Liberty, Penn and Highland Avenues.

12. Judge Forward House (frame with siding), of Vernacular Greek Revival design, was built in 1840. It was the country house of Walter Forward, at one time president judge of Allegheny County and later secretary of the treasury under President John Tyler. *Location:* Squirrel Hill, 2361 Tilbury Street.

13. Arts and Crafts Center, constructed in 1911–12 by Charles D. Marshall, is one of the last of the area's great millionaire mansions to be erected. It was given to the center by the Marshall family in 1945 and houses exhibitions, arts-and-crafts classes, and a shop where works of local artists and craftsmen are sold. It also provides meeting space for many cultural organizations. The R. B. Mellon family donated the park around it in 1946. The only remaining structure on this estate is the carriage house–garage, now part of the Pittsburgh Civic Garden Club. *Hours:* Tuesday–Saturday, 10 A.M.–5 P.M. Sunday, 2–5 P.M. *Location:* Shadyside, Fifth and Shady Avenues.

14. King Mansion (brick), a typical mid-Victorian, successful businessman's house, was the girlhood home of Jennie King, wife of Richard B. Mellon. A four-towered, stone and brick garden structure built by Robert King in 1898 is much dilapidated. After his death in 1954 the home became the King Mansion Conservation Center. It now houses the Pittsburgh Plan for Art. Many works of art by local artists are on display here and may be rented or purchased. *Location:* East Liberty, 1251 North Negley Avenue.

15. Pittsburgh (Presbyterian) Theological Seminary traces its descent from the oldest separate Protestant seminary in the United States, founded in Beaver County in 1794 (see *Service Associate Presbyterian Church,* Beaver County), and from Western Theological Seminary, established in Pittsburgh in 1827. It occupies ten acres—the old Lockhart estate—and has a fine library and a small museum of artifacts from the expeditions of James L. Kelso and Melvin G. Kyle to the Holy Land. Pittsburgh-Xenia Seminary moved to the site in 1954, and the present name was adopted after the church union of 1958. *Location:* East Liberty, 616 North Highland Avenue.

16. Saints Peter and Paul Church (cement block) was built in 1890, its parish having been founded in 1857. The structure, a fine example of Gothic architecture, contains a vaulted ceiling and a beautiful rose window.

1. *Old Post Office Museum*

In 1911 the church was struck by lightning; the towers were saved, but the middle section and roof burned. *Location:* East Liberty, 130 Larimer Avenue.

17. Kingsley House, Pittsburgh's first settlement house, was founded by Rev. George Hodges, Episcopalian; Rev. Charles E. St. John, Unitarian; Rev. Morgan Sheedy, Roman Catholic; and Rev. E. M. Donehoo, Presbyterian. Named for the British clergyman-reformer, Charles Kingsley, it opened December 3, 1893, at 1707 Penn Avenue in the Strip, moved to Herron Hill in 1909, and finally relocated to its present site soon after World War I. *Location:* East Liberty, 220 Larimer Avenue.

Pittsburgh—North Side

1. Old Post Office Museum (stone) was built in 1894–97 as the Post Office of Allegheny City. This impressive building with a central dome, designed by A. W. Aiken, was marked for demolition in the 1960s but was preserved by its sponsor, the Pittsburgh History and Landmarks Foundation. The museum, which includes a garden of architectural artifacts, presents various shows, programs, and exhibits which change every few weeks. *Hours:* Tuesday–Friday, 10 A.M.–4:30 P.M. Saturday–Sunday, 1–4:30 P.M. *Admission charge. Location:* Allegheny Center.

2. Allegheny Library and Music Hall (granite) constructed in 1888–89 at a cost of $240,000, was given to Allegheny City by Andrew Carnegie and is situated on land donated by the city. President Benjamin Harrison spoke at its dedication in 1890. (At that time a special entranceway for his convenience was made between the library and the music hall, and it has been used ever since.) The first municipal organ recitals were held in this structure. They took place over a seventy-year period, having been commenced by organist Dr. Casper Koch in 1904 and continued by his son Paul Koch, organist of Saint Paul's Cathedral in Oakland (q.v.). *Location:* Allegheny Center.

3. Buhl Planetarium and Institute of Popular Science (stone) was built in 1939 by the Buhl Foundation on the site of the old city hall. In addition to sky dramas and science lectures it offers a variety of programs and exhibits, including a miniature railroad and village. Of special note are the iron-industry historical murals painted by Pittsburgh artist Nat Youngblood. *Hours:* Monday–Friday, 1–5 P.M., 7–10 P.M. Saturday, 10:45 A.M.–5 P.M., 7–10 P.M. Sunday, 1–10 P.M. *Admission charge. Location:* Allegheny Center.

4. Community College of Allegheny County, founded in 1966, includes on this campus some notable buildings.

    a. Byers-Lyons House (brick and stone) was built in 1898 by Alexander M. Byers, a well-known Pittsburgh industrialist. The house (two structures fitted together to form a court) cost $500,000 to build, with an additional $90,000 for the lot. In 1941 it sold for $15,000. It now houses offices. *Location:* 901 Ridge Avenue.

    b. West Hall (brick) is almost the last vestige of Western Theological Seminary (see *Pittsburgh Theological Seminary*). It was built in 1875 and used for seminary purposes until after the Presbyterian Church merger in 1958. *Location:* 834 Ridge Avenue.

    c. Jones House (brick and stone) was built by B. F. Jones, Jr., of Jones & Laughlin Steel around 1910. It has forty-two rooms. *Location:* 808 Ridge Avenue.

5. Rinehart House (brick) was the residence of Mary Roberts Rinehart, Pittsburgh's most prolific writer, from her marriage in 1896 to Dr. Stanley M. Rinehart until she moved to the Sewickley area in 1910. *Location:* Allegheny and Beech Avenues.

6. Conservatory-Aviary (brick and glass) is one of the world's finest free-flight aviaries and is operated by the city of Pittsburgh. It contains ecological exhibits, talking birds, and free-flight rooms with exotic specimens from around the world. *Hours:* Daily, 9 A.M.–4:30 P.M., except Christmas. *Admission charge.* Saturdays free to all visitors. *Location:* Allegheny Commons, west corner of West Ohio Street and Sherman Avenue.

7. Mexican War Streets are located on a tract of land originally owned by William Robinson and developed following the Mexican War of 1846–48, as evidenced by the street names. The houses vary from simple Greek Revival to mid- and late Victorian. One three-story house at 1241 Resaca Place has a Romanesque stone facade and carved stone faces on its exterior. The area has been recently redeveloped through the attention of the Pittsburgh History and Landmarks Foundation. *Location:* Buena Vista, Taylor, and Arch Streets.

8. New Zion Baptist Church (brick) was built in 1866–67 by the Union Methodist Church (formed in 1846) which sold it to the Baptist Church in 1961. *Location:* 1304 Manhattan Street at Pennsylvania Avenue.

9. Old Widows' Home (brick and stone) was established in 1860. The Allegheny Widows' Home Association took over the former Allegheny Protestant Orphan Asylum in 1866. Other buildings were added after 1873 on Sherman and Dawson Avenues and in 1903 on Arlington Avenue. The agency is still self-supporting. *Location:* 536 Armandale Street at Garfield Avenue.

10. Calvary Methodist Church (stone), of late Victorian Gothic style, was built in 1892–93 with two spires and is richly carved inside as well as outside. Three large windows were done by Tiffany and before being installed were exhibited at the World Columbian Exposition of 1893 in Chicago. *Location:* Allegheny and Beech Avenues.

11. Emmanuel Episcopal Church (brick), of Romanesque style, was constructed in 1885–86 by Henry Hobson Richardson, who had recently taken the contract for the county courthouse (q.v.). This structure, often called the "bake-oven church" because of its shape, has had a wide influence on Pittsburgh architecture. *Location:* Corner of North and Allegheny Avenues.

12. Allegheny Observatory was built in 1900–12 and is one of the foremost observatories in the world, containing the largest (thirty-inch) spectrographic refractor telescope. Its first building was erected in 1860 near Perrysville Avenue, and in 1865 it was made part of the Western University of Pennsylvania (now the University of Pittsburgh). The present site, along with the park, was donated to the city of Allegheny by David E. Parks. The institution offers lectures, movies, and on clear nights viewing through the tele-

13 & 14. Heinz Plant and Sarah Heinz House

scope. *Hours:* By appointment only. *Location:* Riverview Park, 159 Riverview Avenue.

13. Heinz Plant is the largest food plant of its kind in the world. The firm was founded by the Heinz family in 1869 at Sharpsburg and moved to the present location in 1890. Some of the buildings display remarkable ornamental brickwork. *Location:* Corner of Heinz Street and River Avenue.

14. Sarah Heinz House (brick), a neighborhood club for boys and girls, was founded by Howard Heinz in 1901. He gave the building in 1914 in honor of his mother, Sarah Young Heinz. *Location:* 923 East Ohio Street.

15. Voegtly Evangelical Church (brick), a German church, was erected in 1849 and named for a wealthy benefactor. *Location:* Corner of East Ohio Street and Ahlers Way.

16. Swedenborgian Church, or Church of the New Jerusalem (brick), still uses an organ donated by Andrew Carnegie, the first of many organs provided by him to churches. The congregation's initial building, erected nearby but long since gone, was attended by Carnegie and his parents during his youth. *Location:* 120 Parkhurst Street at Sandusky Street.

Pittsburgh—South Side and West End

1. Pittsburgh & Lake Erie Railroad Station was built in 1898–1901. On the exterior is a large relief of a moving locomotive, "Number 135." The interior contains a fine staircase and foyer, much cut up into offices. *Location:* South Side, at Smithfield Street Bridge and West Carson Street.

2. Monongahela Incline, built in 1869 and rebuilt in 1882, was the first of its kind erected in Pittsburgh. Of the twenty-three original inclines only two remain, this one and the nearby Duquesne Heights Incline, built in 1877 at 1220 Grandview Avenue (same hours and fare as Monongahela funicular). Chartered in 1867, the Monongahela Incline was designed by John J. Endres of Cincinnati, whose daughter Caroline lived at the Monongahela House and supervised construction. This incline has never had a fatal accident. Originally it was constructed of wood with wire cables made by John Roebling but was later rebuilt with steel. It is 640 feet in length, extending 370 feet above West Carson Street. *Hours:* Monday–Saturday, 5:30 A.M.–1 A.M. Sundays and holidays, 7 A.M.–1 A.M. *Transportation fare. Location:* Mount Washington. Runs between Grandview Avenue (top of hill) and West Carson Street near Smithfield Street Bridge.

3. Chatham Village (brick) has been described as the "first large-scale planned residential community built from the ground up in one operation to be retained in single ownership and managed as a long term investment." It was erected on a forty-five-acre tract of land by the Buhl Foundation; 129 houses were finished in 1932 and 68 in 1936. In recent years the foundation has withdrawn from the venture and houses are sold to individuals. The Bigham house, (brick) built in 1843–44 by Thomas James Bigham, serves as the community center for Chatham Village. *Location:* Mount Washington, bounded by Bigham and Olympia Roads, off Virginia Avenue.

4. Ninth United Presbyterian Church (brick), built in 1854, was originally the First Associate Reformed Presbyterian Church of Birmingham. It was closed after the church union of 1958. *Location:* South Side, Bingham and South Fourteenth Streets.

5. South Side Market House (brick) is one of the last two market houses in Pittsburgh, the other being in East Liberty (see *Motor Square Garden).* (A third, the North Side Market, the last to function as such, was taken down for the construction of Allegheny Center.) Built in 1893, the South Side Market House burned about twenty years later and was rebuilt in 1915. It has been a recreation center since 1950. *Location:* South Twelfth and Bingham Streets.

6. Saint John the Baptist Ukrainian Catholic Church (brick) was founded in 1891 and built in 1895, with an addition in 1918–19. Its eight turquoise onion domes lend much charm to the otherwise drab landscape of the area. It is the mother church of all Eastern Rite Catholic churches in western Pennsylvania and the oldest church of the Byzantine Rite in the Pittsburgh area. Its first pastor was Gabriel Wyslecki. The parish cemetery is located in Carrick. *Location:* South Side, 109 South Seventh Street at East Carson Street.

7. Weilersbacher's Hotel (brick), a popular saloon with a fine bar, was built about 1890 by John Weilersbacher. About 1900 it became a club and was purchased in 1918 by Simon Krom, in whose family it has continued ever since. During prohibition days it was an eating place, becoming a tavern again after repeal. *Location:* South Side, 80 South Tenth Street.

8. Old Stone (or Coates) Tavern was built on the Washington Pike about 1793 by James Coates on land purchased by West Elliot in 1768. According to the *Pittsburgh Chronicle Telegraph* of 1903, there was then an inscription on the north side of the building that read, "Old Stone Tavern, R. Smith." Robert Smith, who was associated with Collins Forge, bought the house from Lemual Miller and operated a tavern here for nearly half a century. The Smiths had kept a store in the old house before the tavern was opened. When they moved, George Schad maintained the inn, followed by other proprietors until the Smith family returned forty years later. The stone house is still operated as a tavern.

The area surrounding the tavern was once known as Temperanceville. When Warden Alexander laid out the town, he made a restriction against buying or selling liquor, but a court soon revoked it. *Location:* West End, 434–436 Greentree Road.

9. German Church (brick) was constructed in 1864 by a German Reformed group; it now serves a black congregation, the Jerusalem Baptist Church, organized in 1901 and reestablished in 1945. *Location:* West End, Sanctus and Steuben Streets.

10. Firehall (brick), built in 1874, has a cast-iron front on the first story. It is presently used as a storage facility by the city. *Location:* West End, Sanctus and Steuben Streets across from Baptist Church.

1. Conrad's Radio Station (brick), now the Wilkinsburg Elks Club, was the site at which Dr. Frank Conrad (1874–1941), assistant chief of engineers at the Westinghouse Corporation, built a small radio receiver to hear time signals from transmitters at Arlington, Va., in 1916. A year later he built a transmitter, station license 8XK, over his garage. In 1917 his facilities were used to test military radio equipment being built at East Pittsburgh for the United States and British governments. The outcome of the experiments was one of the first practical vacuum tube receivers. In 1918 he played phonograph records over the air, and it is reputed that the word *broadcast* was coined at this time. As a result of his work, station KDKA, one of the first commercial radio stations, made its initial broadcast from a small building on top of the East Pittsburgh plant in 1920—the returns of the Harding-Cox presidential election. *Location:* Wilkinsburg, 7750 Penn Avenue at Peebles Street.

2. Graham House (frame) was built at the forks of the road in 1830 by James Graham, pastor of Beulah Presbyterian Church (q.v.). His daughter Mary married Dr. Smith Agnew. She and her brother managed a tavern in this house at one time. *Location:* Wilkinsburg, 2015 Penn Avenue at Greensburg Pike.

3. Singer House (stone), a Gothic structure, was built in 1865–69 by steel baron John F. Singer (1834–80), a partner in the firm of Singer, Hartman & Company, which later became Singer, Nimick & Company. In the 1860s Singer bought an estate of thirty acres near Wilkinsburg where he made a large ornamental lake. This structure was the home of artist William F. Singer. Near the house was a private chapel, now a garage. *Location:* Wilkinsburg, 1318 Singer Place.

4. Edgewood Club (stucco) was organized in 1903 as a recreational center for young people. In 1915 it purchased the old C. C. Mellor estate, setting up the present neoclassical building with a grant from the Carnegie Foundation. Here on November 2, 1920, was held the first radio election party (see *Conrad's Radio Station*), with a makeshift loudspeaker and about thirty members present. *Location:* Edgewood, 1 Pennwood Avenue.

5. Beulah Presbyterian Church (brick) was founded in 1785. The early building, still standing, was erected in 1837. Although it was also called Pitt Township Presbyterian Church, its first name was Bullock Pens, since it was near the site of the commissary of Gen. John Forbes in his campaign of 1758. Beef cattle were kept here for pasture and slaughtering. At that time Charles Beatty served as chaplain for Forbes. Later Samuel Barr preached here, followed by the first regular pastor, James Graham. When he began to serve the congregation in 1804, the name of the church was changed to Beulah. An early cemetery was located between this structure, now used as a chapel, and the 1957 church nearby. *Location:* Churchill, on old U.S. 22 about three miles west of Monroeville at Beulah and McCready Roads.

6. The Westinghouse Atom Smasher, decommissioned since 1958, was begun in the summer of 1937 and was operating in full by December 1939. At the time of its construction it was the world's largest unit for conducting experiments in the field of nuclear physics. Consisting of a large pear-shaped tank, thirty feet in diameter and forty-seven feet high, it housed an electrostatic tube through which particles were shot to bombard targets. The structure is sixty-five feet high. Its steel shell was constructed by the Chicago Bridge and Iron Company, with Dr. William H. Wells, head of the Westinghouse nuclear physics program at that time, being instrumental in its design. *Location:* Forest Hills, off U.S. 30 at Westinghouse plant.

7. Rising Sun Stagecoach Tavern (frame) was the first stagecoach stop on the Northern Pike east of Pittsburgh. Across the road where a floral shop now stands is the site of the stable where horses were changed. The tavern was built in 1833 by Abraham Taylor, who operated an inn here. It was later occupied by the innkeeper's daughter and her husband, George Washington Warner. There are fireplaces in every room and hand-hewn logs in the basement.

The community where the inn is located was named for Joel Monroe, the first postmaster in 1857. It was formerly called Patton Township and became a borough in 1951. *Location:* Monroeville, 3835 Northern Pike near junction with U.S. 22.

Note: A stone earthen-bed bridge built in the 1880s is just off old U.S. 22 near Beatty Road.

8. Cross Roads (Old Stone) Church, originally associated with Beulah Presbyterian Church (q.v.) in Churchill, was constructed in 1896–97 partly from stones of an earlier building of 1834. The congregation was organized in 1836 by Revs. Francis Laird and James Graham. The first regular pastor was S. M. McClung. The adjacent cemetery was donated by the Snodgrass and Monroe families. Andrew Mellon (the immigrant) and his family joined this church after breaking with an early Covenanter church near Export (see *Mellon House,* Westmoreland County). In 1969 T. M. Sylves purchased the church property and deeded it to the borough of Monroeville for their historical society and museum headquarters. *Location:* Monroeville, Center Road at Stroschein Road and Northern Pike.

9. McGinley House (stone) was built in 1804 by James McGinley. This landmark, once owned by the Westinghouse Corporation, was turned over to the Monroeville Historical Society and will be restored in the future as a museum. *Location:* Monroeville, on McGinley Road off Greensburg Pike, next to Westinghouse Atomic Power headquarters.

10. Linhart House (double log) was erected in 1782 by Christian Linhart, an early settler whose family owned a sawmill in the Turtle Creek Valley. His daughter, who married into the Metz family, lived in the newer section of the structure, which was built twelve years later. When Indians attacked the area and burned the houses, the family fled to nearby Fort Braddock and their house was spared.

The Linharts' private cemetery is located near Harrison Street, and a memorial park in the area is named for this family. The R. M. Fisher family purchased the Linhart house and built additions to it in 1956, the same year the Century Club erected a historical marker in the front yard. *Location:* Wilkins Township, 221 Farnsworth Avenue.

11. McLaughlin House (log) is reputed to have been constructed in 1775 (deed dates back to 1784) by Edward McLaughlin, who came to America from Ireland at the age of twelve. After living at Fort Pitt, he and his wife Nancy (Wade) moved to this location, taking up a land grant of 236 acres called Groton, where their nine children were born. The house was later owned by their son Edward, followed by their grandson J. W. McLaughlin, whose daughter married John W. Jackson. After the Jacksons lived here, their son A. Ivory Jackson owned it. He deeded it to the Girl Scouts but continues to reside in the neighboring frame house built in 1869. The log house, named Tapawingo by the scouts,

is situated in a scenic meadow surrounded by trees and a stream. Future plans for the site include archeological excavations and restoration of the building. *Location:* Penn Hills, near Unity. From junction of Universal and Meadow Avenues, follow Meadow to Pike Street and continue until road ends at barn. Cabin is nearby.

12. Wilson House (painted brick) was built in 1860 by George Wilson. According to H. C. Bell (in Warner's history), Thomas Wilson resided in Penn Township in 1770 on Wilson's Mount, had a land patent in 1788, and moved to Fort Pitt in 1776. *Location:* Penn Hills, corner of Frankstown Road and Wilson Lane, house no. 11003.

13. Schiller House (brick and log) with curtain chimneys has been owned by the Bishops, the Owens, the Niesleins, and finally the Gerthoffers, who still occupy it. The log kitchen section was built about 1820, and the brick part around 1840. The original springhouse is in the basement. *Location:* Penn Hills, 123 Faybern Road.

14. Penn Hebron Garden Club Barn was built in 1834 of hand-hewn oak constructed with pegs. The structure is situated on a land grant known as The Flying Shuttle on the H. S. Morrow farm. In 1928 it was purchased by the garden club. A historical landmark plaque was placed on it in June 1975. *Location:* Penn Hills, Jefferson Road.

Note: The 1819 Morrow log house is at 11401 Frankstown Road.

15. Wyckoff-Mason House was built of chestnut logs in 1774–75. The land was originally part of a land grant to George Duffield and two others. Duffield deeded a portion of the land to Peter Wyckoff, who built the present house. In 1960 the Mason family purchased it. *Location:* Penn Hills, 6133 Verona Road.

Note: The Isaac Blackadore brick house was built about 1860 at 1235 Blackadore Avenue.

16. Plum Creek Presbyterian Church (brick) was built in 1867–79. The congregation first worshiped at this site in 1791. About 1810 a log meetinghouse was erected, followed by a brick church in the 1850s. *Location:* Plum Borough, 550 New Texas Road.

Note: Logans Ferry Presbyterian Church (frame) was founded in 1854 and the present building was erected in 1856. First meetings were held in homes until the Logan family donated land for a church. Alexander Logan also purchased a tract nearby in 1803 and operated a ferry and an inn. *Location:* Logans Ferry, on Logans Ferry Road and Pa. 909.

17. Globe Powder Storage Building (stone), over eighty feet long, was built along Plum Creek about one hundred years ago. At one time there were five buildings here, one of which blew up. This property was owned by a coal company. (The Plum Creek branch of the Penn Central Railroad, established in 1872, ran alongside this structure. It hauled passengers and freight between Unity and Verona.) The building is now a residence and office of the Kirkpatrick trailer park. *Location:* Plum Borough, 1741 Hulton Road near East Oakmont.

Note: Nearby at 1831 Hulton Road is a restored early log house, partially burned in 1976.

18. Boyce House Site was the birthplace of William D. Boyce, born June 16, 1858. Inspired by the good turn of an English Scout, Boyce brought the scouting movement to the United States and helped make possible the incorporation of the Boy Scouts in Washington, D.C., on February 8, 1910. Although the house no longer exists, the visitor can see remains of a barn and other outbuildings near a deserted farmhouse. *Location:* Two miles southeast of New Kensington, off Pa. 366. One mile south of historical marker on this route, turn left at yellow brick house. At end of lane (one-fourth of a mile) turn right. Continue about 200 yards on disused road. Foundation on left. Other old ruins are located in woods on right, near site of Boyce house.

19. Westinghouse Air Brake General Office Building (sandstone and brick) dates back to 1890, when its first section was built. Destroyed by fire in 1896, it was reconstructed in 1896–97. The new wing of early French Renaissance architecture was added in 1928. The older building is of Richardsonian Romanesque style. A clock is located in the tower overlooking the town. *Location:* Wilmerding, Station Street.

20. George Westinghouse Memorial Bridge, built in 1930–32, is constructed entirely of reinforced concrete, and at the time of its erection the center span was the longest reinforced concrete arch in the country. It is a five-span bridge of the double-ribbed type. *Location:* North Versailles Township, over Turtle Creek on U.S. 30.

21. Wallace-Nasor House (quarried stone) was built after 1790 by James Irwin, who deeded 232 acres of his estates called Veron and Newry to George Miller in 1805. The land was warranted in 1787, surveyed in 1789, patented in 1824, and later owned by James Michael, William Wallace, Mary Lang, and Fred Nasor, in succession. The three-bay house contains six rooms and originally had double porches. Later called Pickup Farm, the property also features a springhouse. The house overlooks Turtle Creek Valley. *Location:* Near Pitcairn, on Moss Side Boulevard (1.r. 02251), 1.9 mile south of junction with Pa. 130 and 993.

Allegheny Suburban—West and Northwest

1. Mansfield Brown House (stone), reputedly Carnegie's oldest home, was constructed in 1822 by Mansfield Brown. In 1842 James Brown and Col. M. B. Brown occupied the building. (The colonel's son Robert, who also lived here at one time, later moved to the mansion site now occupied by Carnegie Library on Beechwood Avenue.) The house has a cavelike structure in the rear, where a "moonshine" still operated during Prohibition days. In 1825 Rev. Joseph Kerr started one of the first seminaries here. In the early 1900s it was a girls' school, later it was made into apartments, and at present it is privately owned. *Location:* Carnegie, 602 Poplar Way.

2. Obey House (frame) was built in 1823 by John Robinson. This old tavern on the Steubenville Pike was later remodeled with a larger addition. According to tradition, Henry Clay played a fiddle and danced here. Other famous guests included Andrew Jackson and Sam Houston. *Location:* Crafton, at Steuben and Obey Streets.

3. Saint Philip's Roman Catholic Mass House (log with brick and weatherboarding) was built by a Mr. Flannigan and used for mass before the first church, named for Philip Smith who donated the land, was erected in 1839. (The site of this old church is near the crucifix in the Saint Philip's cemetery at Crafton Avenue and Steuben Street, next to the present church.) The house, moved to its new location nearby, was where priests from Saint Patrick's Church in Pittsburgh came to conduct mass. *Location:* Crafton, 37 Norma Street near Saint Philip's Roman Catholic Church.

ALLEGHENY COUNTY

4. Frew-Goran-McFall House (stone and brick) was built before 1800 by John Frew with a brick portion later being added to the stone section. A springhouse on the property has been rebuilt. *Location:* Crafton, 105 Sterret Place (off Poplar Street, which is off Noblestown Road).

5. Dixmont State Hospital was the first institution for the mentally ill to be established in Pittsburgh and one of the first in America. Its oldest structure, the administration building, was completed in 1861, after the cornerstone was laid on July 19, 1859. It still contains some of the original furnishings and has an exterior iron-filigree balcony.

Dixmont was founded with the encouragement of Dorothea L. Dix, who selected the site overlooking the Ohio River; and the property was purchased through private and public funds. It began as the mental department of the Western Pennsylvania Hospital and after a series of name changes became Dixmont State Hospital on October 1, 1945. Among the notable people associated with the institution at its founding were Thomas Bakewell, John Bissell, F. R. Brunot, W. M. Darlington, John Herron, John Holmes, John Irwin, George W. Jackson, Governor William F. Johnston, James McCandless, E. W. H. Schenley, and J. H. Shoenberger. *Location:* Kilbuck Township, at Hazelwood Avenue.

6. Saint Stephen's Episcopal Church (stone) of Romanesque and Gothic design was constructed in 1894 and enlarged in 1911. The parish was organized in 1863 and chartered in 1864. In 1863–64 a small frame church designed by the rector, William F. Ten Boeck, was built by the congregation and later replaced with the present structure. *Location:* Sewickley, Broad Street and Frederick Avenue.

7. Frederick Way House (frame) is the home of the famous riverboat pilot and author, Capt. Frederick Way, Jr., whose great-grandfather was Abishai Way (see *Abishai Way House*). Frederick was the pilot of the *Betsy Ann* and the *Liberty,* the last two packet boats to run on the western rivers. He has written numerous books about riverboats and related subjects, and was editor of the *Inland River Record* for many years. *Location:* Sewickley, 121 River Avenue.

8. Stinson-Olver-Foster House (painted brick), of Greek Revival and Edwardian Georgian architecture, was built in 1835 on part of the former Shields estate. Mrs. Mary Olver had established the Edgeworth Female Seminary (which was named for novelist Maria Edgeworth) at Braddock's Field and moved it to East Pittsburgh in 1825. In 1836 she relocated her school in this house. At the time of Mrs. Olver's death in 1842 the seminary closed but reopened in 1846. The two frame wings of the house were destroyed by fire in 1865, thus closing the school permanently. The central section later became the residence of Morrison Foster, brother of Stephen C. Foster; it was subsequently occupied by J. Wilkinson Elliott, an architect who enlarged and remodeled it with a large portico that faces Beaver Road. *Location:* Edgeworth, 420 Oliver Road (street name misspelled from Olver).

9. Abishai Way House (brick), of Greek Revival design with bulls-eye windows, was built in 1838 by Abishai Way, a successful Pittsburgh merchant and business agent for the Harmony Society (see also *Harmony,* Butler County). This house is sometimes mistakenly referred to as the Nicholas Way home (see *John Way House*). It was later purchased by W. L. Jones, followed by Campbell Hall. *Location:* Edgeworth, 108 Beaver Road.

10. John Way House (painted brick) was built in 1810 by Squire John Way and enlarged in 1820. It was operated as an inn called the Sewickley House. John's sons were Abishai, Nicholas, who later owned this house, and James, a riverboat captain. The Walker family purchased the property at a later date. *Location:* Edgeworth, Quaker and Beaver Roads.

11. Newington (brick) was constructed by David Shields in 1816–23 on depreciation land acquired by his father-in-law, Daniel Leet, a major in the Revolution. In 1825 the house became the post office of Sewickley Bottom and was modernized in 1959 by J. Judson Brooks, a descendant of Shields. Shields Presbyterian Church, built in 1868–69, and the Shields Mausoleum are on nearby Church Lane. The Shields brick schoolhouse dates back to 1826. *Location:* Edgeworth, Shields Lane and Beaver Road.

12. Vineacre (Nevin House) (brick), built in 1850 and remodeled in 1916, was the home of Pittsburgh editor Robert P. Nevin and the birthplace of Ethelbert W. Nevin (1862–1901), famous Pittsburgh composer of "Mighty Lak a Rose," "The Rosary," "Narcissus," and other well-known works. Ethelbert lived here for years, and thirty-seven years after his death,

13. Leet's Tavern (Lark Inn)

his widow insisted that his body be disinterred from its burial place in Sewickley, overlooking the Ohio River, and taken to Blue Hill, Maine. *Location:* Edgeworth, Edgeworth Lane and Ohio River Boulevard.

13. Leet's Tavern (Lark Inn) (stone) was built about 1800 by Maj. Daniel Leet, brother of the William Leet who founded Leetsdale in 1796. In 1776 Daniel was commissioned deputy surveyor for Augusta County, Va., and after the Revolution, Pennsylvania authorized him to survey donation and depreciation lands in western Pennsylvania. *Location:* Leet Township, 634 Beaver Road (Pa. 88) at Winding Road.

Note: Near this old tavern is a fine springhouse.

14. D. T. Watson Home (brick) was owned by David T. Watson, one of Pittsburgh's greatest lawyers, who willed it at his death as a home for crippled children. It is an important rehabilitation center, which now includes several other buildings. *Location:* Leetsdale, Camp Meeting Road.

15. Leetsdale Baptist Church (stone) was built between 1850 and 1860 by Gen. Alexander Hays, who was killed in the Civil War in 1863 at the battle of the Wilderness, while leading a group that included the Sixty-third Pennsylvania Regiment, which he had recruited at the opening of the war. *Location:* Beaver Avenue almost at Ambridge line.

16. Settler's Cabin Park, owned and maintained by the county, is the location of three notable early structures.

a. Walker-Ewing House (log), the settler's cabin for which the park was named, is now restored. It was built in the late eighteenth century reportedly by John Henry. In 1785 Isaac and Gabriel Walker acquired the land. Isaac's daughter and son-in-law William Ewing owned the site in 1816. The Ewings' son, J. Nelson Ewing, lived here in 1843 with his wife. *Location:* North Fayette Township, on l.r. 02033. Follow signs to settler's cabin.

b. Ewing-Glass House (frame) was erected in 1855 by J. Nelson Ewing after he had moved from the log cabin. It was later occupied by his grandson, E. W. Glass. *Location:* North Fayette Township, Box 435, on l.r. 02033.

c. Pollock-McGill House (brick) was built by James Pollock in 1837 on a tract of land purchased in 1799. Originally called Mansion Place, it once belonged to Rev. John Riddel. At a later date William McGill acquired the property. *Location:* North Fayette Township, McGill Road off Noblestown Road.

17. Dunlevy-Campbell House (stone) was built in 1814. An oval stone in one gable bears the date. An old barn and springhouse with a log loft above it are also on the property. A later owner, James E. Campbell, lived here all his life. *Location:* North Fayette Township, Box 162, on Pa. 978 (on side of hill looking into valley, approached by winding dirt road and hidden from highway).

18. North Star Hotel (brick), built about 1840, was once known as the Cook farmhouse. In 1914 it became the property of the present owner, who has operated it ever since as a hotel-tavern. It is situated near the village of Santiago (named for a coal company), which was once called Tyre and also North Star (for a railroad station). *Location:* Two miles east of Imperial, on old U.S. 22, near Santiago.

19. Walker-Ewing Grace House (log), not to be confused with the above log house in Settler's Cabin Park, is said to have been built on a tomahawk claim by Isaac and Gabriel Walker. Although the date 1762 is inscribed on the chimney, the house was not finished until about 1787–95. Indians reputedly attacked Gabriel Walker's family at this site in 1782. The property was given by the Ewing family to the Pittsburgh History and Landmarks Foundation in 1973. Open by appointment. *Location:* Collier Township, on Noblestown Road near Robinson Run and Penn Central Railroad (across valley from Nike site, 3.4 miles from U.S. 422).

20. Hyeholde is a labor of love designed and built by William and Clara Kryskill during the depression and completed in 1937. Operated by the Kryskills until 1974, this rustic, charming structure was constructed with materials from the old Stonesifer barn on the Steubenville Pike, which in turn had been fashioned from timbers cut in Westmoreland County and floated down the Monongahela and Ohio Rivers on rafts. Scenes depicting Chaucer's *Canterbury Tales* were sketched by the innkeeper on the interior walls (later replaced by prints). A large walk-in fireplace is located in the main dining room, which also has unique stained-glass windows. Directly in front of this building is another stone house that Kryskill constructed for one of his daughters. The book *Hyeholde,* written by the builder, gives a step-by-step account of the inn's construction and history. *Location:* Coraopolis, 0.5 mile north of Greater Pittsburgh Airport, 192 Hyeholde Drive off Coraopolis Heights Road.

21. Sharon Community Presbyterian Church (frame) was organized in 1817. Its first brick church was dedicated on October 7, 1828, in the village of Sharon, later called Carnot. Its first pastor was Andrew McDonald. In 1868–69 the present large frame building was erected with construction costs that amounted to $8,000, and services were held here until 1965 when a modern sanctuary was built next to it. The old structure is used for youth programs and a nursery school. *Location:* Moon Township, 522 Carnot Road off junction of Pa. 51 and Beaver Grade Road.

Allegheny Suburban—North

1. Saint Nicholas Church (brick), a Latin Rite Catholic church, was built in 1900 by a Croatian parish and remodeled with twin towers after a fire in 1922. The interior contains some interesting murals called *Life in the Old Country,* painted by Maximilian Vanka in 1937, along with a more recent group on American experiences. During the painting of the early series, Vanka claimed that he saw a ghost appear repeatedly in the church. Because of this report the church is closed in the evenings, unless there is a service. *Location:* Millvale, 24 Maryland Avenue.

2. Wilkins House (stone) was erected before 1826 with a late Georgian fanlighted door and a subsequent frame addition. This property was part of a 230-acre tract of land marked "No. 1 of the Jones District Depreciation Land" granted to John Wilkins. A deed of 1826 confirms that two houses stood on the property at the time. *Location:* Millvale Borough, 144 Evergreen Street.

3. Chalfant House (frame with aluminum siding), of Greek Revival design, belonged at one time to the Chalfant family and was moved to this location at an earlier date. The house at present is occupied by a women's club. *Location:* Etna Borough, 89 Locust Street.

4. Shaw House (brick) was built in 1824–26 by Thomas Wilson Shaw, operator of a sickle factory on nearby Pine Creek. His father John Shaw, who owned a blacksmith shop at the Point in Pittsburgh, had bought a 600-acre tract of land from John Wilkins, Jr., and in 1802 he built the low two-story frame house (recently well restored) south of the creek at 1021 Glenshaw Avenue, corner of Old Butler Plank Road. John Shaw and his sons operated an industrial complex, including the sickle factory, a gristmill, a coal mine, a sawmill, a brick factory, and others. The brick house is still occupied by members of the Shaw family. *Location:* Glenshaw, 1525 Old Butler Plank Road.

5. Kirk House (frame) was built in 1885 by James B. Kirk, general auditor of the Baltimore & Ohio Railroad. He made his headquarters at Glenshaw after being sent to the area by John W. Garrett, B & O president, who was financing Henry W. Oliver in the construction of the Pittsburgh & Western (which later merged with the parent road). Kirk, in order to induce his wife to bring their daughters and live in Glenshaw, built an exact replica of her girlhood home in Baltimore. His signature, written with a diamond, is still on a window pane, and some of those who have lived in the house since his death have reported seeing his ghost looking out a window toward the railroad. *Location:* Glenshaw, 1001 Glenshaw Avenue.

6. Isaac Lightner House (brick) is a gem of Greek Revival architecture, built in 1833. One of its features is a cantilevered roof on a walkway to an outbuilding. *Location:* Glenshaw, 2407 Mount Royal Boulevard.

7. Thompson-DeHaven-Leet House (brick in Flemish bond) was built in 1831 or 1836 by Robert Thompson. After Harmar DeHaven purchased it, the house was occupied for two generations by the DeHaven family. The next person to live here was Clifford S. Leet. *Location:* Glenshaw, 3201 Mount Royal Boulevard.

8. Guyasuta Statue was a gift of Henry J. Heinz in memory of Seneca Indian Chief Guyasuta. Gen. James O'Hara had furnished a cabin for the old Indian leader on his estate at what is now Sharpsburg and provided necessities during his last years. When Guyasuta died about 1800, he was buried in an old mound near the north end of the Highland Park Bridge. His skeletal remains were taken to Carnegie Museum when the Pennsylvania Railroad received title to the ground in 1919. Guyasuta is also reported, with some believable evidence in each case, to be buried in two other places: one in Mercer County (see *Indian Burials*) and the other at an unknown spot on the Cornplanter Reservation in Warren County (see *Kinzua Dam*), Cornplanter having been his nephew. *Location:* Sharpsburg, corner of Main and North Canal Streets.

9. Depreciation Lands Museum (brick) was built in 1860 as a sanctuary for the Reformed (Covenanter) Presbyterian Church on property acquired in 1837. The church was vacant from 1925 to 1948 when the Episcopal Church of Saint Thomas in the Fields bought it. A Baptist congregation purchased it in 1963 after the Saint Thomas members moved into their new building. At present it is a museum containing displays and memorabilia from the time when certificates for the depreciation of Continental currency paid to soldiers in the revolution could be used to buy certain lands in Pennsylvania.

The log house next to the museum was moved from Middle Road in Glenshaw. It was built in 1803 by James Armstrong, who paid for his land with depreciation certificates. *Hours:* May–October: Saturday and Sunday, 1–4 P.M. *Location:* Hampton Township (at Wildwood), on Pa. 8 behind bank, one mile south of Pennsylvania Turnpike.

10. Shady Side Academy (brick), a boys' preparatory school, was founded in 1883 at 926 Aiken Avenue in Shadyside. The school was moved to the country soon after World War I, when Wallace H. Rowe, a trustee of the academy, purchased the Hanlin and Prager farms in O'Hara Township, a tract totaling 125

acres. Three buildings were erected here in October 1922. During the twenties two more dormitories, a dining hall, an infirmary, and a gymnasium were added. Memorial Hall was erected in 1954.

In 1940 the academy united with the Arnold School, thus making Shady Side the only boys' college preparatory school in the Pittsburgh area at that time. On the old Lewis estate nearby, overlooking this site and located on Squaw Run Road, is the middle school. The junior school is located on Braddock Avenue in Pittsburgh. *Location:* Fox Chapel, on Fox Chapel Road.

Note: Near the junction of Squaw Run Road and Old Mill Road is "Long Meadow," a 120-year-old log house on a 1786 land grant, later the Ernest Hillman estate.

11. Lawrence Estate (stone), built in 1929, was the home of Mary Flinn Lawrence, daughter of William Flinn, of the infamous Flinn-Magee ring that controlled Allegheny County politics from 1873 to 1909. In 1969 the Allegheny Department of Parks, Recreation, and Conservation acquired this 480-acre estate for $1 million, and since the death of Mrs. Lawrence in 1974, has been planning to open the home with its furnishing, paintings, rare china, and antiques as a cultural center and park for musical and art events. The property, situated high on a hill with a winding driveway leading up to it, contains a great stand of native trees with understory growth typical of the early years of settlement in the county, as well as a variety of wildlife. *Location:* Indiana Township, north of Harts Run Road. Turn left on Saxonburg Boulevard and continue for 1.2 mile. Gatehouse is just off road at left.

12. Cross Keys Tavern (brick), built in 1850, first appeared on an Allegheny County property holders' map in 1851. It was known as the G. F. Thomas Tavern until 1876 and served as a halfway house on what was then the Kittanning Pike. In later years it was operated by a woman and her daughters. After a flourishing life it fell into disrepair, and restoration of this old inn was begun in 1972. The charming establishment now specializes in wild-game dinners. *Hours:* Tuesday–Friday, 12 A.M.–2:30 P.M., 6–10:30 P.M. Saturday, 3–12:00 P.M. *Location:* Fox Chapel, on Dorseyville Road south of Harts Run Road.

13. Bakerstown Presbyterian Church (brick), of Greek Revival and Gothic detail, was built in 1838 and remodeled in 1888. It was built as a Methodist Protestant church.

The slightly younger original Presbyterian church is nearby, built into a later structure, while the MP building still sits apart. *Location:* Bakerstown, on Pa. 8, south of l.r. 02273.

14. Babcock House (frame) was built about 1900 by Edward Vose Babcock, Pittsburgh mayor, Allegheny County commissioner, lumberman, and early conservationist. Babcock is remembered as the "father" of North and South Parks, secretly buying up the land and transferring it to the county at no profit to himself. He also gave Pennsylvania the land for Babcock State Forest in Somerset County (see *Ashtola*) and West Virginia acreage for another state forest, as well as creating the Babcock National Forest in the far West. The house, in a park-like setting, is well maintained but not presently occupied by its owner. *Location:* Near north end of Babcock Boulevard, across from Pine Junior High School.

15. Green Gables (stucco) is an enlargement, much changed, of the Woods family's Tudor house dating from before 1876. About 1890 it was rebuilt into a typical Victorian mansion by one Johnston. Later it was owned by Harry Dipple. Now, renamed Beverly Hills, it is a nightclub with dinner theater. It was severely damaged by fire in 1975, but is being repaired. *Location:* Ross Township, between Evergreen Road and Babcock Boulevard, opposite end of Rochester Road.

16. Evergreen Hamlet, the former farm property of Benjamin Davis, was an experimental commune organized on May 16, 1851, and lasting until 1866. Its members, prominent Pittsburgh businessmen who wanted reasonable country-style homes, paid an initiation fee, a portion of the road assessment, and their share of the purchase price of the property, receiving in return "one building lot and one (undivided) sixteenth in the school lot, and that portion of the farm not laid off in lots." A schoolhouse was built and a community farmer employed. Only four English-type villas remain. Twenty were intended to be erected. In 1879, J. J. Gillespie, a later owner, built a narrow-gauge railroad from Millvale to the hamlet. *Location:* Evergreen, off Babcock Boulevard on Evergreen Hamlet Road (Ross Township).

17. Russell's Pyramid commemorates Charles Taze Russell (founder of Jehovah's Witnesses) who died in October 1916. He was buried, by his own wish, in the United Cemeteries in Ross Township. There is only a small headstone, but beside it is a granite pyramid in which are copies of almost everything he wrote. *Location:* Ross Township, United Cemeteries, Cemetery Lane, off U.S. 19 just above West View.

18. Hilands Presbyterian Church (painted brick) was organized in 1797. The present church was built in 1826, and an education building was added in 1914. In 1936 the church's interior was remodeled, and in 1940 its exterior was redone in the Georgian style. *Location:* Ross Township, 845 Perry Highway.

19. North Hills Unitarian Church (frame) is a remarkable adaptation by John Schurko of a former dairy barn. The barn became the Unitarian-Universalist church in 1960, and it is situated almost out of view from the road on a large tract planted in trees and gardens. *Location:* McCandless Township, on West Ingomar Road near borough line.

20. Thorn Hill School, a penal institution for delinquent boys, was in operation from 1913 until 1973. Most of it is gone, but a few remaining structures serve as maintenance buildings in Thorn Hill Industrial Park. *Location:* Thorn Hill, off Commonwealth Drive near Pennsylvania Turnpike interchange no. 3 (at U.S. 19 and Interstate 79).

21. Harwick Disaster Graves and Monument are a grim reminder of the 1901 mine disaster that took 179 lives. The graves and monument are in the old Lutheran cemetery beside a road leading into the Colfax Power Station of Duquesne Light Company. One granite monument is a fine folk carving of the scene in the mine, with workers and mine mules falling dead from the explosion. *Location:* Cheswick, off Pa. 28.

22. Rachel Carson's Birthplace (frame), the former home of the author of *The Sea Around Us* and *Silent Spring,* is being restored by the Rachel Carson Homestead Association as a museum and a lending and research library. This structure was built in 1840. The original four-room section is on the right side. *Location:* Springdale, on top of Colfax Hill.

23. Allegheny–Kiski Valley Historical Society (stone) is housed in the former American Legion Post No. 85 building, erected in 1931. The museum includes collections of glassware and pottery, military uniforms, models of regional industrial development, early lighting devices, Indian artifacts, early appliances, farm tools, photographs, and other memorabilia. *Hours:* Wednesday, Friday, Saturday, 1–4 P.M. Winter: Sunday, 1–4 P.M. Tours by arrangement. *Location:* Tarentum, 224 East Seventh Avenue at Lock Street.

24. Tour-Ed Mine, an educational museum, presents information on coal mining in the Allegheny Valley from about 1800 to the present. This enterprise, developed and owned by Ira Wood, includes a half-hour tour in man-trip cars through the half-acre mine, with views of displays depicting the various phases of coal-mining development, a series of rooms in a typical coal-mining community, and a mockup of a company store. *Hours:* Memorial Day–Labor Day: daily, 1–5:30 P.M. May and September 1 to October 15, Saturday and Sunday, 1–5:30 P.M. *Admission charge. Location:* One mile west of Tarentum, seven miles from Oakmont interchange of Turnpike (no. 5), off Pa. 28 on Bull Creek Road, across from Woodlawn Golf Course.

25. Burtner House (stone), recently restored, was built in 1821 by Philip Burtner and his wife Anna Negley, the first permanent white settlers in the area. This house, with large stone chimneys on the gable ends, was a polling place at the time of President Lincoln's election. The structure has remained in the possession of the same family until recent years. In the 1970s it was doomed for destruction by the expressway, but at the last minute was saved by public protest. It will be restored as a museum. *Tours:* By appointment only. *Donation. Location:* Natrona Heights, on Burtner Road off Pa. 28 along the Allegheny Valley Expressway (Harrison Township).

26. Natrona Salt Works Buildings (brick), formerly occupied by the salt and soda works which gave the town its name, are now used in the production of chemicals from deposits shipped in from abroad. *Location:* Natrona Heights.

27. Bell Haven is the brain child and endeavor of J. Oliver Elliott, who owns a collection of bells sprawling over most of the acre of lawn which adjoins his house, as well as much of the space within. The octogenarian's philosophy is that bringing joy to humanity is reward enough. The Elliotts ring the bells twice a year—on New Year's Eve and at 2 P.M. on July 4—when they include a two-hour tour of the grounds. *Location:* West Deer Town-

ship. Take Bull Creek Road, off Pa. 28 in Tarentum, and follow Red Belt for seven miles.

28. Bull Creek Presbyterian Church (brick) was erected in 1853. The first services of this congregation were held outdoors in 1796. Their original church, made of logs, was built in 1801, followed by a smaller one in 1833 that was constructed because the first was too large to heat. The 1853 structure was replaced by a new church across the road and is now used as a recreation hall. *Location:* West Deer Township, Tarentum-Culmerville Road.

Allegheny Suburban—South

1. Hugh Jackson House (stucco over stone), a massive and venerable home, narrowly missed destruction when it was almost inundated by an artificial lake that was built around it by the developers of Cedarhurst Manor at the beginning of World War II. Although some evidence seems to date its construction at 1808, the house was most likely built by 1794, because it was mentioned in reports of the Whiskey Rebellion. *Location:* Mount Lebanon, just west of Lindendale Drive on lake bank.

2. Forsythe Log Cabin was built about 1823 in Wilkinsburg. In 1840 it was moved to Penn Avenue near Saint Clair Street in Pittsburgh where it was occupied by Hugh Forsythe and his wife Mary Perchment, daughter of Capt. Peter Perchment of the Revolution. In 1917 it was moved to a location near Negley, on Penn Avenue. Faced with destruction about 1950, it was relocated to the present site by Congressman James G. Fulton. After his death it was acquired by the Upper Saint Clair school board, which has deeded it to the township. For a while it served as a youth center, but its fate in the present location is uncertain. *Location:* Upper Saint Clair Township, on Clifton-Bridgeville (McLaughlin Run) Road, near U.S. 19 across from municipal building.

3. Joy House (brick) was built by Joseph Joy, who devised the first functional mine-loading machine, known today as the Joy Loader, and other mining machinery. Joy took an engineering course from a Scranton correspondence school, the only education beyond grade school that this farm boy had. The company became wealthy on his invention, which revolutionized the mining industry. This house had a specially built-in

7. *Miller Homestead*

laboratory for his use. *Location:* Upper Saint Clair Township, on southeast corner of Iroquois and Comanche Roads (near South Hills Village Mall).

4. Gilfillan House (brick) was built in 1855–57 by John Gilfillan. This three-bay house has a transom doorway and a chimney at each gable end. The original glass windows have been preserved in the structure. Also on the property is a stone springhouse. This is the last piece of farmland in the area still held by the original family. The Gilfillans donated land for the Westminster Presbyterian Church located nearby. *Location:* Upper Saint Clair Township, 1950 Washington Road near Orr Road on Pa. 19.

5. Bethel Presbyterian Church (brick), the western division of Peters Creek Presbyterian Church (oldest congregation of this denomination in the county), was organized in 1796. (See *Lebanon Presbyterian Church*.) John Clark was the area's first regular pastor, serving from 1783 to 1794. A log meeting-house was built in 1779 or 1780; a brick church in 1826; a third, also brick, in 1855; and the fourth and present structure in 1910. Bethel is the parent of five churches in the area. Housed in this building is a fine historical room containing memorabilia relating to the church. A cemetery adjoining the structure is one of the oldest in the area, containing the graves of early settlers and fourteen soldiers of the Revolution. *Location:* Bethel Park, junction of Bethel Church and Marshall Roads.

Note: An early brick manse is at the corner of Marshall and Oakhurst Roads. George Marshall, fourth pastor of Bethel Church (1833–72), lived here while he served the church.

6. Sheplar House (stone) was built by John Sheplar in 1831. It is situated on the early land grant, Mullington, owned by Thomas McMillan (brother of Rev. John McMillan) in 1776. Before erecting the present house, Sheplar lived in a nearby log structure where his twelve children were born. *Location:* Library (Snowden area), 3914 Snowden Road off Ridge Road (South Park Township).

7. Miller Homestead (stone) was built near Catfish Run (a branch of Peters Creek) in 1808 by James Miller, the son of Oliver Miller, Sr. James built a stone addition to the house in 1830. The building remained in the Miller family until the 1920s when it was purchased by the county. The homestead was built on the site of Oliver Miller's two-story log house where the first church service of Peters Creek (see *Bethel Presbyterian Church*) was conducted by Rev. John McMillan in 1776. The stone house was never a manse, though it has been referred to as such over the years.

30

9. Octagon Barn

10. Saint Luke's Protestant
Episcopal Church

In 1794 this area witnessed the first shots of the rebellion over a whiskey tax, fired as a response to federal officers' attempt to serve William Miller (James's brother) a warrant on his unregistered still. Their brother Oliver Miller, Jr., was killed at this time on Bower Hill. *Hours:* Tuesday–Saturday, 12–4 P.M. Sunday 1–4 P.M. Clubs and groups by appointment. *Location:* South Park, on Stone Manse Drive off Pa. 88.

8. Pioneer Inn (log) was built in 1927 presumably on the site of Fort Couch, which was erected in the 1790s and razed in 1890. At first called Fort Couch Inn, the building acquired its present name in 1939. The original fireplace, chimney, and foundation of the early fort have been preserved as part of this structure. During the Whiskey Rebellion of 1794 insurgents planned battle strategy here. *Location:* Bethel Park, 82 Fort Couch Road (south of South Hills Village).

Note: At 3215 Kennebec Road in the Brookside Farms area is a stuccoed stone house built before 1790. It belonged to Sarah Couch Mannes, the daughter of Nathan Couch who built the fort.

9. Octagon Barn (frame), apparently the last of its kind in the county, bears a date of 1897, which appears improbable since this type of structure had gone out of vogue half a century earlier. However, the unusual octagonal peak might indicate such a late date. *Location:* Upper Saint Clair, 2333 Lesnett Road.

10. Saint Luke's Protestant Episcopal Church (stone), the first Episcopal church established west of the Allegheny Mountains, was first built of logs by Col. John Lea for services perhaps as early as 1770. Brig. Gen. John Neville (see *Woodville*) took the lead in building a frame structure and paid for the education of Francis Reno, the first regular Episcopal minister in the west. This second church rotted from neglect. The present stone one, intentionally archaic and rustic in appearance, was built by the diocese in 1851–53 as a memorial of its first congregation. *Location:* Scott Township, on old Washington Pike in Woodville section.

11. Woodville (Neville House) (frame), on the Avenue grant, was built in 1785 by Brig. Gen. John Neville (1731–1803), an officer in the French and Indian War and the Revolution, who was also inspector of taxes for the collection of the levy on whiskey. The nucleus of the house, now a kitchen, is an extremely early log cabin. Several years later the general built another house nearby (Bower Hill) on the Sidge Field grant which was burned by the insurgents during the Whiskey Rebellion of 1794. His son Col. Presley Neville resided in Woodville at that time. The house was purchased about 1820 by John Wrenshall, and is now owned by the Pittsburgh History and Landmarks Foundation. *Location:* Collier Township, 50 Washington Pike at Thompson Run Rd.

12. Railroad Station Library, a former Pennsylvania Railroad station, was con-

11. Woodville (Neville House)

verted in recent years to a public library. A refurbished caboose next to it serves as a children's library. *Location:* Bridgeville, corner of Railroad and Station Streets.

13. Jefferson Memorial Park, the county's largest cemetery of its kind, was founded in 1929–30 by Harry C. Neel and includes 325 acres on a tract originally called Beam Hill. The land patent, signed by Gov. Thomas Mifflin in 1798, went to Jacob Beam who sold it to Aaron Work, the founder's great-great-grandfather. The Neel family has restored the 1782 Beam log cabin with eight of the original logs. The Aaron Work house, built about 1800, also log with stone and frame additions, is nearby. Preserved on a hillside mausoleum are pillars from the Bank of Pittsburgh (1828) together with a bronze statue of Thomas Jefferson by sculptor Frank Vittor. A bronze replica of the statue of George Washington by Jean Antoine Houdon and the steps salvaged from the Henry W. Oliver estate are near another mausoleum. Future plans include the construction of a museum building to house memorabilia of the area collected by the Neel family. *Location:* Jefferson Borough, Jefferson Memorial Park.

14. Payne House (painted brick), once a stagecoach stop halfway between Pittsburgh and Elizabeth, was built about 1802. John Payne, who married a daughter of Henry Large (see *Large House*), lived here. There is a porch on the side of the house, and a later rear patio is the site of an early springhouse. *Location:* Jefferson Borough, on Old Clairton Road at Pearson Road.

15. High Tor (brick) was the home of Andrew W. Robertson, one of the founders of the Western Pennsylvania Conservancy and former chairman of the board of Westinghouse Electric Corporation, in which capacity he was a vital force especially during the depression. A man dedicated to preservation of the nation's natural heritage, Robertson, with his wife Alice, formed the Pleasant Hills Arboretum Corporation in 1950 and donated eight acres of oak forest to the organization for public use. This was followed by another gift of eight acres in 1952, four of which were originally owned by John Shields, who obtained a patent in 1791. In 1953, Dr. O. E. Jennings headed a census of the plant and bird life here. In 1966, on the death of Robertson, the organization's name was changed to the A. W. Robertson Arboretum of Pleasant Hills, in his honor. *Location:* Pleasant Hills, on Old Clairton Road near Dutch Lane. Arboretum entrances are opposite 170 West Bruceton Road and 217 Oakcrest Lane.

16. Torrence House (fieldstone) was built about 1790 by Maj. James Torrence on land given to him for services during the Revolutionary War. His son David obtained the warrant for the land in 1827 and the following year paid $116.64 to the state and received the patent for the 237-acre tract. *Location:* Pleasant Hills, 121 Colson Drive.

17. Large House (painted brick), of Greek Revival style, has a signature stone in one gable end which reads, "J. & E. Large 1838." This home, built by John Large, was later owned by Henry Large, John's grandson, who began operation of a distillery in 1863, engaging in the manufacture of Monongahela rye whiskey, the brand that his grandfather had established. This business was later bought by Abraham Overholt (see *Henry Clay Frick Birthplace*, Westmoreland County). Henry Large married Anna H. Greenly in 1861. *Location:* Large, on Pa. 51 at Westinghouse atomic plant.

18. Round Hill Farm, consisting of 181 acres, is a modern working farm operated by the county, with a variety of barnyard animals. Located here is a brick farmhouse built in 1838 on an original land grant made to Elisha Peairs in 1790. It passed through six generations to Walter Scott. Marjorie Scott, of the seventh generation, lived on the farm with her parents until it was acquired by the county in 1958. The house now serves as the county park police headquarters. *Hours:* Year round: daily, 9 A.M. to dusk. *Location:* Round Hill Regional Park, on Round Hill Road off Pa. 48 near Elizabeth.

19. Van Allen House (brick), of late Georgian style with a fanlight in the front entrance, was built between 1819 and 1823 by David Van Allen. This fine house with an interesting stairway and interior is situated on a high hill looking toward the Monongahela Valley. *Location:* Forward Township, on Mentor Road (l.r. 02036) about one mile off Pa. 136 at Sunnyside.

Note: Also nearby on this road are the Sutton-Wunderlich house, painted brick with a double porch recessed at one end, built in 1860, and the brick King-Stracelsky house, with gable curtains between the chimneys, built about 1830–50.

20. Experimental Mine (U.S. Bureau of Mines), a unique coal-mine testing laboratory founded by the U.S. Bureau of Mines in 1900, has been responsible for the creation of many mine-safety devices and the improvement of accident-prevention methods. *Location:* Bruceton, off Cochran Mill Road.

21. Lebanon Presbyterian Church (brick), known as the Lebanon Meeting House, was built in 1871–72, replacing a brick structure of 1823. The congregation was organized as the eastern division of Peters Creek Presbyterian Church on November 5, 1776, when Dr. John McMillan preached there (see *Bethel Presbyterian Church*). The building now houses administration offices, a learning center, a library, and student personnel services for a branch of Community College of Allegheny County. *Location:* West Mifflin, near old Allegheny County Airport, 0.1 mile South of Lebanon Church Road, at junction of Lebanon School and Old Elizabeth Roads.

22. Saint Sava Church (brick), originally built in 1904, was the first Serbian Orthodox church organized in the eastern part of the United States. The present church was erected in 1950. (See *Shadeland,* Crawford County.) *Location:* McKeesport, 901 Hartman Street.

23. Borland-Jones House (brick) was built in 1831. It has a signature stone bearing the inscription, "JA & NR 1831." *Location:* White Oak Borough, 2683 McClintock Road.

24. Muse Homestead (stone) is restored as a museum in White Oak Regional Park. A plaque at the entrance reads:

Original site of blockhouse built by an area settler as protection from Indians. The patent was acquired in 1788 by one of the builders, Adam Reburn, and became known as "Fort Reburn."

Reburn's 218 and ¾ acre homestead, Galilee, was purchased in 1834 by John Jones Muse, Esq. in whose family it remained until it became part of the Allegheny Regional Parks System in 1967. Muse was a son of the American Revolution. Erected in 1972 by Queen Alliquippa Chap. D.A.R., McKeesport.

Location: McKeesport, White Oak Regional Park, 4222 Third Street.

25. Saint Paulinas Roman Catholic Church (stone), an outstanding example of human resourcefulness, was erected in 1936 through the effort and determination of this congregation. In 1935, when two existing church buildings could not accommodate the membership, an architect estimated the expense of a new building at $300,000, which was beyond the church's means. As a result, the congregation constructed this Norman French building, for the most part on its own. Men, women, and children, together with their neighbors, cleared the ground and collected cast-off stone. The steel-trussed roof was designed by a draftsman in a steel plant, and the architectural plan was copied from photographs of existing churches. Within eighteen months the volunteers had completed the edifice at a cost of only $37,000. *Location:* Clairton, corner of Carnegie and Delaware Avenues and Fourth Street.

Pennsylvania Historical and Museum Commission Markers

Allegheny Arsenal   Pittsburgh, opposite 257 Fortieth Street, Lawrenceville

Avery College   Pittsburgh, 619 East Ohio Street, North Side

Bethel Presbyterian Church   Bethel Church Road between U.S. 19 and Pa. 88

Bouquet Camp   Pa. 380 east of Pittsburgh

Braddock's Crossing   Pa. 837 north of Duquesne at Kennywood Park

Braddock's Defeat   U.S. 30 southeast of Wilkinsburg

Chartier's Town   Tarentum, Pa. 28

David L. Lawrence   Pittsburgh, Point State Park

Elizabeth   Elizabeth, Pa. 51

Ethelbert Nevin   Edgeworth, Pa. 65

Ferris Wheel Inventor   Pittsburgh, West Commons, North Side

Forbes Road (Bouquet's Breastworks)   Monroeville, l.r. 02213

Fort Duquesne   Pittsburgh, Point State Park

Fort Lafayette   Pittsburgh, Ninth Street just north of Penn Avenue

Fort Pitt Pittsburgh, Point State Park

Fort Pitt Blockhouse Pittsburgh, Point State Park

Fort Prince George Pittsburgh, Point State Park

George Westinghouse U.S. 30 near Turtle Creek, east and west ends of bridge

Hand's Hospital Crafton, Pa. 60

James Hay Reed Pittsburgh, at Buhl Planetarium, North Side

Jane Grey Swisshelm Pittsburgh, Braddock Avenue near Penn-Lincoln Parkway

John Scull Pittsburgh, Boulevard of the Allies just west of Market Street

Kier Refinery Pittsburgh, at parklet near Bigelow Square

Neville House Pa. 50 south of Woodville

Pennsylvania Canal Pittsburgh, Liberty Avenue east of Eleventh Street, to the left of Union Station ramp

Pittsburgh On main highways leading into city

Polish Army Pittsburgh, 97 South Eighteenth Street, South Side

Shadyside Iron Furnace Pittsburgh, southeast corner of Bayard Street and Amberson Avenue, Oakland

Shannopin Town Pittsburgh, Fortieth Street at bridge, Lawrenceville

Station WQED Pittsburgh, 4802 Fifth Avenue, Oakland

Stephen C. Foster Memorial Pittsburgh, Forbes Avenue just east of Bigelow Boulevard, Oakland

V.F.W. Pittsburgh, Fifth Avenue and Bigelow Boulevard, Oakland

William D. Boyce Pa. 366, two miles southeast of New Kensington

Yohogania Courthouse Pa. 837 southwest of West Elizabeth

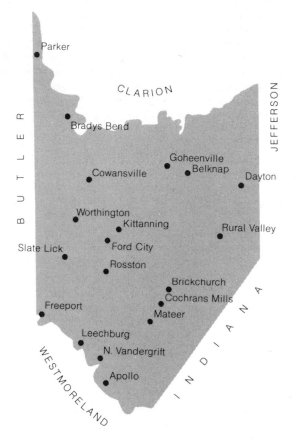

Armstrong County

Capsule History

Armstrong County, named for Maj. Gen. John Armstrong, an Indian fighter who served in the Continental Congress and the Revolutionary army, was formed on March 12, 1800, from parts of Allegheny, Westmoreland, and Lycoming Counties. It has an area of 652 square miles and a population of 75,590.

Before 1740 Pennsylvania traders had established posts in the Indian villages of the area; and in 1749 Céloron de Blainville, a French army officer, was commissioned by the governor-general of France to claim the region for Louis XV by burying lead plates along the Allegheny River.

The county seat of Kittanning, whose name was derived from the Indian word for "at the great stream," was laid out on a famous Delaware and Shawnee Indian settlement which was claimed by the Six Nations by conquest. This Indian village is believed to have been one of the largest of its kind west of the Alleghenies. On September 8, 1756, during the French and Indian War, Armstrong's forces destroyed the settlement on account of atrocities the Indians committed against the English. (One of the earliest medals executed in America depicts this event, the die having been cast in Philadelphia in 1756 or 1757.) Among those killed was the Delaware Indian Captain Jacobs, who lived in a two-story log house in Kittanning (site at 313 Market Street).

Blanket Hill, east of Kittanning, was a stopping point for the troops en route to attack the Indians and the site of an army defeat when a returning party encountered a large Indian force. A monument marks the hill where the soldiers suffered severe losses and abandoned their blankets and other gear. Fort Appleby, built in 1776 at the site that later became Fort Armstrong, was the first United States fort west of the Alleghenies.

Kittanning, together with Ford City and Rosston, was included in Appleby Manor—surveyed in 1769 and one of the forty-four manors reserved by the Penns. The county seat was laid out about 1803–04 and incorporated in 1821. It was the terminal point of the old *Frankstown Path* (locally called the Kittanning Path), which was used by both the Indians and the settlers for years and was a part of a national system of trails, following much the same course from Shelocta to Kittanning as present-day U.S. 422. Other principal Indian trails of the county included the *Great Shamokin Path,* which followed Cowanshannack Creek most of the way from Kittanning to about Nu Mine, thence turning northeast through Barnards, toward Smicksburg; the *Kuskusky Path,* running from Kittanning past Worthington, thence toward Herman; and the *Kiskiminetas Path,* a branch of the Frankstown Path, which cut off east of Shelocta, entered the county near West Lebanon, and followed a course similar to Pa. 56 through South Bend and Spring Church, thence running directly to the Indian town of Kiskiminetas on the river northwest of Vandergrift. (The Baker Trail, a modern hiking path originally starting at Freeport and covering seventy-five miles to Cook Forest, was founded in 1950 by the Pittsburgh Council of the American Youth Hostels.)

Freeport, originally Todd's Town, was laid out by David Todd in 1796. It was traversed by the western division of the Pennsylvania Canal and is the oldest non-Indian town in the county. In the Freeport cemetery (junction of Pa. 28 and Pa. 356, north of Freeport) is the grave of Massa Harbison (see *Massa Harbison Log Cabin,* Westmoreland County).

Among other early settlers of the county were James Clark, William Green, James Kirkpatrick, Michael Mechling, James Claypool, Andrew Sharp, and Absalom Woodward. Others figuring prominently in the county's history were Edward Warren, who established a trading post near what is now Apollo (Conrad Weiser stopped there on his way to "kindle the first council fire with the Ohio Indians"); Capt. Samuel Brady, who was active in frontier campaigns against the Indians; Governor William Freame Johnston (see Westmoreland County); Nellie Bly (Elizabeth Cochran), one of America's great reporters; Dr. David Alter, inventor of spectroscopy; and Margaret Shoemaker, an early feminist.

Natural resources in the area include bituminous coal, clay, salt, oil, gas, sand and gravel, and limestone. Among the principal industries are coal-mining, brick-making, agriculture, lumbering, glass, and iron- and steel-sheet manufacture. Bradys

Bend was the site at which the first iron rails west of the Alleghenies were manufactured. The county had fifteen early blast furnaces. In 1881 the first visible typewriter was invented in Kittanning by J. D. Daugherty and manufactured there for a number of years.

Two flood-control dams in the county form the Mahoning Creek and Crooked Creek reservoirs. The river park at Kittanning is one of the most beautiful waterfronts in western Pennsylvania.

Landmarks

1. Courthouse (stone), erected in 1858–60 at a cost of $32,000, is a late Greek Revival structure with a Corinthian porticoed central pavilion and large domed cupola. The left wing was added in 1871. The first courthouse, of brick, was built in 1809 and remodeled in 1819. The present jail, beside it, with a ninety-six-foot battlemented tower was built in 1873, at a cost of $252,000. Both the jail and the courthouse are of Clarion County sandstone. *Location:* Kittanning, corner of Market and Jefferson Streets.

2. Armstrong County Historical Museum

2. Armstrong County Historical Museum (painted brick), a Federal-style house, was built in 1842 by Thomas McConnell and occupied by his descendants for several generations. It was later known as the McCain house. About 1900 a spacious wing was added. Now a museum, it offers seasonal exhibits, a historical-genealogical library, and an educational classroom center. *Hours:* Wednesday and Saturday, 2–5 P.M. Special tours by appointment. *Location:* Kittanning, 300 North McKean Street at Vine Street.

3. Ford City Glass Factory, a plate-glass industry established by Capt. John B. Ford in 1887, was at one time the largest plant of its kind in the world. *Location:* Ford City, junction of Pa. 66 and Pa. 128 on Allegheny River.

Note: Ford's statue is in the Ford City Park, Fourth Avenue and Ninth Street. One of the oldest houses in the area is at 1201 Third Avenue, Ford City.

4. Ross House (stone) was built about 1807–09 by George Ross, a judge and first permanent white settler in the Kittanning Manor. It is located on the site of Fort Green. *Location:* Rosston. From Fourth Avenue in Ford City bear left before bridge and continue along Allegheny River to Rosston. Take left turn over railroad to first house on right.

5. Christ Evangelical Lutheran Church (brick) was built in 1894. Founded in 1796 as the county's first church, it was known as the German Meeting House, but was commonly called Rupp's after early settlers of the area. Originally, both German Lutheran and Reformed congregations worshiped here, but in 1815 the Reformed Church was absorbed by the Lutherans. The entrance bears the dates 1812, 1847, 1851, and 1894. *Location:* About three miles east of Kittanning, visible south of U.S. 422. (Follow church sign.)

6. Rural Valley Hotel (brick) was operated in 1876 by William Kirkpatrick. Its age is uncertain, but it was probably built before the Civil War. *Location:* Rural Valley, 639 Gourley Avenue at old Pa. 85, across from bank.

7. Myers House (partially log covered with siding) was built about 1810. Fanny Myers was one of the early owners. One room was added before 1850 and another in 1879. In 1970 the interior was remodeled and restored by the present owners who plan to restore the exterior. The house has unusual double sliding doors for front entrance and a fireplace in every room. An old springhouse on the property in now an antique-furniture refin-

37

ishing shop. *Location:* About four miles north of Leechburg, off Pa. 66. At intersection of Pa. 66 and I.r. 03036 turn east (at nursery sign) and continue about 1.5 mile. House is on right.

8. Dining and Keeping Room (painted brick), owned at one time by Elias Miller, was bought about 1830 by James and Robert Coulter. The house and property were assessed for the first time in 1844. The two-and-a-half-acre property was once the Pleasant Valley Stock Farm, where famous racehorses were bred. The house, restored in 1974 by its present owners, conforms with the original architecture. The eight-room structure has a new kitchen wing along with other additions, fireplaces in every room, and a roof of lead and wrought iron imported from Portugal. A brick springhouse is nearby. It was restored by the Gorelli family. *Hours:* Wednesday and Thursday, 5–9 P.M. Friday and Saturday, 5–10 P.M. Sunday, 2–8 P.M. *Location:* Gilpen Township, about 2.5 miles north of Leechburg on Pa. 66.

9. Laneville Gristmill (frame), originally called the Valley Mill, is the third constructed on this site, about 1890. Mills have stood here for nearly two hundred years. The present structure, on the original foundation, is built of timber, some twenty-four feet long, floated down the Kiskiminetas River to Buffalo Creek. The mill used a stone burr, and from 1910 to 1968 had a massive gas engine and a vertical turbine (single shaft). Probably built by Levi Hill, it is now owned by the Freeport Community Park Association, which plans to remodel the structure with a running (not functional) wheel. *Location:* Near Freeport, off Pa. 356. After heading northwest on Pa. 356 beyond Freeport, cross Buffalo Creek and turn right to get to mill.

10. Drake Log House, measuring 18 by 24 feet, was built in the south end of Apollo sometime between 1816 and 1848. The dwelling was purchased from Samuel Wilson of Conneaut Lake in recent years by the Apollo Area Historical Society, and named for Mrs. Sarah Drake, who lived in it for about fifty years. The land for the structure was donated to the society by Robert Halstein, a California resident. The cabin was restored in 1971. *Hours:* By appointment and first Sunday of month, 2–4 P.M. *Donation. Location:* Apollo, off South Kiski Avenue, reached most conveniently from South Warren Avenue. (Look for log cabin signs after turning right off First Street.)

11. Saint Michael's Evangelical Lutheran Church (brick) was founded in 1806 by Michael Steck, Jr., and incorporated in 1850. The first church, built here in 1852, was blown down July 29, 1860, and rebuilt the same year. On the day it was demolished the congregation began reconstruction. An early minister was Daniel Earhart, great-great-grandfather of Amelia Earhart. The old church cemetery is about three quarters of a mile east of church off I.r. 03058. *Location:* Brick-church, at junction of Pa. 359 and I.r. 03052, four miles north of Mateer near Crooked Creek Dam and north of Cochrans Mills.

12. Cochrans Mills House (frame) is the only remaining structure in the original village of Cochrans Mills. Foundation scars of the town are visible near Crooked Creek. *Location:* Turn east off Pa. 359 at Cochrans Mills on I.r. 03053. It is last house on right before crossing steel bridge (north of Mateer).

Note: Two prominent feminists, Nelly Bly and Margaret Miller Shoemaker, lived in Cochrans Mills. Unfortunately their homes no longer exist. Nelly Bly (pen name for Elizabeth Cochran) was a young aspiring reporter and advocate of women's liberation who made a record-breaking trip around the world in 1889–90, completing it in seventy-two days. Working for Joseph Pulitzer, she was known for her colorful exposures in governmental and industrial fraud. Her birthplace was in Cochrans Mills.

Margaret Miller Shoemaker was an excellent business woman who astonished America in the early 1800s (and was much laughed at) by twice requiring prenuptial agreements to protect her children's inheritance before remarrying after being widowed. The agreements also protected the rights of the children of the widowers whom she married. They were legally drawn and scrupulously kept, and covered the separate use, occupation, and management of the respective properties. Following the death of her first husband, George, she married Barnard Davers and later George King. Her home was located on a tract of land called Monmouth on the north side of Crooked Creek near the mouth of Cherry Run. Only a house scar remains. *Location:* South of Cochrans Mills, off I.r. 03503—east of road about two hundred yards before village.

13. Leech House (brick and stucco) was the home of David Leech, founder of Leechburg. The house, which originally faced Basin Street and now faces Market Street, was built in the 1830s, the golden age of the Pennsylvania Canal. It is presently the Masonic Hall. *Location:* Leechburg, corner of Market and Spring Streets (between Hicks and Market Streets).

14. Transylvania Bible Institute (stone) was founded in 1938 by Rev. Henry Shilling. This nondenominational school was built by students, entirely on faith. Two later additions were also constructed by the student body. The school has fathered others of its type, one in Canada and another in Oregon. *Location:* Halfway between village of Slate Lick and Slate Lick exit off Pa. 28.

15. Old Stone Tavern was once a stagecoach stop built by James Sample about 1820. It has been restored by the Kit-han-ne Questers. Worthington, the town where the tavern is located, was originally called Mount Lorenzo and was founded in 1808 on Buffalo Creek. *Hours:* May–October: Sunday, 2–4:30 P.M. *Admission Charge. Location:* Worthington, Main Street (off U.S. 422 near corner of Bear Street).

16. Graff House (painted brick) was built about 1840 by Peter Graff, who came to Worthington from Pittsburgh in the 1830s. In 1844 he purchased the Buffalo Iron Foundry in the village and in 1865 built the Buffalo Woolen Mill to help employ the widows of men killed in the Civil War. The old mill nearby is now an electric printery. The Lutheran chapel in Worthington was built in honor of Peter Graff by his widow. Private residence of a descendant. *Location:* Worthington, west end of Buffalo Creek.

17. Parker House Hotel (frame), formerly the Parker City Hotel, is the oldest building in the smallest city in the state (population 843). Judge John Parker built this structure, which was used by Fullerton Parker in 1824 as a warehouse. With the oil and lumber boom in the 1870s it became a hotel and is still used as a tavern with little change in the original structure and decor. Parker (City) was founded by William Parker shortly before 1800. *Location:* Parker, at Parker's Landing, junction of Pa. 368 and Pa. 268, near Butler County border.

Note: At this location Hogan's Floating Palace (gambling house and brothel) used to operate in mid-river between Clarion and Armstrong Counties.

18. Saint Stephen's Episcopal Church (stone) was built about the time oil was struck

20. *Marshall House*

in 1865. Later used as a community center, it is now an American Legion Hall. *Location:* Bradys Bend, on Pa. 68, about a mile south of river bridge.

19. Calhoun Schoolhouse (red frame), in its original condition, is a one-room country school with the date 1881 scratched into its foundation. It is maintained as a museum by a local group. *Hours:* Summer months: Sunday, 3–5 P.M. Tours arranged. *Location:* Wayne Township, on l.r. 03080. Leave Pa. 66–28 just north of Goheenville and proceed east toward Belknap (northeast of Kittanning). Building is located halfway between Goheenville and Belknap.

20. Marshall House (brick) is reputed to have been built in 1801 by William Marshall, Sr., one of the first settlers in the area. (The unusual architecture suggests alterations or a later date.) His sons Robert and William were among the founders of the Soldiers' Orphans Home and the Glade Run Academy. The house served as an underground railway station prior to the Civil War and is perhaps the oldest home in the county. *Location:* About 0.5 mile south of Dayton, just west of Pa. 839 near Glade Run Church.

Note: William Marshall, Sr., was an elder and one of the founders of Glade Run Church.

21. Thomas Hindman Marshall House (frame) was built after 1850 by Robert Marshall's son. (This property was once owned by John Hays, son of Mary Hays, the legendary "Mollie Pitcher" of Revolutionary War fame.) A large wooden tank, which formerly had water pumped into it by a windmill, has been preserved in the attic. The home is being restored as a museum and meeting place. *Location:* Dayton, State Street.

23. *Saint Patrick's Sugar Creek Roman Catholic Church*

22. Stone Bridge, built in 1895 and recently reopened to traffic, is a fine example of late nineteenth-century masonry. *Location:* Mahoning Township, on l.r. 03224, about two miles west of Pa. 66–28 from the intersection just north of bridge over Pittsburgh & Shawmut Railroad, on Hogback Hill.

23. Saint Patrick's Sugar Creek Roman Catholic Church (log), measuring 22 by 35 feet, was built on land owned by Rev. Sylvester Phelan in 1805–06. A brick church, constructed in 1842 at a new location, was burned by vandals in 1872. The congregation used the old log church as a place of worship for four years after the fire. The structure is now restored and preserved as the oldest existing Catholic church in western Pennsylvania. *Location:* Northwest corner of county, off Pa. 268 near county line. Go sixteen miles north of Kittanning on Pa. 268 to historical marker at junction of Pa. 268 and l.r. 03015; turn south on l.r. 03015 and proceed 4.5 miles to Boyle's Crossroads; continue southwest on l.r. 03030 for 0.5 mile to church. (Follow signs.)

Pennsylvania Historical and Museum Commission Markers

Blanket Hill U.S. 422, 6.5 miles east of Kittanning
Bradys Bend Works Bradys Bend, Pa. 68
Fort Armstrong Pa. 66, 1.8 mile south of Kittanning
Kittanning Kittanning, U.S. 422
Saint Patrick's Church Pa. 268, 6 miles northwest of Cowansville

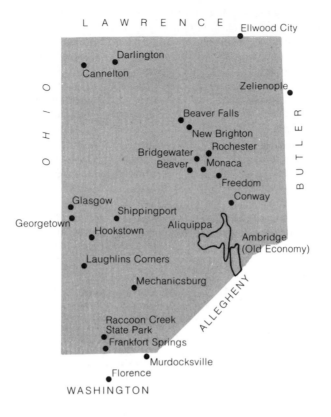

L A W R E N C E Ellwood City

Darlington
Cannelton

Zelienople

O H I O

Beaver Falls
New Brighton
Rochester
Bridgewater
Beaver Monaca
Freedom
Conway

B U T L E R

Glasgow
Shippingport
Georgetown
Hookstown Aliquippa
Ambridge
(Old Economy)
Laughlins Corners

Mechanicsburg

ALLEGHENY

Raccoon Creek
State Park
Frankfort Springs
Murdocksville
Florence
WASHINGTON

Beaver County

Capsule History

Beaver County (named for the Beaver River) was erected out of Washington and Allegheny Counties on March 12, 1800. It decreased in size on March 20, 1849, when Lawrence County was formed, leaving it with 440 square miles. The county's population is 208,418.

Among the early settlers of the land that was to become Beaver County was Levi Duncan, who in 1772 lived near Frankfort Springs. Thomas White resided at Raccoon Creek about the same time.

Logstown, an important trading settlement of the upper Ohio until 1758, was founded during the Delaware and Shawnee migrations of 1725–27. In 1749 Conrad Weiser, a Pennsylvania Indian agent, brought a message to the Indians camped at Logstown proclaiming that the land belonged to the British. The same year the French claimed the area by placing lead plates along the Allegheny and Ohio Rivers. This settlement was the scene of numerous Indian conferences, including the first one between the English and the tribes living along the Ohio River. Both the Delaware and the Six Nations Indians had other settlements near the mouth of the Big Beaver.

Gen. Anthony Wayne trained his army near Logstown (in 1792–93), renaming it Legionville. Montmorin (later Ambridge), above the site of Logstown, was a town projected by Col. Isaac Melcher in 1787. In 1824 the Harmony Society purchased the land and the following year laid out the village of Economy on the site.

Other towns played important parts in the history of the county. Beaver Falls, at the middle falls, was known as Brighton or Old Brighton until 1859, when the Harmony Society purchased the site. It was incorporated in 1861. Beaver, the county seat, was laid out September 28, 1791, and incorporated March 29, 1802. Until 1758 the settlement was known as Shingas Old Town, of the Shawnee and Delaware tribes. During the Revolution it was the site of Fort McIntosh. Monaca (Phillipsburg until 1892) was founded in 1822 by Stephen Phillips, a member of the Phillips and Graham boat-building firm. In ten years his company constructed thirty-two steamboats, including the *Mohawk,* at that time the longest boat on western waters. Other early villages included Darlington, Hookstown, Georgetown, Frankfort Springs, Enon Valley, Freedom, and Blackhawk.

Brodhead Road, built in 1778 by Gen. Daniel Brodhead for military purposes, ran from Fort Pitt to Fort McIntosh, following in part the route of Pa. 51. The Beaver and Erie Canal, built in the 1830s, also helped the area to develop. The Sandy and Beaver Canal left the Ohio River at the western edge of the county.

The Beaver River—which falls sixty-nine feet in five miles—and the Ohio River provided early industrial development and transportation. Shortly after 1800 manufacturing began at the falls of the Beaver River, and by 1835 there were four or five dams and sixteen to eighteen factories in operation. David Townsend erected a sawmill at the lower falls (Fallston) in 1799. Old Economy, final home of the Harmony Society, was a prosperous manufacturing and mercantile center. Boat-building was an important industry along the river for almost a century; and rich coal deposits, together with abundant supplies of building stone, helped promote industrial development. There was a shortage of iron, however, and Beaver County had only three stone blast furnaces in the early period. Today the Jones & Laughlin Steel mill at Aliquippa is one of the largest in Pennsylvania.

Four important Indian trails crossed Beaver County. The *Great Path* followed the right bank of the Ohio, crossed the Beaver near its mouth, and turned west through Blackhawk into Ohio. The *Logstown Path* swung right off the Great Path at Conway and ran northward through Economy Township toward Zelienople. (George Washington and Christopher Gist took this course on their way to Fort Le Boeuf.) The *Mahoning Path* from Beaver followed the left bank of the Beaver River and then cut eastward near Slippery Rock. Finally, the *Kuskusky-Ohio Forks Path* cut across the northeast corner of Beaver County and ran northwest near Fombell toward Wurtemburg.

The county has been traditionally thought of as East, West, and South Beaver, divided by the Ohio and Beaver Rivers.

Landmarks

1. Courthouse (stone) was built in 1875–77. The first court of Beaver County had been held September 6, 1804, at Abner Lacock's tavern and later courts met in the jail (on the northeast side of the square, fronting Third Street) until the original courthouse was built in 1810. The present building was erected west of this site; additions to it were made in 1906–07. Partly burned in 1932, it was remodeled in 1933 with a later addition in 1973–74. The architect of the present courthouse was David S. Geredel of Philadelphia and the contractor was John Schreiner of Pittsburgh. The stone jail is across from the courthouse. *Location:* Beaver, corner of Market and Third Streets.

2. Quay House (brick) was the home of Matthew Stanley Quay, who moved to Beaver with his family in 1840 and became prothonotary in 1856. During the Civil War he was military secretary to Gov. Andrew Curtin. He also served as an assemblyman, 1865–67; secretary of the commonwealth, 1872–82; treasurer of the commonwealth, 1885–89; and U.S. senator, 1889–1904. From 1867 to 1872 he was owner-editor of the *Beaver Radical.* A Republican, he was for decades the ultimate political "boss" of Pennsylvania and gained national prominence as manager of the presidential campaign of 1888. Quay died in 1904 and is buried in the Beaver Cemetery. His house is now a funeral home. *Location:* Beaver, 205 College Avenue at Second Avenue.

3. Johnston-McCreary House (weatherboarded log) is reputed to be the oldest house in Beaver. The original part was built in 1805 on a log foundation and cost seventy-one dollars. An early owner, David Johnston, was the first prothonotary of Beaver County. In 1815 he became the first teacher of the Beaver Academy. *Location:* Beaver, corner of Market Street and River Road, across from site of Fort McIntosh.

4. Fort McIntosh (log) was the first U.S. military post north of the Ohio River and also served as a survey base. It was built in 1778 by Gen. Lachlan McIntosh (1725–1806), commander in chief of the western department during the Revolutionary War, and designed by Le Chevalier de Cambray, chief of artillery in McIntosh's army. This trapezoidal fort with four bastions was built on a 150-foot bluff as a base for launching attacks against the British and Indians in the West. In 1785 it was used as a meeting place for the U.S. treaty with the western Indians, the outcome of which enabled Congress to establish the Northwest Territory and made possible the sale of depreciation lands as payment to Revolutionary War soldiers. The fort was abandoned in 1791, and due to plundering was completely gone in two years.

Members of the Beaver County Chapter of the Society for Pennsylvania Archeology have excavated the site. The original cut sandstone reservoir has been restored at the corner of Wayne and Fourth Streets. The Beaver Area Heritage Board and Beaver Area Memorial Library Association have proposed an outline of the fort on the site, a flag plaza nearby, and a small museum at the Beaver Library. *Location:* Beaver, River Road at end of Market Street on bluff overlooking Ohio River.

5. Dravo House (brick) was built by John F. Dravo, steamboat operator, pioneer in coal-towing, and industrialist, who owned much of the land along River Street (formerly First or Front Street) in the late nineteenth century. The turreted house overlooks the Ohio River. *Location:* Beaver, corner of River and Dravo Streets.

6. Beaver Female College (brick) was opened in 1855, rebuilt in 1868, and enlarged in 1871–73. It became the town high school in 1895 and at present is a middle school. Its first president was Rev. Sheridan Baker, succeeded by Samuel Davenport and then by Rev. R. T. Taylor. *Location:* Beaver, College Avenue (between Third and Fourth Streets).

7. Presbyterian Church (brick) was erected in 1845 and rebuilt in 1879–80. *Location:* Bridgewater, near bridge on Third Street.

8. Wray Homestead (cut stone) was built overlooking Beaner Hollow by Joseph Wray in 1835. An unusual signature stone is inscribed above the front entrance with the date and the builder's name in script instead of print. The original stone sink is still in use in the kitchen, and the windows throughout the house have the original glass. Many of the Wray family's furnishings, including a portrait of the first owner, remain in the home. The last of the Wray family to reside in this house, Joseph's granddaughter, Katherine Wray Peters, willed the property to its present

8. *Wray Homestead*

early lock of this canal remaining in Pennsylvania. The canal basin near the Ohio River can be seen from Pa. 68. *Location:* Glasgow. Just within state limits on Pa. 68, drive 0.95 mile on unmarked cinder road; walk for about two miles over old railroad bed (right of way of Erie & Ohio Railroad). Lock is about 300 feet below tracks along Little Beaver.

13. Stone Boundary Marker between Ohio and Pennsylvania was erected in 1886 to mark the southern extremity of the Pennsylvania-Ohio border as resurveyed. About 112 feet south on the Ohio River bank was the point where Thomas Hutchins, first U.S. geographer, began the first survey of public lands in the United States, September 30, 1785. It was here that he began the system of quarters, sections, square townships, and ranges almost universally used since that time. *Location:* On Pa. 68 at Ohio-Pennsylvania line.

14. Pittsburgh & Lake Erie Railroad Bridge was built about 1910 over the Ohio River. James M. Schoonmaker, head of the P.&L.E. at that time, believed that the most important feature of a railroad bridge was strength. This structure for four tracks gantleted to two is one of the strongest ever built and has defied the ravages of time and changes in equipment. *Location:* Over Ohio River between Monaca and Beaver.

15. Beaver Historical Research Center and Museum (brick) was established through the efforts of county commissioners, the Beaver County Research and Landmarks Foundation, and the Carnegie Library. The center is located in the basement of the Carnegie Library of Beaver Falls, which was built in 1902, the first public library in the county. Rare collections of early Beaver County writings are available. *Hours:* Monday, Tuesday, and Thursday, 10 A.M.–5:30 P.M. Wednesday and Friday, 6–9 P.M. *Location:* Beaver Falls, corner of Seventh and Thirteenth Streets.

16. Harmonist Houses, six stone structures built by the Harmony Society when Beaver Falls was founded, still remain in the town, mostly in good condition. (See *Old Economy* and also *Harmony,* Butler County.) All are private residences. *Locations:* Beaver Falls, 1314 Third Avenue, 1603 Fourth Avenue, 1611 and 1618 Fifth Avenue, 1602 Sixth Avenue, and 1324 Tenth Avenue.

17. Old Main Hall at Geneva College (stone quarried on the campus) was built in

owners. *Location:* Brighton Township, one mile north of Beaver, a quarter mile off Dutch Ridge Road (Market Street extension), 100 yards to left of Beaner Hollow Road.

9. Mount Pleasant (painted brick) was built in 1808 by John Wolf, Jr., who later lived at Fort McIntosh. His son was Squire A. B. Wolf. The home has a double porch, and the property originally included 148 acres. *Location:* Brighton Township, 908 Western Avenue, one mile north of Beaver.

10. Small House (painted brick) is now a part of a housing plan, with the carriage house and greenhouse both remodeled as private dwellings. One of the early owners was in the oil business. A later owner was a Mr. Small, for whom the house is named. *Location:* At north edge of Beaver, on Dutch Ridge Road (Market Street extension).

11. Richmond Little Red Schoolhouse (brick) was in operation from 1844 to 1950. At present it is maintained as a one-room schoolhouse museum by the Richmond Little Red Schoolhouse Organization. It is open to the public and school groups by appointment. *Location:* Brighton Township, near entrance to Brady's Run Park on Dutch Ridge Road (Market Street extension).

12. Sandy and Beaver Canal Lock, No. 53, is located on the Little Beaver near the mouth of Island Run and, though in ruins, is the only

1880 at this liberal arts, coeducational college. The school was founded April 20, 1848, by the Reformed Presbyterian Church in Northwood, Ohio, and was moved to its present location when John Reeves, a representative of the Harmony Society, offered to give it ten acres of land. (Reeves Athletic Field is named in his honor.) The class of 1881 was the first to graduate at Beaver Falls. Geneva College is the only institution of higher learning of the Reformed Presbyterian Church (Covenanter) except for its theological seminary in Wilkinsburg. In 1945 the college awarded an honorary degree to John Duss (1860–1951), the last surviving member of the Harmony Society. *Location:* Beaver Falls, College Avenue (on College Hill).

18. White Home (stone) was built about 1853 by Thomas White, son of John White, first settler of Beaver Falls. *Location:* Beaver Falls, 3925 Thirty-ninth Street at Fourth Avenue (on College Hill).

19. Greenway Farmhouse (painted brick), built about 1830, belonged to Joseph Swartz in 1876. The farm included 150 acres at that time. *Location:* Beaver Falls, 3186 Thirty-seventh Street extension.

20. Mayfield Cottage Farmhouse (log and weatherboards with shingles) was built about 1825. The home has a belfry with the original bell, which was used for calling the farmhands to dinner or in times of distress. The barn, now a garage, once had a date of 1823 on it. Originally consisting of 200 acres, the property was named for Mayfield Station nearby. The Schutte family has owned this property for three generations. *Location:* Beaver Falls, 3181 Thirty-seventh Street extension at Clearview Street (across from Greenway Farm in West Mayfield).

21. Haley House (weatherboarded log) was built by John Haley about 1792, with subsequent additions. An early cupola on top of the house has been removed. *Location:* Beaver Falls, 191 Oakville Road.

22. Greersburg Academy (two sites, stone and brick), under the auspices of the Presbytery of Erie, was chartered by the state of Pennsylvania on February 24, 1806, through the endeavors of Thomas E. Hughes, who was pastor of Mount Pleasant Presbyterian Church at Greersburg (now Darlington) and New Salem Presbyterian Church at the village of Salem Church. He had built a log

22. *Brick Building at Greersburg Academy*

school near his home in 1802 and became the first head of the academy until its incorporation in 1806, when Daniel Hayden succeeded him. William Holmes McGuffey, editor of the famous *McGuffey's Readers,* attended this school. In 1833 the "stone academy" was sold to the Pittsburgh, Marion & Chicago Railroad Company to be used for a depot. For a while it was a private residence.

In 1833 the academy built a new two-story brick building on the corner of Second and Plum Streets, which closed about 1910 and became a public school. Both academy buildings now belong to the Little Beaver Historical Society. *Locations:* Darlington.

23. Greersburg Free Presbyterian Church (brick) was founded by Arthur Bloomfield Bradford, an abolitionist leader and pastor of Mount Pleasant Presbyterian Church in Greersburg (now Darlington) from 1839 to 1847 (see *Bradford House*). In 1847 Bradford withdrew from the pastorate because of a disagreement with the synod on the question of slavery, and organized the Free Presbyterian Church, becoming its first pastor. This house of worship, a charming structure, was erected in 1847. With the dissolution of the Free Presbyterian denomination after the Civil War, the congregation became affiliated with the Reformed Presbyterian Church. *Location:* Darlington.

24. Wallace House (brick) was bought in 1839 by the Wallaces, and it has remained in this family ever since that time. *Location:* Darlington, on Wallace Drive off Market Street.

25. Martin House (frame) was constructed with a double porch and a stone foundation about 1805. Much of its history is obscure.

Location: Darlington, on Rohrmann Road one block from Fourth Street.

26. Douthitt Farmhouse (brick) was built by Joseph Douthitt about 1832 and was a stagecoach stop on the Pittsburgh-Cleveland road. An old stile, or stepping stone, used for carriages stands in the front yard. This property is still owned by members of the Douthitt family. *Location:* One mile north of Darlington, on Hollow Road.

27. Veon House (stone) was built by a Mr. Veon and his son. The elder Veon had been a Hessian soldier who turned patriot during the Revolutionary War, making America his home. Local tradition dates this house from 1850, but its appearance and other factors would indicate a date nearer 1825. *Location:* 1.5 mile north of Darlington, on Hollow Road.

28. Bradford House (brick) was built between 1837 and 1840 by Arthur Bloomfield Bradford, abolitionist and founder of the Greersburg Free Presbyterian Church (q.v.), who was once sent by President Lincoln to China as an ambassador. His home was one of the stops on the underground railroad. The small brick building behind the main house was a "prophet house" used for visiting parsons, who could stay overnight and prepare their sermons. *Location:* About two miles north of Darlington, on Bradford Road off Hollow Road.

29. Alliance Brick Factory (brick) later housed the Federal Steel Corporation. Its two buildings are abandoned. Across the road is a brick house built in 1825. It was once owned by Rankin Martin, a Beaver lawyer. *Location:* Darlington, on Darlington Road near junction with Alliance Road.

30. Morris House (brick) was built by Jonathan Morris. The signature stone on the chimney reads, "Jan. Morris 1837." Later John White (no relation to man of same name in no. 18) bought the property. White incorporated the Darlington Coal Company in 1852 and was its president for the first eight years. A brick smokehouse stands near the home, and both are being restored by the present owners. The White cemetery is nearby on the same side of the road. *Location:* Cannelton, Cannelton Road, in industrial park area.

32. Stone Face

31. Mansfield House (frame), built about 1840, was the birthplace and summer home of Ira F. Mansfield (who died in 1919 and is buried at Poland, Ohio), a prominent coal operator who bought out the Cannelton Mining Company interests in 1865. Mansfield was a Beaver County state representative in 1880–81. In 1887 he moved to Beaver, living in a home with turrets that was at times referred to as the Queen's Castle. This edifice was replaced by the new library building on the corner of College Avenue and River Road. *Location:* Northwest of Darlington, on Ridge Road, 0.3 mile from Cannelton Road near Ohio line.

32. Stone Face was created by Charles Jones, an eccentric who carved the face in a huge rock, with two round hollows for eyes, one for a mouth, and a square depression for a nose, so that water would collect for birds to drink. The rock, facing skyward, sits high on a steep knob, which has partially been stripped for coal. *Location:* 0.5 mile south of Cannelton, off Cannelton Road on unused road behind Morris house (see no. 30). Hill where stone face is located is reached by crossing Little Beaver Creek over stringers of iron bridge with most of floorboards missing. Extremely difficult access, but rewarding climb.

33. Merrick Free Art Gallery (brick) was founded in 1865 by Edward Demptster Merrick. The gallery contains French, German, English, and American paintings of the eighteenth and nineteenth centuries collected by its founder, himself an artist. Today it also houses a library and the New Brighton Historical Society. Unfortunately all Merrick's own paintings were discarded about 1930. *Location:* New Brighton, Fifth Avenue and Eleventh Street.

34. 1823 House (brick with frame addition in rear) has a marker on the front porch bearing the date of its construction. In the back is a stone well with a cement foundation that has Pennsylvania Dutch sayings inscribed on it at a later date. *Location:* New Brighton, 513 Third Avenue.

35. White Cottage (frame) was the home of Sarah Clarke Lippincott, whose pen name was Grace Greenwood, an internationally known journalist who was ahead of her time. Born in 1823, she wrote a number of her books in this house in the 1850s. Some of her work was published in the *McGuffey's Readers*. *Location:* New Brighton, 1221 Third Avenue (marker in front of house).

36. Christ Episcopal Church (stone) was built in 1851 with stone buttresses added later. The first rector was J. P. Taylor. *Location:* New Brighton, Third Avenue next to White cottage.

37. Conway Railroad Yards are the largest push-button railroad yards in the United States. There are no tours, but operations of the yard can be viewed from streets overlooking the site. *Location:* Conway, Penn Central Railroad, running beside Pa. 65 for one mile.

38. Vicary House (cut stone) was built in 1826–28 by William Vicary, a sea captain from Philadelphia. After living in Sewickley, where two of his eight children were born, Vicary purchased from the government about one thousand acres extending from Dutch Run in Freedom to Crows Run, where the stones for his three-story house were quarried. The home has eight rooms, each eighteen feet square, arranged around a wide hall and a winding staircase. The walls are two feet thick.

Vicary's last voyage was in 1803 as captain of the *Liberty,* a trading vessel which sailed from Philadelphia to the East Indies. His experiences at sea included a near-mutiny among his men, which he quelled, and a battle with Chinese pirates. A scar on his forehead was a permanent reminder of the latter encounter. In accordance with his wife's wishes, he finally gave up the life of the sea. In 1837 he laid out the village of Saint Clair,

often referred to as "Vicary Extension," which has been part of Freedom Borough since 1896.

Recently a retaining wall was built to preserve this early landmark, located precariously close to the new Beaver Valley Expressway. The Beaver County Historical Society plans to preserve the house as a museum and headquarters for the organization. *Location:* Freedom, on Harvey's Run Road above Pa. 65, overlooking Conway Railroad Yards.

39. Old Economy, a religious community founded in 1805 by George Rapp (1757–1847), was the third and last home (1825–1905) of the Harmony Society, builders of a large industrial empire. They adopted celibacy in 1807. (See *Harmony,* Butler County). There are many interesting old buildings in this well-preserved settlement, now operated by the Pennsylvania Historical and Museum Commission. *Hours:* Daylight saving time: Weekdays, 8:30 A.M.–5 P.M. Sunday, 1–5 P.M. Winter: Weekdays, 9 A.M.–4:30 P.M. Sunday, 1–4:30 P.M. *Admission charge. Location:* Ambridge, Fourteenth and Church Streets:

a. Great House (brick), having thirty-five rooms, was the home of Father Rapp and some of his successors in office. Its hostess for many years was his granddaughter, Gertrude. The building is furnished in its original style.

b. Feast Hall (brick), the society's cultural center which included a school, museum, and printshop, was built about 1830. The tremendous single room upstairs was used for feasts, band concerts, and other events.

c. Grotto (stone) is a small garden house that contains many symbolic decorations to encourage meditation. It is surrounded by a well-kept garden.

d. Baker House (brick) was remodeled in 1847 at the time that Romelius Baker took over Father Rapp's position. Baker lived here until his death in 1868. It is on exhibit as a typical Harmonist house.

e. Harmonie Associates House (brick), located outside the walled grounds of the original village, is now occupied by the Associates, a volunteer group that presents craft fairs, classes, and similar events.

f. Saint John's Lutheran Church (brick) was built by the society in 1827–31, replacing a wooden structure located on Fifteenth Street. It is not currently open to the public except for church services. A belfry clock with the mechanism for only one hand still keeps good time when in repair. In the front churchyard is a Linden tree planted in 1917 in

39.a. Great House at Old Economy

honor of the four hundredth anniversary of the Reformation. Encircling the tree is a large millstone.

g. A granary, wine cellar, and other shops are also located on the property.

40. Watt House (fieldstone), a long, primitive-looking structure, is composed of three sections, the first of which was built by the Watt family. Thomas, James, and their sister Mary, none of whom ever married, lived in this portion of the house, built in 1851–52. (Date on cornerstone is concealed underground.) The second section was added in 1866 (cornerstone by door), and the date of the third part is uncertain. *Location:* Daugherty Township, on Helbly Road, 0.2 mile from its intersection with Tulip Drive (which is off Pa. 68). House sits 0.1 mile behind buff brick house on Helbly Road.

41. Old Davis Schoolhouse (frame with fieldstone foundation) was probably built around 1890 and used for nearly forty years. Later it became the meeting place for Our Savior Lutheran Church, which was founded in this building. The first church of this congregation was built in 1931 and is located next to the school. *Location:* Near Ambridge, on Ridge Road extension.

42. Providence Baptist Church (brick), the first of that denomination in the county, was constituted November 14, 1801, by Henry Speer, an itinerant Baptist minister. The fourth and present church was built in 1857 and remodeled at a later date. *Location:* 4.5 miles south of Ellwood City (Lawrence County), on l.r. 04110, 0.5 mile east of its junction with Pa. 65.

43. Benvenue (cut stone, quarried on property) was built in 1814 by George Henry Mueller, who came from Baltimore. This twelve-room mansion, situated on a hill near the old Venango Path, was named Benvenue ("welcome here") by Mueller, and at times it was referred to as Mueller's Castle. It was in this home that Saint Paul's Lutheran Church in Zelienople (q.v., Butler County) was organized. In 1902 the property was purchased by the Bethany Bible Society, founded by Mary Moorehead, with its original headquarters in Pittsburgh's North Side. On the same land is Sunrise Cottage, built in 1848 by Mueller for his niece, where the Bible Society operated a printing shop.

Benvenue has had exterior alterations, including the addition of a castlelike cistern, but the original interior has been preserved. The third and present owner of the property is Roger Hogan, who purchased it in 1963. *Location:* Marion Township, 1.3 mile west of Zelienople on Pa. 68 (on Mueller Hill).

44. Oldest Harmonist House in Monaca (brick), with its high stone foundation, was built by Harmonists who separated from their society at Old Economy, partly because of their disagreement with the group's belief in celibacy. Some 250 members withdrew and moved to this section along the Ohio River in 1832. *Location:* Monaca, corner of Fifth and Atlantic Streets.

Note: Also at Monaca is the Mill Creek Valley Historical Museum, on the Penn State Monaca campus.

45. Shippingport Power Plant is the world's first commercial electric-power generating unit to use nuclear energy as fuel. Construction began September 6, 1954, and the plant was in operation in 1957. Later a pit-mouth coal facility was added. One smokestack is 950 feet high. *Hours:* Open for tours Wednesday with advance reservations. *Location:* Shippingport, on south side of bridge.

Note: About a mile downstream from the plant is Duquesne Light's $250 million Beaver Valley Station, No. 1, which began operations in 1975.

46. Georgetown Blockhouse (weatherboarded log) was built in 1796 by Benoni Dawson and until 1900 had two stories. John Bever, an immigrant from Ireland who built the first paper mill in Ohio, purchased and enlarged this house about 1800 and had a tavern and store here. George Henry Loskiel visited here in 1803. *Location:* Georgetown, on Water Street overlooking Ohio River, near Old River Hotel.

47. Old River Hotel (frame) was erected in 1802 by Thomas Foster. A structure with six columns, it is situated high on a hillside overlooking an old Ohio River landing. In 1805 Foster got a license to operate the building as a tavern; Samuel Lyon was a later owner. The house is located where the ferry used to operate, and no doubt this tavern had a thriving business during the era of the keelboat and steam packet boat. *Location:* Georgetown, Market and Water Streets.

48. Poe House (frame), of uncertain date, replaced the original log house on the property erected in 1820 by Thomas Poe, a raftsman. A Methodist church held its first services here. The present seven-bay house with four chimneys does not appear in a town map in an 1876 atlas, but a former owner and Poe descendant believes it is much older. The house is now open to the public as an antique shop. *Location:* Georgetown, corner of Market and First Streets.

47. Old River Hotel

49. Saint Luke's Protestant Episcopal Church (brick), founded about 1800, is the oldest of this faith in the county. Its first pastor was Francis Reno, a protégé of Gen. John Neville (see *Saint Luke's Protestant Episcopal Church,* Allegheny County). Built in 1833, the present house of worship replaced an earlier log church. *Location:* Georgetown.

50. Service Associate Presbyterian Church (brick), now United Presbyterian, is located in a beautiful scenic area overlooking the reservoir of the Ambridge Water Authority on Service Creek. Three wooden crosses were erected in 1963 on the bank in front of the church near the water's edge. The congregation was organized in 1790, and Rev. John Anderson served the church from 1792 until 1833. The first church, of log, was erected in 1793–94. The cornerstone of the existing church reads, "Service A.P. Church, Built 1800, rebuilt 1828, 1868, 1928. Dr. John Anderson first pastor." The present church was constructed with the bricks of the 1868 church, which had burned a few years before 1928.

Next to this house of worship is the John Anderson Memorial Cemetery, where numerous Revolutionary War soldiers are buried. Near the head of the reservoir is a stone marking the site of Service Theological Seminary, founded there by the Associate Presbytery of Philadelphia, April 21, 1794. It was the first such institution west of the Alleghenies and the first Protestant seminary in the United States not attached to a college or university. The seminary continued here with Dr. Anderson as head until 1821, when it was

51. Frankfort Mineral Springs

transferred to Canonsburg; in 1855 it relocated to Xenia, Ohio. It is the earliest forebear of the present Pittsburgh Theological Seminary (q.v., Allegheny County). *Location:* North of Mechanicsburg, on Service Church Road, l.r. 04070, 1.5 mile from Pa. 18.

51. Frankfort Mineral Springs, now consisting of three springs of the original seven, located at a natural solid rock grotto, was at one time the most popular resort and health spa in western Pennsylvania. This scenic area, once the site of wolf dens and steeped in Indian lore, was bought in 1784 by Isaac Stephens (a 400-acre tract) for less than ten dollars.

Later, Edward McGinnis, a ferryman and keelboatman, who found the mineral waters "healing to his ailment," bought twelve acres of the land. Some time before 1800 he built a three-story hotel called the Frankfort House overlooking the glen where the springs are located. Originally the property also included a guest house, a carriage house, a dance pavilion (built in the 1800s), a livery stable, an icehouse, vegetable gardens, a ballfield, a dirt tennis court, and croquet greens. Except for the partly burned and rebuilt guest house, only the foundation scars remain. (Signs have been erected to mark these early sites.) The hotel itself was destroyed by fire.

The stone guest house, the only remaining building of the resort complex, was restored in the 1960s by the Commonwealth of Pennsylvania and the Western Pennsylvania Conservancy. Originally it had three stories, but the fire in 1905 reduced it to one. It has been used as a guest house, a manager's residence, later a store, barber shop, and then a bottling works. In 1884 McGinnis's daughter, Eliza, sold the property to J. Moore Bigger, and in 1912 it was closed as a health spa,

although mineral-water bottling operations continued for some time afterward. Today a scenic walkway leads to the spring grotto below the stone guest house. *Location:* North of Frankfort Springs (town), at Raccoon Creek State Park (a quarter mile south of park office on Pa. 18).

Note: Raccoon Creek State Park is one of the oldest of its kind in Pennsylvania. Over two hundred thousand years ago it was part of an ancient sea bottom. The park also includes a wild flower preserve, where programs concerning conservation and early pioneer life are held. Dr. O. E. Jennings, well-known western Pennsylvania botanist, discovered over five hundred different species of plants here. The wild flower preserve is located along U.S. 30, opposite east entrance of park's day-use area. Tours prearranged.

52. Witherspoon Drovers' Tavern (stucco over brick) was the home of John Witherspoon, who was born in Ireland in 1785, came to America at the age of five, and settled with his family at Canonsburg, Washington County. Some time between 1796 and 1809, they bought land on Travis Creek in Hanover Township. Witherspoon married Margaret Kennedy in 1813, built a house in Frankfort Springs, and operated a popular drovers' tavern here. The house is still occupied by his descendants. *Location:* Frankfort Springs, on Pa. 18.

53. King's Creek or Frankfort Springs Associate Presbyterian Church (brick) was organized in 1790 by Rev. John Anderson, who founded the Service Associate Presbyterian Church (q.v.) about the same time. The first house of worship was a log structure located two miles north of the present borough. The third and present church (now United Presbyterian) was built in 1876. *Location:* Frankfort Springs, on Pa. 18 near borough line.

54. Nelson House (stone and frame) was erected on land granted to Samuel Caughy in 1807. Matthew Nelson, next owner, bought the property in 1810 and hired Cornelius Shane to build the house in 1817. Shane's name and the date are on an exterior signature stone. The frame addition was constructed at a later date. Nearby on the property is a stone springhouse. George Shields, a later owner, replaced the original windows with leaded glass in the 1930s. Private residence. *Location:* Near Hookstown on U.S. 30, about two miles east of Laughlins Corners.

55. Church of Christ (frame), built about 1850, was originally an Associate Reformed Presbyterian Church. An old cemetery is located on the hillside behind the church. *Location:* Near Laughlins Corners and West Virginia line on Tomlinson Run Road.

56. Mill Creek Presbyterian Church (frame), organized in 1784, is the county's oldest religious institution and was attached to the Presbytery of Ohio in 1793. George M. Scott became its first regular pastor in 1799. Dr. John McMillan held one of his last services here in 1833. The congregation has had five church buildings, the first three located at the cemetery (marker on l.r. 04048, about 0.2 mile east of present church), and the last two on the site where the existing structure was built in 1882. In the cemetery is the grave of Andrew Poe, a celebrated Indian fighter who died in 1823. *Location:* Near Laughlins Corners (where Pa. 168 crosses U.S. 30), on l.r. 04048 (follow sign).

57. Locust Grove (Reed House) (cut stone) was built in 1820, costing $100 for labor. The stones for the house, which measures 24 by 40 feet, were hauled from the old Ernest Littell farm. In 1839 Samuel Reed bought the farm from Robert Wright, and it remained in his family until 1937. *Location:* Three miles south of Laughlins Corners. Follow Pa. 168 from Laughlins Corners to sign for Mill Creek Church; turn left on l.r. 04048 and continue past church until first through crossroad (about one mile); turn right on t. 368 and take first lane to left.

58. Standish House (cut stone) marks the area where in 1793 Levi Dungan, first settler in the county, obtained a patent for 306 acres, naming it Turkey Plains. A later owner, Henry Hayes, sold the land in 1823 to Miles Standish (reputed descendant of the Mayflower immigrant), who built the house on the property. *Location:* From Pa. 18, 3.1 miles south of Frankfort Springs, turn west on Purdy Road (l.r. 62071) 4 miles; turn right across small bridge at creek 0.1 mile; make sharp left on unmarked road for 0.5 mile.

59. Ramsey House (cut stone), sometimes referred to as the "still house," was erected by Miles Standish (see *Standish House*). It is reputed that a still was operated in the attic. The heirs of Lee Ramsey, who was born in the house, sold it to Mrs. Bea Carmody, who has had the house restored. There is another

62. Reddick Grave

smaller stone building on this property. *Location:* 5.7 miles northwest of Florence, on Purdy Road (l.r. 62071) at Little Brook Farm.

60. Freshwater House (brick) was built about 1811 with a double front porch and a large fireplace in the basement. *Location:* Across Irwin Road from Ramsey house.

61. Cross House (stone) was constructed in 1832 by James Cross, whose family came from Ireland in 1793, settling on 300 acres of land called Haywood. This house, which replaced a log home, was built on the property with stones hauled from the Levi Standish farm. Susannah Cross, the granddaughter of James Cross, lived in the house until 1913. After standing vacant for eighteen years, the house was bought by James Sutherin, who planted honeysuckle vines around it. Started from sprouts in the woods, these vines now cover much of the house. *Location:* From Freshwater house go 0.9 mile on Irwin Road to unmarked road. Turn right 0.7 mile.

62. Reddick Grave is the spot where John Hoge Reddick, one of the first associate judges of Beaver County, is buried. The grave is enclosed by a sandstone wall several feet away from the West Virginia border. Reddick asked to be buried "with his face toward the east, his head in [West] Virginia and his feet in Pennsylvania," so that if the devil came for him on one side, he could quickly flee to the other. Ironically a resurvey in 1882 showed the grave to be entirely within Pennsylvania.

Legend has it that Reddick feared the devil had heard him boast that a favorite horse could outrun "His Satanic Majesty" and thus would seek revenge. On his tombstone are written the words.

John Reddick
Pennsylvania
Ensign 5 Co. 2 Bn
Westmoreland County Militia
Revolutionary War
War of 1812
1756–1830

A survey boundary stone sits directly in front of the grave site. *Location:* Go south for 3.5 miles on Pa. 168 at intersection of U.S. 30 (at Laughlins Corners); turn west for 2.8 miles on l.r. 04046 to Ross Road, thence left for three quarters of a mile to private lane leading to yellow chalet in West Virginia. Grave is inside stone wall about 150 yards to rear of house, at edge of woods.

63. White's Mill (ruin), once a focal point in establishing the Allegheny County boundary, was built by Thomas White before 1786. White had taken a 400-acre tract of land in this area in the early 1770s and by 1786 there was a settlement around the mill, built on Raccoon Creek near the mouth of Potato Garden Run. The huge log mill operated until 1904, and it was razed in 1950. The stone foundation ruins and vestiges of the dam and race are discernible along the creek. *Location:* Near Murdocksville on Raccoon Creek; on t. 115 (1.6 mile south of junction with U.S. 30 west of Clinton, Allegheny County).

Pennsylvania Historical and Museum Commission Markers

Fort McIntosh   Beaver, Pa. 68

Harmony Society Cemetery 1823–1951   Ambridge, Church Street, in center of cemetery

Harmony Society Church   Ambridge, Church Street near Creese Street

King Beaver's Town   Beaver, Pa. 68

Legionville   Duss Avenue north of Ambridge

Logstown   Duss Avenue north of Ambridge

Matthew S. Quay   Beaver, Pa. 68, 205 College Avenue

Old Economy   Ambridge, Pa. 65

Old Economy Memorial   Ambridge at Old Economy

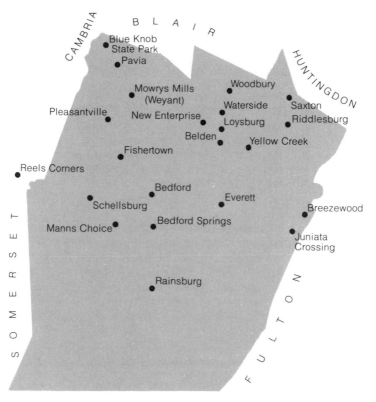

Bedford County

Capsule History

Bedford County, named in honor of John Russell, fourth duke of Bedford, was formed out of Cumberland County March 9, 1771. It embraced almost all of western Pennsylvania. Today the county is 1,018 square miles in area with a population of 42,353.

The county's prehistoric wonders include the sinks of New Paris, where the bones of many animals—some now extinct—have been found, the only known underground coral reefs, at Manns Choice; and artifacts dating from the pre-Columbian period (A.D. 400–1500).

The first settlement of the county took place in what is now Southampton Township. Among the pioneers who arrived in the area in the 1750s were Bernard

Dougherty, George Woods, Joseph Sheniwolf, and David Espy. Robert Ray, an Indian trader, came to Bedford in 1750–51; Garrett Prendergast arrived in 1752 and was burned out by the Indians in 1755. The most fertile of the valleys, Morrisons Cove, was settled largely by Germans in the 1760s. From 1754 until the close of the Revolution, Indians made incursions into this region, which had been their hunting grounds. Here numerous massacres occurred.

The *Raystown Path* was the most important of the Indian trails of the county. The favorite of the fur traders en route to Kittanning, it followed much the course of U.S. 30 in this area, passing through or near Breezewood, Everett, Raystown (now Bedford), Wolfsburg, and Shawnee Cabins. Another main route, the *Warrior's Path,* traversed the county in two and, farther south, three separate branches. One branch entered the county above King, following U.S. 220 past Osterburg and Cessna where it forked, the western course going near Pa. 96 past Manns Choice and Palo Alto, the eastern by Bedford, Bedford Springs, along U.S. 220 to Centerville, and down Shaver Ridge. The other main branch entered the county southwest of Shy Beaver, ran down the Woodcock Valley toward Tatesville and Everett, then followed Black Valley toward Flintstone. Two minor paths ran from the eastern branch into Morrisons Cove, one taking off above King and running past Bakers Summit to Martinsburg, the other below King and going southeast to Salemville. The *Glades Path* left the eastern branch of Warrior's Path at Wolfsburg, going by Dry Ridge, West End, and Brotherton along the general course of the Turnpike and from about Somerset of Pa. 31. The *Conemaugh Path,* from Bedford to Johnstown, ran north to Cessna and Reynoldsdale, turned northwest, and crossed the Allegheny Ridge near the head of South Fork.

In 1758 Gen. John Forbes cut a road roughly following U.S. 30. One Forbes camp was located west of Schellsburg at Shawnee Cabins, a site now covered by Shawnee Cabin Dam.

Bedford, the county seat, was laid out in 1766. Bedford Manor had been surveyed by John Lukens in 1761 and the streets named for members of the Penn family. The town squares, set aside for public parks still exist today. By 1806 there were wooden pipes supplying the town with spring water. There are at least 300 pre-1840 buildings still in use in the county, of which almost fifty are in the borough of Bedford.

Included among the noteworthy residents of the county were Robert J. Walker, senator from Mississippi and governor of Kansas Territory in 1857; John Cessna, congressman and orator; and Maj. Gen. Arthur St. Clair, famed leader in the Revolutionary War. Thomas Bleistein, the beloved "Bozo Snyder" of vaudeville and burlesque, was born in Bedford in 1891. Friedrich Goeb (see Somerset County) lived for some years in Schellsburg and is buried there.

Important early industries of the county included farming and wool-growing. Numerous mills were operated by water power, while iron ore, coal, and limestone were plentiful natural resources. In 1791 William McDermott, pioneer steel manufacturer, built his establishment on the "Caledonia tract" near Bedford Springs. Hopewell Furnace and Lemnos Forge were the county's main iron producers. Altogether there were four early stone blast furnaces in the county. The Riddlesburg iron furances, operating from 1869 to 1943, were among the county's largest. In 1874 an iron industry was developed in Everett (once called Bloody Run).

Of forty-two covered bridges built in the county, sixteen remain. The largest was swept away by flood waters (see *General Washington Tavern*).

Bedford Village, a proposed project, will consist of restored and relocated early buildings. Also a covered bridge now over Dunning's Creek at Reynoldsdale will be rebuilt at the village. This seventy-two-acre tract is bordered by U.S. 220 (Bedford North bypass), the Juniata River, and private lands, with access to the park over the covered bridge and at two other points.

Landmarks

1. Courthouse (brick) is the oldest existing courthouse in Pennsylvania. The first court of Bedford County was held April 16, 1771, in a log courthouse. Not until 1774 were a stone structure and a jail erected. In 1828–29 the present classic brick structure was built by Solomon Filler, for $7,500, and in 1876 it was enlarged. Its second-floor courtroom contains portraits of all the judges who have presided there. Among the early records preserved in its vaults is an Indian deed transferring title to a large area including Pittsburgh's Golden Triangle. The purchase was illegal and became void. The courthouse is open for tours. *Location:* Bedford, Juliana and Penn Streets.

2. Lyon House (brick) was erected in 1833–34 by Solomon Filler as a private residence for the William Lyon family. This structure, flanked by two small buildings, one a former carriage house and the other an office, was later converted into the Timmins private hospital. Following this it was a residence once more, and at present is the courthouse annex. *Location:* Bedford, 214 South Juliana Street.

3. Russell House (brick), with an arched and gabled roof over the front entrance, was built in 1816 by Solomon Filler for James M. Russell, the first burgess of Bedford. Similar in appearance to the Anderson house (q.v.), the structure once served as a mortuary. Its old interior elevator is still operating. *Location:* Bedford, 203 South Juliana Street.

4. Bedford Presbyterian Church (brick), organized before 1783, was constructed in 1829 by Solomon Filler. It replaced a frame structure that had succeeded an 1810 church. The old Presbyterian burial ground (Bedford Memorial Park, South Juliana and East John Streets) marks the site of the congregation's first church. It contains the graves of sixteen Revolutionary War soldiers. *Location:* Bedford, at square.
Note: Next to the church is the Cessna building, erected in 1820. It is now an apartment house.

5. Union Common School (brick), built in 1859, replaced several one-room schools. Originally planned to house eight grades, this building was the county's first consolidated and graded school. In 1889 it was added to and became the first high school of the county. It is among the oldest school buildings in Pennsylvania still in operation. *Location:* Bedford, South Juliana and Watson Streets.

6. Saint Thomas Apostle Catholic Chapel (brick), the oldest Catholic church in the county, was erected in 1817. Though abandoned in 1833 when the congregation moved to another site, it was restored in 1958 as a memorial shrine. The church was first served by a missionary priest, Father Demetrius Gallitzin (see *Gallitzin Chapel and House,* Cambria County). Adjacent to the chapel is an early cemetery. *Location:* Bedford, 225 East Street (between Penn and John Streets).

7. Jacob Krichbaum House (weatherboarded log) is a squat, one-story, gable-roofed structure built in 1816. It is now the Colonial Inn. *Location:* Bedford, 113 West Pitt Street.

8. Steckman House (brick), an early tavern known as the Sign of the Blazing Star in 1784, is at present a discount store. *Location:* Bedford, 114 West Pitt Street.

9. Early Apothecary Shop (stone) was built in 1805 and at present houses a commercial business. *Location:* Bedford, 118 West Pitt Street.

10. Bedford Hotel (brick) was erected in 1836 and now houses a modern hostelry. It is reputed, but of course incorrectly, that George Washington was entertained here in 1794. *Location:* Bedford, 224 East Pitt Street.

11. Graystone Hotel (stone) was built partially on the site of an early log tavern and trading post operated by John and Jean Fraser. Their son William, the first white child born in Bedford county, in 1759, died at age

12. *Anderson House*

14. *Espy House*

85 and is buried near a monument on a farm he owned on Glade Pike west of Manns Choice. *Location:* Bedford, northeast corner of East Pitt and Richard Streets.

12. Anderson House (brick) is a fine example of Georgian post-Colonial architecture, built by Solomon Filler in 1814 for Dr. John Anderson and his wife Mary Espy. This two-and-a-half-story structure, with a seven-bay facade and narrow one-story cast-iron porch added later, is more typical of the South than of Pennsylvania. It has a fanlight in the entrance and the original brass door knocker with the initials "J.A." on it. Anderson, who was a banker, doctor, and postmaster, operated the county's first bank, the Bedford branch of Allegheny Bank of Pennsylvania, from 1814 to 1832. Among Anderson's assets were the Bedford Springs Hotel (q.v.), gristmills, and coal lands. Since 1924 the property has belonged to the borough and now serves as headquarters for the Bedford County Heritage Commission, the Northern Appalachian Crafts Festival, and the Heritage Shoppe. *Hours:* Monday–Thursday, Saturday, 10 A.M.–5 P.M. Friday, 10 A.M.–9 P.M. *Location:* Bedford, 137 East Pitt Street.

13. National House (brick), built in 1800 with an overhead porch, has operated as a hotel ever since its erection. *Location:* Bedford, on East Pitt Street, next to Anderson house.

14. Espy House (stone), a three-bay structure built in 1770–71, housed the office of Arthur St. Clair, first prothonotary of the county, later succeeded by David Espy. During Espy's term in this office in 1794, President Washington made his headquarters here for two nights while inspecting the troops sent to quell the Whiskey Rebellion in western Pennsylvania. According to legend a soldier ran off with the roasted fowl that Mrs. Espy had prepared for a dinner in honor of the president. The only major alteration to the structure has been a store window in front. It now houses the Washington Bakery. *Location:* Bedford, 123 East Pitt Street.

15. Old Mann Homestead (frame) was built in 1771 by David F. Mann and fronted on Mann Square. Contained in the basement of this long, narrow building are what are reputed to be the last remaining vestiges of Fort Bedford. Here exists the original powder magazine of the fort, the main part of which was located about one hundred feet to the south. The homestead is now occupied by a jewelry store. *Location:* Bedford, South Juliana Street.

16. Fort Bedford, for which Raystown was renamed, was built by the British under the command of Gen. John Forbes in 1758. Col. James Burd was supervisor and Capt. Harry Gordon engineer. It served as the supply base from which Forbes's army advanced to Fort Duquesne with 7,580 men. George Washington was an unofficial adviser.

This stockaded fortress had five bastions which guarded the corners of the irregularly shaped structure and covered 7,000 square yards. It was the first British installation to fall to American forces, when Capt. James Smith's "Black Boys," masquerading with blackened faces, made a dawn raid to release friends who had been arrested for opposing official Indian policy. The fort withstood a siege during Pontiac's Rebellion and was later abandoned with little of the original structure remaining (see *Old Mann Homestead*).

In 1958 the present fort museum was constructed at the same location for the fort's bicentennial celebration, and in 1960 it was enlarged. Surrounded by a stockade, this structure contains numerous exhibits, including a model of the fort and one of the original Conestoga wagons which traveled on the old Forbes Road. The Fort Bedford Park and Museum were developed by the community in cooperation with the Pennsylvania Historical and Museum Commission. *Hours:* May 15–October 15: Daily, 10 A.M.–9 P.M.. *Admission charge.* Special group rates. *Location:* Bedford, on Fort Bedford Drive at North Juliana Street.

17. Grand Central Hotel (brick) in later years was renamed the Washington. It originally had a triple-deck porch which was removed along with one floor when it became a savings and loan office. At present it houses a bank and a gas company. *Location:* Bedford, Juliana and Pitt Streets.

18. The Groves (Barclay House) (stone) was built in 1794 and was the home of Hugh Barclay, who entertained Alexander Hamilton during the Whiskey Rebellion. It was enlarged in 1830. Another residence of Barclay is an 1810 brick house on the corner of Thomas and Pitt Streets, and the present public library was also a Barclay home. *Location:* Bedford, Grove Lane and South Bedford Street.

19. Arundale Hotel (stone), which later became the Elks Country Club, still contains an original part built in 1780. During the Whiskey Rebellion, President Washington's troops bivouacked on the plain around it. *Location:* South edge of Bedford, on old U.S. 220 (on way to Bedford Springs).

20. Naugle Mill (stone) was built in 1797 by Frederick Naugle along Shovers Run. On the building is a protruding gable for a grain pulley. The miller's log house, dating back to

21. *Bedford Springs Hotel*

1798, is located across the road. *Location:* Two miles south of Bedford, on Springs Road (old U.S. 220), near Bedford Springs Hotel.

21. Bedford Springs Hotel (brick and frame) was established soon after 1800 by Dr. John Anderson (see *Anderson House*) at a magnesia mineral spring. By 1848 the lodging rooms included adjoining buildings with a frontage of 557 feet.

The structure was known as the summer White House of Pennsylvania's only president, James Buchanan, who here received the first message over the Atlantic cable on August 17, 1858, from Queen Victoria: "Come let us talk together. American genius and English enterprise have this day joined together the Old and the New World. Let us hope that they may be as closely allied in bonds of peace, harmony and kindred feeling." President Buchanan's reply was, "New England accepts with gladness the hand of fellowship proffered by Old England." In 1859 Buchanan announced from Bedford Springs that he would not seek a second term.

Another event that took place here was the Passmore Williamson case, heard by the Supreme Court when it sat here in the summer of 1855—one of the legal actions leading to the Civil War. During World War II the hotel became a naval training center; soon after, personnel of Japanese embassies were incarcerated here.

The spacious structure with a large colonial portico in front adjoins a wooden bridge over the highway to the springs. It is situated on a 2,800-acre estate in the Allegheny Mountains. *Location:* Four miles south of Bedford exit (no. 11) of Turnpike, on Springs Road (old U.S. 220).

22. Mount Dallas (Hartley House) (stone and frame) has a chimney on its right side that, before it was rebuilt about 1940, bore the legend, "I, Thomas Cruille built this house 1755," but this may not represent the actual date of construction. The stone section of the house was built before 1794 by William Hartley. This tavern replaced a nearby log inn run by one Sarah Tussey, where it was reputed that the male traveler was offered more than food, drink, and a place to sleep. In 1794 President Washington stopped at Mount Dallas on his way to quell the Whiskey Rebellion. By 1803 it belonged to Capt. James Graham. In that year Thaddeus Mason Harris described this house as a "neat and commodius dwelling, principally built with limestone, laid in mortar. The rooms and chambers are snug, and handsomely furnished; and the accommodations and entertainment he provides are the best to be met with between Philadelphia and Pittsburgh." *Location:* 4.6 miles east of Bedford's east-limits marker, on north side of U.S. 30; a quarter mile east of Snake Valley Road (old Pa. 36).
Note: There may be many Hartley taverns and homes in the Bedford area. One was a half mile west of Tussey's; and another, now a hotel, is in Bedford at the corner of East Pitt and East Streets.

23. Thropp's Folly refers to an unfinished railroad bridge begun by the Joseph E. Thropp Company, a major blast furnace and foundry operation that was begun in 1890 and went bankrupt in 1924. A large concrete pier is a reminder of the never-finished, two-gauge railroad bridge which would have carried limestone across the Juniata River to Thropp's furnace. Thropp reportedly invested $80,000 in the venture and then ran out of funds. *Location:* Just east of Everett, on north side of U.S. 30.

24. Defibaugh Tavern (stone with stucco and frame), built about 1800, was one of the largest inns along the old Pennsylvania Road and for many years was known as the Willow Grove Tavern. It originally had seventeen rooms and a two-story drovers' porch. The stone section was built for Abraham Defibaugh by his brother-in-law, George Cruille (Croyle), and the five-room frame part was added by Joseph Mortimore. The barroom, unchanged since 1865, includes the original bar top, a single hand-hewn plank, thirty-six inches wide. Since 1912 the house has been a private residence. *Location:* 1.8 mile east of Everett limits, on U.S. 30.

Note: A log house built in the eighteenth century, now weatherboarded, and a large stone barn are across the highway.

25. Weaverling Tavern (stone) was operated before 1790 by Jacob Weaverling (see *J. P. Weaverling House*). *Location:* East of Everett, on old U.S. 30, south of present highway and visible from it.

26. J. P. Weaverling House (stone), with a later two-story porch, was built by Jacob Weaverling's grandson John Peter on property purchased by the family in 1783. A signature stone in one gable reads, "J. W. 1843." The barn, now razed, bore the date 1837. In 1960 an addition was built on the house, at one time called the Old Stagecoach Inn. *Location:* 3.3 miles east of Everett, on U.S. 30.

27. General Washington Tavern (stone) was built in the early 1800s. Early inkeepers at this site were a Mr. Householder, Abraham Martin, and Hugh Dennison (in 1818), followed by George McGraw in the 1840s. McGraw, who was a judge, died in 1872. There is much folklore associated with this building. One early tavern keeper was said to have been a horse thief; and bandit Davy Lewis, arrested for counterfeiting in 1815, is supposed to have stopped here. At one time it was reputed to have been a center for illegal liquor during Prohibition days. A secret room with a door operated by a rope was discovered in the house. The building, now an antique shop, is situated between old and new U.S. 30. Old U.S. 30 ran directly in front of the house at one time, crossing the Juniata River where a famous old covered bridge was washed away by the Saint Patrick's Day flood of 1936. Foundation stones east of the house show the location of this bridge, which had replaced General Forbes's old bridge built in 1758. The present bridge is between the sites of the two early ones. Forbes had built a small stockade, Fort Juniata, half a mile north of the crossing to protect his army. *Location:* Two miles west of Breezewood, on U.S. 30.

28. Maple Lawn Inn (brick), with fanlighted windows between gable chimneys, was built about 1815 by a member of the Rinard family and operated as a tavern for over 150 years.
The inn is located at Breezewood, which was mostly farmland until 1940, when it mushroomed at the Turnpike interchange with tourist motels. The area has been nicknamed Turnpike City. *Location:* West edge of Breezewood just beyond community sign, on U.S. 30.

29. Crawford's Museum (frame) contains an extensive collection of game and wild birds from around the world. Over three hundred specimens, collected by the museum's owners, are on display here. *Hours:* April 16–December 30: daily (except Wednesday and Sunday), 10 A.M.–6 P.M. *Admission charge. Location:* Breezewood, on U.S. 30.

30. Rainsburg Academy (brick), built in 1853–54, housed the Allegheny Male and Female Seminary chartered in 1853. It provided education equivalent to that given in high schools and junior colleges before such schools came into existence in the area. Samuel Williams, born in 1806 in Napier Township, acquired the old Friend tract in 1844 and founded the seminary, which operated until shortly before 1870. It was next bought by the Odd Fellows and later operated as a normal school until 1912. From 1912 to 1952 an elementary school was held here. In 1969 the building was purchased for a private home. *Location:* South edge of Rainsburg, in Colerain Township.

Note: Two old churches are near Rainsburg in Friends Cove: the "twin churches" (brick), the former Lutheran and Reformed (now Lutheran), built in 1833 with its galleries and high pulpit still intact, and the present Cove Reformed Church, erected in 1888.

31. Old Schoolhouse (stone), the oldest in the county, was built in 1803–05 and used until 1879. The exterior has been repaired by the county's Pioneer Historical Society. *Location:* About four miles north of Bedford, turn east from U.S. 220 onto Belden Road and go 1.9 mile straight through Belden to iron bridge; 300 feet past bridge turn right on l.r. 05109 (unmarked); go about 1.6 mile to school.

Note: About halfway on l.r. 05109, near crossing of l.r. 05100, is the Messiah Lutheran Church built in 1906. A signature stone gives the names of the church officials and the bricklayer. The church was organized about 1790.

32. Chalybeate Springs Hotel (brick) was built as a tavern in 1786–87 by George Funk on land where Indians drank from springs having high iron content. In 1867 a new wing was added, at which time the resort became known by its present name. George H. Dauler bought the hotel in 1885 and added another wing in 1886–87. His son George H. Dauler, Jr., became proprietor in 1898, built a ballroom in 1903, and continued to operate

the summer resort until 1913. During the 1880s and 1890s the hotel prospered and became the summer "playground of presidents." Its register preserves the names of at least five incumbent presidents from Hayes to McKinley, along with cabinet members, political leaders, and famous people. A local contractor bought the property in 1947 and converted the hotel into apartments five years later. *Location:* At traffic light on U.S. 220 just north of Bedford, turn east on Sunnyside Road. Go one mile to its junction with Chalybeate Road (can be seen from Turnpike).

33. Double Stone House is a massive but somewhat dilapidated structure with a front porch. The older portion of the house dates from around 1800. An early turnpike tollgate was nearby. *Location:* About one mile north of Bedford, on North Richard extension.

34. Chambersburg Raid Entrenchments, still visible by the roadside, were prepared in June 1863 by militia under Col. J. C. Higgins against threatened Confederate attack toward the railroads at Altoona. *Location:* Five miles south of Loysburg, on Pa. 36 (Snake Spring Mountain Road) at Tussey Mountain near Morrisons Cove.

35. Loysburg Gristmill (frame with stone foundation) was constructed by Martin Loy, who had a tannery here as early as 1818. This mill operated from 1836 to 1952, passing through several ownerships. *Location:* Loysburg, on Pa. 36 on Yellow Creek.

Note: The large brick house across the road from the mill was built by W. H. Aaron, a millwright who had made a fortune in the northwestern Pennsylvania oil boom. Loysburg was formerly called Pattonville.

36. Snyder House (stone) was completed in 1812 by John Snyder, who built one of the first gristmills in Morrisons Cove about 1795. The present large building was erected as a mill, and its six stories were used as separate residences for Snyder's sons and their families. Because not enough water was available for a mill, this structure was known for a time as Snyder's Folly. *Location:* About two miles north of Loysburg in Morrisons Cove, on Pa. 36 at Pa. 869.

37. Waterside Woolen Mill (frame) belonged to Joseph B. Noble, who in 1862 left his partner Jacob Furry (see *Furry Gristmill*) and purchased this property. He tore down a building that had been erected on the property in 1830 and built the present mill in

1865–66. Its floors and machinery are supported by oak girders held together by locust pins. It continued in operation until a few years ago. *Location:* Waterside, on Pa. 866 on Yellow Creek.

38. Furry Gristmill (frame) was built by John Nicodemus in 1856. In 1862 Jacob Furry and Joseph B. Noble purchased the mill, and shortly afterwards Noble bought the Waterside Woolen Mill. Furry lived in the Noble house, a large stone structure near the mill, and the property has remained in the possession of his family. *Location:* New Enterprise, in Morrisons Cove.

39. Mowry-Way Mill (stone) was built on Bobs Creek in 1807 and was operated until 1931. Among millers who owned the structure were Mowry, Way, and Dubbs. The miller's log house, later painted, is located across from the mill. *Location:* Weyant (Mowrys Mills), junction of Pa. 96 and Pa. 869.

40. Keagy House (stone) was built in 1813 by Michael Keagy. A house of similar stone construction, built before 1827 and possibly the home of the ironmaster of Elizabeth furnace, is in the heart of nearby Woodbury. *Location:* South edge of Woodbury, on Pa. 866.

41. Lost Children Monument marks the site where George, age seven, and Joseph, five and a half, sons of Samuel and Susanna Cox, were discovered after being lost in the wilderness near their home at Spruce Hollow close to the village of Lovely on April 24, 1856. Two thousand people searched the area for the children, and during this time Jacob Dibert, who lived at some distance, had a recurring dream in which he envisioned the spot where the boys were to be found. Dibert and his brother-in-law, Harrison Whysong, who recognized the area from Jacob's report of his dream, searched it and found the boys' bodies by a stream on May 8. A monument dedicated May 8, 1906 is at the site where the children died from exposure and starvation. Their graves are in the Mount Union Church cemetery at Lovely. *Location:* Near Pavia, north of Blue Knob State Park. From Pavia go one mile northwest on Pa. 869; turn right on unimproved road at highway maintenance depot; thence 1.5 mile to clearing along the road. Cross two footbridges on left and follow visible path to monument in woods.

42. Octagonal Schoolhouse (frame), called the Eight Square School, was erected

42. Octagonal Schoolhouse

in 1851 and used as a school until 1931. The builders were largely Quakers. Plans for restoration and possible removal to Bedford Village are being made at this writing. *Location:* Near Fishertown, 100 yards north of Chestnut Ridge Elementary School on lane off Pa. 56, about seven miles northwest of Bedford.

43. Miller's House (log and stone) is a very early structure probably built at the same time as a nearby mill, now gone. Currently this is the office of Friendly Village Campground. *Location:* Two miles west of Bedford, on t. 469, 0.5 mile north of U.S. 30.

44. Bonnet's (Forks Tavern) (stone), reputed to have been built in 1762 by John Bonnet, was an early inn at the forks of Forbes and Burd military roads. It was also the site of a former Indian village and military encampment. In 1763 Capt. John Stewart wrote a letter from this four-mile house, and in 1783 Dr. Johann Schoepf "breakfasted with a Bonnet" at this place. John Heckewelder, a Moravian missionary, stopped here in 1786, 1788, 1789, and 1792. Early western Pennsylvania farmers raised a liberty pole in 1794 at this site in defiance of the federal taxation of whiskey. The house has been restored and is presently a restaurant. *Location:* Four miles west of Bedford, at intersection of U.S. 30 and Pa. 31.

Note: A similar stone house, reportedly an old inn built in 1823, is within sight at the Cook farm on U.S. 30 just east of the Forks.

45. White Sulphur Springs Inn (frame) was built in 1884 by John Reed and George Lyon on land warranted to Samuel Barclay and William Lyons in 1847. In 1894 Ross and Michael Colvin bought the property, and between 1884 and 1914 it became known as a summer resort. A log tavern (razed), believed to have been built in 1771, operated on an earlier tract of this property warranted to Peter Wertz in 1844. It was a stopover for drovers on the Packers Trail close to the crest of Wills Mountain. Original logs from the first inn have been built into a sheep stable on the site. Both establishments were named for the famous mineral springs where various Indian tribes once met in peace because they believed it was hallowed ground.

In 1946 Paul and Patricia Cochran purchased the property, made extensive changes, and continue to operate the inn which is located in a picturesque wooded setting. Open year round. *Location:* At Milligans Cove, on Cove Road, one mile west of Pa. 96, south of Manns Choice.

46. Hereline House (log) is an early structure owned by John Hereline at one time. *Location:* Near Manns Choice, on I.r. 05097, seven miles west of Bedford. After crossing Hereline covered bridge, which is 0.5 mile north of U.S. 30, turn east for 0.7 mile along Juniata River.

47. Sleepy Hollow Inn (Hi-De-Ho Tavern) (log) was built in 1775 as a stagecoach inn on the old Forbes Road. Early owners of this log tavern (before 1786) were one Taylor and later Charles Ruby. The structure was covered with siding after the 1820s and uncovered in 1969. At present it serves as a camp store and recreation center for a modern public camping ground. *Location:* Just east of Schellsburg, on north side of U.S. 30.

48. Schell-Colvin House (brick), with a fanlight entrance, was erected about 1820 and operated as a store by J. P. Schell. The Colvin family owned this building at a later date. *Location:* Schellsburg, junction of U.S. 30 and Pa. 96.

Note: Another brick Colvin house of 1855 is across the road.

49. Danaker House (stone) was built in 1828 with a fanlight entrance. Another stone house having a similar doorway is on the same side of the street (U.S. 30), across from the post office. The Thomas Taylor family owned both houses in later years. *Location:* Schellsburg, U.S. 30 and Peter Street.

50. Clark House (stone) was built in 1780 by William A. B. Clark to replace the 1770 brick structure behind the main house. It has a fanlight entrance. Clark, an early settler, operated a steam tannery. His descendants retained ownership of this property until 1968, when the building was sold and became an antique shop. *Location:* Schellsburg, on U.S. 30.

51. Schellsburg Academy (brick), with a portico, was built before 1877. In 1904 Edgar F. Johnson was principal. After closing about 1912, the building was used for a public school but now stands empty. *Location:* Schellsburg, two blocks north of U.S. 30 on Pa. 96.

52. Schellsburg Union Church (log) was built in 1806 on land donated by John Schell. It is the county's oldest church building and the first Protestant church west of the Susquehanna River erected by the German Evangelical Reformed and Lutheran congregations. According to old records the structure was renovated in 1881, at which time it was probably weatherboarded. The church, with the logs again exposed, still contains the early balcony, the wine-glass pulpit, and high-backed wooden pews. Open to visitors. *Location:* One mile east of Schellsburg, on U.S. 30 (in cemetery).

53. Algonkin Gap Indian Relic Museum contains a remarkable display of Indian artifacts collected in Bedford County by R. F. Duffy and his son John. *Hours:* By appointment. *Location:* Near Schellsburg, on Pensyl Hollow Road, just off U.S. 30.

54. Black Lion Tavern (log), built in 1788, was operated by one Ryan (name often confused as "Lyon" because of sign) from an early period. John Heckewelder and Abraham Steiner stopped here on a western tour in 1789. Steiner noted that it was the only inn with a signboard between Bedford and Pittsburgh. "Nothing to be had here excepting a little whiskey, and no oats for the horses." Howell's map of 1792 shows it as the "Lyon." The tavern is in a settlement, later owned by Maj. James Burns, that included a gristmill he built about 1800, a blacksmith shop, a tannery, a store, a post office, and slave quarters. Some of the foundations can still be seen across the road from the house. *Location:* Four miles west of Schellsburg, off U.S. 30, 150 yards north over hillside at foot of Allegheny Mountain.

52. *Schellsburg Union Church*

55. "Shot Factory" House (stone), across from Tollgate Spring at the foot of Allegheny Mountain (Grandview), is an old landmark situated on the sharp curve where Forbes's army built its road straight up the mountain. Gunshot used to be made on this property. Early owners were the Finleys. Traces of the old breastworks built by the British remain on top of the mountain. This house, later purchased by the Shaffer family, now operates as a candy shop. *Location:* West of Schellsburg, on U.S. 30 just east of crest of Allegheny Mountain.

Note: Halfway between this site and the Grand View Ship Hotel (q.v.), on the north side of the road, is the site of an old tollgate on an early turnpike.

56. Grand View Ship Hotel, originally called the Grand View Point Hotel, was built in 1931–32 to give the impression of an ocean liner, since the owner, Herbert Paulson, saw a resemblance between mists in the valley and ocean waves. He had opened a stand here in 1927. Constructed of concrete and steel, with a top-deck promenade, it is known locally as the Ship, providing a view of seven counties and parts of Maryland and West Virginia. *Location:* Seventeen miles west of Bedford, on U.S. 30.

57. Fort Dewart, also known as McLean's redoubt or the breastworks, was established August 1758 as a temporary depot for work parties cutting through the military road for Gen. John Forbes's army. A monument erected in 1930 by the Pennsylvania Historical and Museum Commission is on the site where the outline of the breastworks can be seen. The site is on private property. *Location:* 3.6 miles east of Reels Corners (junction of U.S. 30 and Pa. 160); thence 0.6 mile north on private road off U.S. 30 (about 400 yards from house on this site). (Partly in Somerset County.)

Pennsylvania Historical and Museum Commission Markers

Anderson House   Bedford, East Pitt Street between Juliana and Richard Streets

Bedford Springs   Bedford Springs, old U.S. 220

Bedford Village   On main highways leading into Bedford

Capt. Phillips' Rangers Memorial   At property on Pa. 26 northwest of Saxton

Espy House   Bedford, East Pitt Street between Juliana and Richard Streets

Forbes Camp   U.S. 30 west of Schellsburg

Forbes Road   Junction of U.S. 30 and Pa. 31, 4 miles west of Bedford

Forbes Road (Fort Juniata)   U.S. 30, 6.2 miles east of Everett

Fort Bedford   Bedford, U.S. 30

Fraser Tavern   Bedford, northeast corner of East Pitt and Richard Streets

Gettysburg Campaign   Pa. 36, 5 miles south of Loysburg

"King's House"   Bedford, East Pitt Street between Juliana and Richard Streets

Old Log Church   U.S. 30 west of Schellsburg

Russell House   Bedford, 203 South Juliana Street

Shawnee Cabins   U.S. 30 west of Schellsburg

The Squares   Bedford, 203 South Juliana Street, southeast corner of square

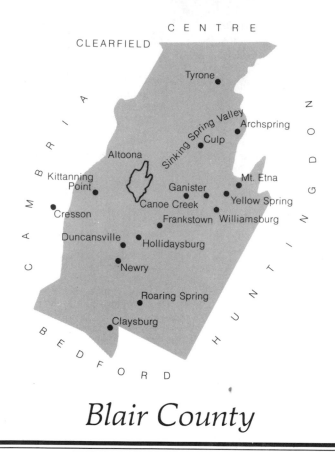

Blair County

Capsule History

Blair is the only county in the state named in honor of a living native resident, John Blair, who served in the Pennsylvania legislature and was active in the development of turnpike and canal-boat transportation. It was erected out of Huntingdon and Bedford Counties on February 26, 1846, and is 530 square miles in area with a population of 135,356.

The first European settlers who entered Blair County before the Revolutionary War were Germans who settled in Morrisons Cove and Scotch-Irish who located in the northern part of the county. Chief John Logan, one of the sons of Shikellamy, famous Indian vicegerent of the Six Nations, was a friend to the white people and lived at Logans Spring.

Numerous Indian trails ran through Blair County, the most important of which was the *Frankstown Path* (Kittanning Trail) running from near Harrisburg to the Allegheny River. It entered the county at Yellow Spring and crossed Canoe Mountain near the mouth of Canoe Creek. The trail ran along a ridge near U.S. 22 to Frankstown and followed the course of that highway to Hollidaysburg; thence it continued through El Dorado and on toward Ashville. The *Bald Eagle Creek Path* turned north from it at Hollidaysburg and ran through Altoona, Bellwood, and Tyrone. The *Frankstown–Burnt Cabins Path* ran by Shelleytown and above Marklesburg. The *Warrior Path* followed the course of U.S. 22 from Water Street to Frankstown, thence south through McKee Gap, near Claysburg and Sproul. The *Raystown-Chinklacamoose Path* followed the same course in Blair County. The northern *Morrisons Cove Path* cut through a corner of Blair County northeast of King.

Situated strategically near the head of the Juniata River Valley and at the portals of mountain ranges (bounded by Tussey Mountain on the east and Allegheny Mountain on the other side), the county became a natural gateway to the West. Blair is noted for its transportation progress. The Indian trails became trader paths, which were superseded by turnpikes, the canal-portage railroad, railways, and modern highways. The Blair-Altoona Airport at Martinsburg was one of the earliest important fields in the state.

Hollidaysburg, the county seat, laid out in 1796 by Adam Holliday, whose brother William's three children were massacred by Indians, became the eastern junction of the Main Line Canal and the Portage Railroad. Altoona was founded by the Pennsylvania Railroad in 1849 and became a thriving village with the completion of the track over the Allegheny Ridge by the Horseshoe Curve in 1852. It became a borough two years later and a city in 1868, after the world's largest railroad shops of that era and a roundhouse were established there. Most of its streets were named for the sweethearts of the engineers.

Abundant ore, limestone, and timber made the Juniata Valley an important iron-producing area. In 1855 there were thirty-two charcoal furnaces, forges, and allied works in the county, including sixteen (possibly seventeen) stone blast furnaces. (One of Pennsylvania's foremost ironmasters, Dr. Peter Shoenberger, built his first furnace in Blair County in 1819.) Additional resources were coal and zinc. Lead-mining centered in Sinking Valley. Later, construction and repair of railroad cars provided major employment.

The county offers excellent views of scenic landscapes at such places as Homers, Riggles, Juniata, Blairs, and Bells Gaps, as well as at the top of Wopsononock Mountain.

Landmarks

1. County Courthouse (stone) was erected in 1876. The first courthouse was put up by Daniel K. Reaney in 1846 and occupied by various county offices the following year. The present courthouse, dedicated in 1877, cost $103,000. It is a three-story structure of Neo-Gothic style, with a high clock tower and spacious corridors. *Location:* Hollidaysburg, corner of Allegheny and Union Streets.

2. Stone Jail was built in 1868–69 by Jonathan Rhule. The first keeper of the jail was Aden Baird. It is a spectacular structure. *Location:* Hollidaysburg, corner of Mulberry and Union Streets.

3. Zion Evangelical Lutheran Church (painted brick) was founded in 1838 by members of the 1824 church at Frankstown. Jacob Garber was the first pastor. The cornerstone of the present church was laid in June 1853. It was remodeled between 1872 and 1883. *Location:* Hollidaysburg, corner of Allegheny and Union Streets.

5. Manahath School of Theology

4. Highland Hall (stone) was originally Hollidaysburgh Male and Female Seminary, founded in 1865 and first opened in the Town Hall since this building was not completed until 1868–70. After 1869 the school was exclusively for girls. In 1911 the original marble marker which bore the title "Male and Female Seminary" was covered with concrete and the new name, "Highland Hall 1867–1911," inscribed. The last commencement for the girls school was in 1940, and from 1942 to 1945 it became an Army-Navy training school and a radio school. In 1945 the Franciscan Fathers of Immaculate Conception province purchased the building, and under their direction a boys school was opened here, continuing until 1957. Presently it is the courthouse annex. *Location:* Hollidaysburg, 509 Walnut Street.

5. Manahath School of Theology (stone), an impressive house with beams showing through the stone and a cupola, was built in 1854 by William Jack, an abolitionist leader who became a colonel in the Civil War. A tunnel connecting the basement and the river was closed in the 1940s. Jack also opened the first bank in the county and owned an iron furnace and other industries. Following his death in 1901, his wife and son and later a nephew owned the house. In 1953 it became a funeral home, and since 1964 it has housed an Evangelical Methodist school, the name being Hebrew for "God's resting place." *Location:* Hollidaysburg, 1111 North Juniata Street at Cedar Boulevard.

6. Railroad Museum is located in the restored Cove Station, formerly on the main line of the Pennsylvania Railroad about ten miles west of Harrisburg. This building and a caboose were moved to the property by Charles Hazlett, who owns the museum. *Hours:* April–

October: Monday–Friday, 10 A.M.–5 P.M. Saturday and Sunday, 1–6 P.M. *Location:* 1.5 mile south of Frankstown, on l.r. 07011 (off U.S. 22 east of Hollidaysburg).

7. Chimney Rocks marks the reputed location where Indians held council meetings. This rock formation of limestone has been owned by the Blair County Historical Society since December 14, 1923. A bronze marker was placed on Pulpit Rock on October 17, 1924, to serve as a recognition of this gift of land to the society and to designate the property for public use. Similar rock formations can be seen at Fayetown on Pa. 866. *Location:* Juniata Valley, south of Hollidaysburg near Pa. 36.

8. Allegheny Portage Railroad, plane no. 6, was a section of this unbelievable road which carried canal boats and other freight from the Pennsylvania Main Line Canal ending at Hollidaysburg to its resumption at Johnstown. This feat was accomplished by a series of levels and ten inclined planes, five east and five west of the summit. Construction was begun in 1831 and completed in 1834, when through rail and canal transport from Philadelphia to Pittsburgh was opened. At first cars were drawn up and let down by ropes, which wore out quickly, until John Roebling (see *Saxonburg,* Butler County) devised wire cables. Later, engines ran on some of the gentler inclines. The total cost of the railroad was $16.5 million. A section of plane no. 6 may be seen at the foot of the hill. This part of the Portage Railroad has been made a national historic site. *Location:* Just east of summit at Cresson, on U.S. 22.

9. Skew Arch Bridge (stone) was built without mortar in 1832–33 to carry the Huntingdon-Blairsville section of the Northern Turnpike over the Allegheny Portage Railroad at the lower end of plane no. 6. It is one of the few arch stone bridges built on an oblique angle in Pennsylvania. Reputed to be the most famous masonry structure in America, it was abandoned in 1922 when U.S. 22 was widened and straightened. Steps leading to the base of the arch are made of stones from the old Portage Railroad bed. A ten-foot monument near the bridge was erected in 1929. *Location:* East of summit at Cresson in Y of U.S. 22.

10. Gallitzin Spring was a favorite stopping place of Father Demetrius Gallitzin, a Roman Catholic missionary who founded Loretto. In 1916 the Knights of Columbus, Knights of

9. Skew Arch Bridge

Saint George Cadets, and other organizations landscaped the site and erected a stone springhouse. *Location:* About one mile east of Allegheny Portage Railroad monument (see no. 8), on west side of U.S. 22, east slope of summit at Cresson.

11. Blair Homestead (weatherboarded log and stone) was built in 1785 by Capt. Thomas Blair on Blairs Gap Run, and the stone part was a later addition. Blair's son John was president of the Huntingdon, Cambria, and Indiana Turnpike (Northern Pike) from 1819 to 1826. He served in the legislature from 1826 to 1830; and as a member of the Committee on Inland Navigation and Internal Improvements, he had much influence in locating the Pennsylvania Canal basin at Hollidaysburg. *Location:* 1.1 mile west of Duncansville, on old U.S. 22, directly south of historical marker on new highway.

12. Vipond's House (brick) is a two-and-a-half-story, L-shaped building in two sections, with a white wooden Doric portico. The older section was built in 1790. In 1914 Col. John Vipond lived here. On this estate is the Fort Fetter Monument (1777), 500 yards southwest of the fort site, where an Indian band met defeat. Seven skeletons were disinterred during the construction of the railroad that runs beside the monument. *Location:* Duncansville, just east of junction of U.S. 220 and U.S. 22.

13. Duncansville Presbyterian Church (painted brick) was organized in 1846, with the present building erected in 1847. This structure, which now serves as the municipal building, is located in the village founded by Samuel Duncan, who flipped a coin with Jacob Walter to see whose name the town would honor. Prior to this time, about 1840, it was called Iron Town for the operations of the old forge here. *Location:* Duncansville, on U.S. 22.

14. Lowry Homestead (stone) was built in 1785 by Lazarus Lowry, of the famous Lowry trading family, who came to the Frankstown region about 1768. In 1788 he owned 400 acres of land and was assessed for two horses, two head of cattle, and one Negro slave. A huge stone fireplace is in the kitchen, and additions, including porches, have been added to the original two-story structure. A stone springhouse, built at the same time as the house, is located nearby. *Location:* 1.1 mile east of Hollidaysburg, on old U.S. 22 (0.1 mile west of Frankstown). House can be seen from U.S. 22, where historical marker is located.

15. Hileman House (stone), built in 1795, first appeared on the tax list of 1820. After Hileman owned this property, it was purchased by Jacob Confer. It is situated in Frankstown, which was named for the early trader Frank Stevens, who established a trading post at the nearby village of Assanepachla. The villagers anticipated that this location would be the eastern terminus of the western section of the Pennsylvania Main Line Canal; but through the influence of John Blair, Hollidaysburg became the site instead. *Location:* Frankstown, on U.S. 22 at corner hillside.

16. Mishler Theater (brick) was built by I. C. Mishler (called "Doc" after his father, a dispenser of herb medicines), whose dream was to have a "safe, perfect, and beautiful" playhouse for the people of Altoona. In 1893 he took over the management of the Eleventh Avenue Opera House, and on February 15, 1906, he realized his great ambition when his new Mishler Theater was opened.

Of French classic design and constructed of red brick in Flemish bond with Indiana limestone trim, the theater was built with the greatest attention to safety. A six-inch water main was run into it, a fire curtain installed, and extra-wide aisles planned. The interior was furnished lavishly with twelve dressing rooms and a 42-by-84-foot stage. The exterior entrance consists of four representations in color of the Muses, separated by Ionic columns and mounted on a stone balustrade. Above these are four circular windows, with carved stone garlands flanked by two life-size stone figures representing the Muse of Tragedy and the Muse of Dance. In October 1907 the building burned but was reopened on January 21, 1907.

Among the famous persons who played here were Ethel Barrymore and the John Philip Sousa Band. It was a legitimate theater from 1906 to 1919, after which it was a movie house and a dance studio until about 1950. In 1965 the building, though scheduled to be torn down, was rescued and bought by the Blair Arts Foundation and the Altoona Community Theater. In 1969, after being restored, it was opened as a legitimate theater and arts center. *Location:* Altoona, 1208 Twelfth Avenue.

17. Cathedral of the Blessed Sacrament (stone), built in 1926 as the seat of the Roman Catholic Diocese of Altoona, is one of the most beautiful of its kind in the United States. It is open for visitors during normal hours. *Location:* Altoona, Thirteenth Avenue and Thirteenth Street.

18. Pennsylvania Railroad Shops (brick) include erecting shops at Juniata, one of the largest car-wheel foundries in the world in South Altoona, and what was at one time

19. Baker Mansion

reputedly the largest roundhouse in the world in East Altoona. Though the complex was very active at one time, much of it has been phased out in recent years. *Location:* Altoona, above south side of Tenth Avenue, from Sixteenth to Seventh Streets, and from Seventh Street east to city line.

19. Baker Mansion (stone) was built in 1846 by Elias Baker, the county's wealthiest ironmaster and co-owner of the Allegheny Iron Furnace. The mansion is one of the finest examples of Greek Revival architecture in the United States. The limestone of the building is set in sheets of lead. An impressive portico with six fluted Ionic columns two and one-half stories high is in the front, with a smaller one in the rear. The interior has black walnut woodwork, and Italian marble trim. Among the furnishings are hand-carved pieces and an inlaid rosewood piano brought from Belgium by Elias Baker. This building now houses the Blair County Historical Society and Museum. In 1941 the society purchased this property from Charles Copeley and Louise Harding of London, England. *Hours:* Thursday, Friday, and Saturday during summer months, 1:30–4:30 P.M. Other times by appointment. *Location:* Altoona, 3500 Baker Boulevard (near Thirty-sixth Street).

20. Allegheny Iron Furnace, built in 1811 by Robert Allison and Andrew Henderson and operated by them until 1818, was purchased by Elias Baker and Roland Diller in

1836. Originally fired by charcoal, the furnace was converted to coke in 1867. Following Baker's death in 1864 his son continued to operate the furnace until it went out of business in 1884. The large stone-furnace stack and the stone combination store and office building, erected in 1837, have been restored by the Women's Club of Altoona, which purchased the complex in 1939. *Location:* Altoona, 3400 Crescent Road, at Pa. 36 near Union Road.

21. Burns House (log covered with siding) was erected by the Cadwallader family. Although the house bears the date 1771 on its side, it was actually built in 1776. The daughter of the family married John Burns, for whom this area (Burns Crossing) is named. Antiques are now sold at the house. *Location:* Near Altoona, on Pa. 764, house no. 7200.

22. Cassidy Log House is reputed to have been built by Patrick Cassidy, who founded the town of Newry in 1793, naming it for his birthplace in Ireland. This private residence has been well restored. A number of other early houses are in the vicinity. *Location:* Newry, corner of Allegheny and Cassidy Streets.

23. Roaring Spring is Blair County's "Old Faithful," fed by an uncharted underground stream. The large stone castlelike building overlooking the lake houses the Blank Book Company, established in 1900 and still in business. The town, named in honor of this spring, contains many early houses. *Location:* Roaring Spring.

24. Claysburg Library (log), the oldest house in this village, was built by John Ulrich Zeth in 1811. Arriving here in 1804, he was the first German settler. He built a sawmill in 1805 and a gristmill the following year. The house is now a public library, perhaps the state's only log library. *Location:* Claysburg, on Church Street near Bedford Street.

25. Royer House (quarried stone) was erected in 1815 for Daniel Royer, owner of the iron furnace nearby on l.r. 07022. This house, like many of the others in nearby Williamsburg, has ornate wrought-iron work. *Location:* 0.5 mile from village of Royer and seven miles south of Williamsburg, on Pa. 866.

Note: William McAllister, the ironmaster, lived in the white frame house near the furnace. In the same vicinity is a frame Methodist Episcopal church built in 1872.

30. *Living Quarters at Mount Etna Iron Furnace Plantation*

26. W. R. Metz House (brick), one of the first houses in Williamsburg, has typical architecture of this area. Many buildings have wrought-iron porch railings with decor that came from the old charcoal furnaces nearby. *Location:* Williamsburg, 500 Second Street at Plum Street.

27. Presbyterian Church (brick), founded in 1816, was built in 1841. The structure is in good condition. *Location:* Williamsburg, on Second Street between Plum and Black Streets.

28. Octagonal Chapel (brick), now serving as a church, was formerly a schoolhouse. *Location:* Near Ganister, on l.r. 07061 (Piney Creek Road), three miles from Juniata Run Bridge on Pa. 866.

Note: Nearby are several early stone houses worthy of study.

29. Patterson House (stone) was built about 1850 by George W. Patterson, who was on the tax list in Huntingdon County as early as 1846. A building next to the house, now used as a garage, was erected much earlier, perhaps 1820. *Location:* About twelve miles east of Hollidaysburg, on U.S. 22 (one mile west of Yellow Spring and six miles east of Canoe Creek).

30. Mount Etna Iron Furnace Plantation includes the first furnace built in Blair County; it was begun about 1807, put into blast in 1809, and went out of operation in 1870. Erected by Canan, Stewart & Moore, it passed through several ownerships before it was purchased by Henry S. Spang in 1837. Spang built a huge stone mansion, a mill (in 1823 to replace a 1790 structure), a large office-store, and a new house twelve windows long, all of stone. Later he sold the property to Samuel Isett and his son, descendants of Jacob Isett of Arch Spring (see *Isett House*). Samuel Isett developed the enterprise created by Spang, and the settlement became the Isett Post Office. *Location:* Turn southeast off U.S. 22 at historical marker near dairy barn, about two miles west of Huntingdon County line. Follow t. 463 for 0.8 mile to site, which includes (in order) a large stone barn, twelve-windowed stone living quarters (four apartments), ruins of blacksmith shop, and furnace stack (one side fell in spring of 1975), all on left. On right are store-office and manager's stone residence. Continue 0.2 mile from furnace to river road and right 0.4 mile on l.r. 07020 to row of log cabins, built for workers and still occupied, and ironmaster's mansion erected by Spang.

31. Horseshoe Curve, opened on February 15, 1854, and still operating, is a feat of engineering built when the westward expansion of the Pennsylvania Railroad demanded a main line connecting east and west. The roadbed was surveyed and the track, 2,375 feet in length, was laid out in 1847 by J. Edgar Thomson and his aides. At the outbreak of World War II, the railroad closed Horseshoe Curve to the public for fear of sabotage. In 1942, a Nazi submarine landed four highly trained saboteurs on the eastern coast of the United States in an unsuccessful attempt to blow up twelve key locations, one of which was this landmark.

In 1925 the Pennsylvania Railroad built a decorative stone horseshoe thirty-four feet long on the hillside. Also on display is a K-4 locomotive, no. 1361, at the curve beside the main line at an elevation of 1,623 feet. Before being made a memorial, this engine had rolled up 2,469,000 miles. A caboose, a 1916 version of the famed Pennsy "Mae West" cabin car, sits at the foot of the curve and is open to visitors. *Location:* 5.5 miles west of Altoona, on l.r. 07023 north off Pa. 764.

32. Glen White Coke Ovens, brick faced, are all that remain of a former bustling coke industry in this area. *Location:* Near Altoona, on l.r. 07023, 1.5 mile west of tunnel at Horseshoe Curve picnic area.

33. Fort Roberdeau (stockade) was originally built in 1778 by Maj. Gen. Daniel Roberdeau near the Sinking Spring Valley Lead Mines in order to protect the miners and settlers from Indian attack. (From 1778 until 1780 Roberdeau operated these mines, which supplied lead for the Continental armies during the Revolution.) In April 1779 a magazine and headquarters for a county militia were established here. The fort is presently being restored. *Location:* Eight miles east of Altoona (one mile south of Culp), on l.r. 07053 in Sinking Spring Valley. (Site of lead mine is on l.r. 07053, 8.4 miles east of its junction with Pa. 220 in Altoona.)

34. Isett House (limestone) is a magnificent mansion built by Jacob Isett, who had come from Bucks County in 1785. A signature stone in the gable of the house reads, "Jacob–Elenor 1805," an unusual instance of a wife's name being included. Jagged stones projecting above the roof edge at the gables give an old-world flavor.

The house is almost the last trace of the former glory of the Sinking Spring Valley, which takes its name from the famed Arch Spring—a stream which sank into the earth and reappeared some distance away as a brook and which provided water enough to turn a mill.

Isett also built a mill before 1788. Rebuilt in 1800, 1824, and 1869, it was torn down in 1943. Samuel Isett, Jacob's son, moved to Mount Etna about 1850 (see *Mount Etna Iron Furnace Plantation*). *Location:* Archspring, two miles west of Pa. 350, on unmarked road. Turn just north of Fort Roberdeau marker.

Note: Across the road is a large two-story limestone store building.

35. Sinking Valley Presbyterian Church (stone and wood) is an unusual structure with the lower part stone and the upper part wood and two peculiar round (bulls-eye) windows. The building dates from 1818, though the church was organized in the 1780s. *Location:* About 0.4 mile east of Isett house.

Note: Nearby is the old frame Arch Spring School, vintage of about 1850 to 1870.

36. Wilson Theater (brick), built in 1913, has been used principally for motion pictures since the end of the road-show era. *Location:* Tyrone, on Pa. 350.

37. Home Electric Plant (brick) is a tremendous complex that includes a trolley-car barn dating from 1901. The power plant was built about 1892. *Location:* Tyrone, near "The Forks."

Pennsylvania Historical and Museum Commission Markers

Allegheny Furnace Altoona, Pa. 36 south of Thirty-first Street

Altoona On main highways leading into city

Altoona Conference U.S. 22 west of Hollidaysburg

Baker Mansion Altoona, Pa. 36 at Mansion Boulevard

Blair Homestead Old U.S. 22, 3.5 miles west of Hollidaysburg; and U.S. 22, 3.3 miles west of Hollidaysburg

Etna Furnace U.S. 22, 0.6 mile east of Yellow Spring

Fort Roberdeau L.r. 07053, 1 mile south of Culp; Altoona, U.S. 220; and Altoona, Pleasant Valley Boulevard and Kettle Street

Frankstown U.S. 22, 0.6 mile east of Hollidaysburg

Gallitzin Spring U.S. 22 eastbound, 1 mile east of Cresson; and U.S. 22 westbound, 1 mile east of Cresson

Juniata Iron U.S. 22, 3.9 miles west of Hollidaysburg

Logan House Altoona, Eleventh Avenue at Thirteenth Street

Lowry Homestead U.S. 22, 1.1 mile east of Hollidaysburg

Portage Railroad U.S. 22, 7.9 miles west of Hollidaysburg

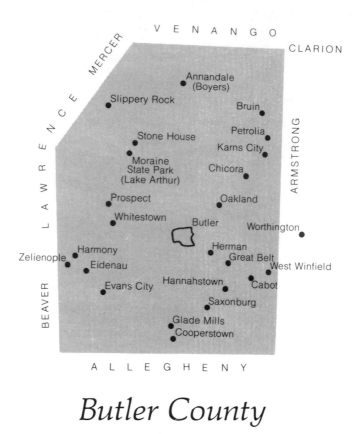

VENANGO

CLARION

MERCER

LAWRENCE

Annandale
(Boyers)

Slippery Rock

Bruin

Stone House

Petrolia

Karns City

Moraine
State Park
(Lake Arthur)

Chicora

Prospect

Oakland

Whitestown

Butler

Worthington

ARMSTRONG

Harmony

Herman

Zelienople

Great Belt

Eidenau

West Winfield

Evans City

Hannahstown

Cabot

Saxonburg

BEAVER

Glade Mills

Cooperstown

ALLEGHENY

Butler County

Capsule History

Butler County, named for Gen. Richard Butler (lawyer, legislator, soldier, and Indian agent, killed in 1791 under the command of Maj. Gen. Arthur St. Clair), was erected out of Allegheny County, March 12, 1800. The land area, much of which lies in the plateau of the Connoquenessing Valley, is 794 square miles with a population of 127,941.

Pennsylvania set apart much of the section north of Pittsburgh and west of the Allegheny River for soldiers of the Revolution as reward for their services. A 1783 act of the legislature divided the territory by a line due west, surveyed under the direction of Surveyor General Daniel Brodhead. Land south of the line was known as "depreciation lands," given to compensate veterans for the depreciation in value of the Continental currency with which they had been paid; and north of it, as "donation lands," given as extra pay for their service. Butler County included both depreciation and donation lands.

Settlement of the county started in 1792 with David Studebaker, James Glover, Abraham Snyder, and one McKinney. Brady Township is named for the Indian fighter Samuel Brady.

Three principal Indian trails crossed the county. The *Kuskusky-Kittanning Path* ran from near Worthington to Butler, passing just north of Herman. It turned north of west through Portersville, and thence a little west of north through Allen's Mill, thence west near Rose Point. The *Logstown Path* entered the county below Zelienople, passing northward through Portersville and West Liberty, crossing Slippery Rock Creek at Crolls Mills, and continuing north through Harrisville. The *Venango Path* from Fort Pitt to Presque Isle followed much the course of U.S. 19 at first and then ran near Pa. 528 and Pa. 8. It entered Butler County above Warrendale, passed through or near Evans City, Whitestown, Prospect, and Muddy Creek, crossing the Slippery Rock, at the mouth of Glade Run. It went through Keisters and Forestville and rejoined the Logstown Path at Harrisville.

Much has been written about Washington's course through the county en route to Fort LeBoeuf in 1753. The best evidence is that he followed the Logstown Path in this area, because more direct ways were blocked by high water. A monument in Forward Township marks the location where he narrowly escaped death when shot at by an Indian on his return by way of the Venango Path.

Butler, the county seat, was settled in 1793 and laid out in 1803, when John and Samuel Cunningham donated 250 acres to the county. It became a third-class city in 1918. Here, through the American Bantam Car Company, was pioneered the development of small, open, lightweight automobiles, the first jeep having been designed and built in Butler.

Since the county embraces part of the rich oil fields of northern Pennsylvania, Petrolia was able at one time to become the "oil capital of the world." The manufacturing of iron and steel and the refining of oil and gas are among its major industries. The county had seven stone blast furnaces. Butler, known as the Buckwheat county, is also one of the leading agricultural counties in the state, with an outstanding mushroom cultivation.

Landmarks

1. Courthouse (stone), of mixed Gothic and French architecture, was built in 1886, costing $117,700. R. B. Taylor of Reynoldsville was the contractor and James P. Bailey of Pittsburgh the architect. It was enlarged and modernized in 1907–08 at a cost of $155,000. This building contains a well-preserved clock 100 years old, which ran mechanically until 1940. A sixty-pound electric motor now operates the hands, though the original works remain in the tower. In 1958 the wood and slate tower shell was replaced by a stainless steel one.

The original log courthouse was located where the Nixon Hotel presently stands, until a brick one was built in 1807. The third building, erected across from the public square in 1855, was remodeled with a clock and bell tower in 1877, but it burned in 1883. *Location:* Butler, on Main Street (Pa. 8).

2. Willard Hotel (brick) is located on the site of an early log tavern. The present structure was remodeled and enlarged from a brick house built by Abraham Brinker in 1834–35. *Location:* Butler, corner of Main and Wayne Streets (near courthouse).

3. Little Red Schoolhouse Museum (brick) was built in 1838, the first brick school in Butler Borough. It has been restored as the headquarters for the Butler County Historical

Society. *Hours:* By appointment only. *Location:* Butler, corner of East Jefferson and South Cliff Streets.

4. Old Hospital (brick), incorporated in January 1897, was opened the following year at a construction cost of $25,000. This large building, now used for apartments, was the first Butler County General Hospital. *Location:* Butler, south end of Main Street bridge, at junction of Pa. 8 and Pa. 356.

5. Saint John's Roman Catholic Church (brick) was erected in 1853, with a spire added in 1877. *Location:* Nine miles east of Butler and six miles west of Worthington, just south of U.S. 422, near Steigner Road.

6. Butler County Mushroom Farm grows mushrooms at two underground locations in limestone mines that have been worked out since 1896. The older of the two is near West Winfield (originally known as Rough Run). Started in 1937, it has fifteen miles of underground roadways connecting eighty acres of rooms. The second and larger one, in operation since 1966, is at Worthington, with 100 miles of corridors and 500 acres of rooms. Both locations use the tray-type growing method at a constant temperature of fifty-six degrees. These farms are the largest of their kind in the world and supply many of the nation's canneries and produce markets. No tours. *Locations:* Near West Winfield, on Cabot-Winfield Road, six miles from Knox Chapel on Pa. 356, and at Worthington, off U.S. 422.

7. Saint Fidelis College and Seminary was founded in 1877 by Capuchin Franciscan Fathers. In 1946 it became affiliated with the Catholic University of America and by 1948 was a four-year college. The first building was erected in 1869 where the church is now located. The oldest existing structure is the faculty residence built in 1886. *Location:* Herman, southeast of Butler, on Pa. 978 near l.r. 10033.

8. Old Hotel Museum consists of restored buildings, including a barbershop, a country store, and the old Black Gold (railroad) Hotel, together with a kitchen house and stone well. Great Belt, where it is located, was at one time thought to be situated on or near an oil belt of the eastern part of the county, hence the name. The post office established in 1870 was also known as Coyle's Station, originally on the Gottlieb Wolf farm. *Hours:* By appointment only. *Admission charge. Location:* Great Belt, Jefferson Township, southeast of Butler (junction of t. 578 and t. 749 at railroad).

9. "Uncle Billy" Smith Monument was erected in memory of William "Uncle Billy" Smith (1812–90), driller of Edwin L. Drake's 69½-foot-deep oil well near Titusville (see *Drake Well,* Venango County). (In 1885 an oil well was drilled at Uncle Billy's home in Double Sales. It was called the "Midnight Mystery" since its flow soon disappeared.) The monument was erected by the petroleum industry in 1959, the centennial of the Drake well. *Location:* Hannahstown, Pape Cemetery, on Pa. 356, 1.5 mile northeast of Saxonburg.

10. Hannahstown Stagecoach Tavern (brick) was built by Nathan Skeer soon after he and Abraham Maxwell founded the town in 1829. Originally a handsome house, it is badly run down and may be lost unless it is soon repaired. *Location:* Hannahstown, on Pa. 356 in Winfield Township.

11. Gibben-Spurling House (log covered with shingles) was built in 1816 before Saxonburg was founded. It once belonged to an early settler, James Gibben, and later to one Spurling. An outstanding feature of the house is its huge stone chimney. *Location:* West Saxonburg (former railroad depot), on l.r. 10019.

12. Cooper House (log), now in poor condition, is the oldest house in Winfield Township. Samuel Cooper built this home in 1800, and his granddaughter Nancy lived here until 1962, when she died at the age of 101. *Location:* Winfield Township, on Cabot-Hannahstown Road. Turn onto t. 677 from Pa. 356 at Pape Cemetery in Hannahstown, continue for one mile to crossroad, and turn left on t. 576. Log cabin sits on left, 100 yards from intersection.

13. Saxonburg was founded by German immigrants in 1832 when Charles and John Augustus Roebling (1806–69) were sent from Saxony to purchase a tract of 16,000 acres in Jefferson Township originally belonging to Robert Morris, financier of the Revolution. It was incorporated in 1846. About 1900, a mineral spring here became a popular health resort. Several original buildings remain.

    a. Roebling House (log covered with siding) was the home of John A. Roebling who laid out the town in 1832. He graduated from the Royal University of Germany and

13.b. Roebling Workshop

came to America in 1831. As the inventor of wire-cable suspended bridges, he improved the Allegheny Portage Railroad by introducing wire cable in place of rope. He was the designer of the Brooklyn Bridge in New York City. Roebling's son Washington, born in 1837, built the structure after his father's death. *Location:* Corner of Water and Main Streets (l.r. 10024 and Pa. 387).

b. Roebling Workshop (frame), its machinery run by hand, was John Roebling's rope factory built in 1840, with a 2,500-foot-long "rope walk" where the cable was wound. The shop, moved to this property from its original location, is in a park diagonally across the street from Roebling's house. In 1848–49 Roebling took his business to New Jersey. *Location:* Corner of Water and Rebecca Streets.

c. Memorial Church (frame), originally German Evangelical Lutheran, was organized in 1837. Built on land given by John Roebling, the present building was completed in 1870. A spire was added later. A few of the original pews made by a church member for fifty dollars remain in the balcony. The sun rises behind the church on the equinox and sets squarely before it. The street extends straight east to the church and divides, continuing on either side of the house of worship. The church stands on the highest point of the watershed; water from the south side of the roof flows to the Allegheny River and from the north side to the Beaver. The congregation became Presbyterian in 1955. *Location:* Main Street.

d. Steubgen House (frame), except for the Roebling house, is the oldest residence in the town. Christian Steubgen started a hotel here in 1848. He was postmaster from 1845 to 1861. The present owner, Helen Steubgen, is a descendant of the family, which settled in

Saxonburg in 1840 after coming from Muhlhausen in the province of Saxony. *Location:* Main Street.

e. Saxonburg Hotel (frame) was built about 1852 with a later addition about 1863. It was known as the Union House from 1861 to 1865. Francis Laube, a musician born in Saxony in 1819, migrated to America in 1837. He rented this hotel in 1865 with E. F. Muder as a partner and called it the Laube House. Squire Laube also owned a brewery on the corner of Water Street and Old Butler Road.

Prior to Laube, George Vogeley and O. M. Raabe had run the hotel. Proprietors following Laube were Hedwig Helmbold, John E. Muder, Milton Newbert, Sam Bernstein, and present owner Dominick Gentile.

The house across from the hotel was a drug store and doctor's office owned by E. B. Mershon about 1888. The property was originally owned by Vogeley. *Location:* Main Street.

14. Robins House (log) is an early structure, but its builder is unknown. It was sold at sheriff's sale in 1810. It was bought by Britnek Robins in 1819. Succeeding owners were James McGowan, the Kingan family, which owned it for nearly a century, Eli Eardly, Robert McGill, Helten T. Patterson, and Florie Lappan, the present owner. A fine spring on the property was ruined by road construction. *Location:* Middlesex Township, on Pa. 228, 1.1 mile east of Glade Mills.

15. Middlesex Presbyterian Church (brick) was organized in 1799, with Abraham Boyd as its first pastor. The present building, similar to the Beulah Presbyterian Church in Allegheny County (q.v.), was built in 1842 with later alterations to the interior. *Location:* North of Cooperstown in Middlesex Township, 116 Church Road (off Pa. 8).

16. Glade Mills House (brick) was built by John Woodcock more than a century ago and bears on its front a U.S. geological survey elevation marker. The present owner is H. P. Starr. In 1877 his grandfather, William Starr, ran a frame sawmill and gristmill, which in 1878 he converted from waterpower to steam (now a lumber store). His sons, J. H. and J. W. Starr, inherited the business. *Location:* Glade Mills, on Pa. 8 at Saxonburg Road. Brick house faces on old Pa. 8 (slightly to east of present highway).

Note: Nearby is a large frame store building erected in 1883 by W. J. Marks during the oil excitement in the area. It is now used as a warehouse.

19. *Evans City Station*

17. North Star Inn (brick), an old stage-coach tavern, was probably built about 1820 on the Pittsburgh Post Road (shown on David Dougal's map of 1817). It sits at about a hundred degree angle with the present highway, facing the old road scar still visible near the spot. Until a few years ago the early stagecoach barn and blacksmith shop were still standing. In 1876 the inn was owned by Simeon Nixon, who sold out in 1882 and built a hotel at Renfrew, where oil had just been struck. Three years later he moved to Butler and built the Central Hotel, relocated by his son, Simeon, Jr., in 1906 and renamed the Nixon. After Nixon's departure the North Star was operated by William Fisher. *Location:* South of Butler, east side of Pa. 8, 0.2 mile south of Airport Road.

18. Phillips Mansion (brick), surrounded by a high iron fence, was the home of T. W. Phillips, Jr., congressman and member of a prominent oil and gas family. The palatial mansion and its appurtenant houses, built about 1922, have recently been converted into a restaurant and recreational club. *Location:* 6.5 miles south of Butler, at junction of Airport Road and Pa. 8 (opposite Butler-Graham Airport).

19. Evans City Station (frame) is said to be the only train station in the country built over water. Erected in 1917, it spans Connoquen-essing Creek in the town. *Location:* Evans City, on Pa. 528 at bridge.

20. Miller Hotel (brick) was built by J. N. Miller, a shoemaker, in 1872. This establishment was one of the finest hotels in the county at that time. In 1880 the roof was blown off the building, which had been converted into apartments. *Location:* Evans City, corner of East Main and Harrison Streets.

21. Miller House (painted brick) was built in 1876 as the successor of the Miller Hotel (see above). The Victorian-style structure still operates as a hotel, run by the original family. *Location:* Evans City, corner of South Washington Street and Pa. 528.

22. Saint Peter's Lutheran Church (brick), at one time the union church of the German Reformed and Lutheran congregations, held its first services, conducted by Rev. John Esensee, in 1845. A frame church, now a residence on Pittsburgh (East Main) Street, was dedicated by Rev. Herman Manz in 1849 and was used for worship until 1869. Nearby this frame church site is a cemetery (between Petroleum Alley and Hill Street), with burial plots arranged according to the ages of the deceased. The second church, also of frame construction, was dedicated in 1869 by Rev. Frederick Wilhelm. It was later destroyed by fire.

The present house of worship, built in Gothic style in 1897 and dedicated in 1898 by Rev. P. J. C. Clatzert, was erected on the former church cemetery grounds (used from 1869 to 1891). An addition was built in 1972. In 1915 an oil well was struck in the church-yard of this congregation. (There were about fifty wells in the area.) *Location:* Evans City, corner of Van Buren and South Washington Streets.

23. Pearce House (brick) was erected by Alfred Pearce around 1875 when Harmony was expected to be the northern terminus of the narrow-gauge Pittsburgh, New Castle & Lake Erie Railroad, which was begun in 1877. Pearce was forced to sell this massive home after the railroad failed in 1879, and it passed to George Ramsey, Jr., who eventually found a way for the Wabash Railroad to run into Pittsburgh for George J. Gould. Later it was bought by the Zieglers and was operated as the Ziegler Hotel. Currently it continues under the name of the Harmony Hilton. *Location:* Harmony, on old U.S. 19, one block east of Bentle House Museum (see *Harmony*).

24. Harmony was settled by the Harmony Society, a religious community founded in 1804 (formally organized in 1805) by George Rapp and some five hundred German followers who came to America in 1803. The settlement under Father Rapp's direction chose celibacy as part of its life-style, in 1807, which inevitably led to its dying out. (In the fifteenth canto of *Don Juan,* Lord Byron refers to Rapp's approval of celibacy.) In 1814 the Harmonists decided to move to Indiana, where the next year they founded New Harmony, finally settling at Old Economy (q.v.) in Beaver County in 1825. Abraham Ziegler, a Mennonite from Lehigh County, and five associates bought the Harmony property in 1815 for $100,000. The following are landmarks of this settlement.

a. Bentle House Museum (painted brick) was the first home of the Harmony Society. This 46-by-36-foot warehouse, with a steeply pitched roof, was built in 1809. It now houses the Harmonist museum and town fire department, organized in 1874. After Abraham Ziegler bought the property in 1815, this house was used as a female seminary. Above the entrance is a picture in relief carved in stone by Frederick Reichert, Father Rapp's adopted son. It is of the Virgin Sophia, a religious symbol of the Divine Wisdom. Included in the museum's collection is the oldest tower clock in the Western Hemisphere,

24.a. Bentle House Museum

brought to America from a German monastery by Frederick Reichert Rapp. The wooden timepiece, built in 1650, was made to run with one hand. The museum is administered by the Harmonie Historical Society. *Hours:* June 1–October 1: Tuesday–Friday, 1–4 P.M. Saturday and Sunday, 1–5 P.M. Winter months by appointment. *Admission charge. Location:* Southeast corner of Mercer and Main Streets (U.S. 19).

Note: An early log house is being restored across the street from this museum.

b. Wagner House (brick), built in 1809, is next to the Bentle House Museum. *Location:* 222 Mercer Street.

c. Stewart House (stucco) was erected in 1805 by the Harmony Society. It burned in 1856 and was rebuilt by Francis Colvert, who used the original foundation and some other parts. It is now owned by Dr. A. I. Stewart. *Location:* Main Street (across from Rapp's house).

d. Shaffer House (brick), built in 1807 or 1809 with the same dimensions as the Bentle house, was used as a store. It had a cut-stone doorway, now bricked in. *Location:* Northwest corner of Mercer and Main Streets.

e. Rapp's House (brick), the last house built here by the Harmony Society, was the residence of Father Rapp. His house has a "Philadelphia" doorway and bricks laid in Flemish bond. Also on the premises are a well and an outside bake oven. *Location:* Main Street, next to old Hotel Beam (now a grocery store).

f. Father Rapp's Chair was carved in the stone on Vineyard Hill and used as a place of meditation by Rapp. According to tradition it also was a lookout for him to watch his workers in the fields below. Originally reached by a stone staircase of about 120 steps, this lovers' rendezvous now has only a precarious dirt path leading to it. This "cell" is high above the Connoquenessing Creek. *Location:* On road northeast of bridge at outskirts of town.

g. Log House is one of the few remaining early homes built in 1805 at the first location in Harmony. There were originally forty-eight of these, measuring 18 by 26 feet. Traces of a mill race can still be seen near the property where a gristmill and barn once stood. *Location:* North of Harmony. At Harmony Mennonite marker on Pa. 19, turn west on Fanker Road and go for less than a mile.

h. Mueller House (brick) was constructed in the early 1800s with an angled corner to allow additional room for wagons to turn on the street. It was owned by Dr. Christopher Mueller, who raised his own herbs. *Location:* Corner of Mercer and Wood Streets.

i. Eidenau Stone Arch is all that remains of an elegant mill of hewn stone built by the Harmonists from 1809 to 1811. The mill arch can be seen along the highway at Minetta Spring, where Harry Etheridge built a monument in memory of his mother-in-law, Mrs. Minetta A. Walsh, which was dedicated October 31, 1932. *Location:* 2.8 miles east of Harmony, on Pa. 68.

j. Harmonist Church (brick) was built before 1820. A two-year supply of grain used to be stored in the attic of this building, as was the custom of the Harmonists. The former doorway through which they drove their wagons into the church is still discernible. A stone doorway dated 1809, once part of another building, is incorporated in the south entrance of the church. The town clock, now in the museum across the street, was originally located in the church tower and later in the public school nearby. *Location:* On south side of Mercer Street, midway between Main and Liberty Streets, on the Diamond.

k. Harmonist Cemetery is enclosed by a cut-stone wall built by Elias Ziegler in 1869, after the Harmonists had returned from New Harmony, Indiana, and had settled at Old Economy in Beaver County. A massive stone gate weighing more than a ton and revolving on a metal pin has inscribed over it, "Hier Ruhen 100 Mitsleiter der Harmonie Geselshaft Gestorben von 1805, bis 1815" (Here rest 100 members of the Harmony Society who died from 1805 to 1815). All the graves within the burial grounds are unmarked, as was the society's custom, except John Rapp's. His stone is attached to the south wall. *Location:* At edge of town, on Pa. 68.

l. Mennonite Church (cut stone) was built in 1825. The first pastor was John Boyer. The Mennonites in the area worshiped with the Harmonists until Abraham Ziegler built their first church in 1816. The present church, with a later addition, and the cemetery are enclosed by a stone wall. *Location:* Just north of Harmony, 0.8 mile north of Zelienople off U.S. 19. (Church is located between old and new U.S. 19.)

m. Stouffer House (stone) was erected in 1825 by one of Abraham Ziegler's associates and was operated as a drovers' inn. It is next to the Gospel Barn. *Location:* About 0.5 mile north of Harmony, on east side of U.S. 19.

25. Lutheran Orphans Home (brick) was organized in Pittsburgh in 1852, and eight boys were moved to Zelienople two years later when Rev. William A. Passavant (see *Zelienople*) and Rev. Gottlieb Bassler bought twenty-five acres of land from Joseph Ziegler. In 1899 another similar institution in Rochester was merged with it. It now receives boys referred by the juvenile court. *Location:* Edge of Zelienople, on Pa. 68 at South Green Lane.

Note: Another Passavant institution, for aged women, is also still active on U.S. 19, at the south edge of Zelienople.

26. Zelienople was founded by Baron Dettmar Basse, later assuming the name Miller (Muller), who bought 10,000 acres of depreciation lands in 1802 and laid out the town in 1803. He built a wooden replica of a German castle which he called Bassenheim (destroyed by fire in 1842) and the Bassenheim iron furnace in 1813. His grandson, born in Zelienople, was Rev. William A. Passavant, editor, philanthropist, Lutheran clergyman, and founder of many hospitals and orphan homes throughout the United States. First called Zelie City, the town was named for Basse's daughter, Zelie.

a. Passavant House (painted brick) was the home of Philip Louis Passavant. Philip married Zelie, daughter of Dr. Dettmar Basse, and they had a son, William A. Passavant. This Georgian-style structure, built about 1814, is now an antique shop. Its present owner is Lester Mohr. *Location:* 243 Main Street.

b. Saint Paul's Lutheran Church (stone) was built in 1826 on land donated by Philip Louis Passavant. The congregation was founded in 1821. In 1913 a tower and transept were added, with a new addition in 1960. The memorial stained-glass windows were donated by Henry Buhl and Joseph S. Seaman. *Location:* 215 North Main Street at Grandview Avenue on the Diamond.

c. Mollard House (brick) was constructed between 1800 and 1805 by an Englishman. The house was later used as a girls' finishing school, a fancy millinery shop, and at present an antique store. John Mollard was a later owner who sold antiques. *Location:* Main Street, U.S. 19.

27. Mount Nebo United Presbyterian Church (brick) was organized in 1805 by Reid Bracken, who was installed in 1808 as the first pastor. The original house of worship, a log structure built in 1808, was replaced by a stone church in 1827. The church cemetery off Pa. 528, 1.5 mile south of Whitestown, marks the site of these two buildings. The third and present church was built in 1859. *Location:* Whitestown, at junction of Pa. 528 and Harmony Road.

28. Saint John's (Old Stone) Lutheran Church (or Middle Lancaster) was organized in 1806. The present church was built in 1829–31. Near the pump in the churchyard are the remains of an old cut-stone lantern post erected in 1829. The first pastor was Gottlieb Schweitgenbarth. *Location:* Over a mile north of Harmony Road and 1.5 mile west of Whitestown on Stone Church Road, off Pa. 528.

29. Prospect is located on the old Venango Indian trail. Andrew McGowan, an early settler, lived here in 1796. Although the White Horse Tavern that once stood here is now gone, many old brick and covered log homes still exist. Among the original buildings that remain are:

a. Edmonson House (yellow frame), a former stagecoach tavern, was once owned by Caleb Edmonson. *Location:* 488 Main Street at Franklin Street.

b. Frazier House (brick), over 130 years old, was formerly owned by the Fraziers and later by the Hays family. *Location:* Franklin (Pittsburgh) Street.

c. Allen House (painted brick) was a tavern owned by Robert Allen in 1845 and by Titus Boehm in 1895. *Location:* Junction of U.S. 422 and Pa. 528.

30. Davis Cabin (log and stone) was built in the 1790s and still remains in a wooded setting on what is now known as the Glacier Ridge Trail, a scenic hikers' path from Jennings Nature Reserve through McConnells Mill State Park past Lake Arthur. It was remodeled in the 1930s. The Davis family owned it when the state purchased the property for a park. *Location:* Moraine State Park, near Lake Arthur at Davis Hollow (behind boat sales office at marina).

31. Muddy Creek United Presbyterian Church (brick) was organized in 1803, with John McPherrin as its first pastor. The present structure, succeeding log ones of 1803 and 1824, was built about 1860, with a new addition in 1954. Mrs. James Wigton and her five children are buried in the churchyard (see *Old Stone House Museum*). *Location:* On t. 414, off Pa. 8 opposite junction with Pa. 138 north.

32. Old Stone House Museum perpetuates a tavern built by John K. Brown in 1822 on land he acquired from Stephen Lowery. Brown built a stagecoach and drovers' inn on the property, which was located at the crossroads of the first two public roads in the county, the Pittsburgh-Franklin and the Butler-Mercer Pikes. Lafayette stopped here on his way from Pittsburgh to Erie in 1825. Due to financial difficulties, Brown's property reverted to the Lowerys, who retained control until the house was brought under public ownership.

In 1843 Sam Mohawk, a Seneca Indian, after becoming drunk at the tavern, went to a farmhouse north of the establishment and murdered Mrs. James Wigton and her five children, who are buried in the churchyard of the Muddy Creek United Presbyterian Church. The Wigton home site (unmarked) is on a nearby golf course.

About this period the first of several groups of counterfeiters, who went only by nicknames, began operations in the area under the leadership of Julius C. Holiday and for a while resided in the tavern. Also in the 1840s and 1850s a group of horse thieves, the "Stone House Gang," had their hideout about two miles southeast of the inn and ambushed many of the drovers going to and from the tavern along the pikes. During the Civil War, another band of counterfeiters led by a character known as "Old Man North Pole" had its headquarters nearby. By 1885, due to the advent of the railroad, which caused a decrease in wagon and coach trade, the tavern became a farmhouse.

The two-story structure with a double front porch was rebuilt with much of the original stone through the efforts of the Western Pennsylvania Conservancy and the Old Stone House Restoration Committee in 1965. Nineteenth-century furnishings have been donated or lent by people in the area. The reconstructed tavern is administered by the Pennsylvania Historical and Museum Commission and is part of the Moraine State Park complex. *Hours:* Daylight saving time: Tuesday–Friday, 8:30 A.M.–5 P.M. Sunday, 1–5 P.M. Winter: Tuesday–Friday, 9 A.M.–4:30 P.M. Sunday, 1–4:30 P.M. *Admission charge. Location:* Twelve miles north of Butler, on Pa. 8 at junction with Pa. 173 and Pa. 528 in Brady Township.

Note: The nearby Jennings Nature Reserve, named for Dr. O. E. Jennings, beloved Pennsylvania botanist, is noted for its rare blazing star flowers which bloom in late July and early August. This relict prairie began during the last ice age and is leased by Slippery Rock State College as an education center. *Hours:* Daily, 10 A.M.–6 P.M. *Location:* Near Old Stone House Museum, on Pa. 528 at junction of Pa. 8 and Pa. 173.

33. Daugherty House (brick) was originally owned and built by a miller. The mill is no longer here, but the house is now a tourist home. *Location:* One mile northwest of Slippery Rock, on Pa. 173 at Slippery Rock Creek crossing.

34. Slippery Rock State College is a four-year liberal arts college located on a campus of 410 acres. The first class of eleven members graduated in 1890, about the time its principal early building, Old Main, was completed. The institution was originally called Slippery Rock Normal School, dedicated in 1889.

The town was first known humorously as Ginger Hill, from an early tavern owner who specialized in Jamaica ginger. *Location:* Slippery Rock.

35. National Storage Mine is a former limestone mine now worked out. It is now a unique underground storage center for historical documents, archives, government and corporate records, and various memorabilia. Visitation only through special arrangement. *Location:* Near Annandale (Boyers).

36. Oakland German Catholic Church, a frame structure with a steeple, was built about 1860 and is now a public health center. On the other side of the road is an English Catholic church, Saint Joseph's, built in 1847 of brick and also having a spire. The German church resulted from a split of the Saint Joseph's congregation. *Location:* Oakland, on Pa. 68.

37. Turner House (stone), of unusual construction for its age, was built by H. R. Turner

before 1875. On a hillside in view of the house and on the same side of the road is a brick house also erected by Turner somewhat earlier. The community here was first known as Martinsburg, surveyed by John Martin in 1837. *Location:* Bruin, on Pa. 268, South Parker Township.

38. Karns City Oil Refineries are located in the city named for Gen. Stephen Duncan Karns of Antietam and Chancellorsville Civil War fame, who promoted the oil pipeline established by Van Syckel and in 1860 built one from Karns City to Harrisburg, to fight the United line. He also controlled the Parker & Karns City Railroad. (One of his oil wells, which happened to be unsuccessful, was drilled on the property of the Old Stone House Museum, q.v.) Today a modern industrial town and oil refineries have replaced the old Karns City of oil boom days. *Location:* Karns City, along Pa. 268.

39. Chicora, in Donegal Township, was founded by James Hemphill of Westmoreland County in 1794. It was first known as Millers Town and later as Barnhart's Mills. When oil was discovered here in 1873, it had the third busiest telegraph office in the state. In its heyday the town had its own oil exchange, organized in 1882 (described in John J. McLaurin's *Sketches of Crude Oil*).

a. Hays Hardware and Furniture Store (frame), which still operates under the same name and with the original cash register, was built in 1892 on the site of the O'Brien House of the oil-boom days of the 1870s. *Location:* West Slippery Rock Road.

b. Octagon House (frame), a fascinating polygon with an interesting and efficient arrangement of interior walls and rooms, was once owned by Andrew Ford. Private residence. *Location:* Grove Avenue.

c. Long Trestle Bridge, which spans Little Buffalo Creek and the town park, originally carried the Butler & Karns City Narrow Gauge Railroad. Built in 1876, it is one of three wooden trestle-type bridges at Chicora. *Location:* Near Chicora Cemetery, on Pa. 68. (Cemetery has an interesting old chapel.)

d. Central Hotel (brick) was preceded by a frame tavern built by Dr. D. T. Book during the town's oil boom. When the great fire of 1874 demolished it, Book rebuilt it of brick, and again it was destroyed by fire. Martin Hoch took over the property and in 1877–78 built this hotel which was operated for five years by Henry Lockhart. In 1883 Hoch Brothers bought it. Still operated as a hotel,

41. Diviner Oil Well

Pennsylvania Historical and Museum Commission Markers

George Washington   Pa. 68, 1.8 mile northeast of Evans City
Harmonist Cemetery   Harmony, Pa. 68
Harmony   Harmony, Pa. 68
Harmony Mennonites   U.S. 19 north of Zelienople
Old Stone House   Stone House, at property, Pa. 8 and Pa. 173
The Roeblings   Saxonburg, Pa. 387
William A. Smith   Pa. 356, 9 miles southeast of Butler
Zelienople   Zelienople, U.S. 19

the building also includes a hardware store. *Location:* Main and East Slippery Rock Streets.

40. Petrolia Store (frame) is one of the few remaining original structures in the former oil metropolis. It was originally a hardware store and now is once more in this trade. One former owner was William Stoughton.

Petrolia was settled in 1872 and chartered in 1873. The boom town grew up around the famed Fanny Jane oil well. Other wells in the area included the Daugherty, and the Taylor and Sutterfield "Boss" wells. This area was the center of the oil region for four years and doubled and quadrupled in size as new wells came in. Much of the town was destroyed by fire in 1889. It has been replaced by a new town of Petrolia. *Location:* Petrolia, in center of town across from post office and next to railroad tracks.

41. Diviner Oil Well, one of the world's oldest, has been producing since February 28, 1874, and still continues. *Location:* Southwest of Chicora. From Pa. 68 turn northeast onto Medical Center Road (l.r. 10130); after 0.6 mile turn left on private dirt road. Well is 0.3 mile on left in wooded area (Donegal Township).

42. Cabot Institute (brick) was built in 1903 by G. L. Cabot on land donated by Webster Keasey. The first principal of this two-story brick building was S. W. Frazier. In 1903 the school had sixty-five students and in 1908, twenty-one. *Location:* At Cabot, go out Marwood Road for 0.2 mile; turn right on land near large old stone house and go 0.1 mile to top of hill.

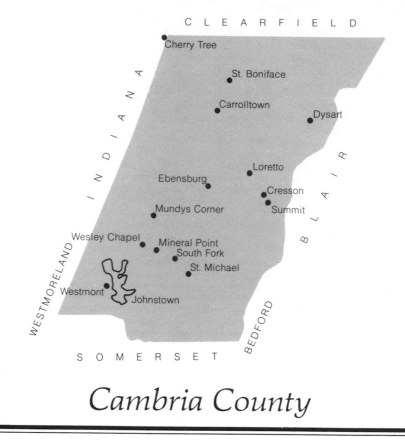

Cambria County

Capsule History

"Cambria" is an ancient name for Wales, so it is not surprising that the county was settled principally by the Welsh, along with the Irish and Germans. Cambria County was erected out of Huntingdon and Somerset Counties March 26, 1804, and remained under the jurisdiction of the latter until January 26, 1807. Surveyors James Gwin and E. A. Vickroy adjusted the much-disputed east and west boundaries in 1849. The county is 692 square miles in area with a population of 186,785.

The first pioneers in the area were Samuel, Solomon, and Rachel Adams, who arrived prior to 1774. While the family was en route to Bedford in 1777, it was attacked by Indians. Samuel was killed and buried near the family home at Elton. Solomon became a county commissioner in 1787.

The first permanent white settlement of importance was at Beulah. This Welsh colony was laid out much like the plan of Philadelphia in 1797 by an agent of Dr.

Benjamin Rush, Rev. Morgan John Rhys (Reese), who had taken a warrant for the land. This speculation failed because of poor soil and lack of roads. Beulah had a library and a newspaper. The first post office and one of the earliest polling places in the county were located here, but today only the old cemetery and a monument mark the site.

The second community was at Ebensburg, the county's geographical center, settled by Welsh led there by Rev. Rhees Lloyd, a religious dissenter, about 1796–97. Lloyd acquired title to the land in 1804 from Thomas Martin, who had taken the original warrant in 1794. After Lloyd laid out the town in 1807, the site was moved to the top of the next hill on the west. Ebensburg officially became the county seat in the same year and the first borough in 1825.

The third settlement was at Loretto. According to tradition Capt. Michael Maguire came in 1768 as a hunter and established a camp about a mile from Loretto. In 1785 he purchased land in the name of Jacob and Adam Good. When Maguire patented the land, he secured an additional 400 acres for Bishop John Carroll of Maryland. Many Roman Catholics moved from that state and, through the help of Father Demetrius Gallitzin, established in 1799 the community named for a celebrated religious shrine in Italy near the Adriatic Sea. Loretto was laid out in 1816 and incorporated as a borough in 1845.

About the same time as Loretto's founding, Johnstown had its beginning. The earliest recorded patent was issued to William Barr in 1788. Though there were no large Indian settlements in the county, a small group of Shawnees migrated from the headwaters of the Potomac in the early 1700s when their chief died. One of their villages, Conemach Old Town, at the confluence of Stony Creek and the little Conemaugh River, later became Johnstown. It was named in 1834 in honor of Joseph Schantz (Johns), who laid it out in 1800; it is the county's only third-class city. Conemaugh Borough was organized in 1849. The great flood of 1889 almost destroyed both, and another in 1936 caused much damage, but a gigantic flood-control project completed in 1943 prevents any recurrence of such disasters.

The town of Cresson was known as the "summer capital" when President Benjamin Harrison spent his vacation there.

The county has had an interesting history of transportation. The old *Frankstown Path,* locally called *Kittanning Indian Trail,* crossed the county from a point near the village of Coupon, on top of the mountain on the east, to a point near Cherry Tree on the west. This path was used by Indians, traders, and settlers in moving from the headwaters of the Juniata River to the Allegheny River at Kittanning. The path entered the county near Saint Joseph's Cemetery, running by Chest Springs, Eckenrode Mills, Baker Crossroads, and Plattsville, and exited 1.8 mile south of Cherry Tree and Pleasant Hill.

In 1820 the Huntingdon, Indiana, and Cambria Turnpike (Northern Pike) was completed, crossing the county from east to west through Ebensburg. Present-day U.S. 22 follows this general direction. A tollhouse, whose site is marked by a tablet, stood from 1820 to 1943 at Lake Rowena.

The Allegheny Portage Railroad, linking the eastern and western sections of the Pennsylvania Main Line Canal between Pittsburgh and Philadelphia, was opened to Johnstown in 1834. The railroad-canal crossed the county from a point near Cresson on the east, through Lilly to Johnstown, and on down along the Conemaugh. It was fed by a reservoir above South Fork. In Johnstown the canal basin covered most of the section bounded by Clinton, Portage, Railroad, Five Points, and Canal (now Washington) Streets. The canal system was abandoned in 1857, soon after the Pennsylvania Railroad crossed the county along much the same course. Several important underground railroad stations were at Geistown, Johnstown, and Ebensburg.

The most important industries in the county are bituminous coal-mining, begun in 1890, and the production of metal and metal products, with Johnstown the center of its iron-and-steel industry. Before the Civil War the county's iron production, with eleven stone blast furnaces, was one of the largest in America.

Lumbering was important in the days of charcoal furnaces. Oak grown in the county provided the raw material for the "shook" stave and shingle business after the Civil War, and many hogsheads used in New Orleans originated in the county. Other than around Ebensburg, agriculture was never important because of the terrain, but in recent years Cambria's potato growers have been among the foremost in the state.

Landmarks

1. Courthouse (brick dressed with stone) was first built about 1808 from logs painted red. The jail was below the courtroom, but because of disturbances from inmates, there arose a need for two separate buildings. Rhees Lloyd donated the land, and his home was used for a temporary commissioners' office until the second courthouse was erected in 1828–30 on Lloyd Street. The third and present courthouse was built in 1880–82 in French Renaissance style at a cost of $109,962.44. The architect was M. E. Beebe and the contractor Henry Shenk. *Location:* Ebensburg, Center Street.

2. Stone Jail was built in 1870 of stones from buildings in Beulah. Contractor William Callan was in the middle of a controversy between Ebensburg and Johnstown over the location of the county seat. After much litigation the structure was finally erected in Ebensburg. *Location:* Ebensburg, corner of Center and Sample Streets.

3. Noon House (stone) was constructed in 1834 on land originally purchased by Rev. Nathaniel W. Sample from Rev. Rhees Lloyd around 1809 for the purpose of building an academy. Successive owners were Jeremiah Mosher and James Ray. In 1834 Ray sold the property to Judge Philip Noon, who built the present house. The home was owned by the judge's daughter Margaret and her husband Philip Collins, a railroad contractor. Collins's second wife, Maude Kittel, owned the house next, followed by a Mr. Parks who sold it in

1907 to the YMCA, which added a rear addition to the structure. It is now used as a youth center. *Location:* Ebensburg, corner of East Highland and Locust Streets.

4. Cambria Historical Society Headquarters, founded in 1924, contains numerous antiques, historical records, books, and other memorabilia. In this building is the oldest French piano in the county, brought over the Allegheny Mountains by a Conestoga wagon. *Location:* Ebensburg, 521 West High Street.

5. William Kittell House (brick) was built before 1830 by Jeremiah Ivory on land which had belonged to Rev. Rhees Lloyd and in 1822 was sold to Stanislaus Wharton. *Location:* Ebensburg, 301 Julian Street at High Street.

6. California House (stone and frame), once a tavern, possibly got its name about the time of the 1849 gold rush. *Location:* Ebensburg, corner of Phaney and High Streets.

7. Stone House (stone and log covered) is an early structure of uncertain date. This house warrants further research. *Location:* Ebensburg, 412 East High Street.

8. Fenwycke Hall (brick) was built about 1876 by Emma Beggs Macnamara as a resort hotel. Around the turn of the century she sold it to Capt. Thomas Davis, who rented it to Sarah Gallaher as a boarding and day school until 1909. In 1910 Thomas S. Davis, the captain's son, divided it, moving one half

3. *Noon House*

down the hill about one hundred feet and selling that part to Attorney Alvin W. Evans who remodeled the interior. Descendants of the two families still own the houses. *Locations:* Ebensburg, 519 and 507 Center Street.

Note: Another resort hotel, Castel Arms, built at about the same period, was later a boys' school and is now an apartment house. *Location:* Ebensburg, corner of Marian and Horner Streets.

9. Johnstown Flood Landmarks

a. South Fork Dam was originally built in 1838–53 and enlarged by the state for a reservoir to supply the Johnstown canal basin and the western division of the Pennsylvania Main Line Canal during the dry summer months. The dam was 300 feet above the level of Johnstown. The reservoir and surrounding property were bought by a group of Pittsburghers in 1879 (see also *1889 Clubhouse*). The dam was raised to impound an area 2 miles long, with more than 540 million cubic feet of water and up to 65 feet deep. This edifice, 931 feet long and 72 feet high, was one of the world's largest earth dams at that time. The faulty, neglected structure gave way May 31, 1889, between 2 and 3 P.M. during a period of heavy rain, contributing to the great Johnstown flood which killed more than twenty-two hundred people and caused property losses amounting to more than $17 million. This was one of the first important disasters aided by Clara Barton, founder of the Red Cross Society. Today one can see the breastwork remains at the edges of a 500-foot gap, a grim reminder of the devastation. A visitors' center is located here. *Location:* About ten miles east of Johnstown, near Saint Michael and South Fork. From Johnstown go east on Pa. 56, then north on U.S. 219, and exit to right at sign one road before Sidman exit.

b. 1889 Clubhouse (frame), with forty-seven rooms and a large porch, once over-looked the Conemaugh Lake at the South Fork Dam where two steam yachts provided excursion trips. It was originally built by a number of Pittsburgh businessmen and industrialists, including Andrew Carnegie, Henry Clay Frick, Henry Phipps, Jr., Robert Pitcairn, and Andrew Mellon, as a summer resort hotel for their South Fork Fishing and Hunting Club, organized May 19, 1879, when they acquired the land. The old building still contains hand-painted murals on cracked walls, depicting the area before and after the dam broke. The establishment, once called Cruikshank's Hotel, is now a tavern. *Location:* Saint Michael, on Main Street (take Sidman exit from U.S. 219).

Note: Nearby are some of the original twenty Queen Anne cottages built by club members prior to the flood. To reach these structures, continue on Main Street; just past the stone church, take a small road to the right.

c. Stone Bridge, a seven-arched structure, withstood the May 31, 1889, Johnstown flood when the South Fork Dam broke. The flood washed up a pile of debris forty feet high, which dammed the stream. Later this pile took fire and its flaming houses have provided the subject matter for numerous artists depicting the holocaust. The Conemaugh River and Stony Creek meet at a point under the bridge. *Location:* Johnstown, along Pa. 56, next to Bethlehem Steel Company.

d. Grandview Cemetery has an "unknown plot" where 777 unidentified victims of the May 31, 1889, Johnstown flood are buried in unmarked graves. There are monuments to these and to many others whose names are known. *Location:* Westmont, on Millcreek Road, west of Johnstown.

e. Johnstown Flood Museum (brick), of French Gothic style, was built with Andrew Carnegie's aid in 1890–91, to replace the former Cambria Public Library building which was destroyed by the 1889 flood. It opened as a museum in 1973 through the efforts of the Johnstown Flood Museum Association, established in 1970 by a group of citizens concerned with preserving the history of Johnstown. The museum contains exhibits dating from 1800, other memorabilia of the area, and throughout the year various special displays. There is a mini-theater, and arts and crafts classes and seminars are offered. *Hours:* Monday–Saturday, 11 A.M.–5 P.M. Sunday, 1–5 P.M. *Admission Charge.* Members free. Special tour rates if arranged

9.c. Stone Bridge (Johnstown Flood Landmark)

in advance. *Location:* Johnstown, at Washington and Walnut Streets.

Note: The Methodist Church that withstood the 1889 flood is still standing on Franklin Street.

10. Cambria Iron Works was formed by King and Shoenberger in 1853. Here the first successful use in America of the Kelly steel converter—a pneumatic process for making steel—began in 1857–58, although it was first pioneered at the Eddyville forge in Kentucky. The hollow pear-shaped iron vessel, developed by William Kelly and similar to that later used in the Bessemer process, once on display in the Bethlehem Steel Company office, is on permanent loan to the Smithsonian Institution.

The first steel rails produced commercially in America were manufactured at this site in 1867. The Cambria works were built expressly to roll "T" rails. Ore was brought here by canal and portage railway from Hollidaysburg. In 1889 portions of the buildings were damaged by the Johnstown flood. An 1850s blacksmith shop still stands on the property.

In 1904 the Bethlehem Steel Company was founded here (and at Bethlehem) by Charles M. Schwab, who served as its first president. *Location:* Johnstown, next to stone bridge (extending for eight miles through city along Conemaugh River bank).

11. Inclined Plane, built for emergency transportation after the 1889 Johnstown flood and used to carry 4,000 people to the top of Yoder Hill during the 1936 Saint Patrick's Day flood, is an "elevator on wheels." It is the world's steepest passenger inclined plane, with a 71 percent grade, linking Johnstown to suburban Westmont, more than five hundred feet above. The structure has two counterbalanced cable cars, one of which moves up the 896-foot-long incline (to a height of 1,693 feet above sea level), as the other descends. Each car accommodates eighty persons and two automobiles. Like those of the Allegheny Portage Railroad, the cars are designed to provide a level ride. An observation deck at the top offers a fine view. *Hours:* Monday–Saturday, 7 A.M.–11:30 P.M. Sundays and holidays, 9 A.M.–11 P.M. *Admission charge. Location:* Johnstown, on Pa. 56 (Vine and Union Streets). Top level accessible from Pa. 271 in Westmont Borough.

12. Johns Log House Model is a small-scale replica of the home of Joseph Schantz (Johns). In 1793 he bought 249 acres at the site of Conemach, an early Indian town, the same year he built a log cabin which was at the site of present Vine and Levergood Streets. In 1800 Johns laid out the town of Conemaugh (now Johnstown). He later moved to Somerset County (see *Johns*

House, Somerset County). *Location:* Johnstown, on Valley Pike off Franklin Street.

13. Staple Bend Tunnel, the first railroad tunnel in the United States, was a part of the Allegheny Portage Railroad between Hollidaysburg and Johnstown. Engineer Alonzo Livermore reported in 1827 that he had discovered a place for a bridge and the tunnel of 750 feet in length could be built. The structure was started in 1833, and on March 24, 1834, the first shipment of cargo by the portage railroad arrived in Pittsburgh from Philadelphia. The rails have been removed, but the masonry of the tunnel is intact. It is presently owned by the Bethlehem Steel Company. *Location:* About five miles north of Johnstown. Go 4.4 miles south on Pa. 271 from its junction with old U.S. 22 at Mundys Corner to Wesley Chapel; thence 2.2 miles on l.r. 11021 to bridge over Conemaugh at Mineral Point. After crossing bridge and passing under railroad tracks, take first (extremely poor) road to right for about two miles to tunnel entrance. (This dirt road with numerous stone blocks is the original portage railroad bed.)

14. Heffley Spring, named after an early settler, continues to produce crystal-clear mountain water, flowing directly from its source above. From this location one can see an excellent view of the Conemaugh Gap. *Location:* Two miles north of Johnstown, on Pa. 56.

15. Carmelite Monastery of Saint Therese of Lisieux (stone), constructed in Norman Gothic style around a quadrangle with a sunken garden, belongs to the discalced Carmelite nuns. The chapel on the property of this sequestered institution is open to the public. *Location:* On west edge of Loretto, near Saint Francis College and Loretto Road.

16. Saint Francis College, founded in 1847 as a boys' school by Franciscan friars, has a replica of the French shrine of Our Lady of Lourdes and a shrine to Saint Joseph the Workman. The bell tower on the 600-acre campus is the only original structure from the early college. Much reconstruction followed two disastrous fires. *Location:* Loretto, on Pa. 53 across from Gardens of Loretto.

17. Schwab Estate and Gardens of Loretto was the country retreat of millionaire steel magnate Charles Michael Schwab (1862–1939), first president of the United

17. Alvernia Hall on Schwab Estate

States Steel Company. This palatial estate, now the Mount Assisi Monastery of the Franciscan Order, is owned by Saint Francis College. The industrialist called his country home Immergrun.

The first house built on the property is a three-story frame dwelling of fifteen rooms and is now called Bonaventure Hall. Schwab's second home, a limestone mansion now called Alvernia Hall, has twenty-six rooms and is surrounded by cascades, fountains, reflecting pools, and exquisite statuary. It was constructed by John Lowry, Inc. (builders of Rockefeller Center and Radio City Music Hall), and designed by architects Murphy and Dana of New York. On the grounds is a shrine to Our Lady of Fatima, which is open to visitors. The original property, of nearly 1,000 acres, included scores of buildings, special-purpose farms, greenhouses, stables, a nine-hole golf course, and an elaborate pumping system. *Location:* Loretto, on Pa. 53.

Note: A nearby stone, castlelike water tower was built by Schwab for his estate. The tower stored his own private supply of water, while the adjacent flat section supplied the town and college. It is near Loretto, off l.r. 11130.

18. Klein Immergrun (brick) was the home of Robert Kimball. The Swiss-style villa was given this title by its owner to indicate "a small ever green estate" in comparison to Schwab's large estate nearby. *Location:* Loretto, one mile north of U.S. 22 and a quarter mile east of Mount Assisi.

87

19. Saint Michael's Roman Catholic Church (gray stone), of Byzantine-Roman architecture, was built in 1899 on the site of a log chapel erected by Father Demetrius Gallitzin in 1800. The prince-priest's tomb and bronze statue are in front of the churchyard. The church, which has a red-tile roof and steeple, was a gift of Charles M. Schwab (see *Schwab Estate*), whose boyhood was spent in Loretto. Schwab is buried in the adjacent cemetery and not, despite tradition, in New York City where he died. The church is open to visitors. *Location:* Southeast edge of Loretto, on Pa. 53.

20. Gallitzin Chapel and House (covered with stucco) was built in 1832 and reconstructed in 1900. It was the residence and private chapel of Father Demetrius Augustine Gallitzin, who assumed the surname Schmet (Smith) on his naturalization papers. Upon a visit to America from Russia, he entered a Roman Catholic seminary at Baltimore, Md., and was ordained in 1795. Sent to Pennsylvania by the Baltimore Diocese, he helped lay out the colony of Loretto in 1799 and built a log chapel (14 by 16 feet) on the site of the present Saint Michael's Church (q.v.) in 1800. After his father died, he refused to return to Russia in order to claim his inheritance. Father Gallitzin died May 6, 1840, and is buried in the churchyard next to the chapel. *Location:* Southeast edge of Loretto, on Pa. 53, next to St. Michael's Church.

21. Peary Monument is a bronze statue of Rear Adm. Robert E. Peary, an arctic explorer who on April 6, 1909, became the first man to reach the North Pole, according to a somewhat questionable congressional decision. The monument, in a memorial park, portrays the hero in furs and parka, leading a husky. Peary was born on May 6, 1856, about 100 yards south of this tribute to him. *Location:* West of Cresson, on Pa. 276 just north of its junction with U.S. 22.

22. Summit Hotel (frame with siding) was the old Allegheny Portage Railroad station house on plane no. 5, built around 1830. The location was once called Summitville, with a post office of the same name. One early owner of this large hotel was Thomas Jackson, who built it in 1846. James C. McGinley was the owner in 1852, when the establishment was called the Summit Mansion House. In an old register of the inn still preserved here, McGinley recorded notes of historical interest after the names of various guests. When President Zachary Taylor's

body was brought through on the portage railroad on the way to Kentucky in 1850, his entourage stayed at this inn. In 1872 William Linton bought the hotel, which was later owned by the Devereauxs and Fishers. It is now a tavern. The three-story building with thirty-two rooms was mentioned in 1836 by Peregrine Prolix (Philip H. Nicklin) in his book *Pleasant Peregrinations Through the Prettiest Parts of Pennsylvania*. *Location:* 0.6 mile west of Cresson Summit, on U.S. 22 (portage railroad historical marker across road from hotel).

23. Cresson Springs had a good reputation for its healing quality. Dr. Robert Montgomery Smith Jackson, a leading scientist and physician, built the Cresson Springs Sanitarium here before 1852. One of his patients was Senator Charles Sumner, who had been beaten unconscious with a cane by Senator Preston Brooks in a dispute over slavery. Here Jackson wrote *The Mountain*. Following his death during the Civil War, the property passed into the hands of Andrew Carnegie, who made his summer home in a small house here. He gave the commonwealth 500 acres, on which a tuberculosis sanitarium was built in 1912–13. Currently it is a school for retarded children. Grace Chapel (stone), built during the TB sanitarium period, is a charming structure well worth a visit. *Location:* Cresson, on west slope at south side of U.S. 22.

Note: Unidentified graves with wooden markers are at a nearby site where 359 patients from the Cresson Springs tuberculosis sanitarium were buried. This cemetery is north of U.S. 22. Take road next to Summit Hotel to cemetery.

24. Lemon House (stone) was built by Samuel Lemon at the time the Allegheny Portage Railroad was constructed in 1834. In 1826 Samuel and his wife Jean had taken title to twenty-eight acres of land at Cresson Summit and built a two-story log tavern on the north side of the Huntingdon, Cambria, and Indiana Turnpike (Northern Pike). When the portage railroad came through, Lemon built the stone house as a residence and tavern at the junction of the ascending and descending planes. In addition to being innkeeper, Lemon also sold the coal on his land, which made him the wealthiest man in the county. Following the decline of the railroad, Lemon moved to Hollidaysburg, where he lived until his death in 1867, when his heirs used the house as a summer home. Later the property was operated as a farm. At present it is the

24. Lemon House

office and museum of the Portage Railroad National Historic Site. Open all year. *Admission charge. Location:* West of Cresson Summit, on U.S. 22.

25. Wildwood Springs Hotel of the Alleghenies (ruin) was a summer resort built in 1850, destroyed by fire in 1860, and rebuilt in 1884. Overlooking Clearfield Creek at an altitude of 2,200 feet, the property at one time consisted of 200 acres with three log cabins in addition to the frame hotel. Today the only remaining structure is the log smoking house where guests were permitted to smoke. The site is now used as a Boy Scout camp. *Location:* About four miles north of Cresson, turn left off Pa. 53 onto l.r. 11082 toward Loretto. Site is on wooded road off l.r. 11082 about 0.5 mile from highway.

26. Flick Birthplace (brick) was the boyhood home of Dr. Lawrence E. Flick (1856–1938) who in 1888 propounded the theory that tuberculosis is contagious and not hereditary. He studied medicine after curing himself of the disease and was the first to point out that sunshine, fresh air, good food, and bed rest were the best cures (before the discovery of penicillin). His idea was to construct screened-in porches for patients in tuberculosis sanitariums so they could get an ample amount of fresh air. Flick was a founder of the White Haven Sanitarium, the American Tuberculosis Society, and the American Catholic Historical Society. (His monument is in the front churchyard of Saint Benedict Catholic Church in Carrolltown, which he attended as a boy.) *Location:* About one mile south of Carrolltown, turn east off U.S. 219; thence about 0.25 mile. House is on left about 100 yards north of road on private drive.

27. Seldom Seen Valley Mine is a bituminous coal pit which provides an opportunity to see a simulated mining operation. Electric mini-cars transport visitors 2,200 feet to the working face. A related museum is also featured. *Hours:* Memorial Day–Labor Day: Daily, 9 A.M.–9 P.M. May, September, and October: Weekends only. *Admission charge. Location:* About 1.4 mile north of Saint Boniface, off Pa. 36. Follow signs.

28. McGough's Sawmill, the first sawmill converted to a tourist attraction in Pennsylvania, provides demonstrations of how giant timber is transformed into usable lumber. Visits by appointment only. *Admission charge.* Special rates for community, church, and social groups. *Location:* Dysart, on Pa. 53, two miles north of Pa. 36.

29. Pennsylvania Purchase Monument stands at the junction of Cambria, Clearfield, and Indiana Counties (see *Canoe Place,* Clearfield County).

Pennsylvania Historical and Museum Commission Markers

Admiral Peary Park On Pa. 276 just north of junction with U.S. 22 west of Cresson
Charles M. Schwab Loretto, Pa. 53
Demetrius Gallitzin Loretto, Pa. 276
Dr. Lawrence F. Flick U.S. 219, 1 mile south of Carrolltown
First Steel Johnstown, Pa. 56 opposite steelmill
First Steel Rails Johnstown, Pa. 56 opposite steelmill
Johnstown On main highways leading into city
Johnstown Flood Pa. 53 at Pa. 869, 1 mile south of South Fork
Lemon House U.S. 22 east of Cresson at county line
Loretto Junction of U.S. 22 and Pa. 276 west of Cresson; and Loretto, Pa. 53
Portage Railroad U.S. 22 east of Cresson
Robert E. Peary U.S. 22 west of Cresson
Staple Bend Tunnel Pa. 271, 5 miles north of Johnstown

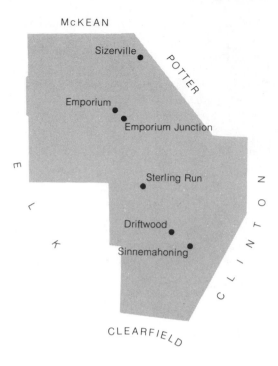

McKEAN

Sizerville

POTTER

Emporium

Emporium Junction

Sterling Run

Driftwood

Sinnemahoning

E
L
K

N
O
T
N
I
L
C

CLEARFIELD

Cameron County

Capsule History

Cameron County was named for Simon Cameron (1799–1887), U.S. senator, secretary of war under Lincoln, and ambassador to Russia. It was erected out of Potter, Clinton, McKean, and Elk Counties March 29, 1860. This area was part of the "New Purchase" lands acquired through the 1784 treaty with the Indians at Fort Stanwix, N.Y. As part of Pennsylvania's last frontier, the region in 1782 was a portion of Connecticut's claim for Pennsylvania land which was settled by the Decree of Trenton.

The county has 401 square miles with a population of 7,096. It was first settled between 1809 and 1815 by Andrew Overdorf, Jacob Burge, Levi Hicks, and John Jordan. Many of the early landowners were veterans of the Revolution and the War of 1812.

Two important Indian trails crossed the county. The *Sinnemahoning Path* followed Portage Creek southward from Gardeau to Sizerville and Emporium and from there traced the Sinnemahoning Creek past Cameron, Sterling Run, Driftwood, and Sinnemahoning to the county line. The upper part of the path, from the "canoe place" (head of navigation) at Emporium to another on the Allegheny River at Port Allegany, was a very important route known as the *Big Portage.*

The main waterway, Sinnemahoning Creek, provided transportation for settlers as well as for timber, which at the time of early settlement covered the entire county. The town of Sinnemahoning, settled by Andrew Overdorf in 1808, was an important river landing in lumbering days.

Emporium, the largest town and county seat, was laid out in 1853 and was incorporated in 1864. It was originally known as Shippen, in honor of Edward Shippen, who owned the land. The first store was operated by Eli Felt in 1848 at Felt Block. Emporium is the hometown of World War II Gen. Joseph T. McNarney, who was deputy chief of staff of the United States Army and later was in command of American forces in the Mediterranean theater. It was for years the headquarters of the Sylvania Electric Products Company, one of the largest manufacturers of radio tubes and electronic equipment in the state, which still has a plant here. Emporium became known as the "powder city" after the Climax Powder Company began operations here in 1890. Dynamite for the building of the Panama Canal was manufactured in a number of powder plants, and ruins of the magazines where gunpowder and dynamite were stored may still be seen in the hills, now declared a wilderness area by the federal government.

Since the county was heavily timbered, its early industries were lumbering and tanning, out of which have risen numerous tales and folklore of this period. Wood-manufacturing industries, sash-and-blind factories, and chemical plants have grown here. With the decline of lumbering, agriculture (especially dairying and livestock-raising) has become important. Naturally colored flagstone from the county's abundant supply was used at Arlington National Cemetery in the walks at the Tomb of the Unkown Soldier.

The major attractions of the county include hunting and fishing, with the rugged mountains bringing in numerous visitors. It is reputedly Pennsylvania's only county where fish are stocked via helicopter. Cameron boasts the largest elk herd east of the Mississippi—about one hundred—in natural habitat at Dents Run.

Cameron County was the birthplace of Katherine Mayo, a well-known reporter and author during the first third of this century.

Landmarks

1. Bucktail Monument, a picturesque commemoration of a famous Civil War regiment, marks the place where companies from Elk, Cameron, and McKean Counties, forming the nucleus of the famous Kane Rifles (Thirteenth Pennsylvania Reserve), started their raft trip to Harrisburg in April 1861. The woodsmen attached buck tails to their hats as a distinctive insignia. The oak tree to which the rafts were tied still stands nearby on the bank. *Location:* Driftwood.

2. *Commercial Hotel*

2. Commercial Hotel (frame), a famous hotel of lumbering days built in 1887, was the

7. *McNarney Birthplace*

gathering place for early Bucktail reunions. It has a solid cherry bar, still in use, and is little changed from a century ago. *Location:* Driftwood, by landing.

3. Little Museum (frame), the former Sterling Run schoolhouse and now the museum of the Cameron County Historical Society, is a depression-days precut building ordered by mail from Sears, Roebuck & Company and used by several generations of students. It contains a treasury of early farming and lumbering tools, and houses the memorabilia of Gen. Joseph T. McNarney, who succeeded Gen. Dwight Eisenhower in the European theater of war, the youngest deputy chief of staff in the nation's history. (See also *McNarney Birthplace.*) In addition, the museum features many works of the famed pen artist Walter J. Filling, a Cameron native. *Hours:* May–October: Wednesdays and Sundays, 1–4 P.M. Also by appointment. *Admission charge. Location:* Sterling Run, on Pa. 120.

4. Memorial Spring, a strongly flowing fountain with a picnic grove, is dedicated to eight youths of the Civilian Conservation Corps who lost their lives fighting a forest fire October 19, 1938. They were Gilbert Mohney, Basil Bogush, Andrew Stephanic, John F. Boring, Howard E. May, Ross Hollobaugh, Stephen Jacofsky, and George W. Vogel. *Location:* Three miles south of Emporium, on Pa. 120.

5. Sizerville Springs was the site of a large sanitarium and a hotel built in 1888, a few years after the public became convinced that mineral water from some of these springs could cure many ills. For many years people came from a wide area to drink the waters. Only the building foundations and the springs remain. *Location:* About 0.5 mile north of Sizerville on unmarked road northwest off Pa. 155 near railroad crossing. Sizerville State Park is located nearby.

6. Emanuel Episcopal Church (frame and stone) was the first church built in Emporium. The original 1867 frame building may be seen directly behind the 1901 stone structure. *Location:* Emporium, Fourth and Walnut Streets.

7. McNarney Birthplace (frame) was the first home of Gen Joseph T. McNarney. It is now used as a medical office. *Location:* Emporium, Fourth and Maple Streets (marked by small plaque).

8. First Sylvania Building (red brick), now deeply imbedded in a larger plant, was used by B. G. Erskine in 1924 when he began the Sylvania Electric Products Company, basing it on the old National Incandescent Lamp Company founded here in 1901. *Location:* Emporium, GTE plant, near railroad.

9. Courthouse (red brick with tower), completed in 1892, incorporates the 1861 courthouse, which was moved back from the street. The earlier one had cost $10,000, half provided by the citizens of Emporium and the remainder by the Philadelphia and Erie Land Company. *Location:* Emporium, East Fifth Street.

10. County Jail (frame and stone) was built in 1862 and rebuilt in 1885. Its first story was built of stone for security; the two upper stories are frame for economy. *Location:* Emporium, next to courthouse.

Pennsylvania Historical and Museum Commission Markers

Allegheny Portage Junction of Pa. 120 and Pa. 155 east of Emporium

Portage Path Pa. 155, 5.5 miles north of Emporium Junction

Sinnemahoning Path Pa. 120, 1.5 mile north of Driftwood; and Pa. 120, 3.8 miles south of Emporium

"The Bucktails" Driftwood, junction of Pa. 120 and Pa. 555

Tom Mix Pa. 555, 3 miles west of Driftwood

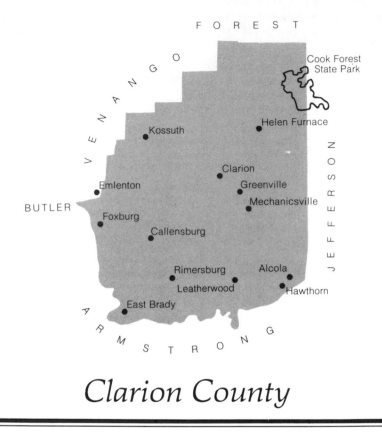

Clarion County

Capsule History

Clarion County was formed March 11, 1839, from parts of Armstrong and Venango Counties and named for the Clarion River (which in turn was so called because of the "clear sound of the distant ripples") after the legislature had rejected the names "Stark" and "Jackson." The county seat, Clarion, was laid out and named later the same year, and courts were organized September 10, 1840, with first elections held October 13. Located on the Allegheny plateau, much cut by stream beds, the county covers an area of 597 square miles with a population of 38,414.

The county's pioneer settlers, predominantly Scotch-Irish, came from the older counties of the state. Absalom Travis, reputed to be one of the first pioneers, arrived in 1792, followed by permanent settlers from Westmoreland and Centre Counties in the early 1800s. Many warrants for land included in the "New Purchase" obtained from the Indians at the Fort Stanwix and McIntosh conferences in 1784–85 were taken out by the Holland Land Company and prominent Philadelphians, including the Pickerings and the Binghams.

Gen. Daniel Brodhead's expedition passed through the area in its campaign against the Indians of the upper Allegheny during the Revolution.

The *Goschgoschink Indian Path* nearly followed the course of U.S. 322 through Corsica and crossed the Clarion River at Clugh's Riffle, two miles east of Clarion. Thence it ran past Helen Furnace and north to Tylersburg and Nebraska. The *Venango-Chinklacamoose Path* followed the same course in the eastern part of the county but turned west at Helen Furnace, passing Lucinda, Fryburg, and Venus. River transportation was also important, especially before the days of the railroad, with the Allegheny and Clarion Rivers and Red Bank Creek providing the main waterways.

The county is notable for the numerous educational institutions that have flourished and declined during its history. These have included the Clarion Academy, 1840–45; Clarion Female Seminary, 1843–44; Carrier Seminary, built by the Erie Conference of the Methodist Episcopal Church in 1868 and later changed to what is now Clarion State College; Reid Institute at Reidsburg; Clarion Collegiate Institute, established in 1858 at Rimersburg; and Callensburg Institute. Of these only the state college remains.

Early industries included lumbering and pine-tar manufacturing. The major portion of Cook Forest State Park, with the largest stand of virgin white pine east of the Mississippi River, is within the county. The forest has an area of over 159,000 acres.

Clarion's growth was largely due to the rise of the iron, lumber, and oil industries. In 1846 its production of pig iron equaled the amount produced in 1831 by the entire state. There were thirty-one stone blast furnaces in the county, which in 1850 was known as the "iron county of the state." President James Buchanan was one of the owners of the Lucinda furnace. The iron industry collapsed following the rise of coke-smelting and the consequent removal of furnaces to cities, beginning shortly before the Civil War.

By 1876 nearly fifty oil wells were reported being drilled in the county. Natural gas and bituminous coal, together with oil, are still plentiful. Glass, clay, stone, and agricultural products are also important commodities.

Clarion is noted for its scenic forest lands and recreational areas. All the county's business has been considerably improved since the opening of the Keystone Shortway (Interstate 80), which traverses the county east and west near its center.

Landmarks

1. Courthouse (brick) was built in 1883–85. The first courthouse of brick cost $10,636.16 in 1841–43 and was replaced after a disastrous fire of March 10, 1859. The second, also of brick and costing $17,220, burned on September 12, 1882, the insurance paying $25,000. The present structure, of a variant Queen Anne style and with a 214-foot tower, was built at a cost to the county of $97,124.27, the contractors losing over $21,000. *Location:* Clarion, on U.S. 322 at Pa. 966.

2. Sutton-Ditz House (brick) is a magnificent white-pillared mansion built in 1847–48 by Thomas Sutton, an attorney who had come from Indiana County and who died in 1853, leaving a wife and two children. The home was successively owned by William J. Reynolds, C. C. Brosius, and Nathan Myers. In 1897 it housed Keller's Academy. It was purchased in 1907 by John P. Reed and in the following year by John A. Ditz, who added a balcony and four Ionic columns in 1910. At this writing a campaign is being held to pur-

2. Sutton-Ditz House

chase the house for the Clarion County Historical Society to use as a museum. *Location:* Clarion, across park from courthouse.

3. Clarion State College was founded in 1867 as Carrier Seminary by the Erie Conference of the Methodist Episcopal Church. In 1886 it was sold to the state for $25,000 and became successively Clarion State Normal School, Clarion State Teachers College, and in 1960 Clarion State College. It has a ninety-nine-acre campus, twenty-five buildings, and one of the largest enrollments of any Pennsylvania state college.
  a. Founders Hall (stone) was built in 1894 as the first additional classroom facility; it is the oldest on the campus, the old Seminary Hall having been razed in 1968.
  b. Becht Hall (brick), one of the older buildings, houses an interesting archeology and anthropology museum largely based on researches in the area.

4. Cook Forest State Park (see also Forest County), of which more than half is in Clarion County, includes the following sites:
  a. Fire Tower originally was built in 1929.
  b. Seneca Spring, a mineral spring located on the Seneca Trail in the forest, was once a favorite of quacks. Mineral waters from this fountain were bottled and widely sold as a cure for arthritis.

c. Indian Rocks, visible at low water in the Clarion River some distance below the bridge, have on them pictures that include a tree and a rider on horseback. These have been authenticated as genuine Indian petroglyphs.

5. Asbury Methodist Church (frame) was built about 1885 on a foundation of large cut stones from nearby Helen Furnace. (Originally Highland Furnace, operating from 1845 to 1856, the stack got its name from a misunderstanding of the Scottish pronunciation of "Hielan." A cold-blast furnace, it produced 756 tons of iron in twenty-six weeks during its last year, but failed because of low prices.) *Location:* Helen Furnace, on Clarion-Cooksburg Road (Pa. 966). Furnace site is marked by Pennsylvania Historical and Museum Commission.

6. Old Turnpike Tavern (painted stone) was built in 1841 (despite the date of 1820 on the garage door) as a tavern on the old Milesburg-Franklin Turnpike. It is presently the home of a Clarion State College professor. *Location:* One mile southeast of Kossuth, on U.S. 322, junction with l.r. 16043.

7. Shortway Bridge (steel arch) on Interstate 80 over the Allegheny River at Emlenton is considered a masterpiece of engineering. Standing 270 feet above the river, it is the highest bridge on a principal highway east of the Mississippi. *Location:* Emlenton, on U.S. 80 (partly in Venango County).

8. Foxburg was founded about 1870 by Samuel Mickle Fox II, son of Joseph Mickle Fox (1779–1845). The latter had purchased more than 13,000 acres in the area from the estate of his father Samuel M. Fox, and came to live here in 1827, after marrying Hanna Emlen, for whose family the town of Emlenton (built on Fox land) was named. He, his son Samuel M. Fox II, and grandsons William L. and Joseph M. Fox II were all civically, industrially, and politically active. In 1870 oil was struck on their land.
  a. Fox Mansion (stone) was built in 1845 by Joseph M. Fox, who died before it was completed. A remarkable building, it was used by the family as a home (later as a summer home) until recent years, when it was sold to a group of investors as the nucleus of a recreational community. *Location:* Behind Allegheny Clarion Valley High School.

8.a. Fox Mansion

b. Memorial Church of Our Father (stone) was built by the Fox family as a memorial to Samuel M. Fox II and his son William. In 1882, before it was completed, Sarah Lindley Fox, William's sister, who had been active in its planning, also died and is buried here. *Location:* On Pa. 58.

c. American Golf Hall of Fame was established at the estate of Joseph M. Fox II, who first introduced the game of golf into America. Fox had learned it in England while traveling after graduation from college. He built a three-hole course on his estate about 1884, inviting his friends to play there. Later it was enlarged to five and in 1888 to nine holes. Fox was first president of the Foxburg Golf Club, leasing the land at a nominal figure. In 1924 the club purchased the land and has enlarged it to eighteen holes. About twenty years ago it organized the Hall of Fame, with a museum that displays golf memorabilia, including some primitive clubs up to 300 years old. The club plans a new museum and golf course. *Location:* Across Pa. 58 from Fox estate.

9. Bradys Bend, a great scenic loop formed by the Allegheny River, takes its name from Capt. Sam Brady, an ardent Indian fighter who received a warrant for 502 acres in the bend in 1785 and gave it six years later to James Ross for defending him in a murder case. Although legend (perhaps growing out of this connection) says the bend was the site of a clash with Indians in June 1779, in which Brady killed a Muncy chief, wounded several other natives, and rescued two captives, better evidence would indicate that the clash occurred beside Red Bank Creek. The bend is a fine sight. *Location:* Viewed from hilltop along Pa. 68 above East Brady.

10. Last Seceder Church (stone and frame) was for many years the last Associate Presbyterian Church east of the Mississippi, until a recent merger with the Reformed Presbyterian (Covenanter). Once very strong in Pennsylvania, the church had been weakened when most congregations left the denomination to form unions establishing the Associate Reformed Church in 1782 and the United Presbyterian in 1858. The Rimersburg church was organized at Cherry Run in 1805 and moved to the village in 1858. The present church was built in 1912. *Location:* North edge of Rimersburg, on Pa. 68.

11. "Leatherwood Horse Thieves," as the Leatherwood Anti–Horse Thief Association was jestingly referred to, was a rural insurance group organized in 1868 to discourage horse theft and indemnify victims. It is known to have had at least two valid claims. For sixty years it has been a quasi-historical group meeting once every year in neighborhood churches or grange halls, and currently has more than one thousand members. A plaque about the group has been set up on the grounds of the Leatherwood Presbyterian Church. *Location of church:* Leatherwood, on Pa. 854, just north of Pa. 861.

12. Nulph Stone House was built about 1825 by Clarion County's first white settler, Henry Nulph, who had settled between present-day Strattanville and Clarion about 1792 but returned to Northampton County after his family was murdered by Indians. He remarried and returned in 1805, but finding his land taken, he settled near Hawthorn. The house is badly dilapidated and only the base is left. His son Henry "Gum" Nulph started a sawmill in New Bethlehem in 1815 and became a prominent citizen there. *Location:* Alcola (near Hawthorn), beside Pa. 28, between highway and railroad, 100 yards northeast of sidetrack grade crossing.

13. Limestone Gristmill (ruin) was built by John and Samuel Sloan in Limestone Township about 1835. It was rebuilt by Henry Smith some years later and once more about 1860 by Washington Craig. The tremendous structure burned in December 1860, but its stone foundations give evidence of its size. *Location:* Greenville, on Pa. 66 south of Mechanicsville.

Pennsylvania Historical and Museum Commission Markers

Bradys Bend   Pa. 68, 1.3 mile east of East Brady, at lookout

Buchanan Furnace   Pa. 368 east of Callensburg

Foxburg Golf Course   Pa. 58 northeast of Foxburg

Helen Furnace   Pa. 966, 7 miles northeast of Clarion

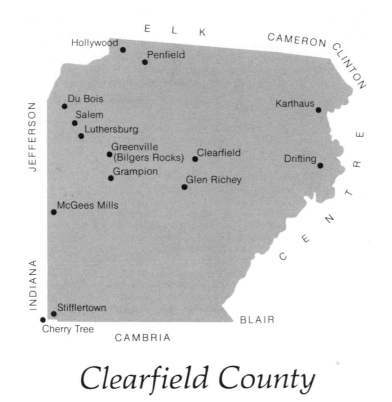

Clearfield County

Capsule History

Clearfield County was named for Clearfield Creek, which in turn came from its large fields cleared of undergrowth by buffalo wallows. It was erected out of parts of Lycoming and Huntingdon Counties on March 26, 1804, and was placed provisionally under the jurisdiction of Centre County. The area had been purchased from the Indians by the Penns in 1754, repurchased in 1768, and though later claimed by Connecticut was awarded to Pennsylvania in 1782. Although Clearfield elected its own commissioners from 1812, complete organization did not occur until January 29, 1822. The county occupies 1,139 square miles, the largest area in western Pennsylvania and the fourth largest in the state, with a population of 74,619.

Three main Indian trails crossed Clearfield County. The *Great Shamokin Path* traversed the county along the course of Pa. 53 near Grassflat (with a short division going south of this course through that village to Kylertown), past Big Sand Spring to Clearfield, and thence by Curwensville, Chestnut Grove, Luthersburg, and Troutville. The *Goschgoschink Path* followed U.S. 322 from Luthersburg past Salem toward Reynoldsville. The *Venango-Chinklacamoose Path* traced the Great Shamokin Path to

Luthersburg and thence the Goschgoschink Path. Marie le Roy and Barbara Leininger, two of the many captives of Indian raiders on the eastern Pennsylvania frontier during the French and Indian War, were taken through the county on these trails.

Among the earliest white visitors were Christian Frederick Post, David Zeisberger, and John Ettwein (Moravian missionaries). One of the first white settlers was Capt. Edward Ricketts, who arrived in 1783 at what is now Bigler Township. The first school and church were in a log cabin built in 1804 at the site of the present McClure cemetery, one of the oldest burial grounds in the county (on Pa. 969 southwest of Curwensville).

Grampian, in Penn Township, was settled first by Quakers beginning in 1805. Dr. Samuel Coleman was one of its early settlers. In 1832 Frenchville, in Covington Township, was launched by pioneers from Normandy and Picardy in France. Luthersburg was founded in 1820 by Germans. John Curwen of Montgomery County founded Curwensville in 1812. William Irvin came to the county in 1818. Karthaus was established in 1814 on Allegheny Coal Company land and is the location of the only stone blast furnace in the county.

The early Indian village of Chinklacamoose, a name perhaps meaning "no one tarries here willingly," was selected by the French as a fort site but nothing was ever built. In 1757 the town was burned. This site later became Clearfield, the county seat, laid out in 1805 on land which had belonged to Abraham Whitmer of Lancaster. The village was part of the old township of Chinklacamoose until 1813, when it became a part of Lawrence Township. In 1840 Clearfield was incorporated as a borough.

Clearfield County's early industries were coal-mining, iron-manufacturing, and lumbering. At one time there were over 400 sawmills in the county. Coal, found mostly in the Moshannon area, is still plentiful, as are building stone, sand, and clay. Tanning, tile and brick manufacture, farming, and dairying are also important.

Landmarks

1. Canoe Place, the upper limit of low-water canoe travel on the west branch of the Susquehanna and the beginning of a portage to Kittanning, was a landmark for the Indians. By the treaty of 1768 at Fort Stanwix, N.Y., it was made the beginning of a line between the west branch and the Allegheny (at a fort at Kittanning) which marked the northern bounds for that area of land ceded to the whites for settlement. It is commonly referred to as the Purchase Line. (Land above "the purchase" was ceded at another Fort Stanwix treaty in 1784.)

This spot, where Cambria, Clearfield, and Indiana Counties meet, was readily identified by an immense wild cherry tree which grew there until it was washed away in a flood in 1838. On June 16, 1893, the state appropriated $1,500 for a monument on the site of the tree, at the mouth of Cush Cushion Creek. Erected the following year, the monument,

24.5 feet in height, bears the names of the three counties, a carving of a canoe, and a suitable inscription. It is surrounded by a small park at which the final meeting and dissolution of the Old Raftmen's Association was held in the fall of 1955. This spot should not be confused with other "canoe places" at Emporium and Port Allegany. *Location:* Near edge of village of Cherry Tree, Indiana County.

2. Saint Severin's Log Church was built in 1851 by Benedictine monks from Saint Vincent Archabbey (q.v., Westmoreland County) and was used until 1891. Formerly in poor condition, it was restored in 1967. Its name came from Severin Nebel, an Alsatian immigrant who gave land for the church and cemetery. *Location:* Drifting, just off Pa. 53.

3. Karthaus Furnace was erected in 1817 by Peter A. Karthaus, who was an associate of

2. Saint Severin's Log Church

1. Cherry Tree Monument at Canoe Place

Dr. Frederick W. Geisenhainer and J. F. W. Schnars in the Allegheny Coal Company. Ore was brought four miles up the river from Buttermilk Falls; and about two hundred tons of pig iron a year were smelted from 1817 to 1822 and again from 1837 to 1839, when the business was closed because of transportation difficulties. The stack has partly fallen. *Location:* Karthaus, mouth of Mosquito Creek (Little Moshannon).

4. Ring Rock Hotel (frame), an early lumbermen's tavern, is still in use. Its date is uncertain, but there is a local legend that Peter Karthaus hanged himself in one of the rooms. *Location:* Karthaus, at bridge.

5. Courthouse (brick) was begun in 1860 to replace the original seat of justice built in 1814–15. Owing to an architect's blunder, most of its high tower had to be rebuilt, and it was not finished for two years. The clock also proved defective and had to be replaced. The building was remodeled and enlarged in 1882. The county jail was built in 1872. *Location:* Clearfield, Market Street.

6. William Bigler home (brick), built in 1845 and now the courthouse annex, was the home of William Bigler until his death. Bigler, who came to Clearfield County as a young newspaperman, was state senator from 1842 to 1847, governor from 1852 to 1855, and U.S. senator from 1856 to 1861. (See *Bigler Graves,* Mercer County.) *Location:* Clearfield, Market Street, two doors from courthouse.

7. County Historical Museum (yellow brick), maintained by the Clearfield County Historical Society in this early residence, contains largely local materials. *Hours:* Sunday. Weekdays by appointment. *Location:* Clearfield, 104 East Pine Street.

8. Raftsmen's Memorial Dam, dedicated in 1974, was named in honor of R. Dudley Tonkin (1880–1973). Born near Cherry Tree, he was a member of a famous West Branch lumbering family and a historian of the rafting and timbering era. *Location:* Lower end of Clearfield, off Pa. 879.

Note: A log-slide trail has been restored in Parker Dam State Park on Pa. 153, north of Clearfield.

9. Mitchell House (cut stone) was the home of John Mitchell, a prominent lumberman; and a signature stone over the door reads, "J. M. 1840." A monument across the road marks the site of the first post office in the area, kept in 1815 by Alexander Read. *Location:* On Glen Richey Road, 1.6 mile north of Pa. 869.

10. Robison Tavern (frame with siding) was built in the late 1850s by two brothers, Samuel and Jerome Robison. It was a stagecoach stop on the Milesburg-Erie Turnpike for many years. After Jerome moved to McKean

County, Samuel continued the business, and the house is still owned by the same family. *Location:* On Pa. 869, about three miles east of Glen Richey Road, near an intersection.

11. Read House (sun-baked brick), believed to have been the first brick residence in Clearfield County, was built by Thomas Read, son of Alexander (see *Mitchell House*). A signature stone in the gable reads, "T. R. 1833." Nearby is Read's barn, the first frame barn built in the county; it was constructed by George Leech, who probably also did the carpentry on the house. *Location:* On Pa. 869, about 0.3 mile from Glen Richey Road.

Note: At this corner may be seen one of the old Erie Turnpike milestones.

12. Bilgers Rocks is a natural formation of large sandstone boulders, many thirty feet thick, forming fissured walls thirty to forty feet high. Crevices lead to a 200-foot corridor where black birch trees have taken root in the rocks. Here can be seen a 500-ton boulder balanced upon a smaller rock. This formation, called "rock city" by geologists, is the result of the displacement of large blocks of rock from the parent ledge. The name is from an early landowner, not to be confused with Bigler. *Location:* 0.8 mile from Greenville, on unmarked road 0.5 mile east of Pa. 861, near Bloom-Pike Township line.

13. Thomas A. McGee House (frame) was the home of pioneer lumberman Thomas McGee. Built about 1835, it has fourteen rooms and was the first in the area to be made of planed lumber. The village had been founded about 1824 by his father James McGee, an itinerant Methodist preacher who held services mostly in schools. Shortly before beginning the house, Thomas (1813–91) built the sawmill from which the town took its name.

His wife, Isabel Holmes McGee (1816–99), had fled Ireland at the age of eight because of the potato famine. She and their daughters sometimes cooked for as many as 100 lumbermen daily in rafting time. She also ran the Chest, Pa., post office in her kitchen. The house is still in good condition and remains in the family. *Location:* McGees Mills, just off U.S. 219.

14. McGee Covered Bridge, one of the oldest of its type and unique in construction, was built in 1873 by Thomas A. McGee for $175. Unchanged, it still crosses the west branch of

the Susquehanna and is used by hundreds of autos a day. It is probably the most photographed span in the state. *Location:* McGees Mills, just off U.S. 219.

15. Merchants Hotel (frame) was built by William Moore in 1853. He was succeeded in its operation by Wallace and Shaw (a partnership), David Johnston, James Ziegler, and H. Wittenmyer. Greatly enlarged from time to time, it came under the management of Daniel Goodlander, who operated it as a "temperance house," although its trade was largely made up of lumbermen. In 1920 it was divided into apartments. In 1940 it became, and still is, a restaurant. *Location:* Luthersburg, Main and Olive Streets.

Note: The famed Big Spring, at the western edge of the village, where Indians met for conference, has been covered and piped into a cistern, with no trace now visible.

16. Old Brady Township School (brick), a one-room building, was one of the first built in Brady Township, perhaps as early as 1840. It was used until about fifteen years ago and is now vacant. *Location:* Salem, on U.S. 219.

17. Du Bois Mansion (frame and stucco) was built in the mid 1870s by John Du Bois, who founded the town in 1872. Originally a frame building in mid-Victorian style, it was enlarged and rebuilt in Italianate style before 1886 by John Du Bois's nephew and heir John E. Du Bois. It was again enlarged and changed to Tudor style in 1900–02. It now houses the offices of an undergraduate center of Pennsylvania State University. *Location:* Du Bois, Fifth Street and Du Bois Avenue.

18. Tyler Hotel (red brick), sportsmen's, lumbermen's, and later miners' hotel, has been operated by three generations of the Tyler family. Gen Ulysses S. Grant, who came to the area soon after being elected in 1868, is reputed to have stayed here. *Location:* North edge of Hollywood, on Pa. 255 near Elk County line.

Note: Nearby is the birthplace of Philip P. Bliss, noted hymn writer, who worked as a lumberman during his youth. Nothing of the building remains.

Pennsylvania Historical and Museum Commission Markers

"Canoe Place"   U.S. 219, 0.5 mile north of Stifflertown

Chinklacamoose   Clearfield, old U.S. 322, east and south

Karthaus Furnace   Karthaus, l.r. 17068

Old State Road   (Milesburg to Waterford)   U.S. 322, 6 miles northwest of Luthersburg

Philip P. Bliss   Pa. 255, 2.2 miles northeast of Penfield

The Big Spring   Pa. 410, 0.5 mile southwest of Luthersburg

Crawford County

Capsule History

Crawford County was named for Col. William Crawford, friend and business agent of George Washington, who served in the French and Indian War, commanded an expedition into Ohio in 1782, and was burned at the stake in western Ohio by Indians. Originally the area was set aside as donation and depreciation lands to be given or sold cheaply to Revolutionary War soldiers for their service (see Capsule History, Butler County). The county was erected out of Allegheny County March 12, 1800, and completely organized three years later. It has 1,012 square miles with a population of 81,342.

The Holland, Pennsylvania, and North American Land Companies bought large tracts within the county. Harm Jan Huidekoper was a representative of the Holland Land Company, formed in 1789. He and his sons bought out the West Allegheny interests of the firm in 1836. Their home, built on Water Street in Meadville, was called Pomona Hall. On the same property was located the company office. Neither has survived. The Huidekopers also owned a gristmill and sawmills in Fredericksburg. Among the county's first settlers in 1787–88 were John and David Mead, Thomas Martin, John Watson, James F. Randolph, Thomas Brant, Cornelius Van Horn, and Christopher Snyder.

The Delaware Indian town of Custaloga was on the west side of French Creek about four miles south of Meadville. Cussewago was a Six Nations town on the site of Meadville.

Meadville, the largest city and county seat, grew out of Mead's Settlement, started by David Mead in 1788 and laid out in 1793 (see *Mead House*). In 1796 Titusville, the county's second city, was settled by Jonathan Titus, a surveyor for the Holland Land Company, who wished to call the town Edinburgh. Edwin L. Drake drilled the first oil well near there in 1859 (see *Drake Well,* Venango County), making it a boom town with the title "Queen city of the oil region." Here along Oil Creek, Indians skimmed the surface oil off the water for domestic uses, and white settlers bottled it and called it Seneca Oil, for medicinal purposes. And this is where the first United States Oil Exchange was organized in 1871 and incorporated in 1880. The "Roberts torpedo," first successful device for increasing the flow of oil by setting off an explosion tamped by water in a well, was pioneered in Titusville.

About 1825 Linesville was laid out as a Quaker community by Amos Line, one-time miller, postmaster, and surveyor of the Pennsylvania Population Company in 1800.

The *Venango Path* was Crawford County's most important Indian trail, entering near Carlton and running through Cochranton and up French Creek to Meadville. Then it divided, one course passing through Saegertown, crossing French Creek, and running through (present) Venango near Cambridge Springs and toward Indian Head; the other branch followed much the same course as Pa. 86. On George Washington's trip to Fort LeBoeuf in 1753, he followed the Venango Path in this county almost to Cambridge Springs, but was forced by high water to detour to the Cussewago Path crossing of Muddy Creek near Little Cooley. He then followed a ridge north, near Ferris Corners, and rejoined the Venango Path near Mill Village. The *Cussewago Path,* from Ohio to Warren, entered the county at Penn Line, running through or near Sandusky, Harmonsburg, and Cussewago (Meadville) and on through Blooming Valley, New Richmond, Little Cooley, and Spartansburg, toward West Spring Creek. The *Conneaut Path* ran north from Harmonsburg east of Conneaut Creek past Conneautville toward Albion.

The county's first highway was the old French military road from Fort LeBoeuf (Waterford) to Fort Machault (Franklin); and in 1809 the Erie-Waterford Turnpike, a part of the Erie-Philadelphia road, was completed. The French Creek Feeder Canal extended from Bemis Park Mill on French Creek to Conneaut Lake, and the Beaver-Erie Canal ran south to north through the western part of the county. During the use of this latter waterway, Conneaut Lake—"the lake of snow waters" and the largest natural body of water in Pennsylvania—served as a source of supply to regulate the level of the canal.

In 1932 Pymatuning Lake was formed when the swamp of the same name (a preglacial lake) was dammed, forming a body of water fifteen miles long with a seventy-mile shoreline and regulating the flow of the Shenango and Beaver Rivers. Seventeen thousand acres of land, rich in Indian lore, make up Pymatuning State Park, located at the lake.

Pioneer industries in the county were lumbering and agriculture. Today the most important products, in order of production value, are metals, textiles, food, and chemicals, and their allied goods. Meadville is the world's largest producer of hookless slide fasteners, the invention of the talon (more popularly called Zipper—a trade name) having been backed by Col. Lewis Walker in 1893. He moved the talon factory from Hoboken, N.J., to Meadville in 1913. Other important industries include dairying; the manufacture of lubricants, oils, and greases; and agriculture, with one of the largest county fairs in Pennsylvania held annually in Meadville. Among notable writers who have lived in the county are Ida M. Tarbell, Maxwell Anderson, and Wythe Williams.

Landmarks

1. Courthouse (red pressed brick, stone trim) was preceded by two earlier ones. The first was built of logs in 1804. A new one, of brick, was constructed in 1825. The present courthouse was begun in 1867 and finished in October 1869, of Renaissance style. Complete with a dome, four clocks, marble floors and an iron fence, it cost $249,000. A statue of Justice bearing scales was also erected, but the scales blew off during a storm in 1938. They were recovered and are stored in the basement. The building was remodeled about 1950. *Location:* Meadville, public square.

2. Baldwin-Reynolds House (frame) was built by Henry Baldwin in 1841–43, based on a sketch of a mansion in Tennessee. Coming to Meadville from New England in 1800, Baldwin assisted in the organization of the first county seat, was the county's first district attorney, served in the U.S. Congress (1816–28), and was appointed a justice of the Supreme Court by President Andrew Jackson (1830–44). In addition, Baldwin was "the father of the American system of high protective tariff."

In 1847 William Reynolds, a nephew of Baldwin's wife, bought the property. The interior of the home includes black walnut woodwork, silver hinges and doorknobs, its own water system, a solarium, and twenty-five rooms on four floors. Crawford County Historical Society purchased the property in 1963 from Mrs. Catherine Reynolds and maintains the house as a museum. *Hours:* Spring, summer, and fall: Wednesday, Saturday, and Sunday, afternoons. Also by appointment. *Admission charge.* School groups free. *Location:* Meadville, 639 Terrace Street.

3. Mead House (frame) was built in 1797 by David Mead, a one-time tavern keeper at Sunbury. An ensign in the Revolutionary War, he later served as a major general in the War of 1812 and was an associate judge at the time of his death. Mead first acquired land on the west side of French Creek near the mouth of the Cussewago in 1788. Shortly after this he moved to Meadville on the east side and built a sawmill in 1789–90. He erected a blockhouse in 1791 overlooking French Creek. It was used as a school between 1798 and 1800. (This site is north of Boynton off Water street slightly north of the present Church of God.) Mead commenced to lay out the town and sell lots in 1793, calling the new town Lewisburgh. It was not until 1795 that its name was changed to Meadville.

Mead donated the land for the state arsenal, built in 1816–17 on the northeast corner of Main and Randolph Streets (present school site). His house, a large, two-and-a-half-story building, now a private residence and apartments, has undergone many alterations, with little of the original structure remaining. *Location:* Meadville, 263 Randolph Street.

4. George Washington Bicentennial Oak was planted March 15, 1932, by the Women's Club of Meadville near a spot where Washington may have stopped on his trip to Fort LeBoeuf in 1753 (see *Washington Sentinel Tree,* Erie County). It is marked by a plaque. *Location:* Meadville, twenty-two feet north of tablet at Mead house.

5. Unitarian Church (brick), also called Independent Congregational, was begun in 1835 and dedicated the following year. Modeled after a Philadelphia Unitarian church (that was later destroyed by fire), this Greek Revival building was designed by Gen. George W. Cullum, architect of Fort Sumter, and built by Edwin Derby for $35,000. A chandelier of whale-oil lamps originally hung inside. In 1973 Carl Heeshen added the

2. *Baldwin-Reynolds House*

14. *Shadeland*

various world religious symbols on the facade. *Location:* Meadville, corner of Main and Chestnut Streets.

6. Christ Church (stone), built in 1884, houses the second oldest congregation in Meadville. It was organized in January 1825 by Rev. John Henry Hopkins of Pittsburgh, who later became a bishop. Its first rector was Charles Smith. *Location:* Meadville, at public square.

7. United Methodist Church (stone), generally referred to as "the stone church," was built in 1868. After being gutted by fire on March 11, 1927, this massive building was restored, with its interior more in keeping with the Gothic exterior, and rededicated April 29, 1928. *Location:* Meadville, at public square.

8. Allegheny College, the oldest college in constant existence under the same name west of the Alleghenies, was named for the Allegheny River basin where it is located. Founded by Timothy Alden in 1815, the college was granted a charter March 24, 1817. It was closed between the years 1831 and 1833 and reopened under sponsorship of the Methodist Episcopal Church.

Bentley Hall (brick) one of the earlier buildings of the school, was begun in 1820 and completed in 1835. It was named in honor of William Bentley, pastor of East Church in Salem, Mass., who bequeathed his library to Allegheny College before his death in 1819. The building, designed by Timothy Alden (first president of the college), is a combination of New England and Greek Revival architecture. *Location:* Meadville, junction of U.S. 6 and U.S. 19 (Park and Baldwin Streets).

9. Meadville Theological Seminary was founded in 1844 by the Unitarian and Disciples of Christ Churches as a nonsectarian school. It began its work in October of that year in Divinity Hall, a rebuilt Cumberland Presbyterian church on Center Street. Later the Disciples Church withdrew. Dr. Rufus P. Stebbins became its first president in 1844. For most of its eighty-two years in Meadville, it averaged from twenty-five to forty students, including those of Jewish, Hindu, Buddhist and other non-Christian religions. The second Divinity Hall was built on Chestnut Street in 1856, and Hunnewell Hall nearby in 1903. The school moved to Chicago in 1926. *Locations:* Meadville. First Divinity Hall (now a warehouse), in lower Talon Corporation plant. Second Divinity Hall (now offices) and Hunnewell Hall (now an employees' club), on Chestnut Street near Arch Street in upper Talon plant.

10. Beaver and Lake Erie Canal System, connecting the Ohio River and Lake Erie, ran through the western part of Crawford County and was in operation from 1842 to 1871. It was connected with French Creek at Bemis Park Mill by a French Creek feeder canal, which utilized Conneaut Lake for part of its course and for a water supply. Evidences of the feeder may still be seen. *Locations of feeder:* About 5.5 miles west of village of Conneaut Lake, on U.S. 6 and Pa. 285.

11. Waterfowl Museum and Fish Hatchery, maintained by the Pennsylvania Game Commission, are on the northeast end of Pymatuning Lake, which is part of the wild waterfowl sanctuary. The state fish hatchery is the largest inland fish hatchery in the world. At the dam spillway ducks literally walk on the backs of the fish because they are so plen-

15. *Cambridge Springs Riverside Hotel*

tiful. *Museum hours:* July–September: Daily, 10 A.M.–7 P.M. May, June, October, and November: Daily, 10 A.M.–5 P.M. Closed December–April. *Locations:* Museum, Linesville. Hatchery, sanctuary area at lake.

Note: The University of Pittsburgh has an on-the-spot field biology laboratory nearby.

12. Adamsville Associate Reformed Church (white frame) has unusual peaked, carpenter Gothic entry and windows and an open belfry. It was built in 1851 and became United Presbyterian in the union at Pittsburgh in 1858. *Location:* Adamsville.

13. White House (frame) was built in 1835 by Dr. James White, a county delegate to the state legislature in 1834 who was instrumental in pushing the completion of the Erie Extension Canal. (Canal remains can be seen a few feet from the house.) The Greek Revival structure, patterned in miniature after the outstanding Dr. Peter Allan house in Kinsman, Ohio, was built on land purchased in 1829 from William Hart, founder of Hartstown. Dr. White lived in the house for forty years and sold it to John W. Case, who occupied the home for sixty-five years. The present owner, Philip M. Hans, restored the building and operates it as the Heritage Antique and Country Store. *Location:* Hartstown, on U.S. 322 and Pa. 18 east, in Crooked Creek Valley.

14. Shadeland was the Powell Brothers Stock Farm, famous for breeding horses and cattle, including the Hambletonian Roadster—a fast, aristocratic carriage horse—and for improving the strains of the Clydesdale and French Percheron. Queen Victoria is reputed to have purchased a pair of their horses. They also raised a fine strain of Holstein cows, one of which produced 103 pounds of milk in a day.

In 1816 Watkin Powell settled here on a 1,500-acre tract, and his grandsons James, William, and Watkin Powell made this stud farm a success. In a nearby field are several boulders marking the graves of their horses. The sixteen barns have been razed, and the main house is at present the Saint Sava Home for elderly Serbian men, under the direction of Saint Sava's Serbian Orthodox Church in McKeesport (q. v., Allegheny County). *Location:* Springboro, eight miles south of Albion, on Pa. 18.

15. Cambridge Springs Riverside Hotel (frame), built in 1886 by Gray's Mineral Fountain Company, was originally 34 by 100 feet. Dr. John H. Gray found the mineral spring in 1884 while prospecting for oil. Later the hotel was enlarged to its present enormous size. From 1895 to 1946 the establishment was owned by William A. Baird. It closed in October 1974, following years of prosperity as a summer health resort. The springhouse, burned in 1941, was later rebuilt. A barn on the property was hit by a cyclone in 1909. *Location:* North edge of Cambridge Springs.

16. Patrick McGill House (red saltbox) was built about 1805 by the area's first settler who had arrived ten years earlier. It is the oldest house in Saegertown and shows New England influence. *Location:* Saegertown, 649 Main Street.

17. Daniel Saeger House (gold frame) is of Greek Revival style, with white pillars and a fanlight. A remarkably well-preserved structure, built by the man who laid out Saegertown in 1824, it is one of the first houses in the village. *Location:* Saegertown, 373 Main Street.

18. Woodcock Methodist Church (brick) was organized in 1810 by Rev. Joshua Monroe. The building, the church's third, dates from 1839. *Location:* Woodcock.

Note: The McPheeters house, a fine brick home from about the same period, is located about a block behind the church.

19. John Brown's Tannery was built in 1825–27 by the famous abolitionist of Osawatomie and Harpers Ferry, and operated by him until 1835. The stone foundation ruins, on a half-acre site, are in the John Brown Memorial Park, enclosed within an ornamental stone wall. Brown's homestead (frame) is located opposite the tannery, and the John Brown Museum is two blocks away on the highway. His first wife and son are buried nearby. *Location:* New Richmond, on l.r. 20118 just off Pa. 77.

20. Crawford County Pioneer Village is owned by the Bechtels and includes a woodworking shop of the 1800s, a carding mill erected before 1822, a log house built early in the 1800s, and an 1856 log house which belonged to Wood Jennings of Chapmanville and now contains a maple sugar display. *Hours:* Memorial Day–Labor Day: Wednesdays and Thursdays, 1–6 P.M. Fridays and Saturdays, 10 A.M.–6 P.M. Sundays, 2–6 P.M. September–October: Weekends as weather permits. *Admission charge. Location* On Pa. 77, about 2.7 miles west of New Richmond.

21. Drake Store and Residence (frame), an early nineteenth-century structure first designed as a store and residence, was later lengthened to serve as a hotel and dance hall. *Location:* Little Cooley.

19. *John Brown's Tannery*

22. Stone Schoolhouse, dating from about 1835, is believed to be the oldest public schoolhouse in Crawford County. It was later used by Dr. W. J. Burgwin to house machinery that provided the village with its first electric power about the time of World War I. *Location:* Guys Mills.

23. Octagon Barn (frame) displays type of construction popular in some areas around 1840. *Location:* On Pa. 27, 0.5 mile west of Venango County line.

24. Edwin L. Drake Monument, erected by Henry H. Rogers of the Standard Oil Company, marks the burial site of the pioneer in the petroleum industry. The famous sculptor Charles H. Neihaus created the bronze figure, called *The Driller,* which was exhibited by the National Sculpture Society in New York before its erection in 1902. The cut-stone monument has two Ionic columns around the statue. On each side is a curved high-backed bench. Drake's body, brought here from Bethlehem, Pa., in 1902, lies with that of his wife in a vault in front of the monument. *Location:* Titusville, near entrance of Titusville cemetery.

25. Ida Tarbell Home (frame) was once the residence of Ida Minerva Tarbell (1857–1944), eminent American journalist. Born in Erie County, she graduated from Titusville High School and from Allegheny College in 1880. She was associate editor of the *Chautauquan* in Meadville from 1883 to 1891. Her books include a noteworthy biography of

Abraham Lincoln and the *History of the Standard Oil Company,* one of the best accounts of the development of that monopoly. *Location:* Titusville, 324 East Main Street.

26. Mather Home (frame) belonged to John A. Mather (1829–1915), a native of England who devoted his life to photographing the oil industry from 1860 on. Most of his surviving work is in the Drake Well Museum (q.v., Venango County). *Location:* Titusville, 407 East Main Street.

27. McKinney Hall (brick) was built in the 1860s by D. H. Cady, a refiner. It was later owned by John D. Archbold of the Standard Oil Company in the 1870s and subsequently by Col. John J. Carter. This Victorian home was remodeled in 1929 as a French chateau by L. C. McKinney, who was in the oil business. The stables were converted into a laboratory. The house is now a classroom. *Location:* Titusville, on University of Pittsburgh branch campus.

28. Titusville City Hall (Greek Revival architecture) was originally constructed as a private residence in 1865. It later became the Bush Hotel and then the city hall, which it has been for the last hundred years. *Location:* Titusville, 107 North Franklin Street.

Pennsylvania Historical and Museum Commission Markers

Allegheny College Meadville, U.S. 6 and U.S. 19 (Park and Baldwin Streets)

Baldwin-Reynolds House Meadville, U.S. 6 and U.S. 19 (Baldwin Street and Reynolds Avenue)

Bishop James M. Thoburn Meadville, Pa. 77

Conneaut Reservoir U.S. 6 and U.S. 322 east of Conneaut Lake

Early Refinery Titusville, East Main Street on Pa. 27

Edwin L. Drake Titusville, Pa. 8 near Woodlawn Cemetery

Erie Extension Canal Pa. 18 north of Conneautville; U.S. 6 west of Shermansville; Pa. 618 south of Conneaut Lake Park; U.S. 6 and U.S. 322 east of Conneaut Lake; U.S. 322 east of Hartstown; and Pa. 18 south of Adamsville

First Oil Exchange Titusville, West Spring Street on Pa. 8 eastbound

French Creek U.S. 6 and U.S. 19 south of Venango; and U.S. 322 southeast of Meadville

French Creek Feeder U.S. 322 south of Meadville; and U.S. 19 south of Meadville

Ida M. Tarbell Titusville, 324 East Main Street on Pa. 27

John A. Mather Titusville, 407 East Main Street

John Brown Tannery New Richmond, l.r. 20118 south of Pa. 77; and New Richmond, Pa. 77

Meadville On main highways leading into city

Oil Creek Titusville, Smock Boulevard on Pa. 8

Roberts Torpedo Titusville, Smock Boulevard on Pa. 8

Unitarian Church Meadville, Main and Chestnut Streets

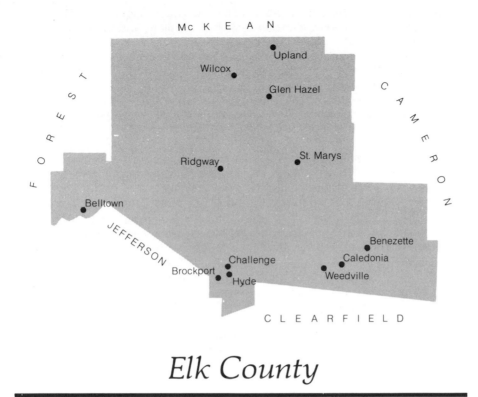

Elk County

Capsule History

Elk County, named for the herds that once roamed the area, was erected out of Clearfield, Jefferson, and McKean Counties on April 18, 1843. It has an area of 807 square miles and a population of 37,770.

Among the first settlers were John Bennett, near Caledonia, in 1787, and John Wade, who arrived at the mouth of Little Toby Creek in present Ridgway Township in 1798.

A year before the formation of the county, Col. Mathias Benzinger of Philadelphia purchased 35,000 acres (later increased to 66,000) in the Saint Marys area to be settled by Catholics from Philadelphia and Baltimore through German Union Bond Societies. He divided the land into twenty-five-, fifty-, and one-hundred-acre parcels, and gave each colonist twenty-five acres and a town lot free. The first group arrived on the Feast of the Immaculate Conception, hence the town's name. Their descendants and those of Irish railroad workers of the 1860s have made the area predominantly Catholic.

Ridgway was named for wealthy merchants Jacob and John J. Ridgway of Philadelphia, who owned over 40,000 acres in the territory; and although it became the county seat in 1843, Wilcox, Brandy Camp, and Saint Marys contended for the honor, with the first court being held at Caledonia. An early settler at Ridgway was Enos Gillis in 1822, and he and James Gallagher established the first tannery there in 1830. The town was laid out in 1833.

Johnsonburg, first known as Coopersburg and then Quay, was settled in 1810 and was named for the pioneer David Johnson. It is the gateway to sixty square miles of the East Branch Valley of the Clarion River, where numerous trout streams are located.

Glen Hazel, settled by Belgian glass workers under the leadership of Count DeHamm, was known as New Flanders and today maintains a summer camp colony. An Indian cemetery was located near New Flanders.

Jones Township was the site of an ancient Indian village, and remains of another have been found near Russell City. The only principal Indian trail crossing Elk County in historic times was the *Catawba Path*. It entered the county near James City, passing near Highland Corners, Sackett and the eastern "teardrop" of Forest County, finally crossing the Clarion River at the mouth of Millstone Creek.

Waterways include the upper branches of the Clarion River and Driftwood Creek, along with a branch of Sinnemahoning Creek. The old Buffalo Swamp extended into the county as far as Daguscahonda.

The county's principal natural resources are fire clay, bituminous coal, oil, gas, silica sand, and lumber. Its earliest industries were lumbering and tanning. Elk Tannery once had branches as far away as Bedford and Warren Counties. Located in Wilcox (on U.S. 219), it once was the largest in the world. Established in 1865, it turned out more than one million tanned buffalo hides between 1866 and 1876.

Today, the county also manufactures paper, metals, leather, and rubber goods. Coal mining began in the 1860s with the opening of the Shawmut mines. The scars of five switchbacks of the Shawmut Railroad, built from Ridgway, may still be seen west of U.S. 219 near Bootjack. Saint Marys is the metropolis of carbon products; Ridgway was long the center of the leather industry, and Johnsonburg is the paper city.

Allegheny National Forest occupies a large portion of the county. It provides lumber (mostly oak and hemlock) and related products; it is also a sportman's paradise. Stands of virgin timber are still in existence there. The first state game lands in Pennsylvania, 6,288 acres bought in 1920 by the Game Commission with money from hunting license fees, are located a short distance north of Glen Hazel.

Landmarks

1. Courthouse (brick), replacing an earlier 1845 structure, was erected in 1879–81 and was modeled after the Warren County courthouse of that day. It cost $65,000, with an additional $700 for the clock. An 1846 stone jail was replaced in 1884 by the present brick one, costing $37,000. In 1890 the first courthouse was moved down Main Street and became the nucleus of the Bogert House, still operated as a tavern. The Elk County Historical Society, very active, is located in the present courthouse. *Location:* Ridgway, Main Street.

2. J. S. Hyde House (frame) was the first town home of this self-made millionaire lumberman and land dealer, who moved into the borough about 1846 from his original base of operations to the south (see *Early J. S. Hyde Home*). In his old age he lived on Hyde Street. *Location:* Ridgway, 21 East Street.

3. James K. Polk Hall (frame), a typical mid-Victorian millionaire's residence, was built about 1890 by J. S. Hyde's son-in-law, a lawyer, banker, lumberman, and land dealer. It is now the American Legion home. *Location:* Ridgway, Main Street.

4. George Dickinson home (frame), a tastefully designed house built by a prominent lumberman in 1855, is now a private home. *Location:* Ridgway, 106 West Main Street.

5. Ridgway Academy (frame) was erected in 1834 for the county's first classical school, which continued in operation until after 1850. Later the building was used as a residence, a church, and a hotel, and is now an apartment house, its original appearance largely disguised by siding and alterations. Originally located on the east side of the street, it was moved to its present site about 1883 to make room for the Buffalo, Rochester, & Pittsburgh Railroad depot. *Location:* Ridgway, 231 West Main Street.

6. Bonifels (stone) was the mansion of attorney and coal-lands dealer Norman T. Arnold. This great granite structure was erected in 1898–99, but its owner lived only a short time to enjoy it, dying in 1906. Now surrounded by the Elk County Country Club, it is occupied by a little theater group. *Location:* 1.1 mile northwest of Pa. 949 in Ridgway, on Laurel Mill Road.

Note: A massive red sandstone structure at the northwest edge of town (0.6 mile from the highway) is its former gatehouse.

7. Early J. S. Hyde Home (frame), a very early structure built over a long period, was occupied for a short time by this pioneer lumberman. The central portion, probably weatherboard over log, is reputed to date from 1801. The two-story newest part was built about 1850. About 1890 it became a hotel. The house is somewhat neglected and may soon be lost. *Location:* Hyde, west side of U.S. 219, 0.3 mile south of Challenge.

Note: The store and home of Harry Hyde, a son, dating from about 1865, stands 0.1 mile to the north and is still so used.

8. Old Belltown Hotel (frame), now disguised with a porch and other changes, was built about 1865 in Elk County's gas-boom

12. *Decker's Chapel*

days, as a drillers' boardinghouse. After the dream of riches for Millstone Township faded, it became a lumberjacks' tavern. It is now used as a hunting and fishing lodge by a Pittsburgh group. *Location:* Belltown, on l.r. 24002, 0.4 mile east of store.

9. Brockway House (frame) was built by Chauncey Brockway, one of the first Elk County commissioners who became a justice of the peace in 1844. (Chauncey Brockway, Sr., operated a sawmill nearby.) This house is presently owned by Raymond Youngdall. *Location:* Brockport.

10. Mount Zion Church (frame), a Greek Revival structure and the first Protestant church in the county, was built in 1855–56 and was dedicated as a Baptist church in 1858 on land set aside by Peter Pearsall in 1832. He came to Pennsylvania in 1817 to seek land for the Holland Land Company with a dream of building a church where all Protestant denominations could worship. Pearsall died in 1838 and is buried in the church cemetery. His son, Alfred, carried out the work of erecting the church. The building is open to all faiths, and Methodists have recently been most active in memorial services. *Location:* 1.6 mile south of Pa. 255 and 2.2 miles northwest of Caledonia, junction of l.r. 24013 and l.r. 24012.

11. Benezette House (frame) was a lumbermen's hotel and store built by Henry Blesh in 1864. It was retained in the family for more than a century. *Location:* Benezette, on Water Street.

12. Decker's Chapel (frame), a 12-by-18-foot white pine church, sometimes incorrectly called the smallest in America, was built in 1856 as a thank-offering by Michael Decker, father of Msgr. M. J. Decker (1839–1914), who preached in the area for many years. In addition to a shrine and pews, it includes a fine collection of historical photographs and other local memorabilia. Always open. *Location:* 1.6 mile south of Saint Marys, on west side of Pa. 255.

13. George Weiss House (stone) is a two-door 1845 house and harness shop, requiring three years to build. It was one of the first businesses in Saint Marys. Twenty years later Weiss moved his business into the 1865 stone house next door. *Location:* Saint Marys, 45 Saint Marys Avenue.

14. Saint Marys Historical Society and Benzinger Township Museum specializes in materials concerning the eastern half of Elk County. *Hours:* Saturdays only, 9–11:30 A.M.; 1–4 P.M. *Location:* Saint Marys, 319 Erie Avenue (in municipal building).

15. Old Saint Benedict's Academy (frame) housed the first girls' school in Elk County, begun in 1853. Later the school moved into the gray (painted) brick building next door. Both are on the grounds of Saint Joseph's Convent, the first house of the Benedictine Sisters in America, which took over an old Redemptorist monastery in 1852. *Location:* Saint Marys, 303 Church Street.

Note: Saint Marys Convent, dedicated to Saint Walburga (see *Saint Walburga Wayside Chapel,* Westmoreland County), is also located in the town.

16. Wilcox House (frame), a tremendous stagecoach tavern opened in 1858 by Thomas J. Goodwin, is one of the oldest hotels in the county and now houses a confectionery store. It was built in several sections, the earliest of which was recently torn down. Since about 1900 it has been operated by members of the Peterson family. *Location:* Wilcox, U.S. 219 and Rasselas Road.

17. Mansion at Upland

17. Upland (both frame) includes two houses. The older one was in turn the home of W. P. Wilcox, Thomas L. Kane, and Capt. Anthony A. Clay. Kane was the founder of Kane, Pa. This modest home to which Kane brought his bride, Elizabeth, in 1856 had been built by Wilcox about 1828. Kane sold it to Captain Clay in 1866. It was moved back from the highway in 1880 by Clay when he built the mansion that stands on the former site. Ulysses S. Grant and Simon Cameron visited Upland in 1868, and the present owner has a photograph of Theodore Roosevelt at Upland about 1906. Unfortunately, both houses are unpainted and badly run down. *Location:* North of Wilcox, on Wilcox-Clermont Road (l.r. 24011), 0.7 mile from McKean County line.

Pennsylvania Historical and Museum Commission Markers

First State Game Lands   L.r. 24013 southeast of Glen Hazel

Iroquois "Main Road"   Pa. 948 east of Pa. 68, Highland Township

Saint Marys   Saint Marys, near the Diamond

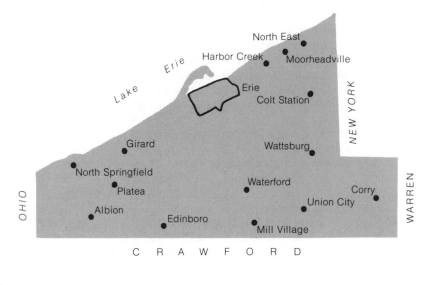

Erie County

Capsule History

Erie County, erected March 12, 1800, and organized April 2, 1803, was originally called Erie Township, then a part of Allegheny County. Named for Lake Erie, which in turn was named for the Erie Indian tribe, the county has 813 square miles with a population of 263,654.

The French claimed the area by discovery under the Treaties of Utrecht and Aix-la-Chapelle. They built forts at Presque Isle and LeBoeuf (Waterford) in 1753. In 1758–59 the British captured Forts Pitt and Niagara, and the French abandoned the Erie County forts, which the English rebuilt. Although the Indians recaptured these forts in 1763, Col. Henry Bouquet's victory at Bushy Run that year and the peace treaty with the Six Nations the following one gave Pennsylvania the right to all of this territory except the Erie Triangle, which at different times was claimed by Massachusetts, Virginia, Connecticut, and New York. In 1792 the Triangle was ceded to Pennsylvania by the United States for seventy-five cents an acre, or a total of $151,640.25 for 202,187 acres—more than William Penn had originally paid for all the rest of the state. This gave Pennsylvania a lake shoreline of forty-six miles.

Following the sale the Indians under Mohawk Chief Joseph Brant resisted white settlement. Finally, following Anthony Wayne's 1794 victory over the western Indians at Fallen Timbers and the Treaty of Greenville, Ohio, the danger lessened and settlement began shortly afterward. The first permanent white settler was Seth Reed. Gen. John Phillips, founder of Phillipsville (near Wattsburg), was paymaster general of the U.S. Army during the War of 1812 and later became canal commissioner of Pennsylvania. He is buried in the Wattsburg cemetery.

The Holland Land Company and the Pennsylvania Population Company purchased large tracts of land in Erie County for settlement.

Mill Village, on U.S. 6 west of Union City (once the chair capital of the world), is built on part of a tract granted to the Moravians by the commonwealth in 1791. However, the land was sold to individuals in 1850. Waterford, formerly LeBoeuf, was laid out in 1794 and was an important shipping point on the route from the Great Lakes to Pittsburgh. The liquefied petroleum gas industry originated in this area in 1912.

Five Indian trails traversed the county. Branches of the *Venango Path,* running past Indian Head and Mill Village, joined at Waterford and followed much the course of Pa. 97 to Erie. This was also the course of the *Presque Isle Portage* from French Creek to the lake. The *Lake Shore Path,* from Sandusky to Buffalo, ran near the lake all the way through Erie County. The *Brokenstraw Path,* from the Allegheny River at Irvine to Waterford, came up Brokenstraw Creek through Spring Creek and Corry; thence it ran down the right bank of the South Branch, crossing the main French Creek west of Union City and joining the Venango Trail a little south of Waterford. The *Conneaut Path* entered Erie County south of Albion, crossed Conneaut Creek at or near that town, and made a fairly straight course toward Conneaut, Ohio.

On the old French Road (which begins on Parade Street in Erie) where French soldiers traveled in 1753 on their way between Fort LeBoeuf and Fort Presque Isle was the Cold Spring well, now capped in a tavern lot in Erie at Twenty-eighth and Parade Streets. The first turnpike in the county was the Erie-Waterford Road, completed in 1821. The building of the railroads resulted in a war over the gauge of track to be used. It was finally settled after several years of conflict in the 1850s.

The Erie extension of the Pennsylvania Canal provided a main artery for transportation from the Ohio to the Great Lakes. Remains of this waterway can be seen along U.S. 20 at Asbury Chapel and followed through Lockport, now Platea. Silas Pratt, contractor for the locks, erected the first buildings of Lockport in 1840. In 1870 the collapse of the aqueduct over Walnut Creek ended the real use of the canal.

Erie, the county seat, was laid out in 1795 by Gen. William Irvine and Andrew Ellicott, the first U.S. surveyor-general; it became a borough in 1805 and a city in 1851. It has grown considerably since World War II and is now Pennsylvania's third largest city and the state's only lake port. Erie has one of the best harbors on the lake, and the county still remains an important transportation center, both for rail and waterborne commerce. In 1813 Oliver Hazard Perry defeated the British during the battle of Lake Erie and gave the United States control over the Great Lakes, making possible the recovery of the Northwest Territory. His fleet was built mainly at Erie.

Among the county's residents have been Henry Thacker Burleigh (1866–1949), eminent singer, composer, and arranger of spirituals including "Deep River" and "Swing Low, Sweet Chariot"; Ida M. Tarbell (1857–1944) (see *Ida Tarbell Home,* Crawford County), biographer of Lincoln and historian of Standard Oil born at Hatch Hollow; Denman Thompson, actor and playwright born near Girard in 1833; Dan Rice (1823–1900), the famous circus owner and clown; magician Harry Keller; and Paul Weitz, astronaut.

In the early days the county's main trade was in salt. It also had two iron furnaces, the first built in 1833. Now it is known for its diversified industries, including metal and related products, paper and printing, electrical machinery, iron and steel forgings, hardware, aircraft, toys and games, plastics, and rubber goods. Presque Isle Foundry, established in 1840, later became the Erie City Iron Works. The Hammermill Paper Company, founded in 1898, is one of the world's best-known makers of fine paper. The General Electric Company built its first plant here in 1911. The county is important for agriculture, especially truck farming, ranking first in the state for the production of grapes and cherries. At North East, a rich fruit-growing area, are some of the largest chrysanthemum gardens in the world.

Presque Isle State Park attracts thousands of vacationers every summer. Outstanding natural phenomena include Six Mile Creek Falls, six miles east of Erie, where an abundance of fossils have been discovered; Howard Falls, five-and-a-half miles south of Fairview; and Oxbow at Elk Creek, a beautiful scenic area steeped in folklore. Four covered bridges remain in the county.

Landmarks

1. County Courthouse (stone) has been in use for court sessions ever since May 7, 1855. The cornerstone of the west wing was laid in 1852; and the building was enlarged in 1889–90, with the east wing added in 1929. Modeled after plans drawn by Thomas H. Walter and similar to the courthouse in Carlisle, Pa., the original structure was designed by a Mr. Porter of Philadelphia, while the later matching section was planned by Walter Monahan of Erie. Another addition is under construction. *Location:* Erie, north side of West Sixth Street, between West Park and Sassafras Streets.

2. Hoskinson House (brick), a double dwelling built in 1840 of Greek Revival style with a twin Doric doorway, was the home of the Hoskinson brothers, James and William. The latter was the general contractor for the west wing of the courthouse. *Location:* Erie, 127 West Sixth Street, across from courthouse.

3. Saint Paul's Protestant Episcopal Cathedral (stone) of Gothic architecture was completed in 1866 and consecrated in 1869. *Location:* Erie, 133 West Sixth Street, across from courthouse.

4. Reed House (brick) was built in 1849 by Gen. Charles M. Reed, grandson of Erie's first settler Dr. Seth Reed, who built the first inn at Erie in 1795 and served in the Revolution. It is now the Erie Club. *Location:* Erie, West Sixth and Peach Streets.

5. Strong Mansion (brick) was built in the late 1880s and early 1890s by William L. Scott (died 1891) for his daughter Annie Wainwright Scott, who married Charles Hamot Strong. It is now the administration building of Gannon College, originally known as Cathedral College. The first classes were held in 1941, with a two-year, arts-and-science term, and in 1944 it became a four-year college. *Location:* Erie, 109 West Sixth Street at Perry Square.

6. Colt House (aluminum siding) was the home of Judah Colt, Erie agent for the Pennsylvania Population Company, who settled at Colt Station in 1797. Colt read the first Protestant service the same year in Erie County. He moved to Erie in 1804 and lived in this house until his death in 1832. Lafayette was entertained here in 1825. The home originally was located at the southeast corner of Fourth and French Streets until it was moved to its present site. *Location:* Erie, 343 East Front Street.

Note: The old Colt Station burial ground is at the junction of Pa. 89 and Station Road.

7. Cunningham House (log covered with aluminum siding) was built in 1806 by Hugh Cunningham (1777–1853), a tailor. After 1868 it became the property of the Witter-Blass families until 1948. *Location:* Erie, 136 East Third Street.

8. Wood-Morrison House (brick) was constructed by Dr. William Maxwell Wood, first U.S. surgeon general and a noted author. His son Charles Erskine Scott Wood (1852–1944) became a soldier, explorer, and nationally known lawyer and poet. This pre–Civil War home stands about twenty yards from the site of the old Erie-Beaver Canal, which ran into the basin at Erie harbor. The building is distinguished by a ship's house cupola. Capt. William Morrison and his wife were the last to reside in the house. Following their deaths, their daughter Mrs. Eric Brooke of Ohio sold it to the Art Club in the 1950s, and it is being used as an art center. Capt. Morrison and Dr. Wood both served on the U.S.S. *Michigan* (see *U.S.S. Wolverine*). Morrison was associated with the early development of Presque Isle State Park. *Location:* Erie, 338 West Sixth Street.

9. Museum, Planetarium, and Art Gallery (stone) are housed in this thirty-five-room mansion, a gift to the Erie School District. It formerly was the Curtze home and became a museum in 1942. The planetarium was founded in 1960. *Museum hours:* Tuesday–Saturday, 10 A.M.–5 P.M. Sunday, 2–5 P.M. *Planetarium hours:* Sunday, Wednesday, and Saturday, 3 P.M. for lectures. *Admission charge* for museum only. *Location:* Erie, 356 West Sixth Street at Chestnut Street.

10. Erie Metropolitan Library (brick and granite) was built in 1897–99. Designed by Alden & Harlow of Pittsburgh in classic Italian Renaissance style, it is located on the site of the first Methodist log church in Erie. *Hours:* Weekdays, 9 A.M.–9:30 P.M. Sundays and holidays, 2–5 P.M. *Location:* Erie, southwest corner of South Park Row and French Street.

11. Saint Peter's Roman Catholic Cathedral (limestone) took twenty years to build. The ground was broken in 1873 and the cornerstone laid August 1, 1875, on Saint Peter's Day. The structure was completed and dedicated in 1893. The four-faced clock on this Gothic edifice is surmounted with an eleven-foot copper cross. Every quarter hour it plays the melody "Chimes of Erie" written by Bishop John Mark Gannon. *Location:* Erie, northwest corner of West Tenth and Sassafras Streets.

12. Joseph M. Sterrett House (brick) was once the home of Horace Greeley, founder and editor of the *New York Tribune,* whose famous words were, "Go west, young man, and grow up with the country." He resided here while working for Sterrett as a printer in 1830–31. In 1936 a tablet in his memory was placed on the building by the Erie Typographical Union. The structure is at present a

14. *Old Custom House or United States Bank Building*

commercial laundry. *Location:* Erie, 414 State Street (directly across from Custom House and Cashier's house).

13. Cashier's House (stone) was authorized to be built as a residence for the cashier of the branch Bank of the United States in 1837–39. Peter Benson, the first resident and cashier, lived here at that time. In later years Samuel Goodwin ran a boardinghouse in the building, and at another time Calista and Louisa Ingersoll operated a select boarding school for girls here. The Samuel Woodruff family occupied the house from 1872 to 1913, when it was purchased by the Ashby Printing Company. From 1920 to 1963 it was the home of the Erie Drug Company. Restored in 1974, this structure, owned by the state, became the headquarters of the Erie County Historical Society the same year. (The Society was incorporated in 1903.) A dining room in the building is named the Reed Room, in honor of an early pioneer family. *Hours:* Tuesday–Friday, 1–4:30 P.M. Saturday, 9 A.M.–noon. *Location:* Erie, 417 State Street, next to Custom House.

14. Old Custom House or United States Bank Building (stone) was designed by William Kelly of Philadelphia and built between 1837 and 1839. It was planned for the Erie branch office of the Bank of Pennsylvania, which succeeded that of the United States. This structure, the first building of the county constructed with native marble, hauled from Vermont via the old Erie Canal, is an example of Greek Revival architecture of classical Doric design, modeled after the Parthenon. (Its parent branch in Philadelphia was also known as the bank of Nicholas Biddle, its president.) Peter Benson was the first cashier. The building was used as a bank

118

until 1840 and was sold to the government for $29,000 in 1849. From 1849 to 1888 it was a custom house. From 1853 to 1867 it also included a post office, and from the early 1890s to 1932 the headquarters of the Grand Army of the Republic. In 1932 it was leased to the Erie County Historical Society, which moved to the cashier's house (q.v.) in 1974. Now a museum, it is managed by the Pennsylvania Historical and Museum Commission. *Hours:* Tuesday–Saturday, 8:30 A.M.–5 P.M. Sunday, 1–5 P.M. (As of October 1975 it has been temporarily closed.) *Admission charge. Location:* Erie, 407 State Street.

15. U.S.S. Wolverine (bow mounted on a base), the first iron-hulled warship of the United States Navy, designed for lake patrol, was assembled in 1842–43 at the foot of Peach Street, where Capt. Daniel Dobbins had built some of Commodore Oliver Hazard Perry's fleet in 1813. This ship, first named the *Michigan,* launched itself on November 9, 1843, after an unsuccessful attempt the previous night by the builder Samuel Hart. It was limited to one gun due to a previous agreement with Canada in 1817.

The ship was the only U.S. war vessel on active duty patrolling the lakes for eighty years, a symbol of peace. During the Civil War the *Michigan* guarded a camp of Confederate prisoners near Sandusky, Ohio. In 1910 it was under its last command, that of Lt. Comdr. William Leverett Morrison (see *Wood-Morrison House*). After the ship was renamed the *Wolverine,* it pulled the restored U.S.S. *Niagara* (q.v.) across the Great Lakes for the 1913 centennial celebration of Perry's victory. It continued to be a training ship until 1923. (Charles Gridley began his naval career on its decks, and Stephen Champlin, commander of Perry's *Scorpion,* ended his career on the same ship.) In 1924 one of the *Wolverine's* piston rods failed while the ship cruised on Lake Huron, but Capt. Morrison managed to get it back to the dock at Erie, where it was maintained until 1927 when the iron steamer was moved to Misery Bay. In 1949 it was sold for scrap. The prow was later brought to the present site. *Location:* Erie, in Niagara Park, foot of State Street near public dock.

16. U.S.S. Niagara, built in 1813 with a 110-foot keel by Capt. Daniel Dobbins, was Commodore Oliver Hazard Perry's second flagship in the battle of Lake Erie during the War of 1812. During the three-hour battle on September 10, 1813, when Perry and his fleet

16. U.S.S. Niagara

found the British ships at Put-in-Bay near Sandusky, Ohio, the *Lawrence,* Perry's first flagship, was damaged. He left it and boarded its twin, the *Niagara,* with his battle flag bearing the motto Don't Give Up the Ship. These words, originally those of Capt. James Lawrence, in command of the U.S.S. *Chesapeake,* were adopted by Perry. After Perry defeated the British, he reported to Gen. William Henry Harrison, "We have met the enemy and they are ours: Two Ships, two Brigs, one Schooner and one Sloop." Perry, who was master commandant at this time, received a promotion to the rank of captain. The *Niagara* was later sunk in Misery Bay upon government orders but was lifted in 1913 and rebuilt for the Perry centennial. Since 1939 the ship has been administered by the Pennsylvania Historical and Museum Commission. In 1963 it was restored again, this time for the sesquicentennial of Perry's victory. The only original portion of the ship remaining is a seventy-eight-foot section of the black oak keel.

The ship now sits on a bank beside the historic canal basin, the northern terminus of the Erie extension of the Pennsylvania Canal system, presently used for small harbor craft. (The adjacent dock, Erie's public steamboat landing, was built in 1909 and extends 538 feet into Presque Isle Bay.) *Hours:* Daylight saving time: Weekdays except Monday, 8:30 A.M.–5 P.M. Sunday, 1–5 P.M. Winter: Weekdays except Monday, 9 A.M.–4:30 P.M. Sunday, 1–4:30 P.M. *Location:* Erie, in Niagara Park, foot of State Street.

·

17. *Perry Memorial House*

19. *Anthony Wayne Memorial Blockhouse*

17. Perry Memorial House (frame) was built by William Himrod after peace was established following the War of 1812. (It is reputed that Oliver Hazard Perry visited this inn.) John Dickson printed Erie's first newspaper here. The Dickson Tavern was one of the leading hostelries in the area for over thirty years, during which time it was also known as the Steamboat House and the Washington Hotel. In 1825 innkeeper Dickson prepared a banquet here for General Lafayette, but due to lack of space tables were arranged on the Second Street Bridge (between State and French Streets) for a banquet hall. The building has the original plank floors, small-paned windows with imported French glass, and handwrought door locks and keys. The walls are honeycombed with narrow stone passages that were used during the pre–Civil War era of the underground railroad. (One of these, now closed, led to the waterfront.) In 1826 the tavern was sold to Josiah Kellogg, in 1841 to the Rogers family, and later to the Stantons. In 1923 the city of Erie purchased it and restored it in 1928. It is administered by the Perry Memorial House Commission. *Hours:* Winter: Saturday and Sunday, 1–4 P.M. Summer: Tuesday–Thursday, 12:30–4 P.M. *Location:* Erie, Second and French Streets, across from Hamot Medical Center.

18. Soldiers and Sailors Home (brick) was established in 1885 and opened in 1886 on a 133-acre tract that includes the Anthony Wayne Memorial Blockhouse (q.v.). Behind the home is a cemetery with a memorial to servicemen. *Location:* Erie, 560 East Third Street at Ash.

19. Anthony Wayne Memorial Blockhouse (log), built in 1879–80, is a replica of the structure which stood on the site of the (northwest) American fortification, Fort Presque Isle, in which Gen. Wayne died December 15, 1796. French and English Forts Presque Isle were located between Parade Street and the mouth of Mill Creek. Wayne, who defeated the Indians in 1794 at the battle of Fallen Timbers, was buried here and later his bones reinterred in 1809 at Saint David's Episcopal churchyard in Radnor, near Philadelphia.

Built in 1795 on Garrison Hill by 200 federal troops from Gen. Wayne's army under the command of Capt. John Grubb, the first blockhouse was part of a defense system being reestablished due to Indian uprisings. Later it was used during the War of 1812. (Other fortifications at this time were located at the mouth of Lees Run, the mouth of Cascade Creek, and on the peninsula, where Perry's monolith stands. There were five blockhouses built at various times in the vicinity.) *Hours:* May 15–Labor Day: Daily, 10 A.M.–4 P.M. Winter: By appointment, through Soldiers and Sailors Home (see no. 18). *Location:* Erie, 560 East Third Street (foot of Ash Street), north of Soldiers and Sailors Home, overlooking harbor entrance.

20. Peninsula Lighthouse (brick and frame) was constructed in 1872 and started to operate the following year, its revolving lenses being visible sixteen to eighteen miles out in Lake Erie. The light is now run automatically by a time-clock system. No lighthouse keeper has lived here since 1941, when the Coast Guard took it over. *Location:* Erie, on peninsula between beaches nos. 8 and 9.

21. Old Land Lighthouse (stone) stands on the approximate site of the first U.S. land lighthouse on the Great Lakes. The original building was erected in 1818 and rebuilt in 1858. The third and present structure was built in 1866–67, originally with an imported $7,000 lens which cast a light seventeen miles out into Lake Erie. The focal point of the lens is 67 feet above lake level; the top, 127 feet. The lighthouse has been out of use since 1885. A later one is in operation today at the channel entrance on Presque Isle. *Location:* Erie, foot of Lighthouse Street or Dunne Boulevard in Land Lighthouse Park (east side).

Note: Near the old stone lighthouse is the site of a War of 1812 redoubt, which stood until 1829.

22. Perry Victory Monument is a memorial to Commodore Oliver Hazard Perry, who defeated the British fleet at Put-in-Bay near Sandusky, Ohio, September 10, 1813, during the battle of Lake Erie (War of 1812). The monolith, rising 101 feet above water level, was built by the state in 1926. Made of reinforced concrete faced with limestone and surmounted by an eight-foot bronze tripod, it stands on the peninsula's Crystal Point, overlooking Misery Bay. *Location:* Erie, in Presque Isle State Park.

23. Old Villa Maria College and Academy (brick), founded in 1891 by the Sisters of Saint Joseph, was established as a college in 1925. This institution, providing elementary, high school, and college training for girls, has been moved to another location (2403 and 2551 West Eighth Street). The old academy building still stands on the original campus. *Location:* Erie, West Eighth Street from Liberty to Plum Street where elementary school is now located.

24. Gridley's Grave is the burial site of Captain Charles Vernon Gridley, commander of the flagship *Olympia* in the Battle of Manila, Philippine Islands, May 1, 1898. This combat in which the Spanish were defeated started when Adm. George Dewey gave his order, "You may fire when you are ready, Captain Gridley." Four bronze eighteenth-century Spanish cannon captured in this battle surround his grave. *Location:* Erie, 1715 East Lake Road (Gridley Circle, in Lakeside Cemetery).

20. *Peninsula Lighthouse*

Note: A granite monument in his honor erected in 1913 is in the middle of Gridley Park (West Sixth Street).

25. Douglas Moorhead House (brick) was built in 1832 by five Moorhead brothers, who came here from Lancaster County between 1801 and 1805. A fine natural-gas well, the first in the county, has provided light and heat for this house for years. In 1906, when U.S. 20 was improved, this house was moved back fifty feet. *Location:* Moorheadville (near North East), about ten miles east of Erie on Pa. 20.

Note: Located a short distance to the west is an identical residence, built the same year, and also a Moorhead home.

26. Lake Shore Railway Historical Society Museum (frame), the largest of its type in the tristate area, is located in a sixty-four-year-old railroad depot. *Hours:* May–September: Saturday and Sunday, 1–5 P.M. *Location:* North East, in old New York Central Railroad depot.

27. Robinson-Hampson House (brick) was built in 1834 by an architect, Royce Tuttle. Later it was sold to W. A. Robinson. In 1893–94 the Hampson family purchased it and lived there until 1967. It is now the property of an insurance agency. *Location:* North East, 55 East Main Street.

28. Franklin Paper Mill (stone remains) was erected in 1833 and operated until 1883. The miller's house is across the street from the mill site, in Paper Mill Hollow. Once owned by the Snyder family, it was later purchased by the Thompsons. *Location:* North East, on North Mill Road off Pa. 5 (Lake Road).

29. Scouller Gristmill (stone remains), built in 1844 by John Scouller, was the largest gristmill in the county. *Location:* North East, on North Mill Road. Remains of mill and spillway are best seen on left just before junction of North Mill Road and Sunset Drive.

Note: Also on Sixteen Mile Creek, within one mile of the center of North East, were a turning works, a table factory, a sawmill, a paper mill (see *Franklin Paper Mill*), a brewery, a cider and vinegar mill, and a tannery, among others.

30. Glass-Sprague House (brick) was built by John Glass, who erected the first iron foundry in the county at the mouth of Sixteen Mile Creek and was active in the underground railroad. Although the H. Churchill family occupied the house in 1865, it is again owned by the Sprague family. *Location:* Freeport, on Pa. 89 (north of Pa. 5) at junction of Old Lake Road.

Note: Spragues Beach, on Pa. 89 near North East, was once a fishing village and is now a summer resort. It was at one time the last stop for Canada-bound slaves. Other interesting early buildings in the area include the Mary Stone house on Pa. 89 and the Old Wine Cellar, now South Shore Inn, on Pa. 89 (about halfway between U.S. 20 and Pa. 5).

31. Grimshaw Woolen Mill (stone remains) was built in 1845 by William Grimshaw, an expert weaver from Leeds, England. During the Civil War many blankets were made here for the federal government. Later the mill was converted to a winery, supplied first by water power, then by steam, and finally by gasoline. The Grimshaw family has lived here for years. *Location:* One mile north of North East, on Curtis Road, close to Pa. 5.

32. Dill House (brick) is a long Greek Revival structure and a former summer boarding house. The original section is the east end. The Victorian trim and porch have been removed. *Location:* Two miles northeast of North East, at end of Dill Park Road.

33. Butt's Octagonal Barn (brick) was built by Alonzo Butt, who was born in 1827. His father, Wendell, a native of Virginia, settled

33. Butt's Octagonal Barn

here in 1817, buying 300 acres from the Holland Land Company. The structure is eighty feet in diameter, and has black walnut and black oak timbers eighteen inches square. A signature stone reads, "A. W. Butt 1879." *Location:* Two miles northeast of North East, on Middle Road, between Pa. 5 and U.S. 20.

Note: Nearby on the property is a brick house constructed in the early nineteenth century.

34. Frog Pond Schoolhouse (frame) was built about 1820 on the farm of B. P. Spooner and used until 1955. The name was derived from the fact that when the fields became flooded in winter the children could skate up to the door. The school is now a private home. *Location:* Three miles south of North East, on Pa. 89 just north of Town Line Road.

35. Corry Area Historical Museum includes among other items a restored Climax locomotive. *Hours:* Saturday and Sunday, 2–8 P.M. *Location:* Corry, on Mead Avenue in Mead Park.

36. Union City Historical Museum. *Hours:* Daily, 10 A.M.–12 noon; 1–4 P.M. *Location:* Union City, east side of Main Street next to municipal building.

37. Humphrey-Rockwell House (frame) was built about 1840 by Dr. Jonas Humphrey, who came to Union Mills (now Union City) from New Hampshire. This Greek Revival home was later occupied by the Rockwell family. *Location:* Union City, 38 East High Street (Pa. 6).

38. United States Fort LeBoeuf was built in 1794 by Maj. Ebenezer Denny under orders from Gov. Mifflin to protect from Indian attacks the state commissioners who were

41. *Judson House*

laying out Waterford and Erie. In 1796 Gen. Anthony Wayne further strengthened the defense already there by erecting another blockhouse, making a total of four. The last blockhouse at this site later operated as the Fort LeBoeuf Hotel until it was destroyed by fire (see *Eagle Hotel*). Most of its foundation was filled in during 1973. This area is unique, for it was under three different flags at various times (see *Judson House*).

The George Washington Monument, dedicated in 1922 and originally erected on U.S. 19, nearby, now overlooks the location of this fort. It is the only memorial of Washington as a young man in British uniform, as he delivered the message of the Virginia governor to the French. *Location:* Waterford, on U.S. 19 (High and First Streets).

39. Washington Sentinel Tree was the hemlock that, according to legend, Gen. George Washington climbed to reconnoiter the French Fort LeBoeuf in 1753 when Governor Dinwiddie of Virginia sent him to the French commander to deliver a message claiming the area for the British and demanding withdrawal of the French forces. As a result Washington was able to observe the fort and write a description of it. Though the tree, over 300 years old, is still standing, its top is missing after being struck by lightning. *Location:* South of Waterford, on U.S. 19, a quarter mile from Eagle Hotel (q.v.) (on private property behind supermarket).

40. Eagle Hotel (stone) was built in 1826–27 (date on signature stone) by Thomas King. Its cut sandstone was quarried on Dr. Vere Worster's property. A stone opposite the signature bears the stonemason's name "E. [Ebenezer] Evans." Evans was a Welshman who built other stone structures in Erie. This fine example of Georgian architecture is the only stone house in Waterford and the oldest hotel that is still operating as a tavern in the county. A large dance hall was constructed on the third floor. In 1868 a demented woman started a fire inside; it spread and destroyed Fort LeBoeuf Hotel (see also *United States Fort LeBoeuf*) along with other structures in town.

A wooden eagle, which identified the Eagle Hotel for years, used to be above the door and once stood on a pole near the road. According to legend, it was carved from a single block of wood by a vagabond in gratitude for having been allowed free accommodations. The eagle is now on display at the state museum in Harrisburg. In 1848 President Zachary Taylor was a guest at the hotel. *Location:* Waterford, on U.S. 19, corner of High and First Streets.

41. Judson House (frame), of Greek Revival style, was built in 1820 by Amos Judson, who migrated from Connecticut in 1795. Judson was the first burgess of the town and a successful salt merchant. He was employed by Holmes and Herriott of Pittsburgh but later opened a store in this house, which was on the sites of French Fort LeBoeuf, built in 1753, and later of English Fort LeBoeuf, built in 1760, and near that of U.S. Fort LeBoeuf (q.v.) built in 1794. The house holds a model of the French fort; French, British, and Indian artifacts; and a library with manuscript material related to the area. A later brick museum building is located nearby on the same side of the street. Both are administered by the Pennsylvania Historical and Museum Commission. *Hours:* Daylight saving time: Weekdays except Monday, 8:30 A.M.–5 P.M. Sunday, 1–5 P.M. Winter: Weekdays except Monday, 9 A.M.–4:30 P.M. Sunday, 1–4:30 P.M. *Admission charge. Location:* Waterford, on U.S. 19 (31 High Street at First Street).

42. Grave of Michael Hare, under a 300-year-old maple tree, has a burial stone that reads:

Michael Hare, born in Armagh County, Ireland, June 10, 1727, was in the French war at Braddock's defeat, served through the Revolutionary War, was with [General Arthur] St. Clair and was scalped at his defeat by the Indians. Died March 3, 1843 AE 115 years, 8 months 13 days.
Elizabeth, his wife, died March 3, 1813, AE 90 years.

Recovering from the scalping, he volunteered for service during the War of 1812 at the age of eighty-five. *Location:* Waterford Cemetery.

43. Lindsley House (frame) was built in 1816 by Moses Himrod, who never lived in the building. It was first occupied by Jesse Lindsley, and for at least six generations this family has lived in the home. To the north of it on the same side of the street is a structure covered with siding which formerly was a store with a blacksmith shop in the back. Both houses are private. *Location:* Waterford, 660 High Street.

44. Saint Peter's Episcopal Church (brick) was built in 1832. The Old Waterford Academy, now gone, stood across an alley from it until 1954. *Location:* Waterford, at East Park.

45. Brotherton House (frame) belonged to some early settlers, the Brothertons, an enterprising family that owned various mills in the area. This house was constructed in the mid–nineteenth century. *Location:* Waterford, on east side of Cherry Street above First Street.

46. The Old Academy (frame) of the Northwestern Normal School founded in 1857 was originally built in 1856 at a cost of $3,200. It

was used as an academy until 1859. On January 26, 1861, the state recognized the institution as a state normal school. By this time several other buildings had been constructed. The commonwealth acquired the school in 1915. In 1926 it became Edinboro State Teachers' College and in 1960 Edinboro State College. It is the oldest institution of higher education in Erie County and the second oldest state-owned college in Pennsylvania. *Location:* Edinboro, on Normal Street at Edinboro State College.

47. Eagle House (frame), once an active stagecoach tavern, was built in 1843 on the site of an earlier hostelry which had burned. In 1896 it became the Robinson house, and later was owned by an auto company. It is presently a commercial business and barbershop. *Location:* Edinboro, 119 Erie Street.
Note: The frame Biggers house, once a hotel, was built in 1850 and is at 148 Meadville Street at West Normal Street. Also of interest is the frame Goodell house built in 1841 at 109 Waterford Street.

48. Vunk House (frame) was built in the mid–nineteenth century by Francis C. Vunk and later owned by the Hencke family. A diner has been attached to it in later years. *Location:* Edinboro, on U.S. 6 opposite restaurant (west of junction of U.S. 6 and Edinboro road).

49. Juliet Mill Pond and a dam are the only reminders of Amos King's gristmill built in 1828. In 1840 W. H. Gray built a woolen mill here. Thomas and William Thornton later owned the property. *Location:* Albion, Main Street (north).

50. Sacred Heart Mission House (brick) was founded as a college for training priests for foreign service. It is presently called Divine Word Seminaries. Across from this building on the south side of U.S. 20 is a stone residence, now a retirement home for missionary priests. *Location:* East of Girard, on north side of U.S. 20.

51. Dan Rice Soldiers' and Sailors' Monument, a twenty-five-foot cylindrical marble shaft, was dedicated in 1865 to the memory of Erie County Civil War servicemen who died in action. Dan Rice, America's most famous comic of the nineteenth century and a native of Girard, donated this monument, which is the earliest Civil War memorial in the county. *Location:* Girard, on U.S. 20 in public square.

52. Universalist Church (frame), of Greek Revival design, was organized a few years before 1850, and the building was erected in 1852. Rev. Charles L. Shipman, who was a leader in the underground railroad during the

Civil War and organized the route from the Ohio River to Lake Erie, served this church for over twenty years. *Location:* Girard.

53. Hutchinson House (brick) was built in 1830 by Judge Myron Hutchinson. It has parapet walls and a later Georgian doorway with fan- and sidelights and a raised keystone. *Location:* Girard, 155 Main Street.

54. Frances Miles House (brick) was built in 1832 on property which had two miles of lake frontage, adjoining the Holliday farm. Frances Miles's nephew, William B. Holliday, presently lives here. A natural-gas well nearby has provided the energy for this house and others in the neighborhood ever since it was drilled in 1898. *Location:* North Springfield, on Miles Road.

55. Holliday House (frame), a "saltbox," was built in 1806 by Capt. Samuel Holliday, who in 1796 had purchased 700 acres of land on Crooked Creek. This house replaced a log cabin where Holliday, his wife, and their six children had lived. Descendants of the family for at least six generations have lived on the property. *Location:* Just north of North Springfield, on Miles Road just south of Miles house.

56. Triangle Marker designates the former (1786–87) northern boundary of Pennsylvania before the purchase of the Erie Triangle. Each of the stone's four sides displays a bronze plaque. The monument was erected in 1907. *Location:* Two miles west of North Springfield and two miles east of Ohio line. Go north for 0.5 mile on dirt road from old Lake Road.

Pennsylvania Historical and Museum Commission Markers

Anthony Wayne   Erie, Pa. 5 at Sixth and Ash Streets

Canal Basin   Erie, north end of State Street

Captain C. V. Gridley   Erie, Pa. 5 at East Lake Road

Circus History   Girard, U.S. 20 at the Diamond

Colt's Station   Colt Station, Pa. 89 at Pa. 430

Drake Well Park   Union City, Pa. 8

Edinboro State College   Edinboro, U.S. 6 and Pa. 99 at College

Erie   On main highways leading into city

Erie Extension Canal   Asbury Chapel, U.S. 20; and Platea, Pa. 18

Flagship Niagara   Erie, at property on State Street

Fort LeBoeuf   Waterford, U.S. 19

Fort LeBoeuf Memorial   Waterford, at property on U.S. 19

Fort Presque Isle   Erie, Pa. 5 at Sixth and Parade Streets

French Creek   U.S. 19 south of Waterford

George Washington   Waterford, U.S. 19

Harry T. Burleigh   Erie, East Sixth Street

Ida M. Tarbell   Pa. 8 southwest of Wattsburg

LP-Gas Industry   Waterford, U.S. 19 at square

Old Custom House   Erie, 407 State Street

Old French Road   Pa. 97 south of Erie

Old State Line   Wattsburg, Pa. 8; Strongs Corner, U.S. 19; Middleboro, Pa. 99; U.S. 20 west of Girard; and Pa. 5 east of North Springfield

Perry's Shipyards   Erie, Pa. 5 at Sixth and Cascade Streets

Presque Isle Portage   U.S. 19 north of Waterford

U.S.S. Wolverine   Erie, north end of State Street

Fayette County

Capsule History

Fayette County was named for the Marquis de Lafayette, a friend of the colonies in their effort to secure independence. It was erected out of Westmoreland County on September 26, 1783, and has an area of 802 square miles with a population of 154,667.

The county's early development was begun by the Ohio Company of Virginia, whose storehouse, The Hangard, was burned by the French after Washington's defeat at Fort Necessity. Christopher Gist, the first settler, arriving in 1754, was a friend of George Washington, who later owned land at Perryopolis. Pioneers started to migrate to the area from the South and from eastern Pennsylvania in 1758. In 1767 Henry and Thomas Beeson came to the area; they built a mill on Redstone Creek in 1772 and erected a blockhouse nearby in 1774. This area was first called Beeson's Mills, then Beeson Town, followed by Union, and Uniontown, which was laid out in 1776, became the county seat in 1783, and was incorporated as a borough in 1795. Several old burial grounds, such as the Great Bethel Regular Baptist cemetery on South Morgantown Street and the Methodist cemetery at West Peter and North Arch Streets, are reminders of early Uniontown churches. Fort Mason was built in 1774–78 by John Mason. The blockhouse was later moved to Main Street in Masontown in 1823.

Brownsville, founded by Thomas Brown who settled there before 1770, was once called Redstone Old Fort. It was an early boat-building center. Fort Burd, built by Col. James Burd in 1759, was fifty yards from the Monongahela River at the mouth of Dunlaps Creek, one and a quarter miles above the mouth of Redstone Creek. In 1793 Zachariah Connell laid out Connellsville at the site of Stewarts Crossing on the Youghiogheny River, where Braddock's army had crossed en route to Fort Duquesne in 1755. Connell's grave is on East Francis Avenue. William McCormick was the first settler in Connellsville in 1770. Perryopolis, named for Oliver Hazard Perry, was laid out in 1814.

Others prominent in the county's history were Albert Gallatin; Col. William Crawford, friend of Washington and owner of a plantation at the site of Connellsville; Dr. John Brashear; Philander Chase Knox (see *Knox House*); and Gen. George Catlett Marshall, U.S. Army chief of staff, secretary of state, secretary of defense, and author of the Marshall Plan, who was born in Uniontown on the site of the Veterans of Foreign Wars Home at 142 West Main Street.

Various Indian paths were located in the county. The *Catawba Path* entered Fayette near Laurelville, passing Prittstown and Connellsville; it followed much the course of U.S. 119 past Uniontown, swinging southwest through Smithfield, Outcrop, and Gans and entering West Virginia near Point Marion. The *Warrior's Path* left the Catawba at Smithfield, running through New Geneva on the way to Moundsville, W.Va. Another branch of the *Catawba Path* followed the northern Redstone Path (see below) to Brier Hill, crossing the Monongahela near East Riverside. *Nemacolin's Path,* from Cumberland, Md., to the forks of the Ohio, followed much the course of the Braddock Road and U.S. 40 to the top of Chestnut Ridge; there it turned through Jumonville to Mount Braddock and followed the Catawba Path to a point outside the county, near Mount Pleasant. The *Redstone Path,* to present-day Brownsville, had two branches, one following U.S. 40 from Nemacolin's Path through Uniontown, the other leaving the Nemacolin's at Mount Braddock and running through Bute and Vances Mill to a junction near Brier Hill.

The Mason-Dixon Boy Scout Trail, dedicated in 1967, follows the original survey completed in 1767 by the English astronomers-surveyors. The old portage path cut by Delaware Indian Nemacolin, later Braddock's military road, became the general course of the Great Cumberland National Road, built between 1811 and 1818 through the efforts of Albert Gallatin and Henry Clay. In the 1920s it became U.S. 40. It extended from Cumberland, Md., to Wheeling, W.Va., passing through Uniontown and Brownsville in Fayette County.

The Monongahela River made possible the transportation of coal, and after the Civil War spur railroads were built into the county in order to tap natural resources. The Youghiogheny River was an important commercial waterway. In Connellsville flat-boats were built for transporting salt, pig metal, hollow ironware, whiskey, and flour. Here the Connellsville Basin, containing the world's finest coking coal, was an early center of the coal and coke industry. At Perryopolis along Pa. 51 are the remains of the world's largest single bank of coke ovens. The first beehive oven in America was designed and built in Connellsville in 1833. The county had twenty early stone blast furnaces.

Glass was an important early industry. On September 20, 1797, Albert Gallatin and Company established the second glass factory in western Pennsylvania. (The first one was in Allegheny County.) It was located on Georges Creek about a mile from New Geneva and shortly after 1810 moved to Greene County near Greensboro. The old American Window Glass Factory, which closed thirty years ago, may be seen at the south end of Belle Vernon, between Pa. 906 and Monongahela City.

Landmarks

1. Courthouse (stone), showing the influence of Richardson's courthouse at Pittsburgh (q.v.), was built in 1891–92 at a cost of $250,000. The first courts were held in a schoolhouse. An early courthouse of uncertain date and construction was sold at auction January 1, 1796, for £15 12s. 6d. The second, of brick, was built in 1797 at a cost of $1,362.53. It burned on February 4, 1845. A brick replacement, built the same year, cost $16,000. The adjacent stone sheriff's house and jail are located at the site of Henry Beeson's blockhouse. A statue of Lafayette is on display in the courthouse. It was carved out of poplar planks, pinned together, at the old West Schoolhouse (q.v.) in 1847 by David Gilmore Blythe, an important genre painter of western Pennsylvania. *Location:* Uniontown, Main Street.

2. West Schoolhouse (log) was built about 1839 by a carpenter, Enos West. George Brown and Noble McCormick were early teachers. The school was restored for the area Girl Scouts and is owned by the Uniontown Service League. Open by appointment. *Location:* Uniontown, 75 South Street.

3. Beeson House (brick) was built in 1847 by Col. Isaac Beeson, a local merchant who owned a hammer and scythe factory. A historical plaque is on the side of this structure, which now serves as apartments. *Location:* Uniontown, near corner of Union and West Fayette Streets (on same side of street as Great Bethel Baptist Church).

4. Mount Vernon Inn (brick) was built in 1785–86 by Jacob Beeson on a tract of land called Mount Vernon. The house remained in the Beeson family until 1831, when it was sold to Daniel Moore, who gave the house to his daughter Mrs. Lucius Stockton. Stockton, the manager of the National Stage Lines (Good Intent Lines) named the house Ben Lomond and added to it. In 1855 Judge Samuel A. Gilmore purchased the property. It became known as Bliss House (or Hill) after his daughter Mrs. Lida Bliss inherited it. Her family resided there until 1946 when it was established as an inn. *Location:* Uniontown, junction of U.S. 40 (Main Street), Fayette Street, and Mount Vernon Avenue.

Note: The apartment building on the corner across from the inn is the site of the log house built by Harry Beeson and later the home site of Princess Lida (née Nichols) of Thurn and Taxis, a niece of J. V. Thompson (see *Oak Hill*).

5. Playford House (brick) was the home of Robert W. Playford, heir to a coal fortune, who killed his wife and five children and himself in this home, due to financial losses during the depression. The mansion, with a widow's walk on top, is now Saint Anthony's Friary of the Franciscan order. *Location:* Uniontown, 115 Oakland Avenue.

6. Frank M. Seaman Mansion (painted brick), with a large front one-story portico, was originally owned by Frank M. Seaman, one of J. V. Thompson's partners, who escaped the coal baron's ruin by withdrawing his personal holdings just before the crash in 1915. The house, formerly facing Ben Lomond Street, was the scene of fabulous parties. The owner once hired the New York Metropolitan Opera Company to entertain on the lawn in a circle lighted by auto headlights. *Location:* Uniontown, 30 Mont View Street.

2. *West Schoolhouse*

7. Uniontown Country Clubhouse (frame) was built in the early 1900s and contains an interesting circular balcony on the second floor. Across from this structure is the site of McCoy's Fort, erected by James McCoy on Flint Hill, warranted to him in 1769. A marker was placed here in 1904 by the Fort Necessity Centennial Celebration Committee. *Location:* Uniontown, 25 Bailey Lane.

8. Oak Hill (Mount Saint Macrina) (brick) was built in the early 1900s by multimillionaire coal baron, financier, and banker Josiah Van Kirk Thompson, who died a pauper. Today this palatial estate is owned by the Sisters of Saint Basil, a Byzantine Rite (Greek Catholic) order. It serves as a sanctuary for the devout, aged, and ill and is visited each fall by 100,000 worshipers from all over the United States and Canada who attend the pilgrimage to the Shrine of our Lady of Perpetual Help. A newer mansion, Fox Hill, also part of the complex, was owned by Thompson's son Andrew. *Location:* About one mile west of Uniontown, on U.S. 40.

9. Jasper Thompson House (brick) was erected about 1850. Thompson was collector of internal revenue and commutation funds under Lincoln, serving two terms. J. V. Thompson (see *Oak Hill*) was born here in 1855. *Location:* 2.5 miles south of Uniontown, off Pa. 21.

10. Searights Tollhouse (brick) is one of two remaining National Road tollhouses. Originally there were six on the Pennsylvania section of the road (see *National Road Toll-*

house, Somerset County). This hexagonal structure was built in 1835, after the road was returned to the state, and was used until 1905. The building has been restored and is operated by the Pennsylvania Historical and Museum Commission. *Hours:* Daylight saving time: Weekdays except Monday, 8:30 A.M.–5 P.M. Sunday, 1–5 P.M. Winter: Weekdays except Monday, 9 A.M.–4:30 P.M. Sunday, 1–4:30 P.M. *Location:* Near Searights, four miles northwest of Uniontown, on U.S. 40.

11. Grace Episcopal Church (brick), built in 1840, is now used as a barn for storing hay. Nearby is the old cemetery, which contains a 1799 stone. The first (log) church was built before 1793. In 1794 Robert Jackson, who had come to the area in 1790, donated the land and most of the money for the construction of the brick church. *Location:* Five miles west of Uniontown, on U.S. 40.

12. Searight's Tavern (remains) was built about 1819 by Josiah Frost. John Gray managed it for a time. He held a memorable political gathering, known as "Gray's meeting," here in 1828. Prior to 1840 many Democratic county meetings and conventions were conducted here. In 1828 William Searight took over the management until 1900. Searight, one of the most wealthy men in Menallen Township at that time, also owned a wagon shop, a blacksmith shop, a large livery stable, and a general store, and operated the post office. He was appointed road commissioner from 1842 to 1852. Other owners were John Risler, Matthias Fry, Joseph Gray (John's son), and two men both having the name of William Shaw but not related. This house, halfway between Uniontown and Brownsville, served as a drovers' stop. It was destroyed by fire in 1944, and the ruins can be seen along the road. The property surrounding the foundation has been excavated by archeology students from California State College. *Location:* Searights Crossroads, on U.S. 40, north side of road.

13. Peter Colley Tavern (stone), one of the oldest inns still standing on the National Road, has a signature stone which reads, "P. & H. Colley, 1796." The original bar, complete with a wooden grill, is intact in the interior. Peter Colley, an early settler and father of Abel, who also owned a tavern (see *Abel Colley Stand*), was reputed to have been the first innkeeper on the National Road to have literally made and displayed a barrel of money. He was born aboard a ship near Philadelphia in 1757 and ran this tavern from two decades before the National Road was built until his death in 1838. Later owners were his son George, Solomon Crumrine, D. Ramsey Woodward, and the Brier Hill Coal Company. The land was excavated by archeology students from California State College, who discovered that the original road was ten feet in front of the tavern doorway, not built to established standards. They also uncovered sites of a granary and a bake oven. The tavern is located in Brier Hill, which has one of the smallest post offices in the country. *Location:* Brier Hill, on U.S. 40.

14. Wallace Tavern (stucco over stone) was first kept by Arthur Wallace prior to 1840. Later Isaac Baily operated it, before he became postmaster of Brownsville and a lawyer. Then George Craft owned the house, but he was not a regular tavern keeper. At one time the eccentric "Jackey" Craft owned it. He was known for "starting out over the road in a sleigh with bells, when there was no snow on the ground." *Location:* Brier Hill, on north side of U.S. 40 west of the Peter Colley Tavern.

15. Johnston-Hatfield Tavern (stone) was built in 1816–17 by Randolph Dearth for Robert Johnston, who kept a tavern here until 1841. William Hatfield operated the inn from 1852 to 1855. He began his career as a blacksmith and formed the iron barrier gates for tollhouses along the pike. *Location:* About two miles west of Searights, on U.S. 40.

16. Abel Colley Stand (stone) was run successfully as a favorite tavern by Abel Colley, though it had been kept by several earlier owners. Abel built a brick house across the road where he retired. His wife Nancy is remembered as a large, amiable woman who habitually wore a Queen-Anne-style cap. Their son W. Searight Colley later lived in the brick farmhouse. Abel's father Peter also operated a tavern east of here (see *Peter Colley Tavern*). *Location:* One mile west of Brier Hill, on the north side of U.S. 40.

17. Sharpless House (stone), built by Jonathan Sharpless, who settled here sometime after 1793, is located across from the site of the first paper mill west of the Allegheny Mountains. The mill was built by Sharpless and Samuel Jackson on Redstone Creek at the mouth of Washington Run in 1794–97 and destroyed by fire in 1842. *Location:* East of Grindstone, on l.r. 26165. House is situated next to railroad tracks at Jefferson Township line.

18. Wilkes Brown Tavern (stone) was built in 1805 by the son of Basil Brown and operated until 1830. A signature stone on an addition at the back is dated 1817, the year before the National Road opened. This was a drovers' tavern, and from its immense size it must have had a good trade. *Location:* South side of U.S. 40, 0.7 mile east of U.S. 40–Pa. 166 Brownsville bypass.

19. Brubaker Tavern (brick) was sold by David Auld in 1826 to a Somerset County "Dutchman" who kept it until his death except for a brief time when it was operated by Alexander R. Watson, who ran an omnibus line between Uniontown and Brownsville. It was later called the White Pillars Hotel, after pillars were added. *Location:* Near Brownsville, on U.S. 40, almost at bypass at top of Brownsville Hill (0.6 mile west of Wilkes Brown tavern).

20. Nemacolin (Bowman's Castle) (brick) was begun in the 1700s and incorporates the original stone trading post constructed by Jacob Bowman in 1787. Containing twenty-two rooms, hallways as long as seventy feet, marble-mantled fireplaces, fine glass chandeliers, and an open circular stairway, this Tudor-style edifice, sometimes known as Nemacolin Tower in honor of an Indian chief, overlooks the Monongahela River. About 1795 President Washington had appointed Bowman the first postmaster of Brownsville, and he served till 1829. Bowman founded the Monongahela Bank in 1812 and served as its president until 1843. This castlelike structure is operated by the Brownsville Historical Society. *Hours:* April 20–October 15: Saturday and Sunday, 1–5 P.M. May 30–September 15: Tuesday–Sunday, 1–5 P.M. *Admission charge. Location:* Brownsville, facing Front Street.

21. Black Horse Tavern (stone) was the location of a meeting, "the first public act in the Whiskey Insurrection," held July 27, 1791. Here David Bradford and others looted mailbags taken by force. The last meeting of the local insurgents was also conducted here August 28 and 29, 1794. Amos Wilson was an early innkeeper. The house has been completely altered and modernized. Private residence. *Location:* Brownsville, on Front Street next to Bowman's Castle.

22. Brownsville Academy (stone) was built as a private residence by George Boyd about 1812. It was later leased by the Episcopal Church for a women's seminary, established in 1866 by Charlotte Smyth. In the 1880s it housed a free-lance publishing company. At another time O. K. Taylor, the president of the Brownsville National Bank, owned the property. *Location:* Brownsville, on Front Street.

23. Knox House (stucco and brick) was the birthplace of Philander C. Knox in 1853. Knox served as U.S. senator and secretary of state under President Taft. *Location:* Brownsville, junction of Fourth Avenue and Front Street.

24. Shreve House (brick) was the home of Henry Shreve, a boat builder who in 1814 constructed the *Enterprise,* first steamboat to return to Pittsburgh after going to New Orleans. Shreve also invented a method of removing tree stumps from rivers which kept boats from being snagged and sunk. Shreveport, La., was named for him. *Location:* Brownsville, junction of Front and Third Streets (below Brownsville Academy).

25. Brashear Tavern (stone) was built about 1796 by Basil Brashear. When Lafayette visited Brownsville in 1825, he addressed the citizens from the door of this house. Basil's grandson John A. Brashear, astronomer and educator, was born here in 1840. The tavern was later owned by James Searight and by Westley Frost. It is now a beer distributor's shop, and the front door has been altered as an access to a garage. *Location:* Brownsville, 519 Market Street (old U.S. 40).

26. Christ Protestant Episcopal Church (stone) was organized in 1785 and at first was served by missionaries. Robert Davis was rector from 1795 to 1805. The congregation purchased property from Charles Wheeler in 1796 and in 1815–23 erected the first building. The present church was built in 1856. Thomas Brown, the founder of Brownsville, is buried near the church door. The brick manse built about 1825 has been restored nearby. *Location:* Brownsville, Church Street and Fourth Avenue.

27. Saint Peter's Roman Catholic Church (stone), patterned after a village church in Ireland, was dedicated April 6, 1845. A fine example of provincial Gothic architecture, it overlooks the Monongahela River and is reached by a long flight of steps. This church was built on the site of an earlier brick house of worship, erected by Father Patrick Rafferty in 1827 and destroyed by fire in 1842. *Location:* Brownsville, 300 Shafner Avenue at Church Street.

31. First Iron Bridge

28. Bar [cq] House (brick), presently the Barr Hotel, stands at the site of the old Kimber house. The present structure was operated as a tavern for many years by Ephraim H. Bar. Other proprietors were Robert Carter (an old wagoner), Thornton Young, George Garrard, Matthew Story, Eli Bar, and W. F. Higinbotham. *Location:* Brownsville (Bridgeport), on Water Street at bridge.

29. Old River Captain's House (brick and stone), of unusual construction, looks out over the Monongahela from a hillside. It was built about 1855 and has a front portico. *Location:* Brownsville, 322 Catherina Avenue.

30. Early Fieldstone House is located next to the Grable blockhouse site. The blockhouse was built in 1788 at the corner of Lewis and Woodward Streets. *Location:* Brownsville, 710 Lewis Street.

Note: Another early stone house, located behind Saint Andrew's Church, next to the parking lot at High and Angle Streets, was originally servants' quarters for the T. S. Wright family.

31. First Iron Bridge west of the Allegheny Mountains was built in 1836–39 at a cost of $39,901.63 and designed by U.S. Army engineer Capt. Richard Delafield. This eighty-foot single-arch structure spanning Dunlaps Creek is still in use as an integral part of the Brownsville business section. It was nicknamed the "neck" because its thirty-foot width used to cause a bottleneck on U.S. 40. It remains a relic of a period when it provided means for immigrants to continue their trek south and west on the Monongahela and Ohio Rivers. William Searight did the stone work for this structure. *Location:* Brownsville, Market Street.

Note: The first iron-chain suspension bridge in the United States was also in Fayette County, built by James Finley in 1801 over Jacobs Creek on the Connellsville-Mount Pleasant Road. This structure has been replaced by the present bridge at the site. A marker commemorating it is located in the Connellsville quadrangle on l.r. 26151.

32. Penncraft, a self-help village from depression days, was launched when the American Friends Service Committee bought 200 acres on Bull Run Road on June 1, 1937, and settled ten unemployed miner families here. Houses, mostly of stone, were built on a traded-work basis; and a knitting mill and cooperative store were launched with thirty-one members and a capital of $165. Within ten years seventeen families had built homes, 165 acres were added, and the store had 550 members and a capital of $22,000. *Location:* Luzerne Township, four miles south of Brownsville, on Bull Run Road.

33. Dunlaps Creek Presbyterian Church (stone) was organized by Rev. James Power in 1774. (About this time Laurel Hill Church on l.r. 26133 near Waltersburg and Tyrone Church on Pa. 819 near l.r. 26104 were also founded by Power.) Rev. James Dunlap was installed in 1782 as the first regular pastor. The present church was completed in 1814 with extensive remodeling done in 1887. In 1962 the panes in all the windows were replaced with stained glass. About 0.2 mile east of this structure just off l.r. 26036 is the cemetery partially enclosed by a stone wall. The site of the first log meetinghouse was half a mile away near the creek.

Near that site is Dunlaps Creek Presbyterian Academy (brick), founded in 1848 and completed in 1849, during the pastorate of Samuel Wilson. It ceased to exist as a school in 1896, and in 1908 the academy trustees turned it over to the church. The restored building (remodeled 1969–73), used for many purposes over a period of years, continues to serve the recreational needs of the church and community. *Locations:* Church: Just east of Merrittstown, at junction of l.r. 26027 and l.r. 26036. Academy: 0.2 mile west of Merrittstown crossroads, on l.r. 26036.

34. Old Manse (stone) was probably built before 1800 by Jacob Jennings, lifetime physician and pastor of Dunlaps Creek Church from 1792 until 1811. It continued to be used as a manse for more than sixty years after his death in 1813. *Location:* Merrittstown, between crossroads and post office.

35. Darnell House (frame and stone) was begun by Caleb Darnell. A log section, replaced by a frame one after a fire, was built before 1790. The stone part was constructed no later than 1810. It has been owned by the Moore family for 150 years. *Location:* Merrittstown, across from post office.

36. Coleman House (stone) was built by Elijah Coleman, who ran a tannery nearby. A frame portion was added later. The Conwell family has owned it since about 1820. *Location:* Merrittstown, just south of post office.

37. Hopewell Presbyterian Church (brick) was organized as Cumberland Presbyterian in 1832 and the present structure was built forty years later. *Location:* Between Merrittstown and Penn Craft, on l.r. 26036.
Note: Just south of this road, about a half mile west is West Bend United Methodist Church, organized in 1830 and built about twenty years later.

38. Davidson's Ferry, now known as the Arensberg Ferry and run by Margaret Mitchell since 1965, is the last to be operated in western Pennsylvania. It was reportedly started in 1814 by David Davidson and remained in the family until 1890. For many years there were six such crossings in eleven miles of river just above Brownsville. They were, in order, Jacobs', Davidson's, Rices Landing, Millsboro, Fredericktown, and Crawford's. In the early years of the telegraph there was a line from Brownsville to offices at Jacobs' and Davidson's ferries.

The brick house at the site was built by Samuel Davidson in 1852. It and the ferry were bought in 1890 by Louis F. Arensberg and operated by him until 1915. For almost half a century the house was heated with gas from a nearby coal mine. *Ferry toll. Location:* At Monongahela River opposite Crucible, on l.r. 26003.

39. Jacobs Lutheran Church (brick), with a signature stone that reads "1846," is said to date from 1773 and was organized twenty years later by Rev. John Stough. The present church replaced the original log meetinghouse. The church was used by both Lutheran and Reformed congregations until 1854. A small replica of the original log church has been erected in the adjoining cemetery. *Location:* Two miles from Masontown and 0.5 mile east of junction of Shoaf and High House Roads.
Note: An early log house is nearby on the same road.

43. Friendship Hill

40. Harmony House (stone) was built by Col. George Wilson in 1773 as a wedding present for his son John, who married Drucilla Swearingen in 1775. (Swearingen's Fort was in Springhill Township near the Cheat River.) This home was later operated by the Harmony family as a tavern, called the Harmony House. Succeeding owners have been the Gans family, George Hager, and Harry Riffle. As a tavern the Harmony House prospered when New Geneva was an important river port. *Location:* New Geneva, 65 Ferry Street.

41. Stone Inn, in disrepair, has a double wooden front porch and may have been owned by the Wilson family. *Location:* New Geneva, junction of Pa. 166 and l.r. 26081.

Note: Across the street is a brick house built about 1856 with a fine doorway, and next to it is the old Davenport general store, built earlier.

42. Old Stone Church was erected in 1810–11. Adjoining it is a walled-in cemetery. Soldiers from the Revolution, War of 1812, Mexican War, and Civil War are buried here. The building has been used by the Methodists, Baptists, and Presbyterians as a place of worship. *Location:* New Geneva, near Pa. 166.

43. Friendship Hill (brick and stone) was built above the Monongahela River in 1789 by Albert Gallatin (1761–1849), who had mi-

grated from Switzerland and joined the side of the colonies during the Revolution. At Wilson's Fort, which he renamed New Geneva, he built a log store and laid out the town in 1794, after purchasing a tract of land in 1788 from Nicholas Blake. In 1789 he and his bride Sophia Allegre moved into their new home, which he called Friendship Hill. Due to his wife's death five months later and his dedication to public service, Gallatin spent little time here until he retired.

Gallatin served as representative to the State Constitutional Convention, was a member of the U.S. House of Representatives, was secretary of the treasury under Jefferson and Madison, served as chief U.S. diplomat for the promulgation of the Treaty of Ghent ending the War of 1812, and was minister to France and Great Britain. Between 1831 and 1839 he was president of the National Bank of New York. In addition, he established the Ethnological Society and was one of the founders of New York University. He operated a gun factory and also a glass works founded in 1797.

A new wing of stone was added to the house by his son Albert, Jr., in 1823. Lafayette addressed 1,000 guests from the building's second-story balcony in 1825. In 1832 Albert, Sr., sold Friendship Hill, and it passed through several ownerships including those of Albin Mellier, Representative John L. Dawson, and Andrew Thompson, son of coal baron J. V. Thompson (see *Oak Hill*).

46. Polly Williams Grave

Gallatin and his second wife, Hannah Nicholson whom he married in 1796, are buried in Trinity churchyard in New York. His first wife's unmarked grave is surrounded by a stone wall in the woods at Friendship Hill. *Location:* One mile south of New Geneva and four miles north of Point Marion, on Pa. 166.

44. Saint John's Evangelical Lutheran Church (brick) was built in 1854 by "Col. Alex. Crow" (according to the signature stone above the door). The building now serves the Pentecostal Apostolic Church. A cemetery is across the road from the church. *Location:* At Morris Crossroads turn off U.S. 119 and go east. 0.5 mile on l.r. 26080.

Note: Nearby at Morris Crossroads is an old hotel that has been a landmark for many years.

45. Hayden House (stone) was built before 1836 by John Hayden (1749–1836), the ironmaster at the Haydentown furnace. Hayden, who served in the Revolution, came to the area in 1784 and was the father of twenty-four children. He donated the land for the cemetery at Little Whiterock Methodist Church. Nearby Haydentown was named for him. In Hopwood (q.v.) is another Hayden house. An old stone dwelling, possibly his work, is situated at the Mountain Road Bridge in Fairchance, behind the site of the log Nixon Tavern, torn down about 1940. *Location:* On Mountain Road, 0.2 mile south of Little Whiterock Methodist Church.

46. Polly Williams Grave is the burial site of Polly (Mary) Williams, who was thrown to her death in 1810 from a sixty-foot cliff, now called White Rocks. Her unfaithful lover Philip Rogers was brought to trial and acquitted. The legend has been perpetuated by ballads and prose tales. A stranger traveling through the area heard the story and carved the following on a stone:

Polly Williams
1792–1810

Behold with pity you that pass by,
here does the bones of Polly Williams lie,
who was cut off in her tender bloom,
by a vile wretch, her pretended groom.

(The original stone was chipped away by souvenir hunters and replaced with another in 1910.) Both Polly and Philip lived near New Salem. *Location:* Village of White Rocks, south of U.S. 40 near Hopwood, in Little Whiterock Methodist Churchyard. (White Rocks can be reached by road on fishing lake near Fairchance.)

47. Tent Presbyterian Church (brick) acquired its name from its first services which were held in an arbor, along what was then the old Catawba Indian Trail. In 1791–92 a log structure was erected. It was replaced by the present church in 1878. *Location:* Four miles south of Uniontown, on U.S. 119.

48. Fort Gaddis (log) was erected on the Catawba Trail in 1774 by Thomas Gaddis, one of the founders of Great Bethel Baptist Church in Uniontown and third in command under Col. William Crawford in the fatal campaign against the Indians in 1782. The stockade around the cabin is no longer standing. Within it were three springs. Basil Brownfield, a relative of Gaddis, built an addition to the dwelling and lived there for many years, as did his descendants. This fort is the only one remaining in the county. It is reputed to have been attacked by Indians several times. Recently students from California State College have excavated the site. *Location:* Two miles south of Uniontown, 300 yards east of U.S. 119, at historical marker.

49. Hopwood, originally Woodstock and later called Monroe after President James Monroe visited here in 1816, was founded by John Hopwood in 1791. This mining and coke-producing center at the base of Chestnut Ridge consists of six original stone houses and other early dwellings along the National Road, in addition to modern structures. A signature stone on one of these stone houses reads, "Wm. Morris September the 7th 1818." (Morris also operated a brick tavern in the community.) The stone structure, an inn, was later run by Joseph Noble, Andrew McMasters, and German D. Hair. Another stone building bears the inscription, "Hayden 1839"; at one time Benjamin Hayden operated a store here. *Location:* East of Uniontown, on U.S. 40.

50. James Barnes Estate (frame) was built in 1906–07 for $1 million by Barnes, one of J. V. Thompson's partners who, like Thompson, went bankrupt as a result of a business deal. A stone gazebo, now in disrepair, is situated by a stream running through the once beautifully landscaped grounds. *Location:* East end of Hopwood, south of U.S. 40.

Note: South of this property on Mountain Road are other interesting log, brick, and stone houses.

51. Watering Trough is located at a well-known spring where travelers still stop to refresh themselves with mountain water, as they have since the early pike days. Here William Downard lived in a stone house (now gone) against the hillside, but did not keep it as a tavern because of lack of land for a wagon yard. He maintained the water trough, although Thomas B. Searight in his book *The Old Pike* states that Downard was eccentric and begrudged use of the water by those he disliked. *Location:* East of Uniontown, on U.S. 40, two thirds of way up Summit Mountain.

Note: A later tavern is in the area of Downard's homesite and next to the watering trough. Remains of the old Turkey's Nest Tavern are visible south of U.S. 40, one third of the way up Summit Mountain (Chestnut Ridge) east of Uniontown, before reaching the watering trough. Once a fine stone tavern, it was destroyed by fire about 1940. It derived its name from a wild turkey's nest found by road workmen constructing the original pike.

52. Mount Summit Inn (masonry and frame) is located on the site of two previous buildings. One of them, the old Summit House, had been an early popular summer resort which formerly belonged to Col. Samuel Evans. He was followed by Ephraim McClean, Henry Clay Rush, Brown Hadden, Stephen Snyder, John Snyder, William Boyd, and Webb Barnet. Mount Summit Inn was built about 1900 as another summer resort. In 1936 the eight-foot-square bed of John Gilbert, idol of the silent movies, was purchased and

48. Fort Gaddis

brought here for the honeymoon room. *Location:* Six miles east of Uniontown, at summit of Chestnut Ridge on U.S. 40.

53. Laurel Caverns, visited as early as 1800, are the largest natural formation of their kind above the Mason and Dixon line. Called Dulaneys Cave prior to 1940, the caverns were developed extensively in 1962. Located on top of Chestnut Ridge, they contain unusual limestone formations, and their entranceway provides an excellent view of seven counties. Open all year. *Admission charge. Location:* Five miles South of Mount Summit Inn. Follow l.r. 26133 for two miles; then go three miles on l.r. 26201.

54. Fayette Springs Hotel (stone), now called the Stone House, was built in 1822 for Congressman Andrew Stewart by masons who had erected the bridges along the National Road. After Stewart's death the property was sold to Capt. John Messmore, followed by Cuthbert Wiggins, John Risler, B. W. Earl, Samuel Lewis, William Snyder, William Darlington, John Rush, Major Swearingen, Redding Bunting, Cuthbert Downer, and others. It was a favorite resort of visitors to the Fayette Springs, about three quarters of a mile away, and many parties of young people from Uniontown visited the hotel during its halcyon days. Marah Ellis Ryan wrote *A Pagan of the Alleghenies* while staying here. *Location:* Midway between the Summit and Chalkhill, on U.S. 40.

55. Downer House (brick) was begun in 1823 by Jonathan Downer, taking seventeen years to build. The Downers had been on their way to Kentucky from Philadelphia when winter set in. After the father had helped his five sons build a log house, he went to Kentucky but was never heard of again. Later, about 1790, the boys erected a small stone house on the Braddock Road near Orchard Camp. After Jonathan built the brick house, he moved the stone one across the road next to it. (This village was named for white clay found when the National Road was built in 1818.) *Location:* Chalk Hill, on U.S. 40.

56. Braddock's Grave is marked by a granite monument surrounded by an iron fence and a grove of evergreens. A footpath north of this site leads to the spot where Gen. Edward Braddock was buried beneath a tree, later called "Braddock's oak," located in the twenty-three-acre Braddock Memorial Park. Here on the west side of the Great Meadows was Braddock's Orchard Camp where his army stayed June 25, 1755, and where he was brought after being fatally wounded in the battle of the Monongahela. His body was buried in the roadbed, traces of which can still be seen, and wagons were driven over the grave to keep the Indians from finding it. In 1804 a party of road workers led by Andrew Stewart (later a congressman) removed Braddock's remains and placed them at the present site, south of the original grave. Some of the bones were later sent to Philadelphia. The Braddock Park Association was formed in 1909, and the monument at the second grave was unveiled in 1913. *Location:* About ten miles east of Uniontown, on U.S. 40 (about one mile west of Fort Necessity Museum).

57. Mount Washington Tavern Museum (brick) was built by Judge Nathaniel Ewing between 1816 and 1818 on a 234-acre tract which George Washington owned from 1769 to 1799 and recommended as being "an exceeding good stand on Braddock's road, from Ft. Cumberland to Pittsburg, and besides a fertile soil, possesses a large quantity of natural meadow, fit for the scythe." The tavern was a popular stagecoach stop for the Good Intent Line. Subsequent proprietors were James Sampey, John Foster, and James Moore. After the business closed, Ellis Beggs purchased the property, followed by Godfrey Fazenbaker. In 1931 the state bought it, and in 1962 the National Park Service acquired it as part of Fort Necessity National Battlefield. On the grounds is a Conestoga wagon, and

inside the building are displays of artifacts and other memorabilia. *Hours:* Daily, 10 A.M.– noon; 1–4 P.M. *Location:* On U.S. 40, just west of Fort Necessity park entrance.

58. Fort Necessity was begun in May 1754 by the Virginia militia commanded by Lt. Col. George Washington. The stockade was quickly finished at the Great Meadows natural clearing, which Washington later bought. On May 28 Washington and his troops had killed or captured a party of ten French soldiers, whose leader Coulon de Jumonville (see *Jumonville*) was among the slain. On July 3 Washington and his men suffered a retaliatory attack by the French and Indians led by Jumonville's half brother, Capt. Louis Coulon de Villiers. After Washington evacuated the fort on July 4, the French burned it. This battle was a prelude to the opening of the French and Indian War, which ended in 1763 with the expulsion of French power from North America.

In 1933 the Fort Necessity National Battlefield was established under the National Park Service. Excavations were carried out under the direction of Jean C. Harrington in 1953, and it was discovered that a circular stockade about fifty-two feet in diameter had been built here instead of a rectangular one as previously surmised. A replica of the original was later built on the site. It is believed that within the battlegrounds are buried the unknown soldiers killed in the action. A modern round structure on the property provides a visitors' center where visual aids depict the events of the battle. *Park, fort, and visitors' center hours:* Daily, 8:30 A.M.–5 P.M. *Location:* Eleven miles east of Uniontown, just south of U.S. 40.

59. Rush Tavern (stone), once a stand for the Stockton Mail Line and later covered with a brick facade, was built on the National Road in 1837 by Judge Nathaniel Ewing. Soon after its completion Sebastian "Boss" Rush moved in as a lessee of Ewing, ran the stagecoach establishment, and later purchased it, operating it until his death in 1878. Rush was appointed superintendent of the road and was township constable. He entertained many distinguished and interesting persons, including P. T. Barnum and the Swedish singer Jenny Lind. Before this tavern was built there had been a frame inn on the site operated by "the widow Tantlinger."

The house, which now is an antique shop, contains the reconstructed bar, and old graffiti were found on the wall under the layers of wallpaper. The 1841 ledger of the National Road Stage Company and the 1858 hotel license of the Rush Tavern are preserved in the house. *Location:* Farmington, at junction of U.S. 40 and Pa. 381.

60. Canaan School Museum (frame) is a one-room schoolhouse built in 1878. The building also served as a church until 1943 and was closed in 1955. Maintained as a museum, it is operated by the Retired Teachers' Association of Fayette County. The structure was restored in 1971, and its original bell is still intact in the belfry. A fine spring is located across the road. *Hours:* May 30–September 30: Weekends, 1–4 P.M. .*Donation. Location:* East of Uniontown, south of U.S. 40 on l.r. 26073, 0.6 mile south of Gibbon Glade Post Office.

61. Gorley's Lake Hotel (masonry and frame), erected in the 1920s, was a famous landmark for years. Presently called Oak Lake, it houses the Society of Brothers, which maintains a toy factory and a publishing company here. *Location:* 0.5 mile east of Farmington, on U.S. 40.

62. John Stone Tavern (stone), built on the John E. Stone farm, was an early National Road house first kept by William Shaw, followed by William Griffin, Charles Kemp, Isaac Denny and William A. Stone. It was later operated by Job Clark. At one time a large carriage house and stables were located across from the house. *Location:* 3.5 miles southeast of Farmington, on south side of U.S. 40 at crest of western slope of Woodcock Hill (near Braddock Road "Twelve Springs Camp" marker).

63. Brown Tavern (stone) was built in 1826 by Thomas Brown, who operated it until the time of his death. Brown, a good fiddler, entertained Col. Ben Brownfield and Gen. Henry W. Beeson, who came here on sleighing excursions. After the Brown family owned the property, Jacob Umberson bought it. The elections of Henry Clay Township were held in this house. *Location:* About seven miles southeast of Farmington, on south side of U.S. 40 just west of its junction with Pa. 281.

64. Conservancy Farmhouse (frame) was built about 1871 by Ross Tissue. In 1940 Edgar J. Kaufmann bought the property, where the tenants ran a dairy business for him. In 1963 Edgar Kaufmann, Jr., gave the farmhouse to the Western Pennsylvania Conservancy, and when that agency started tours of Kaufmann's famous Fallingwater (see below), the farmhouse was used by college students who worked as tour guides. In 1968 the farmhouse was remodeled by the conservancy for the director of the nature reserve. The headquarters for the reserve are in a restored barn. *Location:* Between Mill Run and Ohiopyle, next to Bear Run Nature Reserve on Pa. 381.

65. Fallingwater (sandstone and concrete) at Bear Run Valley was designed and built by Frank Lloyd Wright in 1936 for Edgar J. Kaufmann, Pittsburgh department-store owner. This impressive building, architecturally ahead of its time, features bold cantilevered construction. Perched on gigantic boulders over a rushing waterfall, it blends with the mountainous terrain. It was completed with a guest and service wing in 1939. One of Wright's most widely acclaimed works, this masterpiece was the weekend retreat of the Kaufmann family until 1963. At that time Edgar J. Kaufmann, Jr., donated the property and an endowment was provided by the Kaufmann Charitable and Education Foundation to the Western Pennsylvania Conservancy as a memorial to Edgar and Liliane Kaufmann. Opened to the public in 1964, it is maintained as a cultural center. *Hours:* April–November: Tuesday–Sunday, 10 A.M.–4 P.M. Reservations required. *Admission charge.* A child-care center is provided for visitors' children under twelve. *Location:* Three miles north of Ohiopyle State Park, on Pa. 381.

66. Ohiopyle Falls in the Youghiogheny River was a site reconnoitered by George Washington on his first military expedition in May 1754, while looking for a clear-water passage for his ordnance and supplies from his Great Meadows Camp. Washington's party was forced ashore at these falls, where the river drops sixty feet within a mile. Today this beautiful historic site is part of the nature reserve of the Western Pennsylvania Conservancy. More than 100 acres known as the Ohiopyle Peninsula are located within the loop of the Youghiogheny at the falls. *Location:* Ohiopyle.

Note: Other natural landmarks in the area include Ferncliff Park, also operated by the conservancy on Pa. 381, and Keister Park at Cucumber Falls, on l.r. 26071, 0.5 mile southwest of Ohiopyle Falls.

67. Ora May House (log), once owned by Samuel and Catherine (Enfield) Nicholson, was built in 1856. Ora May and her family moved here in 1915. The hand-hewn structure is held together with wooden pins. *Location:* About two miles from Mill Run, on Hampton Road.

68. Stickel House (frame), commonly referred to as the "big house," was probably erected during the 1860s by a Dr. Gallagher who operated a tannery. This ownership was followed by those of William Dull, Meade Hutchison, A. C. Stickel, and Glenn Work. *Location:* Mill Run, on Pa. 381 across from old post office (now a store).

69. Indian Creek Stone Bridge was built near the early logging town of Indian Creek by Fred Dahl, a stonemason. Although the bridge is still in use by the railroad, nothing remains of the nearby lumbering village along Indian Creek except a few foundation stones where the Stickel general store and the McFarland Lumber Company were located. The lumber mill's floating pond for logs can still be seen along the creek and the railroad tracks. *Location:* Near Mill Run, 1,000 feet down hill across Indian Creek (near church camp).

70. Brotherhood House (brick) is reputed to have been the meeting place of the Pennsville Mennonite congregation before and during the time when its brick church was being constructed in 1852. This house, later owned by the Albright family, is located on what was known as the "Moreland place" and also the "Ganier place." *Location:* Pennsville, one mile south of Mennonite cemetery.

71. Rist House (brick) was built in 1852 by Peter Rist. His father, John, was a Mennonite pioneer who settled in the area around 1790. According to tradition, Peter's wife Sally carried stones in her apron to help construct the wall surrounding this farm, which was later purchased by the Benzio family. *Location:* About two miles north of Connellsville and about 1.5 mile northeast of Broad Ford, on Narrows Road (Bullskin Township).

72. Smith House (brick) was built in 1795 by Jacob and Catherine Galley Smith, a Mennonite couple who raised eleven children on this farm. A small stone structure built earlier than the brick house now serves as a storage building on the property. *Location:* 0.5 mile south of Rist house, on Narrows Road (Connellsville Township).

73. Crawford House (log), constructed in 1975 by the Connellsville Historical Society and Fayette County Manpower program, is a reproduction of Col. William Crawford's home on his plantation. Crawford, who settled here in 1769, was a lifelong friend and adviser of George Washington and was Virginia's licensed surveyor for the West. He was an outstanding officer in Dunmore's War of 1774 and in the Revolutionary War. On the Allegheny River he built Fort Crawford, which was named for him by Gen. Lachlan McIntosh. Crawford took an active part in the 1778 campaign against the western Indians, helped defend Westmoreland County in 1781, and was burned at the stake in the Sandusky expedition of 1782. His son, John, sold the original tract of land in 1787 to Edward Cook, who later transferred it to Isaac Meason. *Location:* Connellsville, junction of North Seventh Street and U.S. 119.

Note: A statue of Crawford stands on the lawn of Carnegie Free Library in Connellsville on South Pittsburgh Street.

74. Meason House (partly stone) was the home of Isaac Meason who laid out this area of town, then called New Haven, in 1796. This structure is presently the West Side Hotel. The stone section is the original house. *Location:* Connellsville, on Crawford Avenue at west end of bridge over Youghiogheny River.

75. Steam Locomotive is a 1930 engine built by the H. K. Porter Company in Pittsburgh. It was once used by the West Penn Power Company. *Location:* Connellsville, North Seventh Street on bank of Youghiogheny River.

76. Stillwagon's Rock Museum (frame), built by Theodore Stillwagon, includes a collection of approximately two thousand mineral specimens, with some two hundred fluorescent stones illuminated by ultraviolet light. Also on exhibit are more than one thousand fossils and Indian artifacts, 80 percent of which have been discovered in the area. Open by appointment. *Location:* Trotter, two miles south of Connellsville (follow signs off Ridge Boulevard).

77. Linden Hall Estate includes a stone mansion built in 1911–12 by Sarah B. Moore Cochran, widow of Philip Galley Cochran, coal baron of the county. It was named for the Linden trees that Mrs. Cochran imported from Germany. This palatial mansion, set on a hill 600 feet above the Youghiogheny River, features signed Tiffany windows, bowling alleys, and an Aeolian pipe organ, and is decorated with gold leaf, sterling and Wedgwood inserts, and marble fireplaces. It is open for tours by reservation. *Admission charge.*

Philip Cochran, born in Lower Tyrone Township in 1849, was the president of the Washington Coal and Coke Company, Brown and Cochran Coke Company, Cochran Coal and Coke Mining, Dawson Bridge Company, and the First National Bank of Dawson. In 1879 he married Sarah, and they had a son Philip who died at the age of twenty-one. Philip, Sr., died in 1899.

The Cochran's original frame house, built in the late 1890s, is now a golf-course clubhouse. A 200-year-old log house on the property is used as a guest house. This estate, where European royalty and financial tycoons were entertained, was later owned by Saint James Church. *Location:* Three miles northwest of Dawson, on Pa. 662 off Pa. 201, 5 miles east of Perryopolis.

78. Abraham Overholt and Company Distillery (brick) was established before 1834 by Abraham Overholt, son of Henry, who came here in 1800. Abraham improved his father's stills and built a grain mill in 1834. The present buildings were erected in 1899. *Location:* Broad Ford, near Connellsville.

Note: A nearby brick house, built in 1832, was the residence of Abraham's grandson Henry Clay Frick, while he worked at the distillery. The smaller red brick house next to it was the former post office. (See also *Henry Clay Frick Birthplace,* Westmoreland County.)

79. Meason House on Christopher Gist's Plantation (cut sandstone), an outstanding Georgian home at Mount Braddock, was built in 1802 by the English architect Adam Wilson for Isaac Meason, the leading ironmaster in the region. Meason owned the Plumsock Iron Works on Redstone Creek in 1815. The main house, with a center hall flanked by one-story servants' quarters on one side and an office wing on the opposite, is one of the finest examples of early post-Colonial architecture still standing in western Pennsylvania. In 1803 it won high acclaim from Francis Asbury, bishop of the Methodist Episcopal Church. The house presently stands vacant, in fine condition but in need of historical preservation.

The land originally belonged to Christopher Gist, who built a house there in 1753. Gist and the Ohio Company intended this area to be the first permanent English settlement west of the Allegheny Mountains, but French occupation of the Ohio in 1754–55 prevented this. This estate, called Mount Braddock, is the site of Gen. Edward Braddock's encampment on June 27, 1755, while en route to Fort Duquesne. Here he issued his last orders before he died at Orchard Camp on July 9. *Location:* About six miles northwest of Uniontown, off U.S. 119.

80. Jumonville, sometimes referred to as Jumonville's Rocks, was the site of George Washington's first combat in which one of his Indian allies killed the French commander Coulon de Jumonville (see *Fort Necessity*). Jumonville's grave is in a glen in the area. Here also is a plaque in memory of the only man whom Washington lost in the skirmish.

The area near the glen later became the site of a Civil War orphans' home, at which time the present stone buildings were erected. It operated here from 1875 to 1880, and was subsidized by the U.S. government. It had previously been organized in 1866 at Madison College in Uniontown. The property is now a training center and camp owned by the Western Pennsylvania Conference of the United Methodist Church and encompasses 275 acres and forty buildings. *Location:* On I.r. 26115, three miles north of U.S. 40 at Summit. A private road leads to some of the sites.

Landmarks include:

a. Great Cross, a 60-foot steel cross (which replaced a wooden one) weighing 35 tons, was erected on Dunbar's Knob in 1950, on a 183-ton, 8-foot-high base. Three states can be seen from this point. The road leading to the cross is scattered with fossils which attest to the area's having been under the sea at one time.

b. Whyel Chapel (stone), built in 1882, was formerly a Lutheran Evangelical church. Now a chapel, it was dedicated to the memory of Florence Williams Whyel, the wife of Harry Whyel who donated the campsite in 1941.

c. Faculty Lodge (frame) was one of the original buildings from the orphans' school.

d. Various stone buildings are classic examples of post–Civil War architecture. (As late as 1939 the YMCA operated a summer hotel called Washington Lodge in one. In 1939 it became a Works Progress Administration training school for young women.)

e. Dunbar's Campsite was used during June and July of 1755 by Col. Thomas Dunbar, who was in charge of artillery for General Braddock's army. At Braddock's defeat, Dunbar destroyed the supplies and retreated. A small cannon was cast from metal artifacts discovered here, and it was used for morning and evening signals when the orphans' home operated. The site is a few hundred yards off Jumonville Glen.

f. Half King's Rocks is the spot where Tanacharison, Delaware Indian chief and friend of the English, met with Washington at the Jumonville victory.

g. Washington Spring, once a landmark, is now in disrepair.

81. Coolspring Stone House was possibly erected by Thompson McKean, who built the Coolspring Iron Furnace before 1820 on Shute's Run. The cut stone from the exterior of the furnace stack was used to build a water reservoir for Uniontown. The furnace was near Coolspring, off l.r. 26115 at the reservoir. *Location:* Coolspring, off l.r. 26115.

82. Three Gaddis Houses, all located near Upper Middletown, were built between 1790 and 1820. The Gaddis family were among the first settlers in Fayette County (see *Fort Gaddis*).

a. John Gaddis House (fieldstone with quarried-stone corners) is a very early structure with an outside fireplace and lintels above the doors and windows. There are large stone chimneys at both gable ends of the house. It was erected by John Gaddis (1741–1827) who had bought 295 acres of land he called Gaddistown. A log house nearby dates back to 1856. *Location:* Near Upper Middletown, on l.r. 26032, 1.1 mile from junction with l.r. 26021.

b. Thomas Martin Gaddis House (quarried stone) is a later house built by T. M. Gaddis. It is a two-bay structure with a stone porch added later. An old stone smokehouse is in the rear. This house was purchased by the Kelley family. *Location:* Near Upper Middletown, on old Pa. 51, 0.6 mile north of new Pa. 51.

c. Thomas Martin Gaddis House (stone) is another early Gaddis home that has stone keystone lintels above the windows and doors and is a two-bay structure. *Location:* Near Upper Middletown, 0.2 mile south of other T. M. Gaddis house (0.3 mile off new Pa. 51, on old Pa. 51, turn west for 0.7 mile to house on left side of road).

83. Sickle House (cut stone) was built at an uncertain date near the bridge over Redstone Creek. A stone wall is in front of this house, and a porch was added about 1940 on one side. Peter Sickle owned the property at one time, followed by H. W. Hamilton. *Location:*

North of Waltersburg, on old Pa. 51 at Redstone Creek bridge.

84. Osborne Log House (covered with aluminum and modern stone) was built in 1790 by Abraham Osborne, Sr. This house, with a central chimney, was built over a spring. Abraham is buried at the Grace Episcopal Church cemetery. The home was later owned by the Holloways, Todds, and McGinnesses, in succession. In 1886 the property was sold to James Vail, followed by Porter Ewing. *Location:* Near Upper Middletown, on l.r. 26032, 0.4 mile from its junction with l.r. 26021.

85. Wetzel-Shanefelter House (fieldstone) was covered with stucco in 1913 and scored to resemble cut stone. There are single-stone lintels above the windows and solid interior walls. It was owned by A. J. Wetzel in 1872. A nearby stone house, later owned by the Duff family, belonged to G. W. Wetzel. *Location:* About nine miles north of Uniontown, 0.4 mile off Pa. 51 on l.r. 26028.

86. Hazen House (cut stone) was built in 1847. The date stone, now obliterated, was found on the chimney. Large stone lintels are above the windows. The family of Abraham and Jacob Hazen owned this property from 1847 to 1941. In 1939 one of their tenants murdered his wife and stepdaughter here with a knife and then shot himself. *Location:* Spillway Lake, on Pa. 51 south of Perryopolis.

87. Patterson-Blaney House (stone) was constructed on a tract of land called Reservation. It was granted to James Patterson in 1785, with a patent two years later. Once called the Old Shotwell Mansion, it was built between 1775 and 1785, with a porch added in 1937. The home was later purchased by Harold and Kate Blaney. *Location:* Just south of Perryopolis, on west side of Pa. 51.

88. Three Harris Houses still remain from an early period. *Location:* All northwest of Perryopolis, on Fairhope Road, a short distance off old Pa. 51.

a. Original House (log) was built by Jacob Harris, who came to Fayette County about 1798. It is of log construction, covered with aluminum siding, and has been added onto though the years. Here, about 1940, social workers found a five-year-old girl who had been tied in an attic chair and fed only on a bottle all her life at the behest of her grandfather, Isaac Harris, because she was her mother's second illegitimate child. This

140

"second-sin-baby" case created world-wide attention. Placed first in a foster home and then in Polk State School, the girl appeared to be developing well but died of pneumonia after about two years. *Location:* At top of hill to right, about 0.5 mile from road junction.

b. Large Brick House was built by Jacob Harris about 1823. Its interior has been considerably altered, and its exterior has been given a modern appearance with tall white pillars. *Location:* On left just before road starts up hill (second house to right, west of 1798 house).

c. Another Brick House, built for a son James about 1840, is not far away on same road.

89. Perryopolis Historical Sites. Ever since it received an inheritance from the estate of Mary Fuller Frazier (see Fuller House below), the town of Perryopolis has been very active in historical restoration.

a. Country Store (weatherboarded log) was formerly the Gue house and is now operated by the Perryopolis Area Historical Society. This historical headquarters, partially restored, also serves as an old-time general store. *Hours:* Memorial Day–October 31: Tuesday–Sunday, 1–5 P.M. Weekends only in November and December. *Location:* Circle and Independence Streets.

b. Snyder House (frame) once belonged to J. Buell Snyder, congressman during Franklin D. Roosevelt's administration. As chairman of War Department appropriations, he did more than any other person to prepare the nation for World War II. *Location:* On Liberty Street across from post office.

c. Fuller House (frame) was formerly owned by Alfred M. Fuller. He and his brother were among the largest owners in the stockyards of New York, Philadelphia, Saint Louis, and Boston, and first in the field as exporters of American livestock to Europe, initiating the shipment of frozen meat. Fuller, a millionaire, was the largest landowner in Fayette County in 1912. Although not a member of any church, he bequeathed funds impartially to various churches in the area. In 1882 Fuller married Margaret Coleman (whose sister Lucy married Andrew Carnegie's brother Thomas). Mary Fuller Frazier, daughter of Alfred, was born in this house. She willed over $1.5 million to Perryopolis and its schools. *Location:* On Circle Street.

d. Old Stone Bank housed one of the oldest banks west of the Allegheny Mountains and one of the few state banks. In 1816 the Youghiogheny Bank of Pennsylvania was established here. Following a bankruptcy in

1820 the building was established as a school, but during Andrew Jackson's administration it was again used as a bank (1829–37). It was later used again as a school, and as a Methodist church, a store, a poolroom, a fruit store, a doctor's office, an insurance office, and a restaurant. At present it is a private residence. *Location:* On Liberty Street.

e. Sisley Blacksmith Shop (frame), one of the few surviving structures of its kind, is located near an old Revolutionary War cemetery and the old Malta Hall schoolhouse. *Location:* On La Fayette Street.

f. Providence Meetinghouse (stone) was founded in 1789 by the Society of Friends as a "preparative meeting of Redstone monthly Meeting." The first log structure was built in 1789 by John Cope. It was followed in 1793 by a stone building that was used until 1872. In 1893 Mary Binns, a descendant of an early Friend, had the present one-story house constructed according to the specifications of the original stone structure, using the stones from the former building. It is located next to a cemetery. The building is operated by the historical society. *Location:* On l.r. 26137, 1.8 mile west of Pa. 51.

g. Washington Gristmill (stone remains) was built for and owned by George Washington. The land deal was made through Washington's friend William Crawford. Construction began on the mill about 1774 and after delays caused by Indian uprisings and the approach of the Revolution, it was completed in 1776. Washington sold the property in 1789. It was leased to Col. Israel Shreve, father of Henry Shreve (see *Shreve House*). The stone foundation of this frame structure, which operated till 1917, is all that remains today. The historical society plans to restore it. A scale model of this mill is on display at the borough building. *Location:* On East Independence Street.

h. Stone Distillery was active during the Whiskey Rebellion days. Plans are being made to restore this structure, which is located next to the Washington gristmill. *Location:* On East Independence Street.

i. Old Stone Bakeshop and Stone House date from the nineteenth century. Only the lower part of the bakeshop remains, with its original stone stove. The second floor was burned. Nearby on a hillside is the stone house, which at one time belonged to a Smith family, the third owners of the property. *Location:* In vicinity of Washington gristmill and stone distillery.

j. Old Stone Fulling Mill was erected by William Searight about 1810. The operation of

89.h. Stone Distillery

93. Alliance Iron Furnace

fulling cloth was carried on in the basement of the building. The first floor contained equipment for carding, and a restored carding machine is on this level. The mill machinery was originally powered by water. In 1968 the historical society purchased the mill, which houses artifacts together with implements relating to the wool and flax industries. *Location:* On Strawn Road, off East Independence Street.

90. Frick Company Colonial Coal Belt was built by the H. C. Frick Coke Company and was in operation until 1956. The remains of the tipple can be seen on the Monongahela River bank. This company was the first to move coal by conveyor belt from inland mines to a river loading dock. *Location:* South of Fayette City (between Gillespie and Brownsville). Go on l.r. 26018 for 0.4 mile north of its junction with l.r. 26012 to unmarked road; thence west on this road for about one mile across P&LE Railroad tracks to site.

Note: On the way to this site is a very early fieldstone house, later stuccoed. Now badly damaged by undermining, this house was reportedly built in 1775 by the Goe family. It has three chimneys and is built in two sections. *Location:* On l.r. 26018, 0.2 mile north of its junction with l.r. 26012.

91. Jackson House (stone covered with stucco) was built in 1785 by Maj. Samuel Jackson, a Quaker. He was a banker, farmer, miller, and boat builder who bought property here in 1777 adjoining land belonging to Thomas Brown and Andrew Linn. More than five generations of heirs have lived in the house. Nearby was the site of the Ohio Company's warehouse, The Hangard. The old brick Forsythe house is a short way north on

the same road. *Location:* Jefferson Township, at mouth of Redstone Creek near Brownsville on l.r. 26018.

92. Cook Mansion (limestone) was built in Rehoboth Valley in 1774–76 by Col. Edward Cook, who came here in 1770. At that time it was the most pretentious house west of the Alleghenies. Former slave quarters have been converted into a parlor, and the sheet-iron ceiling is reputed to be the first rolled in this part of the country. The smokehouse and kitchen washhouse are still standing. This property has been in the Cook family for at least five generations. Edward Cook was a member of both the Provincial Congress (1776) and the State Constitutional Convention (1776). In addition, he was lieutenant of the Westmoreland County Militia (1777–82) and one of the founders of the Rehoboth Presbyterian Church (q.v., Westmoreland County) where he is buried. The large brick house on the same side of the road on the next farm was also a Cook house. *Location:* Near Belle Vernon, 0.9 mile on l.r. 64137 from its junction with Pa. 981; then 0.4 mile on Cook Road.

93. Alliance Iron Furnace (stone) was the first of its kind west of the Alleghenies. It was so named because of its alliance with other business holdings, and was built on Jacobs Creek in 1789 by William Turnbull, Col. John Holker, and Peter Marmie. According to legend Peter Marmie, an avid hunter, drove his faithful hounds into the fiery furnace and followed them after financial failure. However, this tale acutally started at another furnace in the eastern part of the state. In 1792 the furnace provided shot for six-pounders at the Fort Pitt arsenal and in 1793 supplied ammunition for Gen. Anthony Wayne's expedition against the Ohio Indians. It went out of blast in 1802. It was also known as Jacobs Creek Furnace, Alliance Iron Works, Turnbull's Iron Works, and Colonel Holker's Iron Works. Peter Marmie's unmarked grave site is in the First Baptist Church cemetery at Jacobs Creek village. *Location:* From village of Banning, go 2.6 miles on l.r. 26015 to Rough farm on left, across from sawmill; thence to dirt road behind house and continue for over 0.5 mile under railroad to furnace. Or go 1.5 mile east of Perryopolis on l.r. 26191; turn left at Alliance Furnace marker for 0.5 mile on l.r. 26015; turn right on t. 568; thence to railroad track, and proceed on foot under bridge. Furnace is about 100 feet from creek.

Pennsylvania Historical and Museum Commission Markers

Albert Gallatin   Junction of U.S. 119 and Pa. 116 north of Point Marion; and Pa. 166 north of New Geneva

Alliance Furnace   Pa. 819, 1 mile north of Dawson; and l.r. 26015, approximately 6 miles northwest of Pa. 819

Braddock Park   U.S. 40, 2.5 miles northwest of Farmington.

Braddock Road (Dunbar's Camp)   l.r. 26115, approximately 3 miles north of U.S. 40 at Jumonville

Braddock Road (Rock Fort Camp)   U.S. 40, approximately 6 miles southeast of Uniontown at Summit

Braddock Road (Stewart's Crossing)   U.S. 119, 0.2 mile south of Connellsville

Braddock Road (Twelve Springs Camp)   U.S. 40, 3.5 miles southeast of Farmington

Brashear House   Brownsville, U.S. 40, at Market, Sixth, and Union Streets

Brownsville   Brownsville, U.S. 40

Coke Ovens   Perryopolis, Pa. 51

Col. William Crawford   U.S. 119, 0.2 mile south of Connellsville

Dunbar's Camp   U.S. 40, approximately 6 miles southeast of Uniontown, at Summit

Fort Gaddis   U.S. 119, 2 miles south of Uniontown

Fort Mason   Masontown, Pa. 166

Fort Necessity   U.S. 40, 1 mile northwest of Farmington

George Washington   Perryopolis, Pa. 51

Gist's Plantation   U.S. 119, 4.5 miles southwest of Connellsville

Jumonville Defeat   U.S. 40, approximately 6 miles southeast of Uniontown at Summit

Meason House   U.S. 119, 4.5 miles southwest of Connellsville

Mount Washington Tavern   U.S. 40, 1.2 mile northwest of Farmington

National Road   U.S. 40, 1.7 mile northwest of Farmington; and U.S. 40 northwest of Brier Hill

Old Glassworks (Albert Gallatin's)   New Geneva, Pa. 166

Philander Knox   Brownsville, U.S. 40 at Market, Sixth, and Union Sheets

Searight's Tavern   U.S. 40, southeast of Brier Hill

Searights Tollhouse   U.S. 40, 5 miles northwest of Uniontown; and at property on U.S. 40, 5 miles west of Uniontown

Uniontown   On main highways leading into city

Washington Mill   Perryopolis, East Independence Street (l.r. 26191)

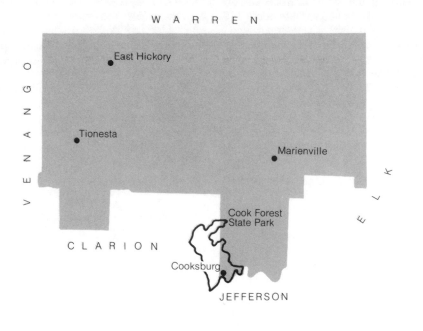

W A R R E N

O
G
N
A
N
E
V

East Hickory

Tionesta

Marienville

K

L

E

Cook Forest
State Park

C L A R I O N

Cooksburg

JEFFERSON

Forest County

Capsule History

Forest County, named for its heavy timberlands, was erected out of Jefferson County on April 11, 1848, and in 1866 it received additional territory from Venango. The county, the most sparsely populated in the state, has an area of 419 square miles and a population of 4,926.

As early as 1749 the French, led by Céloron de Blainville, visited the western section of the county. The Munsees (Delawares) inhabited the area when Moravian missionaries, under the leadership of David Zeisberger, came to convert the refugee tribes. These Indians had fled their villages at the time of John Penn's proclamation in 1764 offering huge bounties for Indian scalps and had settled in the villages of Goschgoschink. (The upper town was possibly near Hunter in Forest County, while the middle and lower towns were probably in Venango County.) These Indians were later driven out of the area.

Cuscushing Indian town was located somewhere between the Tionesta and Little Tionesta Creeks; and Lawunakhannek Indian town was possibly at Tionesta where the first Protestant church west of the Alleghenies was built by Zeisberger in 1769.

Among the earliest white settlers were the Valentine family, who came to Jamieson's (Jamison's) Flats about 1797; John Middleton, the county's first teacher, who arrived in 1802; Eli Holeman, who operated a ferry in 1800 across the Allegheny and later worked for the Waterford and Milesburg Turnpike or Bald Eagle Road; George Siggins, who settled in the West Hickory area in 1818; Poland Hunter in 1805; and George Tubbs. Others came in small numbers between 1815 and 1840.

Cyrus Blood, a surveyor, who had been principal of the Chambersburg Academy, the Hagerstown Academy, and a member of the faculty of Dickinson College, established Blood's Station and later laid out the town of Marienville (see *Cyrus Blood House*). This town was the first county seat, where courts were held from 1857 until 1866, when five townships from Venango County were annexed to Forest. Tionesta, the county's only borough, became the next and present county seat. It derived its name from Tionesta Creek (*Tionesta* being an Iroquois word meaning "it penetrates the land"). The area was acquired by Lt. John Range, Sr., a Revolutionary War officer, who was granted a land warrant, taken out in the name of his oldest son Tehollas Range, in 1785 and settled here in 1815–16. His monument is located at the Tionesta courthouse. The large Tionesta state fish hatchery was opened in 1930, and the Tionesta Flood Control Dam was completed in 1941.

The town of Pigeon acquired its name from the enormous flights of now-extinct passenger pigeons which nested in the beech forest of this area. Cobbtown village remains are along Toms Run. William Armstrong was the founder of Armstrongs Mills (now Clarington), and the German settlement in Green Township was settled in 1842 by Herman Blume. Guitonville was named for Robert Guiton, a noted hunter, trapper, and woodsman.

The *Catawba Path* touched corners of Forest County at Spring Creek and again near the mouth of Millstone Creek. The *Goschgoschink Path* from West Hickory to Clearfield crossed Tionesta Creek at about Nebraska and ran south to Tylersburg. The Allegheny River is the county's chief waterway.

The county contains vast timberlands, amounting to more than two hundred thousand acres, almost three-fourths of its entire area, including part of both Cook Forest State Park and Allegheny National Forest. The firm of Wheeler & Dusenbury built a sawmill near Newtown in 1837 and one in the Endeavor area about 1853. Lumbering was an important early industry, reaching its peak in 1900. Timber still provides a major source of income, and the county has the richest history of lumbering and related folklore in the state. Large stands of hemlock have encouraged the development of chemical industries and tanneries.

Other natural resources include petroleum and natural gas. Harmony Township figured prominently during the oil rush; and Balltown, northeast of Tionesta between Mayburg and Porkey, was the center of the county's oil boom of 1882–83. Forest County had one stone blast furnace. Today important products include gravel, concrete, glass containers, and plastics. With its forests, mountains, and streams, it is an outdoor paradise.

The county's school system claims to have been the first in Pennsylvania to have drivers' training at all its high schools, to close all one-room schools, and to complete joint organization among all its districts.

The Forest County library system has two units, one at Marienville and the other at Tionesta. The library at Tionesta contains a collection of antique tools used in the logging and boat-building era.

4. Cook Homestead

Landmarks

1. Courthouse (brick), built in 1869 and still in use, is the county's second. The first courthouse, a frame structure erected in 1848 when the county seat was at Marienville, was put on ox wagons and hauled across the county when the courts were transferred to Tionesta in 1867. For many decades it sat not far from its successor but was torn down some years ago. *Location:* Tionesta.

2. County Jail (brick), which also contains a home for the sheriff (an old rural Pennsylvania custom), looks much older than the courthouse but was actually built in 1895. *Location:* Tionesta, beside courthouse.

3. Lawrence Tavern (frame), built in 1872 by William Lawrence, was an early river-town hotel with sample rooms, billiard parlor, and barbershop. The proprietor kept six horses and a number of carriages for the use of the guests. About 1930 it was called the Weaver House, and the barroom featured a blood-curdling mural of settlers being massacred by Indians. It may still exist under subsequent layers of paint and paper. It is presently the Towne House, patronized mostly by hunters and summer trade. *Location:* Tionesta, Elm Street.

4. Cook Homestead (frame) was constructed about 1868–70 by Andrew Cook, a judge. His father John Cook, the founder of Cooksburg, came to the Clarion River Valley in 1825–26, built a log cabin and sawmill on this property along Toms Run, and brought his family two years later. His wives bore him a total of seventeen children. John Cook died in 1858 and is buried in the Cooksburg cemetery. The Cook house is now used as a service building and as apartments for the Cook Forest State Park employees. *Location:* Cooksburg, at junction of River Drive and Pa. 36.

5. Cook Forest State Park (see also Clarion County) has one of the largest stands of virgin white pine in eastern America. Although its office and more than half of its area are in Clarion County, it really "belongs" to Forest County.

Anthony W. Cook, grandson of John Cook, whose family had cut thousands of acres of timber, had long planned to preserve the section of forest near his Cooksburg home. On an August day in 1910 he and Maj. M. I. McCreight of Du Bois sat on a log and pledged themselves to save the great trees, some of which had stood there since the disastrous drought and fire of 1644. Four times the Pennsylvania legislature turned down bills to buy the tract at a nominal price. Finally, in 1923 the Cook Forest Association was formed, with S. Y. Ramage of Oil City as president and Taylor Allderdice of Pittsburgh as vice president.

Thomas Liggett, Pittsburgh lumber dealer, led a campaign which raised $200,000—part of it from contributions made by school children. The commonwealth contributed $450,000 and purchased the 6,055 acre tract (later increased to 8,200 acres) on December 28, 1925, exactly 100 years after John Cook had erected his first sawmill in the area. This park was created by an act of Assembly in 1927.

Although the cyclone of August 18, 1956, destroyed some of the finest trees, there are still many in the forest over 200 feet in height and four feet in diameter. A survey taken about 1960 showed the existence of 600,000 trees with trunk diameters of eight inches or more. *Location:* Cooksburg, on Pa. 36 at Forest-Clarion County line.

Among the landmarks in the park are:

a. Shelter No. 1 (frame) was built by the Civilian Conservation Corps in depression days, about 1935. It includes a fine cut sandstone fireplace.

b. Saw Mill Buildings (frame) were constructed about 1940, when timber was still being cut in the forest. Currently one of them is being used as an exhibition building for an arts and crafts group in the area.

c. Memorial Fountain was built in 1950 on the Longfellow Trail in memory of the Cook Forest Association's founders.

6. Cook Mansion (frame) was built by Anthony W. Cook, wealthy lumberman, about 1880. It is still occupied by his descendants. *Location:* Cooksburg, on River Drive.

Note: Nearby is the Cooksburg frame schoolhouse built about 1890.

7. Cook Mausoleum, a marble vault built in 1916 following the death of Andrew Cook, son of John Cook, has spaces for twenty bodies. His was the first to be entombed within. On its back wall is a stained-glass window depicting a log drive out of the mouth of Toms Run, which enters the Clarion River at Cooksburg. *Location:* Cooksburg, at top of village cemetery.

8. Cyrus Blood House (frame) belonged to Cyrus Blood, one of the first land and lumber merchants in Forest County, who named his town Marienville for his daughter. The house was built about 1843 and still contains many of the original furnishings. Blood planted the stately hemlocks that form a lane in front.

8. *Cyrus Blood House*

Fortunately, the house was located far enough from the town to escape the disastrous fires of 1902 and 1913. *Location:* Marienville, off Hemlock Street, at Marienville School.

9. Buzzard Swamp on Muddy Fork is the site of a water fowl and wild animal refuge. It is accessible by automobile to within one mile, and the remainder of the distance can be covered by foot. *Location:* Four miles southeast of Marienville.

10. CCC Campsite, originally a Civilian Conservation Corps camp in the 1930s, was converted into a prisoner-of-war camp during World War II. Later it became a 4-H camp, but at present it is privately owned and is the location for nationally attended horse trail rides. *Location:* Duhring, twelve miles east of Marienville.

Pennsylvania Historical and Museum Commission Markers

Damascus Tionesta, U.S. 62
Goschgoschink U.S. 62, 0.9 mile south of East Hickory
Hickory Town U.S. 62, 2 miles south of East Hickory
Holeman Ferry U.S. 62, 3 miles southwest of Tionesta
Indian Paths U.S. 62, 2.3 miles south of East Hickory
Lawunakhannek U.S. 62, 0.2 mile north of East Hickory
Pigeon Pa. 66, 5 miles northeast of Marienville
Refugee Towns U.S. 62, 0.5 mile south of East Hickory; and U.S. 62, 1.5 mile south of Tionesta Station.

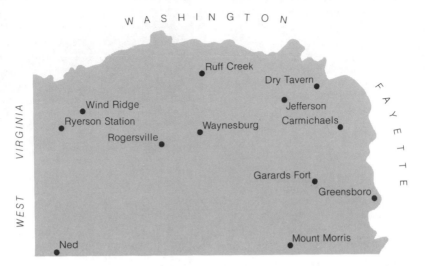

Greene County

Capsule History

Greene County, named for Maj. Gen. Nathaniel Greene, military strategist of the Revolution, was erected out of Washington County on February 9, 1796. It has an area of 578 square miles and a population of 36,090. This southwest corner of Pennsylvania was the scene of both Indian warfare and constant jurisdictional dispute between Virginia and Pennsylvania in the 1700s. Finally, in 1784 the first U.S. scientific survey completed the extension of the Mason and Dixon line and later established the western boundary of the county and the state.

Among the stations or outposts of early settlement were Fort Jackson of 1774 in Waynesburg, Fort Swan of 1774 near Carmichaels, Garard's Fort of 1777 at the town of that name, and Ryerson's blockhouse of 1792 near Wind Ridge. Among the county's pioneers were Creaux Bozarth, first settler on Whiteley Creek (about 1747); Augustine Dilliner in Dunkard Township (about 1754); and Rev. John Corbly. John Spicer, his wife, and five children were attacked by Indians on Dunkard Creek in 1774.

The county was the birthplace of Pennsylvania Governor and U.S. Senator Edward Martin, who also was a major general in World War II, as well as serving in the Spanish American War, Mexican border campaign, and during World War I. (His home is preserved in Washington, Pa.) Native son Albert B. Cummings, U.S. senator and governor of Iowa, acted as vice-president when President Harding died. Arthur

Inghram Boreman was elected first governor of West Virginia. Col. Reese Hill served the county twenty years in the state legislature and seven as speaker of the house. He also was active in securing pensions for widows of the War of 1812 and veterans of the Revolution. Dr. Jesse William Lazear, of Johns Hopkins University, served on the Yellow Fever Commission with Dr. Walter Reed at the time of the building of the Panama Canal and during the Spanish American War. William Thompson Hays began the county's first newspaper, the *Waynesburg Messenger,* in 1813.

A branch of the *Catawba Path* ran south in the county from about East Riverside to Mount Morris, with a fork near Garards Fort leading to the main path near Point Marion. *Catfish's Path* ran north from Brant Summit through Waynesburg and Ruff Creek, following much the course of U.S. 19. *Warrior's Branch Path* ran west from about Greensboro through Luke, Camp, Brant Summit, Bluff, and Nettle Hill to Morford, where it forked, the northern route leading past Rocklick, the southern to Cameron, W.Va. (The latter, a sixty-seven-mile path, is now used as a cross-country hikers' trail and is unique in that it crosses several ridges but not a single waterway. The trail scars were discovered in the 1940s, and the Warrior Trail Association, Inc., created in 1965, is studying the path and Indian artifacts found along the way. The association has also erected trail markers and shelters for hikers, and has located many of the original Mason and Dixon survey stones.)

In 1836 the Monongahela Navigation Company began improving that river for navigation, and the first railroad in the county was constructed in 1877. The county has preserved ten covered bridges.

Waynesburg, the county seat, was laid out in 1796 at the south fork of Ten Mile Creek and named for Gen. Anthony Wayne.

The bituminous coal industry is the most important in the county, which probably contains the richest coal lands in the state, with the Robena mine one of the largest in the commonwealth. The county had one stone blast furnace. Oil and natural gas production are other main enterprises. The Great Tanner Well, drilled in 1866, flowed for fifty years. In addition, Greene is the largest sheep-raising county in the state.

Greensboro was the early glass center of the county, as well as a key shipping point. The first glass factory (New Geneva) west of the Monongahela River and second in western Pennsylvania (see page 128) was moved about 1810 to Greene County (on l.r. 30068 east of Greensboro) where it was operated by James W. Nicholson, Albert Gallatin's brother-in-law and former partner, until 1849. Only the foundation scars remain.

Landmarks

1. Courthouse (brick) originally was constructed of logs in 1796. The second one, built of brick in 1800, was used exactly fifty years. Prior to the first building, courts were held in the home of Isaac Kline on Muddy Creek.

The present structure, erected in 1850, is a classic example of Colonial and Greek Revival architecture; its portico has columns with cast-iron capitals. Samuel and John Bryan, builders of the Fayette County courthouse, were the contractors, receiving $16,000 for their work. Within a copper box in the cornerstone, laid by the Free Masons on June 24, 1850, are memorabilia of the era, including copies of the *Waynesburg Messenger* and *Greene County Democrat* newspapers. The original bell, remolded in 1926, is now inside the building. Bradley Mohanna carved the first statue of Gen. Nathaniel Greene that surmounted the clock tower. A new statue and dome were created following a 1925 fire. In 1952–53 the building was completely restored, at which time the white paint,

7. *Greene County Historical Society Museum and Library*

applied in 1935, was removed from the bricks; and in 1968 it was redecorated. *Location:* Waynesburg, corner of High and Washington Streets.

2. Waynesburg College was founded in 1849, and in 1853 it was the first institution of higher learning to award degrees to women. It is the successor of Greene Academy (q.v.) and Madison College (Fayette County). Rev. Joshua Loughran of Greene Academy was the first president, followed by Rev. J. P. Wethee, former president of Madison. In 1849 the Pennsylvania Synod of the Cumberland Presbyterian Church requested proposals from various towns for contributions toward erecting buildings and endowing professorships for a college. Waynesburg won by volunteering to subscribe $5,000 to build a three-story brick building on a 50-by-70-foot lot on College Street.

First classes were held in 1849 in the Hayes Building, the site now designated by a plaque at the corner of Main and Washington Streets. The college was chartered in 1850 under the auspices of the Cumberland Presbyterian Church, and classes were held in that church. The same year the female seminary of the college met in the Baptist church. In 1851 Hanna Hall (brick), the first college building, was erected on the campus.

The first piano used by the college is on display in the Greene County Historical Society Museum, east of Waynesburg. In Paul R. Stewart Science Hall is one of the finest mineralogy and archeology museums in the county. *Location:* Waynesburg, on College Street (U.S. 19).

3. Mount Pleasant Methodist Church (brick) was built in 1872, the congregation having been organized before 1820. *Location:* Near Waynesburg, about 2.5 miles south of junction of Gordon Hill Road and U.S. 19.

4. Ganiear House (cut stone and fieldstone) was once owned by the Inghrams, John T. Hook, and later by Hiram Wood. At least three generations of the Hiram Wood Ganiear family have lived here. *Location:* Smith Creek, on Pa. 218, one mile south of Waynesburg.

5. J. B. Gordon House (cut stone) was built in 1843 by John Brice Gordon. This unique home of adapted Greek Revival architecture has two columns in front approached by impressive curved-stone steps. A stone stile is in the front yard.

Gordon, who owned much land in the area, sold his coal to J. V. Thompson (see *Oak Hill,* Fayette County). He married Delilah Inghram, who one day noticed that the red-brick house on the hill across the valley was on fire. She

150

rode over on horseback and offered to rebuild the home for the family in need. The same house can be seen from this property.

The present owner, George W. Gordon, is a grandson of the original builder. The family cemetery is on a hill nearby. *Location:* East of Waynesburg. Turn off U.S. 19 onto Gordon Hill Road (old brick); thence 0.6 mile to house on right.

6. George Gordon House (brick) was built about 1860 by George Gordon, son of John Brice Gordon. A stone stile is located in front of the house. *Location:* Near Waynesburg, on side road, 0.3 mile south of Gordon Hill Road, one mile west of J. B. Gordon house.

7. Greene County Historical Society Museum and Library (brick) is owned by the county and operated by the historical society, founded in 1925. This fifty-two-room mansion built in the early 1880s as the County Home (the original section an earlier private residence) was opened to the public in 1971 as a mid-Victorian mansion and museum. This outstanding endeavor includes a large collection of Indian artifacts, hand tools, and spinning wheels; rooms furnished as a country store, schoolhouse and an old-time kitchen; a railroad room; and collections of glass and pottery. Located on the nineteen-acre property is the old Waynesburg and Washington narrow-gauge steam locomotive (formerly situated at the Waynesburg fairgrounds). There are also a carriage house, a one-room brick schoolhouse, a smokehouse, and a large barn, as well as picnic grounds. The library contains three thousand volumes and extensive genealogical records. Plans are being made to move an old covered bridge to the property and restore it. *Museum hours:* Wednesday–Sunday, 1–4:30 P.M. *Library hours:* Wednesday–Saturday, 1–4:30 P.M. *Admission charge. Location:* Three miles east of Waynesburg, on old Pa. 21 (follow signs).

8. Harry House (stone) was built by Jacob Harry before 1831. The present owner is a fourth-generation descendant of the original family. *Location:* East of Waynesburg, on Pa. 188, 3.5 miles from Pa. 21.

Note: Other old stone houses along the same side of the road include the Crayne and Madlock houses. The latter has a stone porch.

9. Jefferson Presbyterian Church (brick), erected in 1845, is typical of many early churches having separate entrances for men and women. A new church building is located in front of the old one. *Location:* Jefferson, on Pine Street.

Note: Near the corner of Green and Pine Streets is the site of Monongahela College, the first Baptist college in western Pennsylvania. It was established in 1867 and operated at different times during the years 1869 and 1894.

10. Hughes House (stone) was built in 1814 with slave labor. The earliest owner of the house was Thomas Hughes, whose homestead later served as a way station for the underground railroad, helping slaves escape to Canada. The house is being restored for public visit. Hughes, who laid out the borough of Jefferson, was the county's first Catholic, and visiting priests occasionally held services at his house. *Location:* Jefferson, on Pa. 188.

11. Murdock House (fieldstone) was constructed in 1824 by the father of Mrs. Emma Syphers Murdock. *Location:* Carmichaels, 303 Old Town Road and Market Street.

Note: Next to the house is a covered bridge spanning Muddy Creek. A mill, converted into a shingle-covered residence, is located on the other side of the bridge. There are many old brick and log-covered houses in this section, called Old Town, which is situated partly on a peninsula formed by a curve in Muddy Creek.

12. Hathaway House (brick) was built in 1844 (date above door) by the Hathaway family and was later used as a store. The home, with the rear entrance surrounded by a courtyard, is still owned by the Hathaways. *Location:* Carmichaels, Old Town, 110 Market Street at Greene Street.

13. Greene Academy (brick and fieldstone) was built in 1790 as an Episcopal church. Through the efforts of James Carmichael, the building was chartered as the county's first institution of higher learning on March 20, 1810. This 25-by-32-foot structure continued to operate as an academy until 1860. Later it became a high school (1890–1930), a GAR headquarters, a private residence, and then an apartment house. The building has been restored and rededicated as the Greene Academy of Art, a nonprofit association founded in 1972. *Location:* Carmichaels, 310, 312, and 314 Market Street, near covered bridge in old section of town.

13. Greene Academy

14. Hartley Inn (brick), built in 1848, was originally a stagecoach stop called the Davidson House. The Jennings family bought the property in the late 1800s. Later owners were John Riley and the Hartley family. *Location:* Carmichaels, corner of Market and George Streets.

15. Biddle House (brick) was erected by Isaac Biddle in 1842 on a farm purchased in 1839. The construction date is above the front door. A large cut-stone and brick fireplace has been restored in the interior of the house. Also, a custom-made ceiling-to-floor cabinet, made exclusively for hat storage at the time one of the Biddle daughters married, has been preserved inside the house, which is still owned by the descendants of the original Biddle family. This property is on the site of Hughes' Fort (1768), which was once attacked by Indians. *Location:* One mile east of Carmichaels, on Jacob's Ferry Road.

16. Harper House (painted brick) was built about 1800 by Samuel Harper, who also constructed a stone springhouse at about the same time. *Location:* 1.2 mile south of Carmichaels, on Pa. 88, at bottom of Glade Hill.

17. Flenniken House (frame) was a hotel owned by Elias A. Flenniken, born in 1824. He had operated a livery stable in Greensboro and later was captain of a steamer on the Monongahela for several years. His wife was Mary Kerr. After leaving the river in the 1850s, he built the hotel and was still running it as late as 1888. *Location:* Greensboro, corner of Main and County Streets.

18. Monongahela House (brick) was a hotel built by John H. Ewing after the Civil War and operated until 1900. On the north side of the road near the Monongahela River is the site where the old ferry used to cross. The roads on both sides of the river are still visible. Among the noteworthy people who stayed at the hotel were Ulysses S. Grant and Grover Cleveland. *Location:* Greensboro, north side of County Street near river.

19. Monon Center (stone) was built as a grade school in 1904. The architect was James Perricho of Italy. In 1965 the school district abandoned the building and deeded it to the borough which in turn transferred it to the Monon Center Society in 1974. This nonprofit organization plans to have two museums. The two at this site will include a pioneer heritage room with Greensboro–New Geneva pottery, Gallatin glassware, Indian artifacts, and coal-mining exhibits. The second museum, pertaining to the Monongahela House (q.v.), will have river-boat models and other memorabilia of this type on display. *Hours:* Will be arranged. *Location:* Greensboro, on Second Street.

20. Blackshere Homestead (frame) originally consisted of 450 acres of land that was a wedding gift from William Gray of Grays Landing to his daughter Eliza in 1859. Eliza married James Edgar Blackshere, who built the house. The foundation is made from hand-cut stone, and the lumber came from pine and hemlock trees on the farm. It is still owned by descendants of this family. *Location:* Three miles north of Greensboro, on Pa. 88.

21. Goshen Baptist Church (brick), the first recorded religious congregation in the county, was organized before April 1771. It is now the John Corbly Memorial Baptist Church, named for its first pastor. The church was constituted by Rev. Isaac Sutton and Daniel Frisbee of the North Ten Mile Baptist Church. Corbly served this church until his death in 1803. The present edifice was built in 1862.

In the churchyard is a monument commemorating the site of Fort Garard, possibly built in 1777. The fort's first settler was Jacob Van Meter who arrived at Muddy Creek in 1769. The land on which the fort was built was warranted to John Garard in 1785.

Corbly's wife Elizabeth, son, and two daughters were killed on their way to church by Indians on May 10, 1782. Two other daughters were scalped but lived for at least three years. Elizabeth's grave is located in this church cemetery; the epitaph reads:

18. *Monongahela House*

Beneath the Indian tommy hawk,
Me and my babe we fell,
Was hurried suddenly away,
With Jesus for to dwell.

(See also *North Ten Mile Baptist Church,* Washington County, and *Turkeyfoot Regular Baptist Church,* Somerset County.) *Location:* Garards Fort, on Pa. 218.

22. Western Terminus of Mason and Dixon Survey is the point at which Indians of the Six Nations stopped Charles Mason and Jeremiah Dixon while they were surveying the boundary line between Maryland and Pennsylvania on June 22, 1767. At this spot, where the Warrior Path met the line, slightly east of what was known as the "second crossing" of Dunkard Creek, the Indians said they could not guarantee the party's safety if they went farther, for their understanding had been that the line should not extend beyond the "War Path." More than fifteen years later the Pennsylvania-Virginia line was completed (see *Pennsylvania Southwest Corner Monument*). A monument marks the Sinclair resurvey (1883) of the Pennsylvania–West Virginia boundary on the spot where the commissioners were stopped by the Indians. During the survey no corrections were made in the original line, but monuments were placed in the original molds. *Location:* Travel southeast of Mount Morris on l.r. 30017 to West Virginia line and continue on this road along Dunkard Creek to old Spencer Fetty Farm (3.3 miles from small bridge in Mount Morris to farm). A lane leads about 1.5 mile farther to marker on ridge.

23. Fort Swan House (painted brick), on land which possibly once belonged to Col. Charles Swan, is an early structure that has a large wooden porch extending across two sides. The Fort Swan site is 1.3 mile east of the historical marker across from the house. The fort was built in 1774 for protection against Indian raids. In 1767 the first settlers—Swan, Van Meter, Hughes, and Hupp—had crossed the Monongahela River into this area. *Location:* South of Dry Tavern, on Pa. 88, north of Carmichaels.

24. Old Stone House, an early structure constructed with fieldstone with a porch added later, is currently being remodeled. It was probably built by David Wise around 1805. *Location:* Just south of Ruff Creek, on U.S. 19.

25. Ross House (brick covered with stucco) first belonged to Thomas Ross. In 1833 Ross contracted with John Andrew to build the house, originally having six rooms, at a cost of $500. Ross hauled the logs for the basement beams with an ox team, and Andrew burned the bricks on the property. The house, with a fieldstone foundation, was built between March and November of 1834. Ross lived in this house only about a month when he died of pneumonia. (Andrew took his pay, went to Ohio, and built a blacksmith shop on one corner, a general store on another, and his home on a third. This crossroads formed the nucleus of Alliance, Ohio.) The Ross house was stuccoed in 1867. Ezra Hoge, the present owner, bought the property from Timothy Ross. *Location:* Near Dunns Station, on Pa. 221, 4.5 miles west of U.S. 19.

26. Old Drovers' Tavern (brick) was built in the 1840s. Later it was operated as the Ryerson Station Inn by one Supler. *Location:* Near entrance of Ryerson Station State Park, on Pa. 21.

Note: Also in this area were three blockhouses erected by Capt. James Paul's company in 1792, the same year that soldiers carrying supplies from Thomas Ryerson's mill clashed with Indians. At Ryerson State Park is an early brick house, now occupied by the park's caretaker.

27. Little Red Schoolhouse (brick), with a belfry and front porch, has been preserved as a memorial to the one-room schoolhouses of the past. *Location:* Between Waynesburg and Rogersville, on Pa. 21.

29. Jacktown Fairgrounds

28. Crow Rock, a large boulder along the side of the road, which has fallen from its original position, bears the inscription, "May 1, 1791 Sus. and Cath. Eliz.—Tina." This was the site where the Crow sisters were massacred by Indians. Two were killed outright, one lived for a few days after being scalped, and the fourth escaped. The Crow house was situated a little way down the road, along Crow Creek. *Location:* On Crow Creek Road, one mile from village of Crabapple (which is three miles on l.r. 30001 from Pa. 21, west of Wind Ridge).

Note: About one-and-one-half miles away is the site of an Indian burial ground, excavated by Carnegie Institute of Pittsburgh.

29. Jacktown Fair was organized July 6, 1866, by the Richhill Agricultural, Horticultural and Mechanical Society. It is the second oldest fair with an unbroken record of exhibitions in the United States. (Jacktown, shortened from Jacksonville, was the original name for the present village of Wind Ridge.) The fair, still sponsored by the agricultural society, is held annually in August as a nonprofit project for the improvement of the community. According to tradition, "you'll never die happy unless you've been to the Jacktown Fair." *Location:* Wind Ridge, on Pa. 21 at the southwest edge of village.

30. Wind Ridge Post Office (frame) has been a wagon shed, a church, and a GAR hall, and at present it is the post office. *Location:* Wind Ridge.

Note: There are many old houses, some covered log, in this community. The main road through town was once a drovers' path. Two early frame hotels still exist here on opposite sites of the street.

31. Pennsylvania Southwest Corner Monument marks the completion of the state's southern boundary by the Mason and Dixon line on November 18, 1784. Prior to this time only a temporary line marked the border between Pennsylvania and Virginia. On August 31, 1779, the states' commissioners agreed that the Mason and Dixon line would be extended to its full length, with Virginia ratifying on June 23, 1780, and Pennsylvania on September 23. (The commissioners for Pennsylvania were John Lukens and Archibald McClean, with James Madison and Robert Andrews for Virginia.) Joseph Reed, president of Pennsylvania, agreed with Thomas Jefferson's "proposal for astronomical determination" of the line. On April 23, 1781, the Pennsylvania commissioners and party were directed to cut a swath fifteen feet wide and mark the large trees. Due to threat of attack by the British, the work was delayed until May 1, 1782, and the line was finally completed in 1784. In 1883 the western extension of the line was resurveyed, and dilapidated and missing monuments were replaced. This square sandstone monument reads, "1883 P WV," "WV," "WV," and "P WV" on its north, west, south, and east sides, respectively. *Location:* Near Ned. Go west from Garrison on l.r. 30037 to its intersection with l.r. 30001; thence on this ridge road (l.r. 30001) through Ned and directly west on poor township road which is intersected by l.r. 30001. Monument is about one mile west on this road.

Pennsylvania Historical and Museum Commission Markers

Fort Jackson   Waynesburg, East High Street at Woodland Avenue

Fort Swan   Pa. 88 south of Dry Tavern

Garard's Fort   T. 616, 0.6 mile east of Garards Fort

Greene Academy   Carmichaels, on Pa. 88 near intersection of Greene and Vine Streets

Monongahela College   Jefferson, Pa. 188 at Greene and Pine Streets

Old Glassworks   L.r. 30068 east of Greensboro

Ryerson's Blockhouse   Wind Ridge, Pa. 21

Waynesburg College   Waynesburg, U.S. 19

JEFFERSON

Smicksburg
Covode
Gilgal
Hamill
Plumville
Cherry Tree
Creekside
Ernest
Cookport
Clymer
Diamondville
Shelocta
Indiana
Camerons Bottom
Brush Valley
Coral
Lewisville
Saltsburg
Josephine
Black Lick
Armagh
Tunnelton
Strangford
Blairsville

ARMSTRONG

CLEARFIELD

CAMBRIA

WESTMORELAND

Indiana County

Capsule History

Indiana County, named for its original inhabitants the Indians, was organized March 12, 1803, out of portions of Westmoreland and Lycoming Counties, although it remained under the jurisdiction of the former until 1806. It now has an area of 825 square miles with a population of 79,451.

About 1727 James Le Tort established a trading post near present-day Shelocta. At Cherry Tree was "Canoe Place," the head of canoe navigation on the west branch of the Susquehanna River. One of the first white settlers to clear a "tomahawk" claim in the county was George Findley in the late 1760s. In 1772 Fergus, Samuel and Joseph Moorhead, James Kelly, and James Thompson moved to the county west of Indiana. The majority of early migrants were Scotch-Irish, coming from the Cumberland Valley. Rev. John Jamison, of the Associate Reformed Presbyterian faith, was the first resident minister in the county, arriving in 1796. German Lutherans, many coming from Virginia, began to settle in the area by 1795.

The county seat, Indiana, was laid out in 1805 on land given by George Clymer, a Philadelphia landholder and signer of the Declaration of Independence. Blairsville, laid out in 1818, became a borough in 1825. (In 1786 James Campbell was granted warrants for a tract of land called "Lisbon" in this area.) Blairsville was important as the western terminus of the Huntingdon, Cambria, and Indiana Turnpike, better known as the Northern Pike. From 1829 to 1860 it was a main depot on the Pennsylvania Canal.

Four principal Indian trails, two of the most important in the area, crossed Indiana County. Most traveled were the *Catawba Path,* the main north-south route, and the *Frankstown Path,* variously called the Kittanning or Armstrong-Kittanning Trail, used more than any other across the mountains. The Catawba Path, running from near Olean, N.Y., to the Carolinas, entered Indiana County below Hamilton, passing through or near Trade City, Georgeville, and Home. It crossed Crooked Creek and intersected the Kittanning (Frankstown) Trail at Shaver's Spring west of the Indiana University campus. Thence it ran through Penoland's Town (Homer City), crossed Black Lick Creek near Palmerton, and forded the Conemaugh close to New Florence. The Frankstown Path entered the county near Emeigh, followed much the course of Pa. 240 to Cookport, forded Two Lick Creek at Shawnee Bottom, and ran thence to Diamondville and Penn Run. From there it went west to Two Licks, passed through what is now the Indiana University campus and near Moorhead's Fort, and followed the general route of U.S. 422 to Shelocta. The *Cherry Tree Portage* ran from the famed tree south for about two miles, then followed the Frankstown Path. The *Frankstown-Venango Path* branched off the main trail east of Cherry Tree and ran through Purchase Line, Marion Center, Frantz, and Smicksburg, thence through the northwest corner of Indiana County.

The county's first gristmill was built on a run flowing into Black Lick Creek in 1773. Agriculture, salt-refining, iron-smelting, coal-mining, grinding of grain, distilling of alcohol, hide-tanning, and lumbering were the main industries before 1850. Salt wells were located along the Conemaugh and Kiskiminetas Rivers. Saltsburg (laid out in 1816 by Andrew Boggs and incorporated as a borough in 1838) derived its name from salt discovered in the vicinity in 1812. The first salt well was drilled in 1813 by William Johnson near Saltsburg and resulted in the Great Conemaugh Salt Works. Coal-mining and agriculture are still thriving industries. The county has had four stone blast furnaces. The dense virgin pine forests of former years have given way to field-grown evergreens, and today the county is known as the Christmas tree capital of the world.

There are four covered bridges in the county: Thomas, built in 1879, off l.r. 32061 between Creekside and Shelocta; Kintersburg, built in 1877, off l.r. 32063 between Gaibleton and Tanoma; Harmon, built in 1910, off l.r. 32072; and Trusal, built in 1870, off l.r. 32072.

Landmarks

1. Old Courthouse (brick and stone), of Second Empire style, was the second Indiana County courthouse, built in 1871 at a cost of $186,000. This structure, with a clock tower, replaced an earlier one dating from 1809. Courts had first been held in the upper story of a stone jail constructed in 1807. The 1871 building was restored by the National Bank of the Commonwealth. A new courthouse was dedicated in 1970 to replace the old one, which is now occupied by offices. *Location:* Indiana, 601 Philadelphia Street at Sixth Street.

2. First National Bank Building (brick), built in the early 1800s, housed Indiana's first banking house, opened in 1857 by John T. Hogg and managed by William C. Boyle. In 1864 the First National Bank was organized here with James Sutton as president (see also *Sutton-Elkin House*). The title to the lot can be traced back to June 15, 1808, when it was sold to William Wrigley of Greensburg. Succeeding owners included William Clark in 1809, William Houston in 1822, George Christy's shoe store in 1865, Henry Hall's news agency and book store in 1870, Houk Drug Store, and James S. Blair in 1920. At present the building houses a restaurant and Republican party headquarters. *Location:* Indiana, Philadelphia and Sixth Streets.

3. Fisher House (frame) was the home of Gov. John S. Fisher prior to his election and until his death. (See *Gov. John Fisher Birthplace.*) *Location:* Indiana, 220 North Sixth Street.

4. Stewart House (brick and stucco) was the home of Alexander Stewart, a prominent citizen and the father of motion-picture star James Stewart. (See *History House.*) *Location:* Indiana, 104 North Seventh Street.

5. History House (brick), also referred to as Memorial Hall, was built by John Sutton and was later the residence of Silas M. Clarke, associate justice of the Pennsylvania Supreme Court. It was built in 1869 on the site of Indiana County's first academy building, opened in 1816. The county bought the home from the Clarke heirs in 1917 for $20,000. After World War I the American Legion removed the partitions between several rooms to increase meeting space. In 1951 the Indiana County Historical and Genealogical Society moved its headquarters into the building, where it also maintains a library and museum.

1. Old Courthouse

On the front lawn is the signature stone from the Alexander Stewart hardware store, which was established in 1853 and stood on the site of the Savings and Trust Company, corner of Philadelphia and Eighth Streets. (See *Stewart House.*) Tours and visits by arrangement. *Location:* Indiana, Wayne Avenue and Sixth Street.

6. Log House Museum was built by Abner Kelly, an ancestor of James Stewart, in Shelocta in the 1840s. It was torn down and reconstructed at its present site in 1961. The following year it was dedicated. Furniture of the pioneer period is displayed on two floors. *Hours:* Memorial Day–Labor Day: weekends, 2–5 P.M. *Donation. Location:* Indiana, Wayne Avenue and Sixth Street.

Note: Nearby is the first community cemetery, known as Memorial Park, which was in use before the town was laid out.

7. Indiana University began in 1875 as a state normal school for the training of teachers. The Student Union Building is on the site of Shaver's spring and is marked by a fountain plaque. The school, noted for its department of music, is the only university in the commonwealth that is completely state owned.

  a. John Sutton Hall (brick), the original college building and one of the finest of its kind at that time, is still standing.

  b. Sutton-Elkin House (brick), known as Breezedale, is the oldest structure on the campus. George Cedric, first passenger agent for the Pennsylvania Railroad in Indiana, sold the property to James Sutton,

9. Moorhead House

brother of John Sutton (see *History House*) and first president of the First National Bank in Indiana. Sutton married Sarah Stansbury, a teacher in Blairsville. This Victorian house was built by 1868. When the Suttons owned it, the estate included a driveway gate that closed automatically. Sutton died in 1870, and the home was sold in 1899 to John P. Elkin, state supreme court justice. Elkin added a law library and a Turkish room, which has a hexagonal tile fireplace. A cupola on top of the third story provides a fine view. The structure became part of the campus in 1947 and was first used as a men's dormitory. It later housed the music, foreign language, and art departments. Since a recent remodeling and restoration, it houses alumni offices, guest rooms, a library, and other rooms. *Location:* School Street between Seventh and Oakland Streets.

8. White's Woods Nature Center is on land originally owned by Thomas White and his son, Harry White, both well-known judges of Indiana County. An English-style estate was planned here but never completed. The foundation of the gatekeeper's house is all that remains on the property, which has been developed with marked trails for nature study. *Location:* Indiana, at end of North Twelfth Street.

9. Moorhead House (stone), a small structure stuccoed at a later date, was built about 1792 near the site of a log fort (blockhouse) erected in 1781. Both buildings were constructed by Fergus Moorhead, who in 1772 came from Franklin County with his family and friends to settle here. While at Kittanning between 1776 and 1777, Moorhead was captured by Indians. His companion, Andrew Simpson, was scalped and killed. This casualty is believed to be the first in western Pennsylvania during the Revolutionary War. After eleven months Moorhead was exchanged for a British prisoner, rejoined his family, and later erected a log blockhouse as his cabin.

In 1907 Ellsworth Brown Campbell bought the property. The stone house was later used for storage of farm implements and is in dire need of attention by some historically minded organization or individual. It is one of the few remaining buildings of its kind in the region.

On the same property are foundation ruins of another early structure and a brick springhouse. This was the site of the first permanent settlement in the area. *Location:* 0.6 mile west of Indiana, on Philadelphia Road extension 0.4 mile east of its junction with Franklin Road (about 150 yards south of historical marker on old U.S. 422).

10. Keystone Generating Station is one of the first and one of the largest mine-mouth, electric-generating stations in the world. Using five million tons of coal annually, the plant is designed to supply power for thirty to forty years. Its twin smokestacks are 800 feet high. It can best be viewed from the Power Vista, an overlook off Pa. 156 near the site that provides information about the plant. *Hours:* May 30–September 15, daily 1–8 P.M. *Location:* One mile south of Shelocta, off Pa. 156.

Note: Another smokestack 1,216 feet high is at the Homer City generating plant.

11. Creekside Station (frame) is a beautiful example of one of the few remaining railroad stations once common along the Buffalo, Rochester & Pittsburgh route, now the Baltimore & Ohio. *Location:* Creekside.

12. Cumming's Dam was built in 1908 by the Buffalo, Rochester & Pittsburgh Railroad to provide a water supply for its steam locomotives. The dam has a span of 455 feet and is maintained to provide fishing and other recreation. *Location:* Near Ernest, off Pa. 110 (in Rayne Township at Blue Spruce Park).

13. Stonehouse Museum

13. Stonehouse Museum was built in 1830, eight years before Saltsburg became a borough. It was purchased in 1968 by the Saltsburg area branch of the Indiana County Historical and Genealogical Society. It is furnished with interesting early memorabilia. *Hours:* April 15–October 15: Saturdays, 1–4 P.M. Group tours by appointment. *Donation.* *Location:* Saltsburg, 105 Point Street.

Note: Another stone house at 214 Salt Street (Pa. 286) was a hotel during the days of the canal, and is located across from an old railroad station.

14. Saltsburg Academy (brick) was built in 1851 and opened the following year. This coeducational school originally cost $3,300 with an additional $300 for the cupola. At first a civic venture (although W. W. Woodend, a Presbyterian, was its principal until 1859), it was purchased by the Presbyterian Church in 1870 and renamed Memorial Institute. It was in operation after 1880, and probably at least for a decade more. The building was used as a public school until 1912. *Location:* Saltsburg, High and Point Streets.

15. Saint Matthews Roman Catholic Church (brick) was built in 1847 and is adjacent to an early cemetery. It is now used for storage. A Catholic church erected in 1960 stands next to it. *Location:* Saltsburg, Cathedral and Washington Streets.

16. Ebenezer Church (brick) was organized about 1790. Joseph Henderson, its first regular pastor, served from 1799 to 1824. The congregation has erected four churches, two log and two brick. The present and fourth structure was built in 1870–71. *Location:* Lewisville, on l.r. 32004 northeast of Saltsburg.

Note: In a nearby cemetery is the grave of John Montgomery, who died November 11, 1840, at age eighty-one. He was born in County Antrim, Ireland, came to America in 1774, and enlisted in 1776, serving as Washington's bodyguard all through the Revolution. His monument is signed, "Littell, S.C. [probably the stonecutter] Blairsville."

17. Pennsylvania Canal Tunnel and Aqueduct (stone) were completed in 1829. The 412-foot aqueduct with elliptical stone arches spanned the Conemaugh River on the western side of the tunnel, which was cut through limestone. The tunnel was 817 feet long, 22 feet wide, and 14 feet high. Its builders were Alonzo Stewart, Hart Stewart, and Thompson Neel. It was the third canal tunnel in the United States, built before any railroad tunnel in the nation. Due to danger of falling rocks, a Gothic stone arched ceiling was added to the tunnel in 1831. The tunnel has been closed since the dam was built, for it would have drained the reservoir. *Location:* About 1.5 mile up Conemaugh River from Tunnelton at Conemaugh Dam, near former railroad bridge now used as access road. (From U.S. 22 take l.r. 64057.) Western portal is visible at foot of hillside and in line with remnants of aqueduct piers in water. Eastern portal is accessible over old Pennsylvania Railroad bed only at times when water in dam reservoir is low.

Note: The Conemaugh Dam was completed September 1953 and is one of the largest flood-control dams in western Pennsylvania. Constructed of concrete, it is 137 feet high, 1,265 feet long, and has 14 crest gates. The maximum pool extends twenty-one miles up the Conemaugh and Black Lick Valleys and can impound 11.76 billion cubic feet of water. Below the dam are the remains of two old railroad tunnels and bridges built in 1883 and 1905.

18. Blairsville Bridge Abutments (stone) are all that remain of the first bridge at this location, built in 1821–22 for $15,000. This 300-foot structure, of Wormweg style, was the largest single-arch bridge in the United States at that time. James Moore was the contractor. The bridge fell in 1874 and was replaced by another in 1875. A third structure was erected in 1889 following the Johnstown Flood, which destroyed the second bridge. The fourth and present bridge, built in 1934–35, is adjacent to the abutments of the original one. *Location:* Blairsville, spanning the Conemaugh River between Indiana and Westmoreland Counties.

19. Marshall House (brick) was built by James Campbell about 1820. Early owners were a blacksmith named Thomas, Sarah Lindsey, Alexander Nesbett, and Samuel Baird. In 1840 Baird sold the property to Dr. Robert Johnson Marshall. The property originally included a granary and stables. Private residence. *Location:* Blairsville, 125 Market Street, between Spring and Main Streets.

20. Saint Peter's Episcopal Church (brick stuccoed), the oldest surviving church structure in Indiana County, was built in 1830, a gift of William G. Davis who was on the building committee. Its contractor was Robert Gregory. Church meetings had begun August 17, 1828, before the church was erected. The first rector was David C. Page, and S. K. Brunot conducted the first service. Alonzo Livermore, one of the promoters of the Pennsylvania Canal, was influential in establishing the church. Unfortunately the earliest records of this church have been lost. The adjacent rectory was built in 1889. *Location:* Blairsville, on West Campbell Street between North Walnut and Spring Streets.

21. Antes Snyder House (brick) was the home of the grandson of Pennsylvania's third governor Simon Snyder. In 1864 Antes Snyder moved to Blairsville and engineered the right of way for the Pennsylvania Railroad. *Location:* Blairsville, 36 East Campbell Street.

22. (Proposed) Blairsville Museum (brick) was originally built as a private residence in 1840. In the future it will be restored as a community museum. *Location:* Blairsville, Spring Street.
Note: "The Conemaugh" hand fire pumper purchased in 1828 by the borough is in excellent condition and is in the nearby firehouse on West Campbell Street.

23. Cunningham House (log completely concealed) was one of the first three homes erected when Blairsville was laid out in 1818. At this time a contest was held in which a free lot was given to the person who built his house first. Among the men who participated—John Cunningham, Issac Green, and James Rankin—the winner was Green. It is now adjacent to a large brick market and is behind the old Lintner house. *Location:* Blairsville, near corner of West Market and Spring Streets. (Structure in front of log house is brick with stucco and faces Market Street.)

Note: Another early house built about the same year is located at 146 South Walnut Street.

24. Artley House (frame) was built in the manner of an early railroad station in 1852 by Daniel Artley, master carpenter for the Pennsylvania Railroad, which ran past the house down old Main Street to the wharf at the river. After Artley's death the house was sold to Samuel Miller, an attorney. It is reputed that President Taft visited the Millers in this house. The Biesingers purchased the property in 1947. *Location:* Blairsville, 304 South Walnut Street.

25. Railroad Station House (frame), converted into a beautiful residence, was built as a station in 1851 when the Pennsylvania Railroad was completed to Blairsville. It later became the home of the Zimmer family, early residents. *Location:* Blairsville, 152 Old Main Street at Liberty Street.

26. Graff House (brick) was owned by Henry Graff in 1837 and was sold to his brother John in 1851. This L-shaped home formerly had four porches and has nine fireplaces. Bricks from an outside oven were used to build an adjacent garage. On the property near the house is a smaller red brick building, originally a stable but later used as a hiding place for escaped slaves. (John Graff was an agent of the underground railroad.) In 1847 John bought the warehouse business belonging to his brothers Henry and Peter. *Location:* Blairsville, 195 South Liberty Street.
Note: John's son Alexander lived in the Graff house at 216 South Liberty in 1857. It was purchased by Charles Graff in 1969.

27. Smith Station House (brick) was built as a summer home by Robert Smith, a broker and coal operator. His grandfather settled in the area in 1797. Robert purchased the property from Moss Stewart in 1825. It is reputed that "Buffalo Bill" Cody visited here while traveling with his show, which performed at the Old Town Hall (now gone) in Blairsville. The house was later purchased by William Torrance. *Location:* About 1.5 mile north of Blairsville, on Socialville Road off U.S. 22.
Note: The old Brainard-Earhart brick farmhouse nearby, built in 1833, has been completely surrounded by strip-mining.

28. Packsaddle Gap was believed in the canal and portage railroad days to be haunted by a man who accidentally shot his girl friend, mistaking her for a deer. A widely known landmark, it was utilized by the Frankstown Path, Northern Pike, Pennsylvania Canal, Pennsylvania Railroad, and William Penn Highway as an access route to the west. *Location:* From Blairsville go east for two miles on Old William Penn Highway; turn south past golf course and through village of Strangford; continue 1.5 mile to open coal field on I.r. 32179 at lower end of village for fine view through gap.

29. Josephine Furnace and Coke Company (brick buildings) was established in 1907 at a cost of $1 million by the owners Corrigan, McKinney & Company two years after the founding of the town of Josephine (originally called Bells Mills). A second blast furnace was erected in 1911. The firm later went bankrupt. During World War I ammunition was made here. At present there is a mill for making rock dust for mines. A retaining wall, built when U.S. 119 was cut through the slag pile, is still existent. *Location:* One mile north of Black Lick, on old U.S. 119 along Black Lick Creek.

30. Luther Chapel (brick) was built on a lot purchased in 1850 for five dollars. It cost $2,500 to construct and was dedicated in 1852. Services had been started in 1828 in the Black Lick School by Rev. Peter Sahm. *Location:* Coral, off U.S. 119 on Power Plant Road.

31. Ewing's Mill (frame with stone foundation) was built in 1821 and put in operation about 1824 by Christian Keller. It was purchased by John Ewing in 1913. It is one of the few early American flour mills still in existence in this area. The structure contains a McCormick turbine, built in 1869, and an Oliver Evans hoist. The original records have been preserved inside the building. The old mill, containing a country store, an 1880 saloon, and a museum, has been restored by Ray Rodkey and William Rodgers as a tourist attraction and is now operated by the William Rodgers family. Tours by appointment. *Location:* Strongstown, ten miles east of Indiana on U.S. 422.

32. Truby House (brick) was built about 1833 by Simeon Truby, who kept a store in this community. The Nesbitt family occupied the home at a later date, and at present it is the Clay Antique Workshop. *Location:* Brush Valley, on Pa. 56 (near center of village).

33. Buena Vista Iron Furnace (cut stone) was erected in 1847 by McClelland & Com-

pany during the Mexican War. In 1853 it was absorbed by Cambria Ironworks, and later owned by Warren Delano, uncle of Franklin D. Roosevelt. In 1957 the Delano Coal Company donated the blast furnace to the Historical and Genealogical Society of Indiana. This is the only remaining one of four charcoal iron furnaces in the county. It is now in deteriorating condition. *Location:* Between Brush Valley and Armagh, off Pa. 56 at Black Lick Creek. Follow U.S. 22 to Armagh and Pa. 56 north 2.25 miles to north end of bridge over Black Lick Creek. Turn left and continue on dirt road 200 to 300 feet. Furnace is below bank on south side of railroad track.

Note: An old blacktop road is within seventy-five feet of the furnace. It was the highway before the bridge was built.

34. Saint Patrick's Roman Catholic Church (frame) was erected in 1872 on land purchased on July 2, 1776, by Joseph Cauffman and another merchant by the name of Cottringer from Philadelphia. Although Cauffman and Cottringer wanted to establish a Catholic settlement here, nothing much was done until 1806 to 1815. In 1806 Cauffman transferred the tract to Mark Wilcox and Rev. Matthew Carr with the proviso it should be held for a house of worship. In 1810 it was transferred to the bishop of Philadelphia. There is evidence that the parish is an offshoot of the Loretto colony of Father Demetrius Gallitzin. A log church was completed about 1821–22. Between 1827 and 1832 a stone church was built, and the Franciscan brothers later maintained an orphanage here until it was moved to Pittsburgh. They also conducted the first seminary for the Diocese of Pittsburgh until Bishop O'Connor transferred it to Pittsburgh. Only traces of the second church's foundation remain in the woods adjacent to the cemetery. The third church was erected in 1852 and, according to tradition, burned in 1869. In 1870–72 the fourth and present building was constructed. Among the many priests who served this congregation were Terence McGirr, Bonaventure Maguire, William Lambert, Richard Phelan (fourth bishop of Pittsburgh), and Augustine Marzhauser. *Location:* Camerons Bottom, 2.5 miles north of old Benjamin Franklin Pike (now U.S. 422), in Pine Township (near Yellow Creek).

35. Diamondville Cut is a man-made gorge for the passage of a branch of the Penn Central Railroad. It was opened about 1901 by the D. F. Keenan Company, which lost money on the project and went bankrupt. Its purpose

42. *McCormick House*

was to eliminate six very crooked miles of railroad. The cut is about one-fourth mile long and one hundred feet deep below the trestle, which is now closed to automobile traffic. *Location:* Diamondville.

36. Stump Fence, composed of stumps pulled in clearing fields, was a type of fence found almost exclusively in northern Pennsylvania. This picturesque row is one of the few remaining anywhere. *Location:* About one mile east of Cookport, on north side of Pa. 240.

37. Cherry Tree Joe McCreery Grave is the burial site of Joseph McCreery (1805–95). Much folklore has grown up around this famous Pennsylvania lumberman; and many of the tales that first evolved about him were later told about Paul Bunyan. McCreery, who served in the Eleventh Pennsylvania Cavalry Regiment of the Civil War, lived in Cherry Tree, an important corner of the 1768 Pennsylvania purchase. *Location:* Cherry Tree Cemetery.

38. Pennsylvania Purchase Monument is at the junction of Indiana, Cambria, and Clearfield Counties (see *Canoe Place,* Clearfield County).

Note: Purchase Line Academy, a boarding school established in 1873 and operated

until 1913, is off Pa. 286 near the village of Purchase Line.

39. Gilgal Presbyterian Church (brick) was organized in 1808 under Redstone Presbytery with James Galbreath installed as the first regular pastor. He served until 1817. The first church of 1810 was of log construction; the second, built in 1838, was brick. The third and present church, with a tower, was erected in 1887. *Location:* North of Hamill. From U.S. 119 turn west 0.1 mile on l.r. 32096 to Gilgal Road; thence 0.6 mile to church.

Note: In the Gilgal cemetery is the grave of Samuel Brady, uncle of the famous Indian scout and one of those who took part in the 1756 Armstrong expedition.

40. Mahoning United Presbyterian Church (frame) was organized about 1825. This handsome building was constructed of adzed timbers and round joists with the bark left on. It is now in poor condition and presently used as a voting place for East Mahoning Township. *Location:* 0.7 mile west of Gilgal, on l.r. 32082.

41. Covode Academy (frame), with a square tower now almost hidden by evergreens, was established by the Presbyterian Church in 1863 and operated until after 1888. From 1870 it was a union effort with the Methodist Episcopal Church. This one-room school, 34 by 42 feet still containing at least one very early wooden student's desk, later became a youth center and is now vacant. *Location:* Covode, at cemetery on U.S. 119.

42. McCormick House (stone) was the home of John B. McCormick, inventor of the water turbine used in early hydroelectric plants, including those in Niagara Falls and Saint Petersburg, Russia. He also published several musical works. One of his turbines operates at Ewing's Mill (q.v.). Inside the house is a model of the 1876 steam Hercules turbine, the design of which is basic to all the hydroelectric plants in the world. This structure was partly built by Judge Joshua Lewis in 1817, and the tower was added by McCormick. The home was later owned by the James Stewart family. *Location:* Three miles northeast of Smicksburg, off Pa. 954 on McCormick Road.

43. Gov. John Fisher Birthplace (frame) was the birthplace of John S. Fisher (1867–1940), whose family still owns the house after more than 120 years. Fisher won the Pennsylvania governorship in 1926 by the largest majority given any man for this office in the state's history. He supported an extensive state road-building program, revised the state fiscal system, and promoted conservation of natural resources. *Location:* From Plumville go north for 0.9 mile on Pa. 210; turn right 0.2 mile on Fisher Road.

Pennsylvania Historical and Museum Commission Markers

John B. McCormick   U.S. 22 west of Armagh

John S. Fisher   Pa. 85 east of Plumville

Moorhead's Fort   Old U.S. 422, 0.6 mile west of Indiana

Purchase of 1768   Cherry Tree, U.S. 219

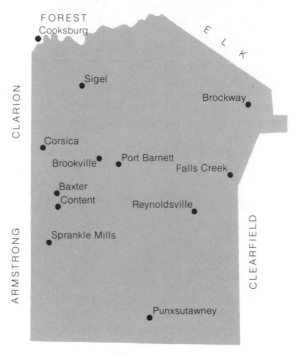

Jefferson County

Capsule History

Jefferson County was named for Thomas Jefferson, who was president at the time of the county's founding on March 26, 1804. The county was erected out of Lycoming, and by the same act attached to Westmoreland. This political jurisdiction was transferred to Indiana County in 1806 and lasted until 1830, when Jefferson became independent. In 1824 the county began to vote for its own officers, with John Jenks, Andrew Barnett, and John Lucas elected as commissioners.

The county was diminished in size in 1843 when a part of Elk County was taken from Jefferson and again in 1848 when Forest County was derived solely from Jefferson. Then in 1868 its acreage was increased by a small section of Clearfield County. Today it has 652 square miles with a population of 43,695.

The first pioneers were Joseph and Andrew Barnett, who came from central Pennsylvania in the 1790s and settled on Sandy Lick Creek. Here, at the village known

164

as Port Barnett, was the site of a sawmill built in 1795 by the Barnett brothers and Samuel Scott. Joseph Barnett became the first postmaster and owner of a hotel and store there. Near this site is a roadside park developed by an industrial firm. Many early settlers in the county were Revolutionary War soldiers who sought land and had come by way of the Susquehanna and Waterford Turnpike or on the Susquehanna and Allegheny Rivers.

Several Indian trails crossed the county. The *Catawba Path* entered near Clarington and followed much the course of Pa. 36 past Sigel, Brookville, and Stanton, then turning toward Worthville and Hamilton. The early Olean Road to Kittanning followed this path. The *Goschgoschink Path* followed the general course of U.S. 322 by Corsica and Brookville and north of Rathmel. The *Great Shamokin Path* (over which Marie Le Roy, Barbara Leininger, and other captives were led on their way to Kittanning in 1755) entered near Troutville, running through or near Big Run, Punxsutawney, and Trade City. The *Punxsutawney-Venango Path* ran past Frostburg and Ringgold, toward Hawthorn. The *Venango-Chinklacamoose Path* followed the Goschgoschink through Brookville, thence by or near Emerickville, Sandy Valley, and on to West Liberty.

In 1814 soldiers under command of Maj. William McClelland encamped at Soldiers Run near Reynoldsville and at Port Barnett on their way to Erie on the old State Road.

Brookville, due to its location on the Erie Turnpike and the confluence of the Sandy Lick and North Fork Creeks, was chosen for the county seat and laid out in 1830. It is reputed that Moses Knapp, a settler who came to Port Barnett in 1796 and operated a gristmill, built a log house here in 1801. Col. A. A. McKnight of Brookville organized the famous Wild Cat Regiment of the Civil War in 1861.

The county's oldest and largest town is Punxsutawney, settled in 1814 by John Jacob Fisher and in 1816 by Abraham Weaver, Dr. John Jenks, and Rev. David Barclay. It was laid out in 1819–21 by Barclay at an old Indian village. The name is derived from the Indian words *Ponks-utennick,* meaning "the town of the Ponkies" or "gnat-town." According to legend, the Indians told a Moravian missionary, John Heckewelder, that an old Indian sorcerer, Chinklacamoose, frightened people by appearing in grotesque forms. The sorcerer was finally killed and his ashes burned and scattered in the air. The ashes turned into "punkies." This area was mentioned in diaries of Moravian missionaries Christian Frederick Post, who visited here in 1758, and John Ettwein, who passed through in 1772.

Many stories have been told concerning wolves, bears, and panthers in the county, along with hunting expeditions, especially those of hunter Bill Long, who died in 1880. Other tales have been related about the halcyon lumbering days.

The log railroad era began here, with the first such railroad operating in 1874 in Jefferson County and Pennsylvania's last in 1948 in Elk County. The rich timberlands brought from New York and New England numerous individuals and companies making heavy investments at the headwaters of the Clarion River. After much of the forest land was depleted, coal, natural gas, and building stone provided resources for mineral industries. Coal was first discovered in the county at Pine Creek Township by a man named Douglass.

Today mine and quarry products are the main industries, followed by glass and clay products. The county has a varied economy, with slightly more invested in agriculture than in manufacturing.

Landmarks

1. Courthouse (brick), the county's second, was built in 1868 at a cost of $78,742, not counting $668 for a bell and $725 for a clock. It was extensively altered in 1927. The first courthouse, a brick structure, was built in 1832 at a cost of $3,000 and was two stories high, with a one-story wing. An addition was made about 1850. It was torn down in 1866. *Location:* Brookville.

2. Marlin's Opera House (brick) when built in 1883 was one of the finest in northwestern Pennsylvania. Now the Marlin Building, it houses a clothing store and offices. *Location:* Brookville, 233 West Main Street.

3. Jefferson County Historical and Genealogical Society Museum (brick) is located in the Brady Craig house, built about 1840. This headquarters also houses a library and displays antiques and artifacts of the area. This is one of the first brick houses built in the area and is currently painted buff. *Hours:* Sunday, 2–5 P.M. or by appointment. *Location:* Brookville, about 236 Jefferson Street, above and behind courthouse.

4. McKnight House (white brick, painted gray), a typical Victorian house dating from shortly after the Civil War, was the home of Dr. W. J. McKnight, civic leader, historian, and physician. During the early years of his practice, he and other young physicians dug up the body of a man who had died of fever and began dissecting it. Discovery of this act shocked the town but helped to promote the 1867 legislation permitting dissection for scientific purposes. The home is still in the McKnight family. *Location:* Brookville, 105 West Main Street.

5. White Elephant, a tremendous, white brick theater, was built in 1915 to provide a place for Chautauqua troupes and other traveling shows. After motion pictures killed off road shows, it was used for boxing matches and other entertainment. It now houses an industrial plant. *Location:* Brookville, Sylvania and Mabon Streets, on flat across North Fork from business district.

6. Brookville Locomotive Works (brick), almost the last in America making narrow gauge as well as standard gauge locomotives, was founded at Brookville in 1919. It has occupied its present plant, the old Brookville Foundry, since 1936. *Location:* Brookville, on Pickering Street, at railroad.

8. Biblical Carvings

7. Litch Mansion (Fleeger Art Studio) (frame) was built in 1850 by lumber baron T. K. Litch for his son Edward, a playboy and later an eccentric recluse. A big and remarkably well-built home, it has survived five fires, has been struck by lightning, and was abandoned for fifteen years, during which it was stripped of its fireplaces, stained-glass windows, and most of its doors. About 1920, as the mansion was being torn down, it was rescued and made into apartments. It is now occupied by a museum, with an art supply store and an extensive art collection, and is gradually being restored. *Hours:* Daily except Monday, 1–8 P.M. *Location:* Brookville, 16 Taylor Street.

Note: The Litch summer cottage, behind the ball field up the hill, is occupied and in reasonably good condition.

8. Biblical Carvings were the work of Douglas Stahlman, a teacher in 1890 at Clear Run School who became fanatical following a head injury received during a controversy with a lumberman. Stahlman wore a steel plate in his head, and about 1900 came under the influence of Dr. John A. Dowie, Chicago faith healer and founder of Zion, Ill. With

166

hammer and chisel Stahlman carved over 500 biblical passages—still legible—with references on beech trees and stones (mostly along or near streams) between 1907 and about 1914. Before 1920 he was committed to Dixmont Hospital at Pittsburgh, where he became an inmate librarian. He died about 1937 and is buried in Temple Cemetery. *Locations of carvings:* All in Brookville–Port Barnett area. (1) Old Brookville Park, along Sugarcamp Run, between North Fork and junction of two township roads near Pa. 968 (on rocks); (2) on U.S. 322, south side of road in wooded lot just east of and across from the Pinecreek Fire Hall (large beech tree just east of stucco bungalow); (3) south of Pa. 28, 0.5 mile from junction with U.S. 322, just east of McCullough farm (area of rock carvings equivalent to two city blocks); (4) at Port Barnett east and south of Humphrey Charcoal office, which stands where pioneer Joseph Barnett had his inn and store (on rocks); (5) along Pennsylvania Railroad at deserted lumbering village of Bells, near Sandy Lick Creek and south of Pinecreek School (rock carvings cover area of possibly two miles on hillside).

Note: Near Temple Cemetery at Cat Rocks on the Hazen-Brockway Road are rocks with potholes believed by many to have been Indian gristmills.

9. Bee House (frame) was built in 1903 by Alonzo M. Applegate, a beekeeper. A quintuple hexagon, this house is made up of modules patterned after the cells of a honeycomb.

Reynoldsville, where the house is located, was named in 1873 for its founders, David and Albert Reynolds, sons of Woodward Reynolds who came here with his bride from Kittanning in 1838 to occupy a farm of 300 acres given him as a wedding gift by his father. *Location:* Reynoldsville, 820 East Main Street.

Note: The Soldier Run mine nearby, now exhausted, was at one time the most productive bituminous mine in the world, with a daily output of 8,000 tons.

10. Gobblers Knob is the home of Punxsutawney Phil, the weather groundhog since 1887. Each February 2 it is the weather capital of the world as devotees and newsmen gather to see if Phil will see his shadow and delay spring for six weeks. *Location:* South of Punxsutawney, on l.r. 33078, 1.9 mile east of U.S. 119 and 0.8 mile east of crossroads.

11. David Brown House

11. David Brown House (variety stone) was erected by Brown, an eccentric widower, oilman, and lumber tycoon, who traveled twice around the world collecting stones from many countries and almost every state, receiving many as gifts. From 1914 to 1916 he had these built into a singular but livable house with ornate fireplaces faced with stones and shells. The dining-room fireplace has his name and picture worked into it. *Location:* Punxsutawney, 906 East Mahoning Street.

12. Clawson House (frame), built in 1825 by Mathias Clawson, sits far back from the street. Its east wing was once used as a school. *Location:* Punxsutawney, 808 East Mahoning Street.

13. McKibben House (brick and frame), with square white decorated columns, was built by Stanford White in 1903 for Edwin McKibben, last manager of the Punxsutawney Iron Works. Bought in 1918 by retired hotel man Thomas E. Bennis, it remains in his family. *Location:* Punxsutawney, 401 West Mahoning Street.

14. Fisher House (stone) is a big, shapeless structure built about 1890 by Jacob Fisher, and for years it was the home of photographer and journalist Florence Fisher Parry. It was later a public library. *Location:* Punxsutawney, 219 West Mahoning Street.

15. Winslow House (brick) was the home of Reuben Winslow, a prominent attorney, coalmine operator, and railroad promoter, who was involved in a famous railroad right-of-way suit. He began this fantastic Victorian house before the Civil War and finished it after the conflict ended. The plate glass in the downstairs windows came from France to

New Orleans, then up the Mississippi, Ohio, and Allegheny to Kittanning. The house was the first in town to have electric lights. Now apartments, it is rather run down. *Location:* Punxsutawney, East Gilpin and Pine Streets.

Note: A previous Winslow house (frame), said to date from 1850, is a charming carpenter Gothic structure, with batten board and three arched front doors in one. Later a summer home, it is located at 95 Cherry Street, on the hill overlooking the other house.

16. Jenks House (frame), built in 1819 by Dr. John W. Jenks, is still in the same family. It is the oldest house in town and an original two-story Greek Revival structure. *Location:* Punxsutawney, 100 Jenks Avenue.

17. Sprankle Viaduct, constructed in 1911, carries the Pittsburgh & Shawmut Railroad over Little Sandy Creek at Sprankle Mills. It is 142 feet high, 1,430 feet long, and is constructed of 1,467 tons of steel. The railway hauls three million tons of coal from Jefferson County over the bridge each year. *Location:* Sprankle Mills, on l.r. 33016.

18. Octagon Barn (frame), erected about 1850, is one of three of its type in the county. Barns of this kind were built for economy of lumber and as a status symbol. Said to be the best-preserved octagon barn in the state, it is on reclaimed land stripped by the R. D. Baughman Coal Company. *Location:* On l.r. 33010, 0.7 mile from l.r. 33011 at Content, three miles off Pa. 28 at Baxter.

19. Gable Tavern (frame) was a lumbermen's tavern built about 1850 by Hiram Gable. It was sold about 1860 to Andy Slike, who operated it for many years in a Prohibition township. It is now a residence. *Location:* Sigel, at crossroads.

20. Truman General Store (frame) was built by Henry Truman, who came here as an orphan from Nottingham, England, in 1848 at the age of twelve. He fought in the Civil War and in 1865 opened a store in a log cabin until the present store, also a residence, could be finished. He became an associate judge and, in 1881, a postmaster. The building has been in his family ever since. On the second floor the present Henry Truman maintains for his friends an interesting museum of early life in the area. *Location:* Sigel, at crossroads.

21. Three Wilderness Wonders should be visited together, preferably in good weather, as much of the road is unpaved.

a. Beartown Rocks, a large group of gigantic boulders deep in the forest, are located on the crest of a hill, providing an excellent view of a mountainous area along the Clarion River. *Location:* From Pa. 949 about one mile northeast of Sigel, take Clear Creek Road (marked) east 1.1 mile to Spring Creek Road; follow this northeast 1.4 mile to Corbett Road; turn north 0.3 mile to sign for rocks, a short walk.

b. Laurel Fields, on the old Tillotson farm, is now owned and maintained as a tourist attraction by National Fuels Gas Company. It is the site of the Northwestern Pennsylvania Laurel Queen crowning, in connection with the annual Laurel Festival in Brookville the second full week of June. *Location:* Near Sigel. At Corbett Road, continue on Spring Creek Road 1.8 mile to sign for Laurel Fields.

c. Slyhoff's Grave is the burial place of Richard Slyhoff. According to a legend traceable back to a 1936 picnic program, Slyhoff, who died on January 2, 1867, at age forty-three, had been such a wicked man that he had asked to be buried beneath a giant leaning boulder, in the belief that at the last trump it would fall on him, putting him out of reach of the Devil. With passing years the rock has gradually moved nearer to a vertical position instead of falling on him. Unfortunately for the legend, close inspection of the marble tombstone indicates that it gives the age as thirteen, not forty-three. That Richard was a boy and not a man is confirmed by the length of the grave—less than four feet, but the spot is an interesting one. *Location:* From Laurel Fields, continue on Spring Creek Road 1.9 mile to Munderf Road; turn right 0.9 mile to house. Ask permission to follow path about a furlong to grave (Polk Township).

22. Historical Museum (brick) is operated by a young but active organization with a good collection of materials on area history. *Hours:* Sundays and holidays, 2–5 P.M. *Location:* Brockway, in Memorial Park.

23. Clarke Home (frame) was built about 1860 by A. M. Clarke, miller, teacher, and surveyor, who laid out the town in 1836, naming it for Alonzo and Chauncey Brockway, lumbermen, who settled here in 1822. *Location:* Brockway, 900 Ninth Avenue.

24. N. B. Lane Mansion (frame) is a typical lumber baron's home, with six white pillars probably added later. It is occupied by descendants, who have retained the original lumbering records. *Location:* One mile southeast of Brockway, on Broad Street extension (visible from U.S. 219 east of town).

25. Beechwoods Church (frame) was organized in 1832. The second building, an early 1850s structure, is incorporated in the present one, which was erected in the 1880s. *Location:* Four miles west of Falls Creek on Pa. 830, turn north 0.8 mile on l.r. 33029.

26. James Smith Home (frame), dating back nearly a century and a half, was built by Smith, an early Irish settler who helped scores of later arrivals from his homeland find homes in Pennsylvania. The house originally faced away from the present road. An 1820s log and stone springhouse is in the original front yard of the house. *Location:* Northwest of Falls Creek and 1.9 mile from Beechwoods Church, on l.r. 33064, which intersects l.r. 33029 at church.

27. Game Commission Training School, founded in 1936, was the first school of its kind in America. It is supported wholly from license fees. Visitors are welcome. *Location:* On Game Commission lands north of Brockway (Snyder Township), on l.r. 33067.

Pennsylvania Historical and Museum Commission Markers

Cooksburg   Pa. 36 near the Clarion River Bridge

Great Shamokin Path U.S. 119, 4 miles northeast of Punxsutawney

Iroquois "Main Road"   Pa. 949, 3.8 miles north of Corsica

Olean Road   Corsica, U.S. 322

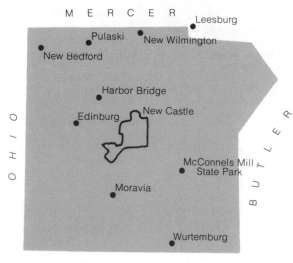

MERCER

Leesburg

Pulaski New Wilmington

New Bedford

Harbor Bridge

Edinburg New Castle

OHIO

McConnels Mill
State Park

Moravia

BUTLER

Wurtemburg

BEAVER

Lawrence County

Capsule History

Lawrence County was organized March 20, 1849, and named for Capt. James Lawrence of the U.S. Navy. His famous command, "Don't give up the ship," aptly applied to the county's struggle to become organized in the face of strong political opposition. Taken from parts of Mercer County to the north and Beaver County to the south, it now has an area of 367 square miles, the smallest county in western Pennsylvania. Its population is 107,374.

Situated around the confluence of three rivers, the Shenango, Mahoning, and Beaver, this area was a favorite location for Indians since it was accessible from many directions by canoe. According to legend the Delawares named Neshannock Creek, and the Senecas first called the Shenango River by its name.

A network of Indian trails radiated from Kuskuskies (present-day New Castle). The *Kuskusky-Chartiers Path, Kuskusky-Kittanning Path,* and *Kuskusky–Ohio Forks Path* ran together down the east bank of the Beaver past Chewton and Wurtemburg. The *Kuskusky-Cussewago Path* ran up the east side of the Shenango River past Pulaski. The *Kuskusky-Venango Path* followed much the course of U.S. 422 past Rose Point and McConnell's Mill and then turned northeast to join the Venango Path near Harrisville. The *Mahoning Path* came up the west side of the Beaver River to New Castle, thence up the north side of the Mahoning toward Youngstown, Ohio.

170

Following Col. John Armstrong's expedition of 1756, which destroyed the Delaware village of Kittanning, Indians living there moved to Kuskuskies and made it their capital until it was abandoned in 1773. Gen. Edward Hand's campaign of 1778 against the British near Cleveland, Ohio, ended here when an old man and a woman, the only remaining Indians at Kuskuskies, were killed. This fiasco acquired the name "squaw campaign." A monument in the Y at U.S. 224 and Pa. 551 marks the farthest point reached by Hand.

Following Christian Frederick Post's visit in 1758, two other Moravian missionaries—David Zeisberger and Gottfried Senseman—ministered in 1770 to the Indian village of Friedensstadt (meaning "city of peace"), which was established through the influence of a convert by the name of Glikkikan. A year later a mission chapel was built there. (In 1834 the town of Moravia, halfway between New Castle and Ellwood City, was laid out near this site.) In 1773, due to internal disturbances, the missionaries, including John Heckewelder, and their converts left and went to the villages of Gnadenhütten and Schoenbrunn on the Muskingum River in Ohio, where some of them were massacred in 1782.

After Gen. Anthony Wayne's victory over the Indians of the northwest in the battle of Fallen Timbers in 1794, white settlers, including Edward Wright, began to make permanent homes in this area. Among the early arrivals in 1798 were John Carlyle Stewart (who built a small iron forge on Neshannock Creek and his first log cabin at Falls Spring on North Mill Street in front of the present Trinity Episcopal Church parish house of New Castle), his brothers-in-law John and Hugh Wood, John McWhorter, and Joseph Townsed, Jr., all from New Castle, Del. In the early 1800s the Sankey family moved to the area. David Sankey was a leader in the movement to erect Lawrence County, a state senator in 1847, and the contractor for Harbor Bridge, completed in 1853. He was also president of the Bank of New Castle and publisher of the *Lawrence Journal.* His son Ira D. Sankey (1840–1908) was a famous hymn writer and singer, a fellow worker with Dwight L. Moody. Ira, who was born in Edinburg, donated the YMCA building (replaced in 1911 by a new one) to the city of New Castle in 1885. In later years the county was settled by many Amish.

New Castle, the geographical center of the former Indian town of Kuskuskies (one of four such villages), became the county seat in 1849. The only city in Lawrence County, it was laid out on fifty acres in 1802 by John C. Stewart, who had discovered this tract of land overlooked in any survey and without private ownership. It was named for Stewart's home in New Castle, Del., and Stewart became the first justice of the peace. In 1825 it was incorporated as a borough and became a city in 1869.

The construction of canals from Pittsburgh to Erie and Youngstown, Ohio, supplemented the natural waterways of this region. The Beaver and Erie Canal traversed the county south to north through New Castle, and the Pennsylvania and Ohio Canal, or "Cross-Cut" Canal (1838–72), bisected the former at Lawrence Junction. Western Reserve Harbor, established in 1833 on the Beaver and Erie Canal, was the shipping point for freight for the Western Reserve in Ohio. (Many of the early settlers of Lawrence, Crawford, Erie, and Mercer Counties were from Connecticut, and these areas are often referred to by the same term as Ohio's Western Reserve area.) Harbor Creek was the northern terminus of the Beaver division of the Pennsylvania canal system, which was completed to this point in 1834. The *Isaphena,* launched in 1840, was the first steamboat to operate on the canal. It was built by Daniel Frisbie in New Castle for Dr. Joseph Pollock and named for the doctor's daughter.

Natural resources in the area include coal, iron ore, clay, and limestone. The iron industry, employing charcoal furnaces, flourished from 1840 until after the Civil War.

The county had ten stone blast furnaces. New Castle is one of the largest manufacturers of chinaware in the United States, and once was known as "the tinplate capital of the world." Other products of local industries include chemicals and allied products, leather goods, lumber, and dairy and agricultural goods. The Neshannock (also Mercer and Gilkey) potato, a choice variety once widely known, originated on the farm of John Gilkey. (Gilkey's orphan sister, Peggy, after growing up in Washington County, was caught in a blizzard December 24, 1804, on her way to find relatives whose address she did not know. She stopped at a cabin for shelter and found it was the home of her brother James.) One of the largest greenhouses in the world under a single span is located two miles from New Castle.

Landmarks

1. Courthouse (brick) has a signature stone that reads "1851." The structure was completed in 1852 at a cost of $32,000. Another wing was added in 1885. Of Greek Revival design, the building has two stories and an Ionic portico with six columns. The first court was held in the First Methodist Episcopal Church on South Jefferson Street in 1850. *Location:* New Castle, on Court Street.

2. Hoyt Institute of Fine Arts (brick) is located in the former residence of coal heiress May Emma Hoyt, built in 1914–17 at a cost of about one quarter of a million dollars. Plans for the structure were started by Charles Owsley of Youngstown, Ohio, and finished by Frank Foulke, an architect from New Castle. There are twenty-two rooms, several of which are concealed, with a ballroom on the third floor. The dining room is paneled in French Provincial walnut, the living room in Italian Provincial walnut, and the hand-carved stairway, hall, and office are of English oak. The home, built on one-and-a-half acres, was donated to the Lawrence County Cultural Association in January 1965 by Mr. and Mrs. Alex Crawford Hoyt. In 1968 the center was incorporated as the Hoyt Institute of Fine Arts, which provides a permanent art gallery for the works of local artists; an arts and crafts shop of institute work; adult and childrens' classes; and lectures, recitals, film showings, and art exhibits. *Location:* New Castle, 124 East Leasure Avenue.

3. Scottish Rite Cathedral (brick and Indiana limestone trimmed with terra cotta) was opened in 1926 and was built at a cost of over $2 million. The Greer memorial organ was donated the same year by George and Charles H. Greer. The building, of Renaissance style, has a ballroom and banquet room that accommodates over 1,000, together with a large auditorium. *Location:* New Castle, corner of Highland and Lincoln Avenues.

4. Kennedy Square was first named the Diamond, later Central Square, and then Pershing Square after World War I. After John F. Kennedy was assassinated, the area was renamed. A Civil War monument, completed December 15, 1897, by the Lawrence County Veterans Association, is located here. Charles Andrews, a resident, posed for the soldier statue. *Location:* New Castle, central area.

5. First Christian Church (Disciples of Christ) (brick) was organized in White Hall. The main structure, including the sanctuary and spire, was built in 1864. Later additions were made in 1911 and 1962. The sanctuary once had a domed ceiling, which has since been lowered. The old pipe organ at one time was one of the largest in this part of the country. *Location:* New Castle, next to Kennedy Square.

6. Shenango Ceramics, Inc., one of the nation's largest producers of chinaware, started with the organization of the New Castle Pottery Company in 1862. Founded by Harmon and Hill, the original company continued in operation for two decades. In 1901 the New Castle China Company, a six-kiln plant, was founded in this area and lasted about four years. Then in 1905 the Shenango China Company was organized. Due to financial difficulties it became the Shenango Pottery Company. This company had similar problems, and in 1908 James M. Smith, Sr., reorganized the business and became its first president. In 1912 it purchased the old defunct New Castle China Company. After

172

2. Hoyt Institute of Fine Arts

Smith's death, his son James, Jr., took over the management, followed upon his early demise by Bowman and Long, who bought the plant and renamed it Shenango Ceramics, Inc. In 1968 the company and its subsidiaries were purchased by International Pipe and Ceramics Company of Parsippany, N.J. For many years the seventeen-acre plant manufactured all of the Haviland china sold in the United States. It was also a large producer of Castleton china. *Tours:* 10 A.M.–1:30 P.M. (no children under twelve). *Location:* West edge of New Castle, on U.S. 224 near railroad tracks.

7. McConnell's Mill (frame) is located in Slippery Rock Gorge, which was carved out in the glacial period. The scenic gorge is seven miles long and from 300 to 500 feet deep. Johnson Knight built the first mill here in 1824–25, and Alexander McConnell the second in 1857. Following a fire in 1867, the third and present mill was erected in 1868 by Thomas McConnell whose son, James, acquired it in 1875 and operated it until 1928. His employee Mose Wharton kept it open as a tourist attraction until 1953 when the Western Pennsylvania Conservancy purchased the original 2,000 acres and turned it over to the commonwealth. The park was dedicated in 1957, and the mill was restored in 1964 along with the reconstruction of the dam. A picturesque covered bridge is near the mill. *Hours:* Summer until September 1: Weekdays,

12:30–4:30 P.M. Mondays by appointment. Tours conducted every half hour from 10 A.M.– 6 P.M. on weekends and holidays during summer. *Location:* In McConnells Mill State Park, just south of U.S. 422, between New Castle and U.S. 422 interchange of U.S. 79.

8. Slippery Rock is visible only when the creek is low in the fall. This rock, steeped in folklore, has given rise to the name of a township, a town, and a college in Butler County, as well as a creek, an oil field, an oil sand, and a favorite football team. It appears on J. P. Lesley's Slippery Rock Creek map of 1874. Moravian missionary, John Heckewelder, wrote that the Delaware Indians called the creek "Wescha-cha-cha-polka," meaning "slippery rock." *Location:* Near Wurtemburg, on Slippery Rock Creek on John Eicholtz property. It can be seen from Glasser bridge on east bank of creek or from southern tip of Camp Allegheny, looking across downstream, on west bank.

9. General Store (brick), built in canal days, was at one time owned by Thomas Murray. In later years the building was used for a market. *Location:* Edinburg, junction of Pa. 551 and U.S. 224.

10. Westminster College was chartered in 1852 by the Associate (now United) Presbyterian Church. It was one of the first two colleges in Pennsylvania to grant degrees to

12. Ten-sided House

women and the first to grant them the A.B. degree, in 1857 (see *Waynesburg College, Greene County*). Some of the brown sandstone buildings are of Collegiate Gothic design. Hillside, a dormitory, is the oldest building. Another early structure is "Old 77," the gymnasium, where seventy-seven undefeated basketball games were played in succession. Old Main was erected in the late 1920s on the site of an earlier building which was destroyed by fire. *Location:* New Wilmington, on Market Street (Pa. 956).

11. The Tavern (frame) was built in the 1830s or 1840s by Dr. Seth Poppino, a physician who served as a surgeon in the Civil War. Many papers and other relics of this era were found by the Ernst Durrast family when they purchased the property. Poppino had his office and apothecary shop in his residence. This building has been operated as a restaurant by Cora Durrast for over forty-three years. It is open daily, except Tuesdays. *Location:* New Wilmington, on Pa. 208.

Note: This area has been settled by many Amish families. About one mile east of New Wilmington on the Volant Road is an early cut-stone house across from a one-room brick Amish school. Presently owned by John Reed, this house is worthy of further research.

12. Ten-sided House (brick), with two stories, was built by William Walker, who was born in 1819. He married Anna Jane Bailey in 1848, erected the house not long afterward, and lived here until 1903. William's father James was a leader in the Free Presbyterian

Church (q.v.) and an abolitionist. Another early owner of this home was Frank Phillis. It was later purchased by Thomas Rupnick. *Location:* Near Pulaski, on old U.S. 422, 1.2 mile from Pa. 208 at New Bedford.

13. Brown House (brick) was built by George Brown. James Brown, of the same family, was an early settler here. A log house foundation is nearby. *Location:* Two miles west of Pulaski, on Pa. 208.

14. Twelve-sided House (brick) was built about 1860 by Joseph Brown, a stonemason. The two-story polygon has five rooms on each floor. *Location:* Near Pulaski, on Pa. 208.

15. Free Presbyterian Church (frame) was organized before 1850 as a protest against slavery. Services were held here until 1871. The motto of the congregation was, "Anyone can worship here." James Walker (see *Ten-sided House*) was active in this church, which was one of the first of its kind organized in the United States. This building was later a town hall, which "anyone desiring to discuss a public question" could use. *Location:* New Bedford, on Pa. 208.

Pennsylvania Historical and Museum Commission Markers

C. Frederick Post   Pa. 18 and Pa. 108 south of New Castle

"Cross-cut Canal"   U.S. 224 north of Edinburg at bridge

Friedensstadt   Pa. 18 north of Moravia (2 markers)

Harbor Creek   U.S. 422 northwest of New Castle

Ira D. Sankey   Edinburg, junction of U.S. 224 and Pa. 551

Kuskuskies Towns   Junction of Pa. 18 and Pa. 108 south of New Castle; and Edinburg, junction of U.S. 224 and Pa. 551

Neshannock Potato   U.S. 19 south of Leesburg

"Squaw Campaign"   L.r. 37091 south of New Castle

Westminster College   Intersection of Pa. 18 and Pa. 208 west of New Wilmington; and New Wilmington, Pa. 208 at Market and Neshannock Streets.

174

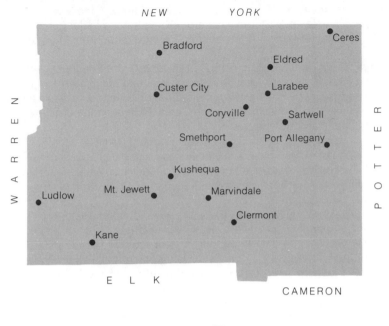

NEW   YORK

Ceres
Bradford
Eldred
Custer City
Larabee
Coryville
Sartwell
Smethport
Port Allegany
Kushequa
Mt. Jewett
Marvindale
Ludlow
Clermont
Kane

N W E R R A W

R E T T O P

E   L   K

CAMERON

McKean County

Capsule History

McKean, the "governor's county," was named for Thomas McKean (1735–1817), chief justice of the state supreme court, president (governor) of Delaware, and a signer of the Declaration of Independence. McKean was governor of this state when the county was erected out of Lycoming on March 26, 1804, with judicial authority remaining temporarily with the parent county. In 1814 McKean and Potter Counties were given common commissioners, and in 1826 McKean became independent. It has 992 square miles with a population of 51,915.

Although few Indians lived in this county, the area was known as "Seneca Land" and provided excellent hunting grounds for the Iroquois. There were three main Indian trails crossing the county. The *Catawba Path* entered McKean below Knapp Creek, passing six miles east of Bradford, crossing Kinzua Creek at Tallyho, and running through Cartwrights and East Kane. The *Forbidden Path,* a route to Olean, N.Y., long off limits to any white man, cut the northeast corner of the county from near Shinglehouse to Ceres. The *Oswayo Path* followed the same route at this point. One of the Iroquois paths used in pigeon-hunting touched the county near Ludlow.

Early settlers in the county came mostly from New England and New York, often along the Allegheny River Valley or up the Susquehanna. Others came from southeastern Pennsylvania. In 1861 Thomas Leiper Kane (later a major general) recruited the famous Bucktail Regiment (Forty-second Pennsylvania) from McKean and adjacent counties.

The first school was opened in 1809 at Instanter, and Smethport Academy was chartered in 1837. The county seat, Smethport, was laid out in 1807 by Francis King, land agent and surveyor, and named for Theodore de Smeth, who was a member of a Dutch banking firm with investments in the Ceres, Susquehanna of Connecticut, and the United States Land Companies.

Bradford was named for the former New England home of John F. Melvin, who arrived in 1827. Dr. W. M. Bennett built the first log cabin there the same year. In 1875 the county's first oil well was drilled in this area by Jackson, Walker, and Urquart. Two years later the first oil exchange was established in 1877 in Bradford. The world's first monorail was operated there.

Teutonia, laid out in 1843, and Ginalsburg were founded by Henry Ginal, agent of the German Co-operative Society of Industry. No vestiges of either settlement remain today. Ceres was founded by Francis King and Quaker friends in 1797 on John Keating's property. King's house was a stopping place for Quaker missionaries.

The county was a leader in the oil industry and today is the largest single producer of world-renowned Pennsylvania crude oil, as well as much natural gas. Chief products are lubricating oils and greases, gasolines, and oil-well supplies. Other outstanding industrial products include wooden toys, chemicals, powder and explosives, and glass and clay products. Beef and dairy cattle provide most of the county's agricultural income.

Lumbering was the first important industry. The county is among those having the largest wooded acreage in the state, most of which is included in the Allegheny National Forest.

Port Allegany, known to the Indians and pioneers as a "canoe place," was an important rafting center at one time. Early settlers in this area, Samuel Stanton, his son Daniel, and Daniel Webber, established the first sawmill at the site in 1824.

Landmarks

1. Courthouse (brick and stone) is an expansion and remodeling of the county's second. The first one was built of brick in 1827–31, with Solomon Sartwell as contractor, at a cost of about $5,000. In 1850 it was enlarged to almost three times its original size, at a cost of $20,000. It was torn down and a new one erected of brick and stone, begun in 1879 and dedicated September 12, 1881, at a cost of about $75,000. The east wing was added in 1914 and the west in 1938. The front part of this structure was destroyed by fire February 12, 1940, and the present courthouse, incorporating the back and two wings of the former one, was built at a cost of $400,000 and dedicated June 15, 1942. It was paid for in cash.

The sheriff's house and jail, in the rear, dates from 1870. The stone part is not older, as might appear, but was built for strength.

The McKean County Historical Society, with headquarters in the courthouse, is open to the public on Tuesday and Thursday afternoons, and contains many old-time tools and other types of furniture and equipment used by the pioneers of the area. *Location:* Smethport, Main Street.

2. Hamlin House (frame) is a charming structure built in 1860 by B. D. Hamlin, an attorney, land dealer, and banker. His father, Orlo J. Hamlin, was a state legislator from

2. Hamlin House

1831 to 1833. All the paneling and trim was made by hand on the job by his employees. This home, later owned by attorney E. L. Keenan, is now an educational office. *Location:* Smethport, 325 West Main Street, next to Hamlin Bank.

Note: Several later and more pretentious Hamlin mansions built by his heirs are to be found in Smethport.

3. McKean Manor (frame), a tremendous structure with tall Doric pillars, was built in 1905 by Charles McKean, a lumber baron perhaps distantly related to the governor. The rooms are finished in a variety of woods from a wide area. It is now the Colonial Hotel. *Location:* Smethport, West Main and Mechanic Streets.

Note: An early stagecoach tavern, completely disguised by a modern brick face, is on a nearby corner.

4. Old Kilns still show the great size of an early clay plant that began about 1890 as the Clermont Sewer Pipe Company, later becoming the Clermont Clay Products Company. About 1900 it was bought by the Kaul Clay Products Company and principally made tiles. It was unique in that the same strip operation which provided coal as fuel also gave the clay which was the company's raw material. It was closed after a disastrous fire in 1963 destroyed much of the plant. *Location:* Clermont, on l.r. 42013, about 0.5 mile from Pa. 146.

5. Port Allegany Hotel (frame covered with gray shingles) was a tavern built well before the Civil War by Lodowick Lillibridge, whose 1825 tavern and residence nearby has recently been allowed to rot down. Still operated as a tavern, this house has many of its early registers. Ole Bull, the famous Nor-

wegian violinist, once played a concert here. *Location:* Port Allegany, on north side of U.S. 6 at public square.

6. Benton Mansion (frame), with twenty rooms, was built in 1859 by A. M. Benton, lumberman, politician, and railroad promoter. It is a striking house with a square tower and wide overhanging eaves. Later a hotel, it was the scene of a still-unsolved murder in 1924 when E. J. Fetterly, who was operating it as Maple Shade Inn, was shot while playing cards with a group of friends, one of whom was wounded by a stray bullet. *Location:* Port Allegany, 500 West Main Street.

7. Gold Eagle House (frame painted gold) was built about 1893 by Harry Oglevee. It was a typical "railroad house," complete with bar, poolroom, barbershop, rental rooms, and ladies' parlor. Oglevee gave it the name because of his opposition to the "free silver" policies of William Jennings Bryan. Frank Slavin bought the hotel in 1908, and it was in his family for many years. *Location:* Eldred, on Railroad Street at railroad.

8. Saint Mary's Church (frame), of carpenter Gothic style, was built between 1869 and 1872, replacing an earlier structure built in 1848. It is the oldest Catholic church in the area and looked upon as the mother church of those at Bradford, Eldred, Smethport, Port Allegany, Duke Center, and Austin. Missionary priests from Elk County held services here soon after the first seven Irish families settled on Newell Creek in 1842. The parish was organized in 1847. Inside the church are paintings of the stations of the cross formerly at Saint Bernard's Church in Bradford. *Location:* Sartwell (Annin Township). From Turtlepoint, turn northeast on Newell Creek Road off Pa. 155 at Saint Mary's Church sign and travel 1.3 mile on blacktop (t. 1463), keeping right on t. 1517 at "Y." Or from Larabee, turn left off Pa. 155 at church sign, 1.2 mile, keeping left onto t. 1517.

9. Crook Farm includes a farmhouse (frame) that is believed to be the oldest existing structure in the Bradford area, dating from 1856. It was continuously occupied by the Crook family until it was deeded to the Bradford Landmark Society in 1974. It is based on a post-and-beam skeleton, with thin board curtain walls. It has the original shingles and most of the original trim and hardware. The Crook farm is the site of the Olmsted (cq) well, first large producer in the Bradford field. The

177

10. Bradford Landmark Museum

society plans to construct a replica oil-field village with early drilling rig and pumping equipment. There will also be nature walks and cycling paths. *Location:* Foster Township, on Seaward Avenue extension, about three miles north of Bradford. Watch for sign.

10. Bradford Landmark Museum (frame) was earlier Gus Herbig's French bakery, which he opened here in 1876. His granddaughter, Mrs. Virginia Loveland Miles, gave the building (second oldest in Bradford) to the Bradford Landmark Society ninety years later for a headquarters. It includes a museum store, the original bakery (except for ovens, restored after a fire), upstairs living quarters, and an extensive collection of early women's clothes. In the rear is a restoration of Frances A. Crook's candy store, with its original equipment. A display room is being added. *Hours:* Wednesday through Saturday, 1 to 4 P.M. *Location:* Bradford, 45 East Corydon Street, back of public library.

11. Penn-Brad Oil Well Park, a museum of the history of oil in McKean County, is sponsored by the Bradford District Oil Producers Association and the Desk and Derrick Club. It displays early drilling and shop equipment set up for operation, as well as photos, curios, and other memorabilia of the county's early oil days. *Hours:* June 1–October 1: Weekdays, 10 A.M.–5 P.M. Sunday, 12–5 P.M. *Location:* Just north of Custer City, on U.S. 219.

12. Kinzua Viaduct over Kinzua Creek was the old Erie-Lackawanna Railroad bridge, once among the biggest in the world. This famous viaduct, built in 1882 by the Bradford, Bordell & Kinzua Railroad, is 301 feet high

and 2,051 feet in length. It has 20 lower spans of 38.5 feet in length and 21 intermediate spans of 61 feet each. The bridge is an impressive sight, and the more courageous visitors may walk across it. In 1974 the area was made into Kinzua Bridge State Park, with picnic grounds and sanitary facilities. *Location:* Near Mount Jewett. From U.S. 6 take l.r. 42006 past Kushequa to l.r. 42047, and follow it to park (total of about two miles, and there are signs).

13. Seneca Indian Spring was a stopping place on the Indian trail which crossed the Big Level on the way south, once the main route from Onondaga, the Iroquois capital, to the Ohio and the Carolinas. It still sends a fine flow of water into a rather poorly kept pool. *Location:* From southeast edge of Kane, take Pa. 321 south about 100 yards to Wetmore Township line marker. Walk another 100 yards to right on old road, swampy in places, to spring.

14. Kane Manor (buff brick with columns) was the former estate of the town's founder, Gen. Thomas L. Kane, who died December 26, 1883 (see *Old Presbyterian Church*). Built in 1870, this house was reconstructed after a fire in 1896. Inside the Victorian, two-and-a-half story building, with numerous wings, chimneys, and a side portico with tall white columns, is a fine exhibition of Arctic paintings by Elisha Kent Kane (Thomas's brother, who went in search of Sir John Franklin). Also included in the collection are letters to the Kane family from five presidents and Brigham Young, and many Civil War relics. On a front step is the inscription, "Dure la vida que con ella todo se alcanza" ("Let life last, because with it all can be accomplished"). Over a fireplace a descendant of the builder has put a plaque that reads, "Life is like iron. Use it, it wears away. Use it not, it rusts away." The manor is now a restaurant with rooms for overnight guests. *Location:* Kane, 230 Clay Street.

15. Old Presbyterian Church (stone), of Gothic design, now the Kane Memorial, was organized November 15, 1874, and built soon afterward by Ann Gray Thomas, aunt of General Kane (see *Kane Manor*), as a memorial to her father Thomas Leiper. General Kane, his grandfather's namesake, laid the cornerstone. The Mormon Church bought the building in 1970 as a memorial to General Kane, who had helped its members in many ways, especially on their westward migration about 1850. He is buried just in front of the church. The bronze statue is a replica of the one of Kane in Utah State Capitol. *Location:* Kane, on Chestnut Street near Edgar Street.

16. Olmstead Manor (wood and stone), built by George Welsh Olmstead of Ludlow, was finished in 1917. Olmstead came to the town as the young secretary at the tannery built here in 1872 by John J. Curtis, associate of Thomas L. Kane and Samuel M. and William L. Fox (see *Foxburg,* Clarion County) in railroad and other industrial ventures. Olmstead took over the plant after Curtis died around 1904. Later he was president of the Long Island (N.Y.) Lighting Company. He died in 1940, and the tannery closed in 1956.

After Olmstead's wife died, the family gave the manor to the Methodist Church in 1969. It is now a retreat center open to all faiths. Another part of the estate, given to the village of Ludlow, has become Wildcat Park, a community recreation area. *Location:* Southeast edge of Ludlow, on U.S. 6.

Note: Under the small bridge on the street to the south, almost across from the manor, may be seen well-preserved timbers of the tannery's dam, under the waters of Two-Mile Run.

Pennsylvania Historical and Museum Commission Markers

Allegheny Portage   Port Allegany, at junction of U.S. 6 and Pa. 155

"The Bucktails"   Smethport, U.S. 6 at courthouse

Ceres   Pa. 44 near Ceres at bridge

Mount Equity Plantation   Pa. 155, 3 miles northwest of Port Allegany

Port Allegany   U.S. 6, 0.2 mile west of Port Allegany; and Port Allegany, at square

Seneca Spring   Pa. 321 south of Kane

Smethport   Smethport, U.S. 6 at courthouse

Tidewater Pipe Company   Pa. 446, 13 miles southwest of Coryville

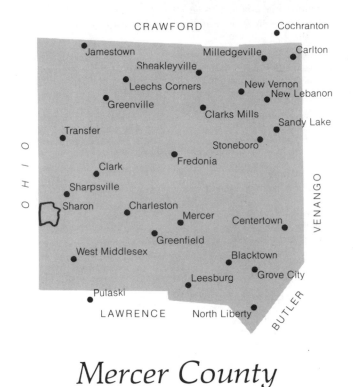

CRAWFORD Cochranton

Jamestown Milledgeville Carlton

Sheakleyville

Leechs Corners New Vernon
New Lebanon

Greenville Clarks Mills

Sandy Lake

Transfer

O H I O

Stoneboro

Clark Fredonia

Sharpsville

VENANGO

Sharon Charleston

Mercer Centertown

Greenfield

West Middlesex Blacktown

Leesburg Grove City

Pulaski

LAWRENCE North Liberty BUTLER

Mercer County

Capsule History

Mercer County, named for Brig. Gen. Hugh Mercer, a Scottish surgeon and commander during the Revolution, was formed March 12, 1800, from Allegheny County and organized in February 1804. The county encompasses 670 square miles, bordering the Ohio line for 32 miles, and has a population of 127,225.

Indian trails that traversed the county included the *Cayahaga Path* from Franklin to Akron, which entered the county near Sandy Lake, followed its north shore to Pymatuning (now flooded by the Shenango Reservoir), one-and-a-half miles west of Big Bend, and turned southwest to West Middletown, following Pa. 318 to the state line. The *Kuskusky-Cussewago Path* ran by Pulaski, West Middlesex, Clark, and Greenville, thence northwest to the county line.

The Wyandot and Delaware Indian village, Shenango Town, was situated on the river bank (marker on Pa. 18 near West Middlesex) in 1750–85 and was under the control of the Seneca Indians, of whom a few remained in the area until 1812. Pymatuning Delaware Indian Town, at Big Bend, was located in 1764 to 1785 on the Shenango River at about Clark (marker on Pa. 258 east of Clark).

The Beaver and Erie Canal traversed the county, following the course of the Shenango River north to Greenville and thence to the Crawford County line via Little Crooked Creek Valley.

The county had "depreciaton lands" and "donation lands" (see Capsule History for Butler County). Benjamin Stokely, deputy surveyor for the county, surveyed some of these lands in 1785. The Holland Land Company and the Pennsylvania Population Company, among others, were active in the region. The county had few settlements until after 1795, when Anthony Wayne signed the Treaty of Greenville with the Indians.

Many of the first settlers were Scottish Presbyterians. Others came from Washington County and introduced sheep-raising, with the county ranking third in the state in wool-growing as late as 1868. William McMillan, one of three trustees appointed to conserve the assets of the new county and son of Rev. John McMillan, erected a blockhouse in Coolspring Township and several area churches. In 1885 a large number of Italians settled in Sharon and Farrell when a pipeline was laid from the Butler and Venango County oil fields through Sharon to Youngstown, Ohio.

Among the prominent residents were James Pierce, of Hickory Township, who helped develop the bituminous coal industry in the mid 1800s; Jonathan Dunham, who settled in Sharpsville in 1798; and James Sharp, an original landowner of the area. Benjamin Bentley came to Sharon in 1803, and William Budd laid it out in 1819. Alfred Landon, governor of Kansas and Republican candidate for president, was born in West Middlesex. The Bigler family, whose two sons became governors on the same day, lived near Greenville (see *Bigler Graves*).

The borough of Mercer, in the area of a former important Indian village and centrally located, was laid out August 24, 1803, by John Hoge, who donated 200 acres for the county seat. In 1805 the Junkins family built the first mill here. The Harthegig health springs were well known in the area for years. In 1825 General Lafayette was entertained in Mercer on his visit to the United States.

The county's two third-class cities are Sharon and Farrell, with Greenville, Grove City, and Sharpsville its larger boroughs. Sharon, first settled in 1803 by Benjamin Bentley, was laid out by William Budd in 1819. Farrell, a company town originally incorporated as South Sharon, was renamed in 1911 for James A. Farrell, a noted steel manufacturer. Greenville, formerly West Greenville, honors Gen. Nathaniel Greene. Wheatland, first settled by the Henry Shilling family prior to 1797, was laid out by James Wood in 1865 and named in honor of the Lancaster estate owned by President James Buchanan. West Middlesex was settled in 1821 and laid out in 1836. Hickory Township was created in 1832, and Shenango Township, originally plotted in 1866 as Atlantic City—derived from the Atlantic and Great Western Railroad—had much land set aside for railroad terminals.

The iron and steel industries, largely in Sharon and Farrell along the Shenango River, have promoted county growth. There were once fifteen stone blast furnaces in the area. Among the important products of the county's industries are iron and steel ingots and bars, railroad cars, gas and gasoline engines, and electric machinery. The 300-ton transformers for the Colorado Boulder Dam were built at one of Sharon's electrical manufacturing plants. Mercer County once ranked high in bituminous coal-mining, paper and printing products, and agriculture.

4. Magoffin House

Landmarks

1. Courthouse (brick and stone) was built in 1909. The first court was held in the home of Joseph Hunter of Mercer in 1804, and the original courthouse was built in 1807–08. It was replaced by a second building in 1866–67, which was destroyed by fire in 1907. The third structure is in use today. *Location:* Mercer, on square.

2. Bingham House (brick), built about 1805, was the birthplace of John A. Bingham (1815–1900). He presided as judge advocate at the trial of Mary Eugenia Surratt and other alleged conspirators in the assassination of Abraham Lincoln. Bingham, a Republican, was also U.S. minister to Japan and was counsel in the impeachment of President Andrew Johnson in 1868. This house is now the county Republican headquarters. *Location:* Mercer, south side of Courthouse Square on South Diamond Street.

3. Old Stone Jail, a square two-story building with narrow windows and a hip roof, was built about 1810 by Thomas Templeton. It served the county until about 1868 when a man by the name of Lafferty bought it for a hotel. At present it houses commercial offices. The second jail, built of brick in 1868, is near the courthouse on Diamond Street. A new one has recently been built. *Location:* Mercer, 107 West Venango Street.

4. Magoffin House (frame), of Georgian style, was built in 1821. It is the former home of James Magoffin, Jr., who with his father and Dr. Beriah Magoffin operated a doctor's office here. The south wing is the older section, and the rooms in the back were added after the Civil War. This house, constructed on the old Butler-Erie Pike, was donated by Mrs. Henrietta Magoffin to the county and dedicated in 1951 as the headquarters for the Henderson Historical Center, which includes a museum, print shop, memorial chapel, historical library, county records, Indian artifacts, pioneer displays, and other memorabilia. *Hours:* Tuesday–Saturday, 1–4:30 P.M. Friday, 7–9 P.M. *Location:* Mercer, 119 South Pitt Street.

5. McClain Print Shop (frame), which once set ads for the *Saturday Evening Post,* was owned by Squire T. W. McClain and later by his son T. W. McClain, Jr., until his death in 1965. The building, donated to the Mercer County Historical Society in 1973 by the McClain family, was moved from its location on South Diamond Street to its present site and dedicated in 1974. *Location:* Mercer, on South Pitt Street, at Henderson Historical Center.

6. Helen Black Miller Memorial Chapel (frame), formerly Grace Episcopal and later Saint Edmund Martyr Episcopal Church, is now nondenominational. It was dedicated in 1973 as a memorial to Mrs. Miller, a local musician and vocalist. The church was originally located on Venango Street on property donated by Charles W. Whistler (see *Whistler House*). The restored church, built about 1884 and purchased by the county historical society, contains the original pews with doors and is now part of the Henderson Historical Center, dedicated in 1973. (The land was a gift from Mr. and Mrs. George M. Henderson. Restoration funds for the church were donated by William W. Miller of Mercer.) The church is used for weddings and other special services. *Location:* Mercer, South Pitt Street.

7. Stewart-McLaughry House (frame), of New England Greek Revival architecture, was built in 1853 by William Stewart, a lawyer and state senator. The Stewart family later rented the house to Judge James McLaughry who bought it in 1911. In 1953 the Beringer family restored the building. *Location:* Mercer, 237 West Market Street, at corner of North Maple Street.

8. Congregational Church (frame) was originally built by this congregation in 1852. From 1887 to 1960 the Reformed Presbyterian Church owned the building. Later a Baptist church sold it as a private residence. In recent years the Cooper Evans family restored the interior and exterior historical features including stained-glass windows. *Location:* Mercer, on West Market Street.

9. Hanna-Small-White House (brick) was constructed in 1839 by Robert Hanna. This house and the Hanna one next to it (built about 1818) are both made of locally fired bricks. Later Edward Small, an abolitionist minister of the United Presbyterian Church who married Mary, the daughter of Robert Hanna, lived in the house with his family and operated an underground railroad station for escaping slaves. Years later a secret room hidden under the kitchen was revealed when a loose stone was discovered in the foundation. During the Civil War a ten-foot addition was constructed. Scratched on a first-floor window is the inscription, "F.H.S. 1870." This residence, later purchased by the Yeager White family, is described by Anna Pierpont Siviter in her 1861–68 *Recollections of War and Peace. Location:* Mercer, 245 South Pitt Street.

Note: Another house (frame) which was used as an underground railroad station is the Kilgore home located on South Erie and Beaver Streets.

10. Herrington House (glacial stone) was erected in 1812 by Jacob Herrington and operated as a stagecoach stop. It was in the attic of this home that the Masons of the county held their secret meetings during the anti-Masonic excitement. The Robinsons restored the house in 1962. *Location:* Mercer, 208 North Pitt Street.

11. Whistler House (frame), of Greek Revival style, was built in 1840 by Samuel and Fred Hays. Several years later it was sold to David W. Findley, a Mercer merchant, county prothonotary, clerk, and associate judge. David Grier, a Presbyterian clergyman, bought it next, followed in 1890 by Capt. Charles W. Whistler, hotel owner, captain in the Civil War, and editor of the *Western Press* (Mercer's Democratic party newspaper). The house is presently owned by Whistler's great-grandson. *Location:* Mercer, 317 North Pitt Street.

12. Garrett Cenotaph, a family monument resembling a small pyramid and dating back to the 1830s, is over eight feet in height. Its unusual construction, of the Greek Revival mode, is noteworthy. The family is buried elsewhere. *Location:* Mercer, at junction of U.S. 62, U.S. 19, and Pa. 58 in old Presbyterian cemetery.

13. Logan-Johnson House (frame), over 100 years old, formerly was a summer mansion for the Logan family. The house cost the original builder so much to erect that he went bankrupt before it was finished. It was bought at a later date by the Virgil Johnson family. *Location:* Mercer, 235 North Shenango Street.

14. Pew Estate belonged to Joseph Newton Pew, founder of the Sun Oil Company and president of the board of trustees of Grove City College (q.v.). For about forty years the buildings had remained unoccupied but well maintained. The landmark house has been razed and now only the frame tenant house, barn, and a few outbuildings remain. *Location:* Southeast of Mercer, on Pa. 58.

15. Boston Tavern (brick) was built in 1833 by John Crill. With a distillery on his farm, Crill supplied spirits for the Saint Cloud Hotel in Mercer, which he ran. In 1845 Crill's daughter Christeena inherited the farm, and she, with her husband Adam Boston, son of an innkeeper of Delaware Township, converted the farmhouse into a tavern.

Sometime in the 1850s a peddler with a carpetbag containing valuables stayed overnight at the inn. According to legend, he mysteriously disappeared early the next morning before the arrival of the stagecoach, leaving blood stains on the floorboards. Following this occurrence, bricks began to fall periodically from the wall above where the peddler stayed. Claude Eckman, who has completely restored the inn, removed the paint which a former owner had applied over the stains, replaced the bricks, and has never been haunted by the peddler ghost. The home, still owned by the Eckman family, is now called Candlewood. *Location:* 2.7 miles south of Mercer, on Mercer–Slippery Rock Pike (South Pitt Street extension, Finley Township).

Note: Another early brick house which is being restored on the same road is the old David Gilson property, originally called Green Knoll Farm. Gov. Thomas Mifflin signed a patent for the land in 1794 to Daniel Stever as "signee of John Yost, private, for lot number 504 in the third donation district in Allegheny County." A two-story bay window was added in 1850. *Location:* Blacktown, junction of l.r. 43017 and l.r. 43024.

16. Stranahan House (stone) is situated on donation land issued to James O. Kane in 1789. He sold the land in 1828 to Thomas Newcomb, who built the house. In 1851 Newcomb transferred the property to Andrew

Stranahan, who retained it as a farm for over half a century. *Location:* Three miles west of Mercer, off Pa. 62 (first road to left) in Hells Hollow School area, East Lackawannock Township.

17. Byers-Bartholomew House (brick), a large structure built by the A. M. Byers family, was formerly a general store. When it was operating commercially, one half of the building was also used as a post office. *Location:* Greenfield, on Pa. 318 (at Bartholomew Orchard) southwest of Mercer.

18. Clay Furnace House (brick), once owned by the Grandy family, could have been the residence of one of the ironmasters—Vincent and Himrod—who built Clay Furnace (named for Henry Clay) in 1845. Raw bituminous coal instead of charcoal was first used successfully in 1846 at this site near the house. *Location:* From Mercer travel west on U.S. 62 eight miles to historical marker on right side of road (west of Charleston); turn north on t. 496 for 2.2 miles. House and furnace ruins are against hillside in pasture on right.

19. Sellers House (frame) was built in 1860 by an Englishman named Sellers, exactly halfway between Pittsburgh and Erie. The family lived in a smaller saltbox house on the property while this home was being constructed. A brass pike marker north of the farmhouse was placed by the side of the road (now under the highway) in 1812, presumably to mark Commodore Perry's route to Lake Erie or the exact midway point between the two towns. In 1915 the location was resurveyed by the U.S. government, using the bull's-eye window of the house and by consulting century-old notes to help calculate where the marker was situated. The house was later purchased by the Owen Clair Neal family and has large additions in the rear. *Location:* North of Fredonia and Mercer, on U.S. 19 just past Mercer greenhouse on right side of road (Delaware Township).

20. Hunter's Choice (log), reputed to be the oldest house in the county, was built on a 500-acre tract in 1786 by Dr. Absalom Baird, a surgeon who had received the land as a Revolutionary War grant October 8, 1785. The property was patented in 1807 to Jacob Stroud as Hunter's Choice. In 1913 it was purchased by George C. Hinckley, one of the engineers who designed the Roosevelt Dam, and nicknamed Yellow Breeches Farm. The

21. Kidds Mills Covered Bridge

Hinckleys had offers from the Ford Foundation to purchase the log cabin and move it to Dearborn, Mich., but they decided to preserve it at its historical location. Later it was sold to Donald and Valeria Dukelow. The house, of oak and poplar logs, had a loft which was converted to bedrooms; a porch and a kitchen were added at another date. *Location:* Near Fredonia. At Mercer greenhouse on U.S. 19, turn east onto l.r. 43043 (District Road) and continue 1.7 mile to Furnace Road; thence west 0.1 mile to lane on right, where Dukelow farm is located (Fairview Township).

Note: Nearby is the site of the Harry-of-the-West Furnace, built in 1838 by J. G. Butler and William McKinley, father of the president. Originally called Temperance Furnace as a compliment to Butler's wife, it acquired its later name in tribute to Henry Clay.

21. Kidds Mills Covered Bridge, built in 1868, is the county's only remaining covered bridge. Known as the "Smith-Cross-Truss" bridge, it spans the Shenango River. *Location:* South of Greenville, on l.r. 43120 northeast of l.r. 43039 between Pa. 58 and Pa. 18. (It can be seen at historical marker on Pa. 58.)

22. Mann-Stewart House (frame), built in 1854 of Greek Revival style with a pedimented front portico and a fanlight window, was the home of Robert Mann. The property was purchased by Vance Stewart at another time. *Location:* Greenville, 115 Columbia Avenue at Vance Street.

23. Thiel College opened its Greenville campus in 1871 in the old Greenville Academy building. Prior to this, Thiel College, of the Evangelical Lutheran Church, the oldest institution of higher education of this sect west of the Allegheny Mountains, was located in Phillipsburg (now Monaca, Beaver County). It had been opened as a "classical school" in 1866 at a former summer resort purchased by Rev. William A. Passavant, acting for the Lutheran Synod. A. L. Thiel, a member of the Second Lutheran Church of Pittsburgh, donated the money for this endeavor, and the school was incorporated as Thiel Hall in 1870, the year it was opened as a college. At that time the citizens of Greenville, through a gift of seven acres and $20,000, induced the Pittsburgh Synod to move the school to Greenville. The oldest remaining structure on campus is Greenville Hall (brick), erected in 1872–74. *Location:* Greenville, on College Hill.

24. Irvin Mansion (brick), of Greek Revival and New England style, was built in 1846 by Himrod and Woodworth and purchased by William Irvin, whose brother Lot became the ironmaster in the family business. When their concern went under in 1851, the original owners bought back the property; and Lot Irvin, despondent over the failure, hanged himself in the bridge house of the deserted furnace. It was said that this lavish house, not his furnace, led to his downfall. The grave of Lot, a thirty-year-old bachelor, is in Shenango Valley Cemetery. In the 1860s George Bittenbanner bought the house and built twin wings at the rear and a thirty-five-foot, three-story turret on the south side. Later the twenty-room house was divided into apartments. The furnace was fifty feet from the house over the bluff. *Location:* Greenville, on bluff, North Front Street.

25. Waugh House (brick), a large structure with chimneys built in steplike fashion at the gable ends, was the home of Judge William Waugh, who was one of the first graduates of the University of Pittsburgh, one of the founders of the National Bank in Greenville, and editor and proprietor of the *Mercer Whig* from 1845 to 1848. His house was built in 1843. *Location:* Greenville, corner of second and Main Streets.

26. Bigler Graves are the burial sites of Jacob (d. 1827) and Susan (d. 1851) Bigler. They were the first parents in America to have reared two sons who became governors of two different states during the same year. William Bigler was governor of Pennsylvania from 1852 to 1855 (see *William Bigler Home,* Clearfield County), and John Bigler was governor of California from 1852 to 1856. Shortly after moving to Fredonia in 1814, the family was swindled in a land deal and lived for some time nearly in poverty. Their frame house is still standing nearby in Delaware Township. *Location:* Three miles southeast of Greenville, in Bigler Cemetery, on Pa. 58 at Mercer and Salem Roads (near historical marker).

27. Gibson House (brick) was the residence of a local physician, Dr. William Gibson (1813–87) and his wife Susan. This mansion was built in 1855. Gibson was a stockholder in the Pittsburgh & Erie and the Franklin & Jamestown Railroads, an officer of a Stoneboro coal company, treasurer of a metallic and lumber company, president of the Jamestown Banking Company, and operator of a drug store across from his house. The Gibsons met Mark Twain on a round-the-world tour in 1867 and became the focus of ridicule in Twain's book *Innocents Abroad.* The author is reputed to have been a guest in the Gibson home after a speaking engagement in Sharon in 1869.

The doctor and his wife erected an enormous ninety-foot monument for their grave sites in 1884 at the Jamestown Cemetery, on a knoll south of Pa. 58. It cost the Gibsons between $95,000 and $100,000 to build, with a special railroad spur constructed to transport the materials to the cemetery. The monument and tracks are still at the cemetery.

Their house later became an inn known as Mark Twain Manor. A brick carriage house on the property is now a commercial business. *Location:* Jamestown, 210 Liberty Street at Main (Pa. 58).

28. Duncan House (frame), also referred to as the Tidewater Manor on the crest of Prospect Hill, was built by James Duncan, who followed an architectural style popular in South Carolina, where he lived after he had served in the Revolution. The structure, with log beams in the basement, has five marble fireplaces. Duncan, who died in 1835, is buried across the road from the house near a barn in a private cemetery with an iron fence around it. *Location:* West of Transfer, on Rutledge Road 0.2 mile from its junction with Pa.

30. *Koonce House*

846 (Greenville-Sharon Road) (Pymatuning Township).

29. Caldwell One-Room Schoolhouse was built in 1880 of brick fired on the Ball farm, four miles southeast of the site. The building, donated by Delaware Township, was dedicated in 1962 by the Mercer County Historical Society in commemoration of the more than 225 former public one-room schools which operated in the county from 1800 to 1900. It is furnished with the original desks, an iron stove, a pipe organ, and other memorabilia. A reconstructed well and bake oven are also on the property. *Hours:* June–September: Sundays and holidays, 1–5 P.M., and by special appointment. *Location:* Five miles south of Greenville, on Pa. 58.

Note: Another early brick one-room schoolhouse, built in 1888, is near Greenville at the junction of Porter and East James Streets (Pa. 58).

30. Koonce House (painted brick) is a Greek Revival mansion built in 1854 by Charles Koonce, coal and real-estate dealer, on the property of his parents, who came to the area in 1808. Charles Koonce, Jr., a Youngstown lawyer, extended the porch and added large columns in 1923. The building at one time housed a television station and is at present used for offices.

Since 1963 the village of Clark (formerly Clarksville settled by Samuel Clark in 1804) has been almost completely submerged by the Shenango Reservoir developed in 1960. Albert Bushnell Hart, distinguished scholar, historian, and Harvard professor, was born nearby in 1854. *Location:* Clark, junction of Pa. 18 and Pa. 258.

31. Pierce Lock (no. 10) is on the Beaver–Lake Erie Canal, which operated from 1844 to 1871 between Pittsburgh and the Great Lakes. The lock, adjoining dam no. 1 and made of huge, hand-chipped, fitted stones, was built in 1835–38. It is the only extant lock masonry of the canal in northwestern Pennsylvania and was important to the western Pennsylvania iron industry before the rise of railroads. In the 1880s, James and Frank Pierce, sons of Gen. James Pierce, a coal and iron tycoon, bought the lock and towpath for a spur of the Pittsburgh, Shenango & Lake Erie Railroad, but it never materialized. *Location:* Sharpsville, on Bridge Street just south of Shenango Reservoir dam. At bridge take dirt path for about 150 yards into wooded area along Shenango River.

Note: See the list of historical markers for locations where the canal is visible.

32. McFarland House (brick) was built in 1860 by Ebenezer McFarland at a crossing named for him. Constructed on Western Reserve land, the home has original black walnut and chestnut woodwork in its interior. A hidden room is underneath the stairway. A large cupola on top of the house provides a fine view of the countryside. *Location:* Three miles northeast of Pulaski and four miles southeast of West Middlesex, at junction of Pa. 468 and Pa. 18.

33. Bell House (brick), with five gables, was built in 1882 by a former legislator, John Bell. His son William S. Bell lived in the house, which was subsequently purchased by the Hopkins family. A bull's-eye window, also called a "wedding-ring light," is above the date stone over the front entrance. The house is situated at what used to be called Battle Row, in a schoolhouse area named for its typical school-yard squabbles. *Location:* South edge of West Middlesex, on Mitchell Road (t. 412) near its junction with Gilkey Road.

34. Stevenson Mansion (sandstone) was erected in 1898–99 by John Stevenson, who had come to Pittsburgh from Glasgow, Scotland, in 1872. The sandstone was first cut in 1891 by Stevenson for a house in New Castle on East Lincoln Avenue. Seven years later, seeking more land, the industrialist had the stone hauled by rail to Sharon and rebuilt into a house with twenty-two rooms on the west hill, which originally belonged to an early settler, Isaac Patterson. Andrew Carnegie

31. Pierce Lock (no. 10)

and President Taft were entertained in this mansion. The building was later used for a kindergarten and nursery. It was damaged by fire in 1961. Again plans were made to move the house owned by Sacred Heart Church, this time to Saint Mary's Cemetery, but it remains at its second site. *Location:* Sharon, 109 North Irvine Avenue.

35. Boyce House (painted brick) was built in 1866 for $15,000 by George Boyce, a construction engineer on the Erie Extension Canal. He operated the Sharon furnace, built in 1846, at the present Westinghouse plant site and the Shenango furnace near Sharpsville. The house was described as "tall, square, and butter-colored, with a hipped roof, iron brackets, eight uneven rooms, and black marble mantels." Boyce maintained numerous greenhouses on the property. *Location:* Sharon, on Silver Street (formerly Boyce Street) at Second Avenue behind Buhl Club.

36. Old Express (frame) is a former Pennsylvania Railroad station that was opened in 1972 as a restaurant. Included on the property are a Pullman car complete with baggage, a locomotive, and a freight station. *Location:* Sharon, 110 Depot Street.

37. Sharon Iron Company was organized and built in 1850. In 1851 it bought the controlling interest (640 acres) in Iron Mountain, Jackson County, Mich., and also controlled sixty acres of land at Iron Bay and the firm's harbor on Lake Superior. In 1853 the company brought seventy tons of Lake Superior ore to the Clay and Sharpsville furnaces, before the Sault Ste. Marie Canal was completed. In 1861 Joel B. Curtis, the president, bought the business and four years later sold it to the Westerman Iron Company. Following additional ownerships, National Steel Company purchased it in 1899. *Location:* Sharon on Sharpsville Avenue.

38. Buhl Mansion (gray sandstone) was built in 1896 for $60,000 by Frank H. Buhl, steel maker and public benefactor who heavily endowed the Sharon Valley. Styled like a French castle, the fourteen-room mansion was designed by Charles Owsley of Youngstown and decorated with furnishings from a castle in France. While the many-turreted landmark was being built, the Buhls stayed in the ten-room house on the property, now the caretaker's residence. In 1936, following the death of Mrs. Buhl, the mansion became the home of Henry B. Forker, Jr., Mrs. Buhl's nephew. The Forkers converted the building into apartments. *Location:* Sharon, 422 East State Street.

39. Whispering Pines (brick), with fourteen rooms and a tower originally having a cupola, was built in 1855 by Robert Stewart, who gave it its name. Stewart, a dealer in sheep and lumber, gradually increased the size of the property. The structure has been a residence since its construction except from 1922 to 1935, when the front section was operated as a tea house by the Jesse Wilsons. Included on the property are the servants' quarters and a garage once used as a carriage house. *Location:* Near Sharon, in Hickory Township, 5465 East State Street (U.S. 62).

40. Johnston Tavern (stone) was built on the Pittsburgh-Mercer Road in 1831 by Arthur Johnston, who had come from Ireland. He no doubt had operated a log tavern prior to this one, for he was issued a license in 1827. Johnston managed the stone tavern until 1842, calling it the New Lodge Inn. It served workmen from the Springfield iron furnace nearby. In 1836 the Springfield post office was opened in the building, with the innkeeper as postmaster. (The post office was moved to Leesburg in 1845.)

Restored by Charles M. Stotz under the direction of the Western Pennsylvania Conservancy, the building is administered by the Pennsylvania Historical and Museum Commission. The front entrance, with a fanlight above the door, has been reconstructed as it appeared originally, and the furnishings are from the Andrew Jackson period. *Hours:* Day-

40. Johnston Tavern

light saving time: Weekdays except Monday, 8:30 A.M.–5 P.M. Sundays, 1–5 P.M. Winter: Weekdays except Monday: 9 A.M.–4:30 P.M. Sundays, 1–4:30 P.M. *Admission charge. Location:* Three miles south of Mercer, on U.S. 19 (Perry Highway) about one mile north of Leesburg.

41. Schollard House (frame) was built in 1850 by William Schollard, the first Springfield furnace operator. The furnace was built by Seth and Hill about 1837, and Schollard took over management in 1846. This family lived in the house until 1944. It has been restored by the Thompson family. *Location:* Springfield Township, on U.S. 19 just north of Leesburg.

Note: The outline of the old furnace, which had a thirty-eight-foot waterwheel, can be seen at Springfield (north on U.S. 19 through Leesburg to its intersection with l.r. 43012; thence continue on t. 335 to Springfield Falls).

42. Fleming House (frame), built before 1850 by the first postmaster of Grove City, William Fleming, served as his home and was also used as a tannery and harness shop, as well as a select school (1858 to 1876), with Richard M. Thompson the first teacher. Classes were held on the third floor. Later the school was moved to its present location and renamed Pine Grove Normal Academy, fore-

runner of Grove City College (q.v.). The house is now owned by Young's Dairy. *Location:* Grove City, 455 Liberty Street.

43. Grove City College began in 1876 (chartered in 1879) as Pine Grove Normal Academy, a teacher-training institution under the auspices of the Presbyterian Church. In 1884 the academy became Grove City College. It was founded by Dr. Isaac Conrad Ketler, former principal of the Select School (see *Fleming House*). Ketler was president of the college from 1876 to 1913, and his son Weir Ketler was president from 1916 to 1956. WSAJ radio station, owned by the college, started broadcasting in 1920 and was one of the first established in the United States.

The institution has been generously supported by Joseph Newton Pew (see *Pew Estate*) and his son John Howard Pew, both presidents of the board of trustees. (Joseph Newton Pew had taught school in a one-room brick building at London, junction of Pa. 208 and l.r. 43023, and one of his students was Isaac Ketler. The school is now used as a garage.)

Cunningham Hall (brick), of Greek Revival style, is the oldest building on the Grove City campus. It was built in 1854 by Squire James Glenn Cunningham and replaced a frame house of 1840. James's parents, Valentine and Margaret Glenn Cunningham, came to this area from Huntingdon County, built a log cabin on land taken up by squatter's rights, and ran a grist- and sawmill. Their sons James and Charles laid out the town of Pine Grove in 1844 (changed to Grove City in 1883). The college purchased the property in 1888. This ivy-covered home, once used as a dormitory, is now a faculty residence. *Location:* Grove City, Main Street.

44. George Junior Republic is one of three institutions endowed by William R. George of Freeville, N.Y., to involve delinquent boys in a situation where they are given responsibility and the opportunity to direct their own rehabilitation. The other two are in New York and California. The Pennsylvania George Junior Republic, founded in 1909, is one of the most successful efforts of its kind in America, with boys sent by juvenile courts of many states and a nationwide reputation. One of its prominent supporters was Dr. Morgan Barnes. The small square flat-roofed brick jail became the printing school in 1950. In 1914 the brick chapel beside the jail and close to the road was dedicated to the memory of Jeremiah Sturgeon. The Donald Lobaugh Auditorium resulted from the bequest of an alumnus killed in action in Korea, who had made out his insurance to the Republic as "next of kin." *Location:* Grove City, on Pa. 58 (Mercer Road).

45. Courtney-Lindley House (shingle siding), of Georgian architecture with a double front porch the length of the house, was built by David Courtney about 1819. It is overshadowed by huge pines that match the house in age. Courtney, who came from Franklin County, erected Courtney's Mill on Wolf Creek in 1803. In 1953 the house was bought from Courtney's great-grandson by John W. Lindley, who restored it in 1959. *Location:* North Liberty, junction of Lindley Lake Road and l.r. 43020 off Pa. 258. Lindley Lake is nearby.

46. Octagon Barn (frame) was built by Jason and Robert Coleman in the late 1800s. A two-story springhouse that served as a post office was across the road from this structure. *Location:* One-fourth mile west of Centertown, on south side of l.r. 43027 (Scrubgrass Road).
　　Note: Another early octagon barn was on l.r. 43074 off l.r. 43075 south of Carlton. It was burned in recent years by an arsonist, but a smaller barn of this type still remains across the road from the site on the Heydrick farm.

47. Freedom Road Cemetery contains the graves of a number of slaves who escaped from the South by the underground railroad and settled near here about 1825 and later. After 1855 most of the rest moved on to Canada. Their cemetery lies a short distance south of the road. As a result of this settlement, nearby Stoneboro, on the south side of Sandy Lake, was once called Liberia. *Location:* Southwest of Sandy Lake, on Pa. 62 (Sandy Lake–Grove City Road) across from Stoneboro fairgrounds.

48. Carnahan House (brick) was built in 1836 for Gen. James M. Carnahan by John Hawthorn, John Henderson, and John McKean from bricks made on the property. It was the first house of its kind in the area, then known as Kerrtown. In later years this house was purchased by the Crawford family. *Location:* Mill Creek Township. About three miles north of Sandy Lake toward Cochranton, take first dirt road to left off Pa. 173. House is on right at crossroads.

49. New Lebanon Institute (brick), a large Victorian structure with five gables and bull's-eye windows, was erected in 1880 at a cost of $7,000. It was incorporated as McElwain Institute in 1883, honoring its most liberal supporter, John McElwain. An academic school for both men and women, it continued until shortly after 1909. It presently serves as a nondenominational church. *Location:* New Lebanon, on Pa. 173.

50. Indian Burials contains a monument to Chief Guyasuta that bears the following inscription:

> Guyasuta, a Chief of the Delaware Indians, had his town here known as Custaloga "he was buried here before 1810."

> Erected by descendants of Charles H. Heydrick. History of Venango County, Page 28.

A burial stone nearby with an outline of a hatchet reads, "Guy a sooter—1810 H.S." Another stone simply has written on it, "Boy." The Indian buried here and thought to be Guyasuta is more likely Custaloga, whose town was about twelve miles northwest of here, south of Meadville. Guyasuta, who was actually chief of the Senecas, is more widely believed to have been buried near Sharpsburg (Allegheny County) where his cabin was located. The bones of an old man, believed to have been his, were dug up in 1919 at

Sharpsburg and are now preserved in Carnegie Museum in the Oakland section of Pittsburgh. *Location:* Halfway between Milledgeville and Carlton, turn east off Pa. 173 and go 1.7 mile on l.r. 43075 to Scout reservation on Heydrick farm.

Note: Nearby is the brick Heydrick house, built in 1871 on donation land given to Charles McConnell Heydrick in 1787 for service in the Revolution.

51. Fairfield Presbyterian Church (frame) was the first church established in the county, with its first service held in 1799 by Rev. Joseph Stockton and Rev. Elisha McCurdy. The congregation adopted the name Fairfield in 1800. William Wiley from the Ten Mile settlement in Washington County was the first pastor, installed in 1802. At that time New Vernon was called the community of "Ten Milers" for the settlers who came here in 1798 from a creek by that name. The present church, built before 1876 adjacent to the cemetery, is on the site of the original structure. *Location:* New Vernon Township, off Pa. 285.

52. Clark's Gristmill (frame) was built in 1852. Giles Clark established the first mill here in 1838. Originally run by waterpower, the present structure continues to operate as a mill powered by electricity. *Location:* Clarks Mills, on Mill Road off Pa. 258.

53. Sheakley Halfway House (frame), once a tavern built in 1820 by Moses Sheakley, where General Lafayette was entertained in 1825, was the home of James Sheakley (1829–1917), fourth territorial governor of Alaska in 1893–97. He also served as U.S. commissioner of schools for Alaska in 1887–92. *Location:* Sheakleyville, on U.S. 19 in center of town near bridge.

54. Old Salem Methodist Church (frame) was organized in 1798. The present building, erected in 1850, retains the original architecture. *Location:* Leechs Corners (northeast of Greenville), on l.r. 43046.

Pennsylvania Historical and Museum Commission Markers

Albert Bushell Hart   Clark, Pa. 258

Bigler Graves   Pa. 58 southeast of Greenville

Bigler Home   Pa. 58 southeast of Greenville

Clay Furnace   U.S. 62 west of Charleston

Erie Extension Canal   Wasser Bridge Road 0.3 mile east of Pa. 18, south of Greenville; and junction of Pa. 18 and Pa. 518 east of Sharpsville

"Freedom Road"   U.S. 62 southwest of Sandy Lake

James Sheakley   Sheakleyville, U.S. 19

Johnston Tavern   U.S. 19 north of Leesburg

Pymatuning   Pa. 258 east of Clark

Shenango Town   Pa. 18 southeast of West Middlesex

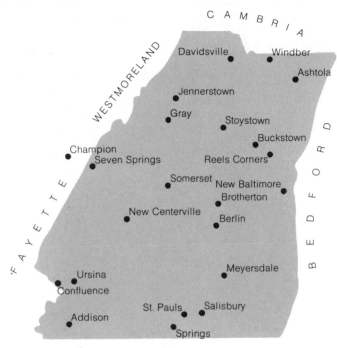

Davidsville Windber
Ashtola
Jennerstown
Gray
Stoystown
Buckstown
Champion
Seven Springs Reels Corners
Somerset New Baltimore
Brotherton
New Centerville
Berlin
Meyersdale
Ursina
Confluence
Addison St. Pauls Salisbury
Springs

CAMBRIA

WESTMORELAND

FAYETTE

BEDFORD

MARYLAND

Somerset County

Capsule History

Somerset County was named for Somersetshire in western England. It was erected out of Bedford County, April 17, 1795, and was reduced in size in 1804 when Cambria was organized in part from Somerset. It now has 1,078 square miles with a population of 76,037.

The earliest land surveys were made in 1767; and the first settlers, who were German of the Reformed and Lutheran faiths, came to the vicinity of Berlin about 1769. In 1780 a number of Mennonites migrated to the county. John Yoder, nicknamed "Axie" Yoder, was an early resident who made and signed more than 5,000 axes. The first permanent settler at the village of Somerset was Harmon Husband, a Quaker from North Carolina. Jeremiah Sullivan Black (1810–83) was born in the county near Brotherton. He served as chief justice of the Pennsylvania Supreme Court and under President James Buchanan as U.S. attorney general and secretary of state. The Black

191

family cemetery and a memorial park named in their honor are located on Pa. 31. Friedrich Goeb, who built a log cabin at the site of 151 West Main Street in Somerset, printed the first Bible west of the Allegheny Mountains in 1813 in German. Abner McKinley, President William McKinley's brother, lived in Somerset (129 East Main Street) from 1892 to 1904.

Five principal Indian trails traversed the county. The *Raystown Path* ran completely across it, following much the course later taken by U.S. 30. The *Conemaugh Path* cut the northeastern corner of the county from Pleasantville, above Ogletown and Windber, toward Johnstown. The *Fort Hill Path* ran from Sailsbury to Fort Hill through still wild country over Negro Mountain. The *Turkeyfoot Path* entered the southeastern corner of the county near Pocahontas, running by Engles Mill, Salisbury, south of the highest peak of Mount Davis, and north of Listonburg to Dumas and Harnedsville. *Nemacolin's Path* cut across the southwest corner near Addison.

Braddock's, Burd's, and Forbes's early military roads traversed sections of the county; and several military camps along the last-named highway later became the villages of Stoystown, Buckstown, and Jennerstown. (Near Stoystown, now under the present Quemahoning Reservoir, was the site of Delaware Chief Kickeney Paulin's cabin, a sleeping place on an early traders' path.) The Great Cumberland National Road (now U.S. 40) passed through the southwest tip of the county.

Somerset County has preserved eleven of its covered bridges as well as numerous log houses. At Fort Hill, three miles northeast of Ursina, two palisaded Indian villages dating from the Discovery Period have been excavated.

Lumbering was an important early industry in the county, later succeeded by agriculture. Limestone was another natural resource. The county has had five stone blast furnaces. Today the leading industries include coal-mining, dairying, and farming. Oats, buckwheat, and maple syrup are among the leading products.

Landmarks

1. Courthouse (brick) was erected in 1904. The earliest court in the county was held on December 21, 1795, in a room in the Webster Tavern in Somerset. The first courthouse was built in 1798. Construction of the second building began in 1851 and was completed in 1852. The third and present structure is on the site of the second. *Location:* Somerset.

2. Coffee Spring Farmhouse (frame) was the home of Harmon Husband, a leader of North Carolina's revolt against the British shortly after the Stamp Act was passed in 1765. Husband wrote the resolutions adopted by the Regulators who hoped to solve public grievances. In 1771 under an assumed name, Toscape Death, he fled to Pennsylvania. As the town of Somerset's first settler, he built the farmhouse in 1773. During the Whiskey Rebellion, Husband became a pamphleteer

and was Bedford County's delegate to the Parkinson Ferry meeting. In 1794 he was one of thirteen insurrectionists who were taken from Bedford to Philadelphia where they were imprisoned for about eight months. He died in 1795, shortly after being released.

Husband's farm acquired its name from the fact that years ago Indians dug wild chicory roots near the spring which still flows on the property. Inside this house is preserved an oil painting portraying the natives gathering their "coffee" to dry for a beverage. Above the fireplace is a mural depicting the life of Harmon Husband. This house, which at one time operated as an inn, continues to take in overnight guests. *Location:* Somerset, 555 East Main Street (junction of Pa. 31 and U.S. 219).

3. Lumber Railroad Tunnel dates back to 1883 when Andrew Carnegie and William H. Vanderbilt planned the South Pennsylvania

2. Coffee Spring Farmhouse

Railroad through Cumberland, Franklin, Fulton, Bedford, Somerset, and Westmoreland Counties to break the Pennsylvania Railroad's stranglehold on Pittsburgh freight rates. But while Carnegie was in Europe, Vanderbilt sold the railroad to the opposition, and it was only half-built. Later, six of its nine tunnels were used by the Pennsylvania Turnpike (one through Laurel Hill, now unused, was in Somerset County). This is the only one of the nine ever used by a railroad—the Pittsburgh, Westmoreland & Somerset, principally a lumber railroad developed by Andrew and Richard B. Mellon in 1906. The end scars of it, almost covered over, can be seen by looking sharply at the north edge of the turnpike. *Location:* About three miles west of Somerset, on Pennsylvania Turnpike halfway between 106- and 107-mile markers.

4. Somerset Historical Center is an indoor-outdoor museum exhibit pertaining to mid-eighteenth-century life on the Laurel Highlands frontier. It was developed and is administered by the Pennsylvania Historical and Museum Commission. It also serves as headquarters for the county historical society. In the late 1960s Dr. and Mrs. Earl O. Haupt sold sixteen acres of property adjacent to their home to the state along with an 1804 log house that they had bought after it had been used in the 1954 county sesquicenten-

nial celebration. The center also displays a bridge originally built in the 1850s at Walters Mill, ten miles south of here and relocated at the site in 1961; a maple-sugar camp of 1840; and a lean-to barn, all from the unique Haupt collection. In 1969–70 the modern stone exhibit building and batten-board administrative offices were opened to the public, along with nature trails. *Hours:* Tuesday–Saturday, 9 A.M.–4 P.M. Sunday, 1–4:30 P.M. No admission charge for citizens over 65, children under 12, and Friday school tours. *Location:* Four miles north of Somerset, on old U.S. 219.

5. Beam's Reformed Church (brick) was organized in 1844 and built in 1847. It is now the Mount Laurel United Church of Christ. William Conrad was the first pastor of this church, which was erected on the Beam farm. The Beam flax and gristmill was at one time located nearby. *Location:* One mile from Gray, at junction of l.r. 55072 and l.r. 55107, just south of Jennerstown.

6. Rauch House (painted brick) was built in 1806 and is now an antique shop. It was formerly the home of Squire Henry Rauch, who conducted a hearing here on charges against Joseph and David Nicely, who posed as constables and killed Herman Umberger, after finding $16,000 in his house in February 1889. The two brothers were convicted and hanged in 1891, after escaping and being

3. *Lumber Railroad Tunnel*

4. *Log House at Somerset Historical Center*

captured twice. After the hanging the noose was taken to the courthouse for preservation. *Location:* Jennerstown, on U.S. 30.

7. Mountain Playhouse (log) **and Green Gables Restaurant** (stone) had their beginning in 1927 when James, Robert, and Louise Stoughton, then in their teens, built a roadside restaurant on the old homestead farm belonging to the family since 1795. Their Green Gables establishment won a $3,000 prize in a highway-beautification contest sponsored by the Rockefeller Foundation, and the prize launched them on a lifetime career. In 1938 James and his sister Louise Stoughton Maust purchased the Cronin-Grover log gristmill, built in 1805 and in use until 1918 at Roxbury, near Berlin, thirty miles away. (It is similar in construction to the 1806 Simon Hay's mill which was erected on Blue Lick Creek near Meyersdale.) After it was rebuilt on their property it became a summer theater, opened in 1939, and the Jenner Art Gallery. This is one of the oldest summer-stock theaters west of the Alleghenies. The 2,500-acre recreation complex was enlarged in 1950 to include a lake built by Robert Stoughton, an additional dining room, and an old barn converted into apartments and guest rooms. The theater is open from late May to mid October, and the restaurant daily, year round. *Location:* On old U.S. 219, 0.5 mile north of Jennerstown.

8. Seese's Museum (partly frame) is a primitive building in a rustic setting. Privately owned. Visits by appointment. *Admission*

charge. *Location:* About three miles north of Jennerstown on Thomas Mills–Jennerstown Road.

9. Johns House (frame) was the last home of Joseph Schantz (Johns), a Swiss Mennonite who came to America in 1769 at the age of twenty. (See *Johns Log House Model*, Cambria County.) He moved in 1806 to this site, the Stock Farm, north of Davidsville, which had been laid out by David Stetzman. Behind the house is a Johns family cemetery enclosed by a picket fence. *Location:* Just north of Davidsville, turn off Main Street onto East Campus Street. House is a quarter mile on left.

10. Lohr Barn (frame) has interesting Pennsylvania Dutch round louvres decorated with cut-out hearts and stars on both sides, and is reminiscent of the barns of the early German settlers in this area. J. W. Lohr built the structure about 1875. *Location:* Near Davidsville. Turn west off Main Street onto West Campus Street and continue for almost 0.5 mile to barn on right.

11. Kline Gristmill (frame) was built in 1801 by a man named Bell. Joseph C. Kline bought the establishment in 1896 and operated it for thirty-four years along with a blacksmith shop. The mill has an overshot wheel. A steel turbine wheel, still existent, replaced the original wooden one. The property is still owned by the Kline family. The present Mrs. Kline is the granddaughter of Squire Henry Rauch (see *Rauch House*). *Location:* Base of

Laurel Hill on Forbes Road (l.r. 55092) near Lutheran church camp. From U.S. 30 at Sliding Rock Country Club Road, take first road to left at Forbes marker; thence 0.6 mile to mill on left.

12. Seven Springs Resort was built after World War II by Helen and Adolph Dupre and is still owned by this family. It now has the largest ski lodge in the United States, a glass-enclosed ski-side swimming pool, and accommodations for 800 overnight guests. *Location:* Eight miles east of Champion, on l.r. 64074.

13. Farm Equipment Museum has a fine collection of steam traction engines, threshers, and other nineteenth- and early twentieth-century farm machinery. A regional display is held here each summer. *Location:* New Centerville.

14. Turkeyfoot Regular Baptist Church (frame), the oldest of its sect in the county, was also known as the Jersey Baptist Church, since a group of Baptist settlers from New Jersey organized it June 14, 1775. At that time Rev. Isaac Sutton and John Corbly met with the congregation gathered at Moses Hall's house and formed the Turkeyfoot and Sandy Creek Glades Union Church. The first house of worship was built in 1788, the second in 1838, and the present one in 1877. Nearby are two covered bridges. *Location:* 1.7 mile on l.r. 55021 from its junction with Pa. 281 in Ursina (on Jersey Road to Ohiopyle).

15. "Great Crossings" Bridge (stone), once spanning the Youghiogheny River at Somerfield (formerly Smithfield) and leading into Somerset County, was built in 1817–18 by Kinkead, Beck & Evans. It was dedicated July 4, 1818, by President Monroe, followed by much celebration in conjunction with the holiday. The structure, 375 feet in length with three arches, has since been covered by the waters of an artificial lake and replaced by another bridge south of the site. The old bridge is visible during dry seasons when the water is low. A marker located at the National Road tollhouse (q.v.) reads:

About one-half mile above this point is the "Great Crossings" of the Youghiogheny River, where George Washington crossed Nov. 18, 1753, when sent as envoy by Governor Dinwiddie of Virginia, to the French Commander at Fort LeBoeuf. Washington, on his military expedition to the Ohio, encamped there with his forces May 18 to 24, 1754, and

11. *Kline Gristmill*

from that point explored the Youghiogheny. There, also Major General Braddock, with his army crossed June 24, 1755, on his march against Fort Duquesne. [Tablet placed by Great Crossing Chapter, DAR, May 18, 1912]

Location: Somerfield, on U.S. 40, 0.5 mile west of Addison.

16. National Road Tollhouse (stone), a two-story, seven-sided structure joined to a one-story wing, was built in 1835 when the state took control of this section of the National Road (U.S. 40). (The only other existing tollhouse of the original six built on this road in Pennsylvania is Searights in Fayette County [q.v.].) This well-preserved structure with its old toll rates still posted on the exterior was restored and is maintained by the Great Crossing Chapter of the DAR. Iron toll-gate posts removed from the building were taken to a cemetery to be used for an entranceway. Visits by appointment. *Location:* Addison, on U.S. 40.

Note: The Turkeyfoot (confluence of the Youghiogheny and Casselman Rivers and Laurel Hill Creek at Confluence) was a famous landmark in pioneer days.

17. Mount Davis is the highest point in the state, with an altitude of 3,213 feet. It is marked by a column of rocks with a brass plate indicating the landmark. Negro Mountain, at its base, was reportedly named by a Maryland hunting party in honor of a black member who was killed during an Indian attack. A forty-five-foot observation tower provides a view of the countryside. *Location:* At Mount Davis Recreation Park, near Salisbury. Take l.r. 55008 from Meyersdale to Summit Mills; continue on this road and watch for signs to rock. Nearby is large picnic area on south side of road, connected to tower site via High Point Trail, a mile-long footpath.

18. Springs Museum (cement-block) houses collections of thousands of items depicting early life in the Casselman Valley. It was founded in 1957 and established here on an abandoned poultry farm in 1964. The museum is operated by the Springs Historical Society. The adjoining grounds are the site of an annual folk-art festival held the first Friday and Saturday in October. The community of Springs, settled between 1760 and 1775, is the state's highest unincorporated village, lying at the foot of Negro Mountain at Mount Davis. *Hours:* Memorial Day–October: 11 A.M.–5 P.M., daily except Sunday, and by appointment. *Admission charge. Location:* Springs, on Pa. 669 halfway between Salisbury and Grantsville, Md.

19. 1795 House (frame) is easily recognized by the date of construction written in bold letters across one gable end of the house. It may have been built by Peter Shirer, who was a business associate of Joseph Markley, the founder of the former mining village of Salisbury. The home was later purchased by Samuel S. Garlitz. *Location:* Salisbury, on Pa. 669.

20. Keagey House (stone) was built in 1815 by John Keagey. It was later owned by the Haselbarth family. *Location:* Salisbury, on Pa. 669 (across from 1795 house).

21. Compton's Grain Mill (frame) was operated by Samuel Compton (born 1827), who purchased the Hostetter mill in 1868. In 1872 he erected the present structure, which was a "burr" flouring mill, and added a sawmill to the plant. Compton also served as justice of the peace. His father Phineas invented the first meat grinder in the county. *Location:* Near Saint Pauls, about two miles on l.r. 55047; halfway between Saint Pauls and Pa. 669.

22. Beachy House (frame) was erected by Peter Beachy (originally Bitsche, 1793–1854), a dairy farmer. Known as "River Pete" he was the only son of Abraham (died 1833) and Barbara Beachy. Abraham had migrated from Switzerland by way of Philadelphia. At least six generations of the family have lived in this house. *Location:* On Pa. 669, 0.5 mile south of West Salisbury.

23. Maple Manor (frame) is the oldest house (about 1785) in Meyersdale, which was laid

23. Maple Manor

out in 1844 and named for Peter Meyers, son of Jacob, an owner of the house. Andrew Berdreger, prior owner, had built a mill nearby. The house is the headquarters of Festival Park. It has a fine collection of antiques. Here also is a cobbler's shop, a typical doctor's office, and a country store in addition to a sugar camp. Each year in March the state maple festival is held here, the maple capital of Pennsylvania. *Location:* Meyersdale.

24. Berlin was laid out on a tract called Pious Springs, owned by the Lutheran and Reformed congregations of Brothers Valley Township. In 1784 the members established the town with the stipulation that the parishioners build their houses with frontages of at least twenty-two feet and with stone chimneys "so that there will be no danger of fire." Those who did not abide by this order were to forfeit their land or lot to the village for the use of the church and school. The manufacture of hats for southern markets was the town's largest industry until the Civil War. The existence of two market squares is a result of an early dispute among the settlers. Today the principal activity is maple-sugar production and farming.

a. Trinity Reformed Church (brick), now the United Church of Christ, was built in 1883. In 1777 the congregations of the Trinity Reformed and Lutheran churches agreed to worship in the village schoolhouse until each could erect a house of worship. Rev. John W. Weber was the first regular pastor of the Trinity Reformed congregation. In 1794 Rev. Cyriacus Spangenberg, pastor of Trinity, fatally stabbed an elder, Jacob Glessner, in a church dispute. Despite the statement often made that he was hanged, Spangenberg received a pardon and moved to the northwestern part of the state. *Location:* Corner of Vine and Main Streets.

b. Holy Trinity Evangelical Lutheran Church (brick) was built in 1889, replacing the first two-story log structure, erected in 1800. *Location:* Corner of Fifth and Main Streets.

25. Saint John the Baptist Catholic Church (brick), served by the Carmelite Monastery of the Franciscan Order of Monks, was organized in 1824, and the present edifice was dedicated August 15, 1890. Its interior, including the ceiling of the sanctuary, is constructed mostly of wood by local craftsmen. This picturesque church sits high on a hill overlooking the German village of New Baltimore and the turnpike. *Location:* On the Pennsylvania Turnpike at New Baltimore, about twenty-five miles east of Somerset. It can be reached from turnpike by long flight of steps or from Bedford exit (no. 11) by Pa. 31.

26. Tunnel Spring was a popular spot for refreshment from the time the turnpike was opened until a second tunnel was cut at the east end of Allegheny Tunnel some years ago. Another spring sends a fine flow of pure water down a cemented trough about 100 feet farther down the mountain, emptying into a drain under the road. *Location:* Eastern portal of Allegheny Tunnel on turnpike (water readily visible on south side of road).

27. Shade Church (frame) housed congregations of Lutheran and Reformed faiths, later Reformed only. The first church organization was in 1835, but there had been preaching at an earlier date. The building was erected in 1822–23, but looks more modern, having been completely renovated and repaired in 1884. *Location:* One mile west of Reels Corners turn north off U.S. 30 at church sign, and follow Shade Church Road for 1.7 mile.

Note: Nearby an army oven has been reconstructed at the site of Fort Bellaire near Kantner. It is off l.r. 55152 about two miles east of Pa. 53.

28. Windber Museum (frame), with a double front porch, is the oldest house in the borough, which owns the structure. It was built by David J. and Rachel (Holsopple) Shaffer in 1869. The Shaffers at one time owned most of the area which is present-day Windber. (Johnny Weissmuller, champion swimmer and movie actor, was born in Windber.) *Hours:* Tuesday–Sunday, 1–4 P.M. *Donations accepted. Location:* Windber, 601 Fifteenth Street.

Note: The Christ of Gethsemane, a painting by Lawrence L. Whitaker, is in the United Brethren Church in this borough. Whitaker, a member of the church, donated it in memory of the congregation's founders.

29. Ashtola (frame, partly covered with original hemlock slabs) was built as a summer vacation home by E. V. Babcock (see *Babcock House,* Allegheny County). (The town of Ashtola was named by Mrs. H. L. Baer at the time of her wedding. She was impressed by the abundance of ash trees in this region. Her son married into President McKinley's family.) *Location:* Ashtola, in Ogle Township, on l.r. 55095, 3.5 miles northeast of Pa. 160 near Hagevo or 3.5 miles southeast of Pa. 160 at Windber.

Pennsylvania Historical and Museum Commission Markers

Adam Schneider Somerset, northwest corner of square

Ankeny Square Somerset, Patriot Street at cemetery

Braddock Road Addison, U.S. 40

Early Bible Somerset, 151 West Main Street

Forbes Road (Edmunds Swamp) Buckstown, U.S. 30

Forbes Road (Fort Dewart) U.S. 30 near Bedford County line

Forbes Road (Stony Creek Encampment) U.S. 30 east of Stoystown

Forbes Road (The Clear Fields) U.S. 30, 1.3 mile west of Jennerstown

Fort Hill Pa. 281, 3 miles northeast of Ursina

Great Crossings U.S. 40 at the Youghiogheny River

Harmon Husband U.S. 219 east of Somerset

Jeremiah S. Black Pa. 31, 6.5 miles east of Somerset

Log Grist Mill U.S. 219, 0.5 mile north of Jennerstown

National Road U.S. 40 southeast of Addison near state line

Toll House Addison, U.S. 40

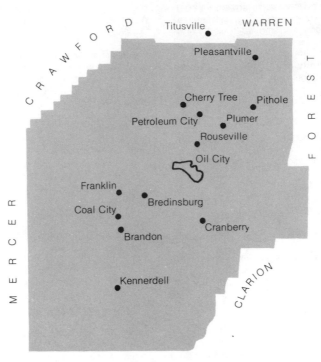

Venango County

Capsule History

Venango County, named for the old Indian town at the mouth of French Creek, was erected out of Allegheny and Lycoming Counties, March 12, 1800. Although Franklin was chosen as the county seat at that time, Crawford County had jurisdictional authority over Venango until 1805. The county has 678 square miles with a population of 62,353. The formation of other counties from Venango has reduced its original 1,390 acres by about half.

George Washington in 1753 was sent here by the governor of Virginia to reconnoiter the French forts and to order the French out of northwestern Pennsylvania, a territory claimed by Pennsylvania, Virginia, and the French. The forts of the county, all within Franklin, included Machault (French, 1756–59), Venango (English, 1760–63), Franklin (American, 1787–96), and Old Garrison (American, 1796–99).

The county's most famous Indian road was the *Venango Path,* which came up the course of Pa. 8 from Harrisville by Wesley, Springville, and Mays Mills, then cut over Gurney Hill to Franklin; crossing French Creek there, it followed the east bank toward Cochranton. The *Kuskusky–Venango Path* followed the same course in this area. The *Frankstown–Venango Path, Punxsutawney–Venango Path, Venango-Chinklaca- moose Path,* and *Venango–Kittanning Path* all came up along the course of U.S. 322 from Kossuth. The *Cayahaga Path* followed U.S. 62 to the county line. The *Corn- planter–Venango Path* followed Pa. 417 to Titusville, thence ran along a ridge east of Caldwell Creek. The *Venango–Conewango Path* ran up the Allegheny River all the way past President.

In 1785 Gen. William Irvine and Andrew Ellicott surveyed donation lands in the county set aside for Revolutionary War soldiers (see Capsule History, Butler County). Also the Seneca leader Chief Cornplanter was granted land on the east bank of Oil Creek for his service during the treaty talks with the Indians in 1784–89. During the War of 1812 he brought 200 Indian volunteers to serve in the conflict.

Franklin, the county seat, was once the Indian village of Venango, where an early settler, John Fraser, lived from 1742 to 1753. Joncaire, a French officer, had his headquarters at Fraser's cabin when Washington visited the site in 1753, and it is believed that this structure was embodied in the French fort. Another pioneer was George Power who settled here in 1790. In 1864 John Wilkes Booth boarded at the Webber house (corner of Buffalo and Thirteenth Streets) in Franklin before going to Washington to assassinate President Lincoln. Booth owned the Dramatic Oil Com- pany in Cranberry Township. Pennsylvania's second oldest and largest mental institu- tion, Polk State School, was founded in 1897 along U.S. 62 west of Franklin.

The world's first well drilled specifically for oil was established in Venango County just south of Titusville (Crawford County) in 1859 by Edwin L. Drake. Oil City, the county's largest city once a rafting center, became an important oil exchange, but a great fire on May 26, 1866, destroyed most of the original structures of this town. Two other oil-boom communities were Pithole and Petroleum Center, which was also a famous gambling place where $64,000 was bet on one throw of the dice.

The Van Sykle Pipe Line was the first in the world to successfully carry crude oil. It ran from Pithole to the Miller Farm, where Andrew Carnegie purchased property and first invested in oil. The line, built in 1865 by Samuel Van Sykle, followed a straight course for about five and a half miles and revolutionized the transportation of petroleum. Definite traces of the original trenches can still be seen along the course of the old pipeline.

The county is still an important oil industrial center. Natural gas, limestone, glass and molding sand, and gravel are also abundant resources. It has had twenty-five stone blast furnaces and was once known as "the iron county."

Landmarks

1. Courthouse (brick), the county's third, was built in 1868–69. The architects were Sloan and Hutton. Col. James S. Meyers and John S. McCalmont were the orators for the ceremony at the laying of the cornerstone July 15, 1868. The structure has double towers, one taller than the other. The first courthouse was erected in 1811; the second, in 1847. *Location:* Franklin, Twelfth and Liberty Streets.

Note: Franklin has many fine old homes.

1. Courthouse

2. First Church of Christ, Scientist (stone), of uncertain date, is reputed to be the oldest structure in Franklin. This congregation was organized in 1894 and its charter secured in 1899. It acquired this stone house for a church home in 1903. This property was partly the site of the Old Garrison, built in 1796, where troops were maintained until 1799. The fortress was used for a jail from 1805 to 1819 and razed in 1824. *Location:* Franklin, Elk and South Park Streets (near courthouse).

Note: The Samuel F. Dale house (brick), built in 1875, is at 1409 Elk Street.

3. Venango County Museum (brick) opened in 1961. Here French, English, and Colonial flags represent those once officially flown over this area. The building was originally the law office of John S. McCalmont. Born in 1822 he was admitted to the Venango County bar in 1844 and served in the Civil War as a colonel. His home, which is now the Franklin Library next to the museum, was remodeled for its present use in 1921–22. The museum contains models of Fort Venango and Fort Machault, as well as other displays. *Hours:* April 1–October 30: Tuesday–Saturday, 1–5 P.M. Sunday 2–5 P.M. Open evenings by appointment. *Location:* Franklin, 417 Twelfth Street.

4. Franklin Club (brick) was built in 1866 by Dr. J. W. Stillman, who later sold the house to a Mr. Troller, succeeded by the White family. In 1889 the Nursery Club purchased the property from the George H. White family for $8,000. (Early histories of the county refer to the town of Franklin as the "nursery of great men.") This social organization, which had 100 members, had been established in the Hancock Building in 1877 and now is known as the Franklin Club. Before the structure was occupied by this group, a ballroom had been added to the house. In 1910 other alterations were made by Corrin and Wilt. *Location:* Franklin, on Pa. 8 (Liberty Street) one block from its junction with U.S. 322.

5. Franklin Pioneer Cemetery was set aside as a burial site at the time the town of Franklin was laid out in 1795. Buried here is one of the first settlers of the county, George Power (1762–1845), who had helped build Fort Franklin in 1787. Also at this location is the grave of an old soldier of Napoleon's army who came by stagecoach to Franklin and died at George Power's inn before anyone learned his name. The cemetery was restored in 1952 by the Venango Chapter of the DAR. *Location:* Franklin, Otter and Fifteenth Streets.

6. Duncan McIntosh Mansion (stone) is a typical oil millionaire's home of the post–Civil War era. In 1954 the White Sisters of Africa bought this estate for their order. At present it houses the Venango County Human Services, operated by the Department of Welfare. *Location:* One mile from bridge at Franklin, on Pa. 322 east.

7. River Ridge (stone) was the estate of Joseph Crocker Sibley, who was an agent of the Galena Oil Works at Chicago. In 1873 he lived in Franklin, developed the Signal Oil Works, and later was elected mayor of Franklin. He was director of the American Jersey Cattle Club, president of the Franklin Opera House Company, and a director of both the Railway Speed Recorder Company and the First National Bank of Franklin. He was under house arrest the latter part of his life. This huge structure with angled wings looks out over the Allegheny River. In 1948 the property was converted into a seminary by the Roman Catholic Society of the Missionaries of Africa. At present it is operated by a conservative religious group as a Bible school. *Location:* 5.5 miles north of Franklin. From Franklin turn left across bridge on Pa. 322 toward Oil City. Just north of Bredins-

3. Venango County Museum

burg, proceed west on golf course road and go 0.2 mile; thence 1.8 mile on unimproved road.

Note: A stone carriage house with an attached portico over the driveway is nearby. All along the dirt road to the estate, in the wooded area, can be seen evidences of secondary oil recovery from early rich oil fields.

8. De Bence's Antique Music Museum and Old Country Store are both located in an old barn which has been remodeled and includes a fine collection of musical instruments and memorabilia. *Hours:* Summer months by appointment. *Admission charge* for museum. *Location:* About two miles south of Franklin on Pa. 8 (Pittsburgh Street) in Sandy Creek Township.

9. Indian God Rock on the left bank of the Allegheny River is a twenty-two-foot-high sandstone with prehistoric petroglyphs on its surface. It was first recorded in the annals of western Pennsylvania history by the French army officer, Céloron de Blainville, who in 1749 arrived in the Upper Ohio River Basin and claimed it for Louis XV, king of France. Father Joseph Pierre de Bonnecamps, who accompanied Céloron on his mission, wrote in his journal:

> In the evening after we disembarked, we buried a 2nd plate of lead under a great rock, upon which were to be seen several

figures roughly graven. . . . Our officers tried to persuade me that this was the work of Europeans; but, in truth, I may say that in the style and workmanship of these engravings, one cannot fail to recognize the unskillfulness of savages.

The lead plates have never been recorded as found, and the rock has been disfigured by erosion, vandalism, and graffiti. A sketch from this rock made by Capt. S. Eastman in 1853 has been preserved in *Archives of Aboriginal Knowledge,* vol. 55. It represents one of the oldest written records of man in western Pennsylvania. *Location:* Several miles south of Franklin. Go 6.5 miles south on Pa. 257 from its junction with U.S. 322. Turn right onto l.r. 60076 and continue through Coal City to Brandon, 6.4 miles, where road ends at railroad tracks. From here walk about two miles up (to right) Pennsylvania Railroad tracks to 115-mile stone. Rock is at river's edge directly below and is best seen from boat.

10. Kennerdell Area Recreational and Cultural Center is located in the town of Kennerdell, known as "the little Switzerland of Pennsylvania." A gift of twelve acres by W. B. Wilson who died in 1970, this natural wooded setting provides the background for an annual music and art festival that commenced in 1955. The Memorial Art Center and native stone monument were erected in

201

7. *River Ridge*

honor of Harry Hickman, Sr., who was the art director from 1955 to 1964. For twenty years Eugene Reichenfeld, the founder of the musical program, has conducted orchestra concerts here in the woodlands. *Location:* Kennerdell, at Wilson Park near Allegheny River.

Note: A picturesque waterfall known as "Little Niagara" is next to the Rockland-Kennerdell Road near a famous lookout point.

11. McClintock Oil Well, no. 1, the world's oldest producing oil well, was drilled in August 1861. The well is across the railroad tracks west of the historical marker on the highway. *Location:* Rouseville, on Pa. 8 south of bridge.

Note: Also on Pa. 8 north of Rouseville is the old frame Rynd Farm schoolhouse, a two-story structure with a bell and belfry.

12. "Coal Oil Johnny" Steele House (frame), on the old Culbertson McClintock oil farm, was inherited in 1864 by John Washington Steele from his aunt after she was burned to death while lighting her kitchen stove with kerosene. Steele acquired his nickname from a Philadelphia newspaper, and he sported a bright red carriage decorated with flowing oil derricks and tanks on its sides. Long after he had squandered his fortune, all within a year, he admitted, "I spent my money foolishly, recklessly, wickedly, gave it away without excuse; threw dollars to street urchins to see them scramble"—a reflection of the early opulent waste of the oil industry. He became a respected railroad stationmaster in Nebraska. *Location:* North of Rouseville, across Oil Creek from Pa. 8.

13. Pithole, sometimes spelled Pit Hole, was created in 1865 by the discovery of oil when the United States or Frazier oil well started producing 250 barrels per day on Thomas Holmden's property. The town site was laid out May 24 and by the summer of that year had a population of 15,000. It at that time was reputed to have the third largest post office in the state and had two banks, countless saloons, about fifty-seven hotels, three churches, the county's first daily newspaper, a water system, and a railroad. The oil wells began to go dry in less than a year, and decreased oil production along with numerous fires caused the inhabitants to move away. Today the only remains of this ghost town are street grades, foundation scars, and signs which were placed in recent years to locate the original streets. The last building to be torn down was the Methodist church in 1939.

In 1957 James B. Stevenson, publisher of the *Titusville Herald,* purchased the Holmden farm and opened the main streets to visitors. Stevenson deeded the site to the state in 1963. It now has a modern museum and one producing oil well administered by the Pennsylvania Historical and Museum Commission. *Hours:* By appointment. *Admission charge. Location:* North of Plumer. Go 1.8 mile on Pa. 227 to l.r. 60049, thence two miles to site.

14. Pithole Schoolhouse (frame) was built several years after the decline of Pithole. A few stone foundation ruins of the ghost town can be seen up the road from this school. *Location:* At Pithole site, off Pa. 227.

15. Cherrytree Presbyterian Church (frame), now a Bible church, was organized in 1837 with thirteen members. This early structure originally had a belfry which was destroyed in recent years when it was struck by lightning. *Location:* 0.3 mile north of Cherry Tree and one fourth mile off Pa. 8.

16. Free Methodist Church (frame) with a spire is a fine example of mid–nineteenth-century design. It was built in 1848. *Location:* Pleasantville, end of Main Street.

17. Drake Well was the world's first drilled specifically for oil, sunk and operated by "Colonel" Edwin L. Drake (see *Edwin L. Drake Monument,* Crawford County), general agent of the Seneca Oil Company, which was organized March 23, 1858. Drake, who later lost his oil fortune in speculation, came to western Pennsylvania to observe salt-well

11. McClintock Oil Well, no. 1

operations and to drill for oil. On August 27, 1859, his driller William A. Smith (see *"Uncle Billy" Smith Monument,* Butler County) struck oil here at sixty-nine and a half feet. This well, whose derrick was designed and built by Smith, yielded eight to ten barrels of petroleum a day. Its success ushered in a new industry which provided an efficient illuminating and lubricating oil. A replica of Drake's original derrick and engine house occupies the exact site of the well.

Nearby in the 229-acre Drake Well Memorial Park is a museum-library, the largest single depository for historical records and relics of the oil industry (collected since 1934). It is operated by the Pennsylvania Historical and Museum Commission. *Hours:* Daylight saving time: Weekdays, 8:30 A.M.–5 P.M. Sunday, 1–5 P.M. Winter: Weekdays, 9 A.M.–4:30 P.M. Sunday, 1–4:30 P.M. *Admission charge. Location:* 1.5 mile south of Titusville, along Oil Creek. Go 0.5 mile south on Pa. 8; thence 1.25 mile southeast on l.r. 60052.

18. The Great Petroleum Shaft was built in the early oil days above the best wells of Oil Creek Valley. This shaft was constructed down to the level of the oil-bearing strata so that oil could be collected in a large pool and then pumped out. Welsh coal miners from Pennsylvania's anthracite region started the work. Huge foundation stones were set around the top of the shaft for ventilating machinery, and threaded steel rods were inserted in these stones to hold the machinery in place. The money ran out after 150 feet of digging and the project was abandoned. The stones and shaft (partly filled up to keep out stray cows and horses) can be seen in the woods. *Location:* Southeast of Petroleum Center, 0.5 mile south of l.r. 60046 on hillside.

Pennsylvania Historical and Museum Commission Markers

Drake Well Park   Cranberry, U.S. 322; and on property in Venango County southeast of Titusville

First Oil Pipeline   Pa. 227, 4 miles southwest of Pleasantville

Fort Machault   Franklin, Eighth and Elk Streets

Fort Venango   Franklin, Eighth and Elk Streets

Oldest Producing Oil Well   Pa. 8 just south of Rouseville

Old Garrison   Franklin, U.S. 322, South Park and Elk Streets

Pithole   L.r. 60049 on hill

Pithole City   At property off Pa. 227 on l.r. 60049 at Pithole, southeast of Titusville

Pithole Fabulous Ghost Town   Intersection of Pa. 227 and l.r. 60049, 5.6 miles southwest of Pleasantville

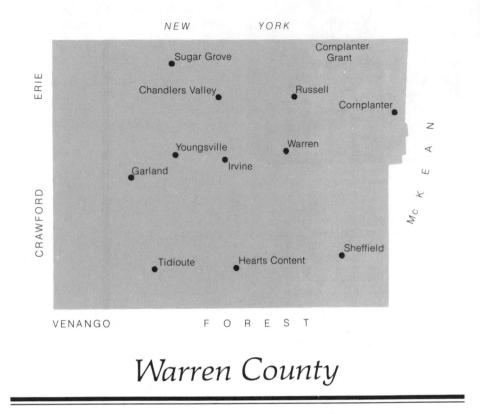

Warren County

Capsule History

Warren County, named in honor of Maj. Gen. Joseph Warren, a doctor killed at the battle of Bunker Hill in 1775, was erected out of Lycoming and Allegheny Counties on March 12, 1800. Separate judicial arrangements were finally made in 1805 when the county was attached first to Crawford and then to Venango. In 1819 Warren acquired its own judicial authority with the community of Warren selected as the county seat. Warren County is 905 square miles in area with a population of 47,682.

The first to arrive here were French explorers who came from Canada to the mouth of the Conewango by way of Lake Erie and Lake Chautauqua. They were followed by many Scotch-Irish settlers after the Revolution.

Baron de Longueuil's expedition through this area was in 1739. This led to the one by Céloron de Blainville in 1749 at the mouth of Conewango Creek, where he buried lead plates claiming the region for France. However, Pierre Paul de Marin, commander of the French military expedition to the Ohio the following year, rejected Céloron's route and forbade the erection of a fort due to the shallow water of the Conewango.

Most of the Indian inhabitants were Senecas from the Iroquois nation and Munsees, a subtribe of the Delawares. In 1779 Gen. John Sullivan drove the Indians northward after the so-called "Wyoming massacre"—actually a regular military action in which British and Indian troops went against American garrisons. Gen. Daniel Brodhead made a similar expedition into the county in the same year and had a skirmish with the Indians at Thompson's Island, the only Revolutionary battle in northwestern Pennsylvania. He destroyed the remains of the Buckaloons Indian town (Irvine) and burned the deserted village of Conewango, where in recent years burial mounds have been excavated. (This area later became Warren, the county seat which was laid out in 1795 and became a borough in 1832.) Sugar Run Mounds at Cornplanter have also been excavated, revealing another village site.

Four Indian trails traversed Warren County. The *Brokenstraw Path* entered just east of Corry, followed Hare Creek to a crossing at its mouth, thence down the left bank of Brokenstraw to Youngsville and the right bank to its mouth at Irvine. The *Cornplanter Path* from Warren went up Conewango Creek and Hatch Run, turned along Quaker Ridge to Scandia, and passed down Hodge Run and up the Allegheny River to the mouth of Cornplanter Run. The *Cornplanter-Venango Path* entered northeast of Titusville, following a ridge east of the East Branch of Caldwell Creek to Pittsfield, thence down the left bank of Brokenstraw to Irvine and up the Allegheny River to Warren, finally following the Cornplanter Path. The *Venango-Conewango Path* followed the Allegheny River from below Tionesta to Irvine and Warren.

Early industries in the county were lumbering and tanning, together with oil production after 1859. That year in August at oil spring north of Tidioute, J. L. Grandin began the second well (which was dry) drilled specifically for oil, after Col. Edwin Drake's discovery. Succeeding wells nearby proved successful. Triumph Hill, above Tidioute, was producing oil in the 1870s, and Cherry Grove had a boom in 1882 and 1883, where the famous "646" well was located (l.r. 61032 nine miles west of Weldbank). During the oil boom the Harmony Society (see *Old Economy,* Beaver County, and *Harmony,* Butler County) made $6 million in this county when oil was struck in 1860 on their timber tract in Limestone Township. Their Economy Oil Company and village enterprise was liquidated in 1895. A monument at the site of the world's first flowing oil well (1860) is across the river from Tidioute just below the bridge.

Today natural gas, petroleum, wood and metal products, and glass are important. In the line of agriculture, potatoes, poultry, cereal grains, and dairy products are noteworthy. In addition, the county is a hunting and fishing paradise.

A recent study has been made on a number of early existing structures in this county. Further information can be obtained in a series of books entitled *Historic Buildings in Warren County,* edited by Mary Putnam and Chase Putnam and published by the county historical society.

Landmarks

1. Courthouse (brick and stone) is an Italian Renaissance building (replacing an 1828 structure). Begun in 1875, it was completed two years later at a cost of $97,434.59, with furnishings costing $6,000 more. It has a large dome with four clocks and a 1,600-pound bell. A statue of Justice stands 125 feet above the sidewalk. Additions were made in 1916 and 1925. *Location:* Warren, Fourth Avenue and Market Street.

3. Historical Society House

2. New Mansion House (cut stone), built in 1833 by Ebenezer Jackson, is a fine building which opened as the Warren Hotel in March of 1834. A year later it became the Lumberman's Bank, and after that institution's failure in the Panic of 1837, it became, successively, the Tanner House and the Diamond House. After the closing of an earlier Mansion House (1814–56), the newer building adopted its name. For a time it was also the Temperance Hotel. It has served as a women's club and a music club, and its upper story was once a ballroom. *Location:* Warren, 215 Fourth Avenue.

3. Historical Society House (brick, white wood trim) was built in 1870–73 by Thomas Struthers as a wedding gift for his daughter Anna, wife of George H. Wetmore. She died in 1880, her husband in 1890, and their only child, Thomas Struthers Wetmore, in 1896. Struthers died in 1892. The house was occupied by the Charles Schimmelfeng family from 1893 to 1950, when it was sold to Warren County for offices. It has been occupied by the historical society—a most active organization—since 1964. *Location:* Warren, 210 Fourth Avenue.

4. Struthers Library-Theater (red brick) was a gift to the Warren community in 1884 from Thomas Struthers, lawyer, land baron,

railroad promoter, politician, banker, and foundry operator. The cost was over $80,000, besides the $7,050 raised by public subscription to buy the ground. The building, which had a tower, was designed to include store and office spaces to provide income for maintenance and improvements. *Location:* Warren, Third Avenue and Liberty Street.

5. Charles W. Stone House (brick), a 1905 Greek Revival structure with Ionic columns, was the home of Charles Warren Stone, attorney, legislator, lieutenant governor from 1879 to 1882, and member of Congress from 1890 to 1899. In 1974–75 it was completely restored by J. H. DeFrees. *Location:* Warren, 505 Liberty Street.

6. Hazeltine House (frame), perhaps the oldest house in Warren, was built about 1823 by Dr. Abraham Hazeltine, who in 1834 sold it to the Summerton family. From 1925 until it was bought in 1934 by Dr. Hugh Robertson, it belonged to the Moose Club and was leased to Ora and Oleta Brown, who operated a tearoom there. *Location:* Warren, 412 Third Avenue.

7. Philadelphia & Erie Depot (brick, stone, and frame), erected in 1869, five years after the beginning of passenger service, was in use for ninety-six years, until its abandonment in 1965. It has recently been designated as a national landmark. *Location:* Warren, between Fourth and Pennsylvania Avenues.

8. Roscoe Hall (brick) is one of the few remaining theaters that blossomed all over the oil region of Pennsylvania during the boom of about a century ago. It was built by Orris Hall and named for his son, a sergeant in the Bucktails (Forty-second Pennsylvania Infantry) who was killed August 30, 1862, at Second Bull Run. The hall occupied the third floor of the Keystone Block. Blind Tom played here, as did local and many touring theatrical troupes. Bret Harte lectured here March 1, 1873. Following the opening of the Struthers Library-Theater (q.v.) in December 1883, Roscoe Hall faded from the theatrical scene. For a while it was a National Guard armory, a roller rink, and an Eagles Club home. Currently it houses the Sons of Italy in America. *Location:* Warren, Pennsylvania Avenue near Hickory Street.

9. Revere House (brick and frame), a thirty-three-room, three-story structure erected in 1872, was a typical railroad hotel in the palmy days of rail passenger traffic. It sits across the street from the P & E station. Built by Frank Metzgar, who first intended to call it the Allegheny House, it was named the Revere House until 1951 when it became the Riverside Hotel. Under almost a score of owners, it has been continuously operated for more than a century. *Location:* Warren, 914 Pennsylvania Avenue, West.

10. The Pines (stone) was erected in 1839 by Lansing Wetmore, Warren County prothonotary, as a magnificent summer home. It was originally a square structure of four rooms. On his death in 1858 it passed to his son Lansing D. Wetmore, who remodeled and enlarged it in 1900. It is now the Barley Nursing Home. *Location:* North Warren, South State and Weatherbee Streets.

11. The Locusts (brick) was begun in 1831 by Guy C. Irvine, the "Napoleon of the lumber business," and his brother-in-law Rufus Weatherby. Weatherby's death in 1833 delayed its completion until 1835. Clay was dug nearby, and bricks burned by William and John Thompson, who, with John Voverse, made all the woodwork by hand. The trees surrounding the house were planted at the time it was built. *Location:* 1.5 mile south of Russell, on U.S. 62.

7. *Philadelphia & Erie Depot*

12. Robert Russell House (brick) was built about 1825 by Robert Russell, who had operated a sawmill in the area since 1806. He died in 1847. The property was purchased in 1875 by Erastus Weatherby, whose family has occupied it for a century. *Location:* Russell, old U.S. 62.

13. Miller Home (frame) was erected originally as a saltbox about 1821 by Richard and Cynthia Miller to replace an 1814 log cabin. In 1828 they had it enlarged, paying Orrin and Morgan Hancock $190 ($50 in cash and the rest in leather, livestock, and grain) to hew timbers and frame the house. Miller agreed to lay the foundation; haul the timber; provide the boards, nails, and glass; board the hands; and "find whiskey for the raising." Miller, an agent for the Holland Land Company, died of fever in Maysville, Ky., June 10, 1832, aged forty-one, while on a lumber-selling trip. Cynthia, with five children, lived more than half a century and kept the family together. Miller descendants owned the home until 1944. *Location:* Sugar Grove.

14. Old Lutheran Church (brick), the Hessel Valley Lutheran Church, which held services in Swedish until 1933, was organized in 1853 and built in 1883–85. It has a hand-carved pulpit showing the ascension of Christ and a mural behind the altar. *Location:* Chandlers Valley.

19. Industrial Boarding House

15. Old State Hospital (red brick) was established in 1874, and the front part was built in 1900 as the Warren State Hospital for the Insane. It has towers on both sides. It is now the Warren campus of Edinboro State College. *Location:* 3.5 miles north of Warren, on U.S. 62.

16. Cobham Castle (frame) was built by George Ashworth Cobham, who came to America in 1834 and was called Lord Cobham, having descended from a nobleman. An attorney, he planned a castle, which he built with the help of two stepsons, cutting the timbers and lumber for the house and barn at a sawmill they operated for the purpose. Begun in 1856, it was completed seven years later. Cobham died in 1870, and the "castle" passed from his family in 1912. Visitors are not permitted. *Location:* Northeast of Warren, 3.5 miles north of U.S. 6, on Park Avenue at Cobham Road.

17. Kinzua Dam (masonry), completed in 1966 at a cost of $114 million, is 2,000 feet long and 80 feet high; it impounds a lake 27 miles long, holding 61 billion gallons of water. It provides a defense both against low water from drouth and against floods. The lake almost completely inundated the Chief Cornplanter grant of 779 acres, one of three made to him in 1791 by the commonwealth. Cornplanter (John O'Bail, son of a Seneca woman and a Dutch trader) died on the grant in 1836, probably at about the age of eighty-five, though his chronology is much confused. His half brother, Handsome Lake, initiated the Seneca "Good Message" religion here. After much litigation, Cornplanter's descendants were removed to the Seneca reservation in New York. His body and others, and the monument erected to him in 1866 by the

state, were moved to the Riverview-Corydon Cemetery at the New York state line. *Location:* East of Warren, on Pa. 59, 6.7 miles east of U.S. 6.

18. Allegheny River Hotel (brick) was built in 1885 by C. B. Willey on the site of the Glade Run House, where a slab tavern had been operated by Solomon Hudson from 1844 until Orren Hook built a more modern house in 1850, which burned in 1875. This hotel was enlarged some time previous to 1905 and has been run by various hosts. (The Jacob Johnson family operated it the longest, from 1911 to 1969.) It was much used by raftmen and traveling salesmen, and for a time it housed a ticket office for the railroad and electric cars. It is still a popular tavern. *Location:* East of Warren, on Hemlock Street and Pennsylvania Avenue, at river and Mead Township line.

19. Industrial Boarding House (frame with siding) has sixteen rooms and a large attic; it was once the Elk Tanning Company boarding house. Mrs. Ida Miller operated the house from about 1900 to 1932. She and her daughters fed and washed clothing for almost 250 men, who slept two to three to a bed, four beds to a room, with many beds in the attic during rush times. It went out of business with the closing of the tannery during the depression. *Location:* Sheffield, 219–21 Horton Avenue.

20. Irvine Presbyterian Church (buff stone), a charming structure with a fanlight, was built in 1838–39 by Dr. William Armstrong Irvine (1803–86) for his wife Sarah, who died after childbirth before it was quite finished and whose funeral was the first held here. Regular services have been conducted here ever since, but it continued in the possession of the Irvine family until 1963, when (under a 1916 will) it passed to the Presbytery of Lake Erie. *Location:* Irvine.

21. Miller's House (stone) is a very early structure, the two-story central portion probably dating from 1840, the two one-story wings at either side added somewhat later. *Location:* Across Brokenstraw Creek from Irvine, on U.S. 62.

22. Rouse Farm was named in honor of Henry R. Rouse of Enterprise, who lost his life in the first great oil fire of April 17, 1861, in Venango County. He left his fortune to Warren County, half for the benefit of the poor and half to improve the roads. The farm is now a home for aged, indigent men and women and is operated by the county. *Location:* East end of Youngsville, just off U.S. 6.

23. Village Inn (frame) is an old stagecoach tavern with square posts dating from about 1850. Its earliest remembered name is the Clancy House. *Location:* Garland.

24. Indian Paint Hill contained large deposits of red ochre which, along with adjacent petroleum springs, provided the Indians with materials for face and body paint. *Location:* Three miles northeast of Tidioute, on U.S. 62.

25. Courson Home (frame) was erected by Anthony Courson, farmer, lumberman, and tavern keeper, who came from Centre County in 1825. He built this home immediately after his first house burned. It is still occupied by his descendants. *Location:* Tidioute, 333 Main Street.

26. Tidioute Presbyterian Church (frame) is an interesting carpenter Gothic structure dating from about the time of the oil boom of 1870. *Location:* Tidioute, 200 Main Street.

27. Grandin Opera House (brick) was built in 1872 by two sons of Samuel Grandin, a lumber baron, following the discovery of oil on their father's land. The first floor served as a bank, the second had offices, and the third was a remarkable opera house, where road companies and home talent performed until the death of William J. Grandin in 1904. It was used for high school productions until 1927. *Location:* Tidioute, 90 Main Street.

28. Angus Gillis House (frame), an early settler's home, dates from about 1840. It was once Gillis post office. *Location:* Pa. 337, set far back across road from junction with l.r. 61042, just north of Old Plank Road School.

29. Heart's Content is one of the two remaining stands of virgin timber in Pennsylvania with evergreens over 160 feet high. One tree is believed to be over five hundred years old. The Wheeler and Dusenbury Lumber Company, a pioneer concern, sold about two-thirds of its last timberlands to the United States in 1922, together with a gift of twenty acres of virgin pine, hemlock, and hardwood "as a memorial to three generations of the families connected with the company." In 1929 the government augmented the gift with

27. *Grandin Opera House*

the purchase of 100 more acres of virgin timber from this company. The purchases and the gift are a part of 500,000 acres comprising the Allegheny National Forest (see also *Cook Forest State Park,* Clarion County). *Location:* Halfway between Warren and Tidioute, on l.r. 61031, 3.6 miles east of Pa. 337.

Note: A fine spring is on the east side of Pa. 337 a short way below its intersection with l.r. 61031.

30. Wagon Wheel Inn (frame covered with siding) was a roadside tavern built in 1885 by the Salmon family. The community is named Slater for John and Robert Slater, lumbermen, who later operated this place and were the only two postmasters. The Slater post office was discontinued in 1887. *Location:* Ten miles south of Warren, on Pa. 337.

Pennsylvania Historical and Museum Commission Markers

Buckaloons   In Buckaloons Park near U.S. 6 and U.S. 62 east of Irvine

Céloron's Expedition   Warren, U.S. 6 at Pennsylvania Avenue and Hickory Street

Conewango   Warren, U.S. 6 at Pennsylvania Avenue and Conewango Creek bridge

Gen. William Irvine   Irvine, old U.S. 6 west of U.S. 62

The Grandin Well   U.S. 62, 0.4 mile south of Allegheny River bridge near Tidioute; and Pa. 127 north, 0.6 mile northwest of Tidioute

Indian Paint Hill   U.S. 62, 3 miles northeast of Tidioute

Thompson's Island   U.S. 62, 9 miles southwest of Warren

209

BEAVER

Murdocksville

Florence

Paris

Candor

A L L E G H E N Y

Cross Creek

Venice

Bishop

Pattersons
Mill

Hickory

VIRGINIA

Avella

Canonsburg

Morganza

Independence

Houston • Strabane Venetia

Gastonville

Elrama

WESTMORELAND

West Middletown

Buffalo

Hill Church

Finleyville

Wolfdale

Meadow Lands

Mingo Creek Park

Washington Eightyfour

Monongahela

Budaville

Donora

Taylorstown

Laboratory

Belle Vernon

WEST

East Buffalo

Gabby Heights Glyde

Speers

Claysville

Lagonda

Chambers

Bentleyville

West Alexander

Baker Station

Lone Pine

Scenery Hill

California

Beallsville

Prosperity

Amity

Centerville

Daisytown

West Brownsville

Dunns Station

Marianna

Malden Inn

Old Concord

Zollarsville

Fredericktown

Millsboro

FAYETTE

G R E E N E

Washington County

Capsule History

Washington County, organized during the Revolution, was named in honor of George Washington, commander in chief of the Continental Army, and was at first claimed by both Virginia and Pennsylvania. Erected out of Westmoreland County on March 28, 1781, it originally included all of Greene and Beaver Counties, together with a large portion of Allegheny. It now has an area of 857 square miles with a population of 210,876.

Most of the early settlers came from Virginia by way of the Monongahela River as well as the Ten Mile and Big Whiteley Creeks. Abraham Teagarden established a ferry across the Monongahela at the mouth of Ten Mile (now Clarksville). Prior to 1781 John Canon, militia officer and member of the state assembly, operated a gristmill (called Canonsburg Milling Company since 1802) and laid out the town of Canonsburg in 1787. In 1774 George Washington purchased 2,813 acres in Washington County. When Pennsylvania erected the county, the state countered an attempt to set up the disputed territory as a new state, which would have been called Westsylvania. The dispute between Pennsylvania and Virginia over territorial claims was settled in 1779 and a temporary border survey run in 1782.

Washington, the county seat often referred to as "Little Washington" to avoid confusion with the national capital, was laid out by David Hoge in 1781, incorporated as a borough in 1810, and chartered as a city in 1923. Originally called Bassett Town, it was settled at the Indian village known in the 1770s as Catfish's Camp, since the Delaware chief Catfish lived there. The first (Virginia) county court west of the Monongahela River was held at Augusta Town, a few miles southwest of Washington at present-day Gabby Heights.

The western section of the county was the scene of many Indian uprisings, including one by Mingo Chief James Logan who attacked settlers in 1774 during Dunmore's War after the murder of his brother and sister. Jacob Wolfe erected a stockaded house southwest of Washington in 1780. At Jacob Miller's blockhouse (site east side of Dutch Fork Fishing Dam), there was a retaliatory attack by Indians whose fellow tribesmen had been massacred at Gnadenhütten in 1782. The Miller family burial plot includes the memorial stone of Ann Hupp, who led a heroic defense here. One of the last battles of the Revolutionary War took place at Rice's Fort in 1782.

Monongahela is the site of several Indian burial mounds which have been excavated in recent years. Once known as Williamsport, it is the oldest settlement in the valley where James Devore and Joseph Parkinson operated a ferry. Parkinson also built a mill one mile from Monongahela on Pigeon Creek, where the Van Voorhis homestead is. Whiskey Point at Main and Park Avenues was the scene of a 1794 Whiskey Rebellion meeting of 226 insurgents.

Two important Indian trails traversed the county. The *Catfish Path* ran from below Amity past Braddock to Washington, thence east of Chartiers Creek to a crossing south of Canonsburg, and west of the stream toward Bridgeville. The *Mingo Path* ran across the county from Brownsville to West Alexander very close to the course of the old National Road (U.S. 40).

In 1806 Congress authorized the construction of the National Road, which began at Cumberland, Md., in 1811 and was completed to Wheeling in 1818. It was a state toll road from 1835 to 1905. Authentic murals of the early history of this road have been preserved inside the George Washington Hotel in the city of Washington. These murals were painted by Malcolm Stevens Parcell, a native of Washington and an internationally known artist.

Among the noteworthy people who lived in the county during its early days were David Bradford, leader of the Whiskey Rebellion; William Holmes McGuffey, author of the renowned *McGuffey's Readers,* born south of Claysville (McGuffey's birthplace was purchased for Henry Ford's Greenfield Village Museum in Dearborn, Mich.); James G. Blaine, who narrowly missed election as president, born in West Browns- ville; Capt. Philo McGiffin, born in Washington and father of the modern Chinese navy; Col. George Morgan, Indian agent during the Revolution; John Doddridge, who erected a fort in 1773, and his son Dr. Joseph Doddridge, who wrote an outstanding account of pioneer life; Edward Acheson, an eminent American chemist; Elisha

McCurdy, the great revivalist; John McMillan, Presbyterian minister and political leader of the area; Governor and U.S. Senator Edward Martin; and David Reed, leader of the Covenanter squatters on lands owned by George Washington.

Washington has always been a prosperous agricultural section, and sheep-raising has remained important over the years. Its natural resources include bituminous coal, natural gas, petroleum, sand, and clay. Rich deposits of coal had been discovered before 1800, when it was mined near Canonsburg and Washington. Alexander McGugin owned the first natural-gas well (1882) in the county. The Gantz oil well was the first in the county, drilled in 1884 at West Chestnut Street and Brookside Avenue in Washington.

Washington and Charleroi produce glassware, while Canonsburg is noted for its pottery, china, and tin and terneplate. Donora was once one of the world's largest manufacturers of steel wire. Standard Industries (now defunct) in Canonsburg, visited in 1921 by Madame Marie Curie, co-discoverer of radium, was one of the largest early radium producers.

The county has preserved twenty-six covered bridges. There are also a great number of early log, stone, and brick structures.

Landmarks

1. Courthouse (stone), the county's fourth, was erected in 1900 for $1 million. The first courts were held in the home of David Hoge, and the first courthouse and jail were constructed of logs in 1787 and destroyed by fire in 1790. The second building was erected in 1791–94 and enlarged in 1819. In 1839–42 the third courthouse was built; it was enlarged in 1867. *Location:* Washington, South Main and West Beau Streets.

2. Washington Town Hall (painted brick) was begun in 1869. Land for the structure had been purchased in 1842. In 1868 Dr. Francis Julius Le Moyne had offered to give $10,000 for a public library provided the town would erect a suitable building with a fireproof vault. The cost was $31,518. President Grant and his wife were visiting their friends, Mr. and Mrs. William W. Smith (see *Trinity Hall Academy*), at the time of the cornerstone-laying and this honor was given to Grant. In 1870 the Citizens' Library Association was granted a charter, and the library was formally opened in the town hall in 1872. Originally the structure was built on the corner of Main Street and West Cherry Avenue, but it was moved in 1897–98 to make way for the present courthouse. The second floor was removed in 1932, and the building remodeled into a one-story structure. In 1965 the

library was moved to a new location on South College Street. The hall now houses the city's police department. *Location:* Washington, West Cherry and Brownson Avenues.

3. Washington and Jefferson College was incorporated as Washington Academy on September 24, 1787, and chartered March 28, 1806. Classes were first held in the courthouse in 1789 with Rev. Thaddeus Dodd serving as principal. In 1792 Benjamin Franklin donated fifty pounds to the college for the purchase of books. From 1827 to 1833 the Washington Medical College of Baltimore functioned under the charter of this school. In 1852 by an agreement between its Board of Trustees and the Synod of Wheeling, the school became a synodical college of the Presbyterian Church. On March 4, 1865, Washington merged with Jefferson College (see *McMillan's Log Cabin School*) at Canonsburg, and by 1869 all classes were held in Washington. *Location:* Washington, on Wheeling, Lincoln, East Maiden, East Beau Streets, and College Avenue.

a. Academy Building (stone), originally 30 by 35 feet, was erected at Washington Academy in 1793 on land donated by William Hoge. In 1816 wings were added to this structure, which now houses the administrative offices.

b. McIlvaine Hall (brick) was originally Washington Female Seminary, founded No-

3.a. Academy Building at Washington and Jefferson College

vember 26, 1835, on land purchased from Alexander Reed. It now houses the English department of the college.

4. First Presbyterian Church (painted brick) was formally organized in 1793, with Matthew Brown its first regular pastor from 1805 to 1822. First services were held in the old administration building of Washington Academy. The third and present church was built in 1868 on lot no. 102 of David Hoge's original plan of Washington, one of two lots presented by Hoge to George Washington. The chapel was built in 1886. *Location:* Washington, southeast corner of Wheeling and College Streets.

5. Trinity Episcopal Church Rectory (brick) was built about 1840, and beginning in 1887 it was the city's first hospital. It is now used as church offices. *Location:* Washington, North College Street near East Beau Street.

6. Boyle Gristmill (frame), originally operated by steam and constructed of hewn timbers, was built in 1844 by millwright Daniel Boyle. It was run by Samuel Hazlett and Daniel Dye until 1849. Later owned by the Zelt family from 1885 to 1910, it stopped functioning as a mill in 1915. At present it is used as a woodwork shop and auction center. *Location:* Washington, corner of Oregon and West Wheeling Streets.

7. Le Moyne House (cut stone), a fine example of early Greek Revival architecture, was built in 1812 by Dr. John Julius Le Moyne, a French physician who came to America during the French Revolution and settled in Washington in 1797 after four years of practice in Gallipolis, Ohio. In 1823 his only son, Dr. Francis Julius Le Moyne, bought the property, which remained in the family until 1943 when it was inherited by the Washington County Historical Society. While Francis Julius, an ardent abolitionist, lived here, the house became one of the first stops on the underground railroad. As many as twenty-six slaves were concealed in a secret room on the third floor of what appears to be a two-story house. *Hours:* Monday–Friday, 1–5 P.M. *Donation. Location:* Washington, 49 East Maiden Street.

Note: The brick home directly across the street was built in 1826 and was also a Le Moyne house.

8. Le Moyne Crematory (brick), the first in the United States, was constructed in 1876 at a cost of $1,500. Built under the direction of Dr. Francis Julius Le Moyne, the one-story structure is divided into two rooms—a reception room and a furnace room. Because of the controversial nature of the building, it had to be erected at night. Between 1876 and 1900 there were over forty-two bodies cremated here. The first cremation was of Baron de Palm, a Bavarian nobleman, with Dr. Le

7. *Le Moyne House*

13. *Bradford House*

Moyne the third on October 16, 1879. A granite monument, a memorial to the founder, is located in the front yard. Le Moyne's philanthropies included Le Moyne College, Washington's Citizens' Library, and a school for blacks in Memphis, Tenn. *Location:* Washington, South Main Street (l.r. 62131), opposite Presbyterian Home.

9. Paul-Linn House (brick) was built in 1838 by the Houston Paul family on land purchased in 1825. The same family that owned the Linn house on Brehm Road (q.v.) were later occupants of this home. *Location:* Washington, 1004 Redstone Road (l.r. 62131).

10. Martin House (brick), easily identified by the words "Governor's House" written above the door, was the home of Maj. Gen. Edward Martin, who was a U.S. senator, governor, and veteran of the Spanish-American War, Mexican-border campaign, and of World Wars I and II. *Location:* Washington, corner of Le Moyne Avenue and Lockhart Street.

11. Baird-Acheson House (brick with round corner), built about 1825, was the birthplace of Edward Acheson, an eminent American chemist born here in 1856. He was awarded many medals for his invention of Carborundum, artificial graphite, and other valuable products of the electric furnace. The house, also owned at one time by Thomas Baird, has an outstanding curved stairway. *Location:* Washington, southwest corner of Maiden and Main Streets.

12. Waynesburg & Washington Railroad Station (brick), now occupied by a builders' firm, is within sight of the Washington stone depot and a frame one, both on the same side of the street—a unique situation, for within one block are three railroad depots of three different types of construction and on their original sites. The "Waynie" was a narrow-gauge road, with so many curves that a wag wrote of it:

> It doubles in and doubles out,
> And leaves the traveler in doubt
> Whether the snake that made the track
> Was going out or coming back.

Location: Washington, Main Street at railroad yards.

13. Bradford House (stone), of early Federal design, was built in 1787–88 by David Bradford, a successful lawyer, businessman, deputy attorney general (district attorney of the county), and leading figure of the Whiskey Rebellion. Bradford lived here from 1788 to 1794 when, according to legend, he jumped from a rear window of this house to escape from a cavalry detachment sent by President Washington to subdue those protesting against high excise taxes. (These taxes fell especially hard on the grain producers of western Pennsylvania.) Bradford fled to Spanish West Florida and sold his house in 1803. One of the later owners was Rebecca Harding Davis, a well-known author who was born in the house in 1831. The structure was used for a store at one time. In 1959 the Pennsylvania Historical and Museum Commission assumed control of the building and restored the front to its original appearance. The interior still retains the beautiful mahogany staircase. A well discovered on the property has been reopened near the house. *Hours:* Daylight saving time: Weekdays except Monday, 8:30 A.M.– 5 P.M. Sunday, 1–5 P.M. Winter: Weekdays except Monday, 9 A.M.– 4:30 P.M. Sunday, 1–4:30 P.M. *Admission charge. Location:* Washington, 175 South Main Street.

14. Blaine's Temporary Residence (painted brick) was the home of James G. Blaine, congressman, party leader, secretary of state, and presidential candidate, while he attended Washington College in 1843–47. In 1854 he moved to Maine. The house can be identified by a glass-covered plaque on the side of the building, which now houses a glass company. *Location:* Washington, 331 South Main Street, near South Street.

15. Three Ridges Church (brick) was erected in 1840. A plaque on a tree stump in the churchyard bears the following inscription: "1785–1936 Site of oak tree under which the first religious services were held in community by the congregation of Three Ridges by Dr. John McMillan, Rev. John Brice and others, as early as 1785." In 1795 land was purchased for the first church, and three houses of worship were built on the same site. The first pastor, Brice, is buried in the cemetery. *Location:* West Alexander, on old U.S. 40 (Main Street).

16. Morgan's Tavern (frame) was built on the National Road and is still operating as a tavern. *Location:* One mile west of West Alexander, on U.S. 40.

17. Murray Brothers Store (brick) belonged to J. W. and William M. Murray, who started a business in this early building in 1871. It was later occupied by the Vensel family and is still a store. *Location:* West Alexander, Main (old U.S. 40) and Liberty Streets.

Note: Next to the store is a long frame structure which is reputed to have been a ladies' seminary at one time. There are many old buildings in this town, which was laid out by Robert Humphreys in 1796 and named for his wife Martha Alexander.

18. Valentine Tavern (frame), one of the favorite wagon stands, was built about 1812 and kept by John Valentine, whose brother Daniel was a tavern keeper in Washington. A

14. Blaine's Temporary Residence

second brother, Charles, was a wagoner on the National Road. *Location:* One mile east of West Alexander, on north side of Pa. 18 (old National Road).

19. Wheeling Hill Church (frame) was built in 1866. The structure, with a fieldstone foundation, has two front entrances. It was an early United Presbyterian church. The "C P" on the building apparently resulted from confusion with the old Windy Gap Cumberland Presbyterian Church nearby. *Location:* Near Good Intent, on l.r. 62137, 2.8 miles from Pa. 231 and 6.3 miles south of Claysville.

20. Claysville was named for Henry Clay, champion of the National Road, and founded by John Purviance in 1817. Because the National Road went through Claysville on Main Street, there were numerous early taverns. The four houses below could have been operated as taverns by the following proprietors in stagecoach days: John Purviance (first tavern keeper), James Sargent (1821, at sign of Black Horse), Basil Brown (1836), James Dennison (1840), David Bell, John Walker, James Kelley, Stephen Conkling, John McIlree, a Walkins, a Walker, and the widow Callahan.

a. Brick House at Cooper's corner was once owned by D. M. Campsey. *Location:* Corner of Main and Greene Streets, adjacent to insurance office which faces Main Street.

b. Painted Brick House was built about 1818, the time of the opening of the National Road. *Location:* Corner of Bell Street (Pa. 231 south) and Main Street (old U.S. 40).

c. Old Brick Tavern. *Location:* 139 Main Street (old U.S. 40).

d. Brick Tavern has a front gable. *Location:* Corner of Main Street and Highland Avenue, next to market.

21. T. C. Noble House (frame), with a cupola and captain's walk on top, was built prior to 1876 and is pictured in an old atlas of that date. *Location:* Claysville, West Main Street (old U.S. 40) on same side of street as Methodist church and across from antique shop.

22. Porter-Montgomery House (frame), a Victorian gingerbread house with an unusually ornate tower, was built in 1879–80 by a contractor and carpenter, Robert Porter. His love for fancy woodwork is reflected in the style of this house, which was owned at a later date by the James Montgomery family. *Location:* Claysville, on West Main Street (old U.S. 40) next to Catholic church.

Note: Next to this building is the Margaret Derrow house, a nineteenth-century structure with Gothic windows.

23. S. White's Sons Building (frame) is believed to be the nation's oldest firm of monument makers, founded by Alexander White as early as 1800, although the first documented date is 1811. In early years stone from the old quarry at the nearby Finley farm was used. Among the noteworthy memorials made here is one for the famous racehorse Adios at The Meadows racetrack and the miner statue at Fairmont, W.Va., representing coal miners of ten counties who lost their lives in the mines. *Location:* Claysville, on North Alley.

24. Dutch Fork Christian Church (frame), built in 1863, was an outgrowth of the movement founded by Alexander Campbell. This congregation was established about 1830. Its first church was erected in 1836. *Location:* Budaville, east of Claysville, near Rice's Fort site on l.r. 62108.

25. Caldwell's Tavern (brick and stone ruins) was built about the time the National Road opened in 1818 by James Caldwell and was operated by him until his death in 1838. His widow Hester continued the business until 1873. It was later owned by J. A. Gordon, also a tavern keeper, who kept his house as one of the favorite resorts along the way. At one time it was a children's home. In later years it was called the Rosemire until it was destroyed by fire. It was partially recon-

structed but never completed due to the operation of an illegal still on the premises. This tavern inspired J. N. Matthews to write the poem "The Old Country Inn." Claire Elliot was the last owner of the tavern. *Location:* On old U.S. 40 (south side of road), west of S-Bridge (no. 26) and across from McGuffey High School.

Note: Across the road is another old brick house, built after the tavern. It was an antique shop owned by a Mr. Ullom and later purchased by Recco Luppino.

26. S-Bridge (stone), completed in 1818 and so named for its double-curve design, was built to carry the National Road over a branch of Buffalo Creek. At one time there was an S-Bridge post office located nearby, and taverns operated at both ends of the structure during the height of travel. Today there are two early buildings on the west end and one near the east end which may have been taverns. When U.S. 40 was relocated, the bridge was no longer used, and the west end was demolished, although pedestrians may yet walk over it. *Location:* About five miles southwest of Washington, at junction of Pa. 221 and U.S. 40.

Note: Nearby is Taylorstown, a one-time oil-boom village.

27. John Miller Tavern (brick) was built in 1812 with a fanlight in the front entrance. It was kept before 1836 by Levi Wilson, who entertained the first wagoners on the road. In 1836 John Miller moved here from a wagon stand east of Cumberland, Md. His daughter married a son of Levi Wilson, and the couple lived here after the establishment was no longer operating. *Location:* About 4.5 miles west of Washington, on north side of U.S. 40, east of S-Bridge at top of Mounts Hill.

28. Martin's Tavern (brick) was a popular hostelry with twelve rooms and a spacious front porch. It was built in 1825 on the National Road by Jonathan Martin. Andrew Jackson and the celebrated theologian Alexander Campbell both stopped here. Martin operated the tavern until business closed on the road, except for a brief time when J. W. Holland managed it in the 1840s.

The community where the tavern is located was first called Pancake for George Pancake, who kept a tavern here as early as 1800. Prior to being named Laboratory, the village was also called Martinsburg in honor of Jonathan Martin. *Location:* Laboratory, 1871 East Maiden Street extension.

32.a. Century Inn

Note: The Nadar homestead (painted stone with frame addition), across the street, was built in 1818.

29. Little Tavern (brick), with an earlier brick house behind the main building, was kept by a Mr. Little. Today a modern tavern is located next to it. *Location:* About four miles east of Washington, near junction of U.S. 40 and Myers Road.

30. Weaver House (brick) has a signature stone that reads, "Adam & M. Weaver, June 14, 1837," and is one of the few on which the owner included at least his wife's initial. This house, with a double porch in front of half of it and a cut-stone foundation, is still in the same family. *Location:* Near Scenery Hill. 2.5 miles south of U.S. 40 on Weaver Run Road (l.r. 62083, also called Scenery Hill–Marianna Road).

31. Charley Miller's Tavern (painted brick) has a signature stone over the front door which reads, "For G. & S. Tombaugh, 1832." Later it was operated as a tavern by Henry Taylor followed by Charley Miller. At this time parties of young people drove ten miles from Washington to eat and dance at Miller's. His meals were sumptuous, and peach brandy was his specialty. After Miller's death the house was purchased by David Ullery. *Location:* About one mile west of Scenery Hill on south side of old U.S. 40 (t. 449). (Old U.S. 40 is immediately in front of house and parallel with new U.S. 40, next to it.)

32. Scenery Hill, originally Hillsboro, resulted from the building of the National Road in 1819, although its first name came from a tavern that antedated that highway by a

quarter century. The town was almost exactly halfway between Brownsville and Washington.

a. Century Inn (stone) was originally Hill's Tavern, one of the oldest on the National Road, and has been in continuous use as a public house since 1794. It was first kept by Stephen Hill, for whom the tavern and town were named, and later by his nephew Thomas Hill. When Thomas retired, Samuel Youman, a stage driver, took over. Suceeding proprietors were John Hampson, John Gibson, William Dawson, and Oliver Lacock. In 1825 General Lafayette and Andrew Jackson were among its celebrated guests. It was for a number of years the leading tavern in the area and continues to exist today as a well-known inn. In later years Dr. Gordon F. Harrington bought the building and restored it, uncovering a large fireplace with the original hand-forged crane and utensils intact. *Location:* Near center of town, on north side of U.S. 40.

b. Wilson Tavern (brick) was possibly kept by John Wilson and later operated by Stephen Phelps and David Powell. *Location:* On south side of U.S. 40, across from Century Inn.

c. Riggle Tavern (brick) was founded about 1820 by Zephania Riggle, who owned taverns at several locations on this highway (see *Zephania Riggle Tavern*). Later a Dr. Clark owned this house. *Location:* On south side of U.S. 40, about one block east of Century Inn.

33. Madonna of the Trail Monument is one of twelve memorials "to the pioneer mothers of the covered wagon days" erected by the National Society of the Daughters of the American Revolution. The statue is ten feet high, weighs five tons, and has a six-foot-high base weighing twelve tons. Created by the sculptor A. Leinbach, this is the only one of these monuments in Pennsylvania and the tenth to be unveiled (on December 8, 1929). It depicts a pioneer woman with a baby in her arms and a boy clutching her skirt. *Location:* 3.9 miles east of Scenery Hill, on U.S. 40, at eastern edge of Beallsville and opposite Nemacolin Country Club.

34. National Hotel (brick), also known as Greenfield stand, was kept by William Greenfield until his death. This famous inn on the National Road was a stop where a traveler could always get a good cup of coffee, a rare thing in a tavern at that time. Greenfield was not only an innkeeper but a banker as well.

33. Madonna of the Trail Monument

His bank, known as the Beallsville Savings Bank, was operated in his tavern with the safe being his pocket. The pressure was too much for the proprietor to withstand, and his banking business did not last long. The famous Ringgold Cavalry started from this hotel for the Civil War. The building, with a wooden balustrade surrounding the second-story porch, is now used as a store and residence. *Location:* Beallsville, southwest corner of junction of U.S. 40 and l.r. 62018.

35. Miller's Tavern (brick) was kept as early as 1830 by Charley Miller and subsequently by a Mrs. Chambers, who ran "a quiet, orderly, and aristocratic inn." Following this ownership, Moses Bennington occupied the tavern. It was later operated by Benjamin Demen and Charles Guttery, the last old-time tavern owner at this site. *Location:* Beallsville, junction of U.S. 40 and l.r. 62018 (on southeast corner across from National Hotel).

36. Keys Hotel (painted brick) was first kept by Andrew Keys, followed by Thomas Keys, prior to 1840. Subsequent tavern owners were Robert Cluggage, James Dennison, Moses Bennington, and Charles Guttery in 1854. The old hotel had a commodious wagon yard at one time. *Location:* Beallsville (north side of road) on U.S. 40 near its junction with l.r. 62074 (second house from Bentleyville Road).

37. Welsh-Emery House (stone) was built about 1815 on a 1781 land grant by William Welsh, son of John Welsh, a fine cabinet maker, and his wife Eleanor, both of whom came from Ulster County, Ireland. The Welshes named their land Enniskillen for their former home, and at first lived in a log cabin about two hundred yards behind the present house. William, one of seven justices of the county in the early days, had an office in the front of this dwelling. He was also president of the first library west of the Alleghenies and the father of eight daughters and two sons, all of whom were well educated for that period.

The kitchen was a one-story addition of stone on the east side of the house, which was later enlarged to two stories. In 1878 William's son Joseph Bud Welsh remodeled the house; and in 1909 Geraldine and Helen Emery remodeled it completely, enlarging rooms and adding a two-story portico in the front with an iron railing. The house is now owned by Joseph B. Welsh's daughter, Mrs. C. W. Theakston. The Rankin Playhouse Olde Trail Players operate in the barn next to the house. *Location:* Halfway between Centerville and Madonna of the Trail monument, on old U.S. 40 (now called Emery Road) 0.2 mile south of its junction with new U.S. 40.

38. Centerville, laid out in 1821 halfway between Uniontown and Washington, has many interesting old buildings.

   a. Rogers Tavern (brick covered with siding) was the first tavern in the village kept by John Rogers, father of Joseph Rogers of Bridgeport. John's other son Robert succeeded his father in the business and died in possession of the house, with his son-in-law Solomon Bracken and a Mr. Wilson occupying it at intervals. The tavern was known as a quiet, orderly, well-kept establishment. *Location:* Junction of old U.S. 40 and Pa. 481 (north side of road), house no. 902.

   b. Zephania Riggle Tavern (brick) was the leading wagon stand in the village with a wagon yard in the rear. It was destroyed by fire but promptly rebuilt while Riggle owned it. He was succeeded in 1845 by Peter Colley (see *Peter Colley Tavern,* Fayette County), Henry Whitsett, Jacob Marks, William Garrett, Jesse Quail, and Joseph Jeffreys. John

Strathers was the last to operate the tavern; it closed in the 1930s. *Location:* Old U.S. 40, house no. 935.

c. Hiram Smith House (frame), with the original front porch removed, was built in 1830. *Location:* Old U.S. 40, house no. 947.

d. Taylor-Linton House (quarried fieldstone) was begun in 1797 by a Mr. Taylor. The second section, constructed largely of fieldstone, was built by Samuel Taylor in 1843. Taylor, who established a bank in Brownsville, owned this property until about 1870, when Malin Linton and his wife Elizabeth bought it. The third and present owner is William Spray, who bought and restored the house in 1949. The large front porch was added in 1909, with another addition made to the house in 1912. Large triangular stone fireplaces with six flues help support the house. Nearby is a stone springhouse, and on the road leading to the house is a fence of fine old Osage orange (hedge apple), typical of early pioneer plantings. *Location:* From old U.S. 40 in Centerville, turn north on unmarked road opposite Vestaburg Clinic sign, and continue about 0.5 mile to house.

39. Wheeler-Taylor House (fieldstone and brick) dates back to before 1808. The original stone section was built by Dr. Charles Wheeler. When Bishop Asbury visited Taylor Methodist Church (q.v.) in 1808, he stopped here to see Dr. Wheeler, who had fallen from a horse. The Oliver Knight Taylor family built the front Victorian brick addition in the 1870s. *Location:* About 0.5 mile east of Centerville, on north side of U.S. 40, across from restaurant.

40. Harrison House (brick), of Victorian design with a towerlike front, was built about 1880 by Joseph and Oretto Harrison, whose memorial window is in nearby Taylor Church. This house has fluctuated between times of prosperity and poverty. At one period Andrew Carnegie paid taxes on the property. Harrison's daughter married a musician, Carl Von Retter, and lived here with him. *Location:* About one mile east of Centerville, on old U.S. 40 (t. 949).

41. Taylor Methodist Church (brick) was founded between 1772 and 1784 as Hawkins Chapel on the William Hawkins property, later owned by William Taylor. Early circuit riders in the area were Eli Shickle, John Cooper, and Solomon Breeze. In 1786 Robert Ayers preached here. The congregation has had four buildings: the first of log (reputedly 1772), the second of stone (1810), the third of brick (1857, destroyed by fire in 1872), and the present building (1872, remodeled in 1904, 1928, and 1959). The chair that Bishop Francis Asbury sat in when visiting here in 1808 is preserved in a glass case inside the church with other historical memorabilia. The earliest gravestone in the cemetery is that of Joseph Woodfil (1754–98), who according to his descendants preached his first sermon here in 1772 at the age of eighteen. His sister, who was killed by Indians, is also buried at the site. Nearby in the cemetery is the Mc-Cutcheon monument (q.v.). *Location:* 1.4 mile east of Centerville, on old U.S. 40.

42. McCutcheon Monument, often referred to as the "spite monument," is a granite memorial ordered built by James Shannon McCutcheon (1824–1902), a miserly farmer who made his money in coal land. Because of a family feud he left his entire estate to buy as expensive a monument as could be erected, with any money left over going toward the construction of four granite columns around the obelisk. His two brothers were paid $1,000 each for the construction. McCutcheon died before its completion and is buried in front of the structure. The eighty-five-foot memorial, with a base over forty-five feet square, blew over in a 1936 storm (the winds also taking off the roof of the Taylor Church, q.v.), and today only eighteen feet of the original structure remain in the cemetery. *Location:* 1.4 mile east of Centerville, on old U.S. 40 (in Taylor churchyard).

43. Jeffreys House (quarried stone), with a frame addition and alterations, was built before 1820 by the father of Joseph Jeffreys, a tavern owner (see *Zephania Riggle Tavern*). The old family cemetery is near the house. *Location:* East of Centerville. Go 1.5 mile east on U.S. 40 and one mile north on Daisytown Road.

44. Isaac Morris House (fieldstone) has a signature stone which reads, "E I & M 1811." In 1804 the Morris family, who were Quakers, built a log barn near the house. The Binns family later bought the property. *Location:* About two miles southeast of Centerville, on Ridge Road.

45. Theakston House (stone) has a stone springhouse on the property. Another early stone house of this family is the Welsh-Emery house (q.v.). *Location:* Two miles southeast of Centerville, turn off Ridge Road onto Binns

46. Malden Inn

houses are in use by various firms. *Location:* West Brownsville, junction of Pa. 88 and old U.S. 40.

Road and continue about one mile to house; Binns Road is almost directly across from Isaac Morris house.

46. Malden Inn (stone), a large impressive building with H chimneys and a court in the back, was built as Kreppsville Inn, since John Krepps, the builder, assumed that a village of this name would grow up around the inn. The town was called Malden, reportedly from emigrants encamping nearby who imagined that the area reminded them of their native town by that name in Massachusetts. The western and original section of the tavern was built in 1822 and the eastern in 1830. The second part bears a unique stone tavern sign built in the front portion. It reads "Kreppsville, 1830" above a moldboard plow; beside the plow is an eagle with "Liberty" inscribed between the wings, and beneath it are sheaves of wheat. Another signature stone in the gable end of the first section is also engraved with an eagle and three sheaves of wheat.

The tavern was first kept by Bry Taylor. His daughter Kizzie was accidentally killed in this house by a gun fired by her brother James, who in later years was shot by a U.S. marshal. Following Taylor, Samuel Acklin, Samuel Bailey, William Pepper, William Garrett, and James Britton operated the inn.

A stone barn, where a large wagon yard had been, is west of the inn. Once a residence, it is now a restaurant. *Location:* 2.5 miles west of Brownsville, junction of old U.S. 40 and I.r. 62178.

47. Sam Thompson Distillery (brick), now vacant, was where the famous Sam Thompson whiskey was made. The business first started at Kinder's mill (see *Kinder Stone Gristmill*) and was later transferred to West Brownsville. Some of the distillery ware-

48. Krepps Tavern (stone) was built before 1800 and operated by Vincent Owens, a Revolutionary War soldier, followed by Samuel Acklin, John Krepps (see *Malden Inn*), and Morris Purcell. The father of Vincent Owens was murdered in this house while his son ran the tavern. Krepps ferry was operated here in conjunction with the inn until 1845. The house was later used for the Sam Thompson Distillery office and is still an office building. A fill on the highway has obscured the first story on the side away from the river. *Location:* West Brownsville, near Sam Thompson Distillery buildings, junction of Pa. 88 and old U.S. 40 (now fronts on Monongahela River).

49. Saint John's Episcopal Church (frame) was built in 1860–70 in carpenter Gothic design. It began with Sunday school work in 1850. The parish was organized in 1860, the same year a lot was donated to the congregation by John Cock. The church took ten years to build due to the Civil War. It is now a Methodist church. *Location:* West Brownsville, 124 Pittsburgh Street.

50. Trinity Hall Academy (brick) was established by William Wrenshall Smith at his estate in the fall of 1879. Smith had purchased this house, built about 1866, and twenty-five acres of land from Joseph McKnight in 1876 for $16,500. This Victorian home, with a large cupola, contained twenty-five rooms and was one of the best built in the United States at that time. R. M. Copeland of Boston landscaped the property, which was said "to be the most beautiful of any private residence in the state." It was called Spring Hill until 1879 when Trinity Hall was established. At that time, Smith, a widower, decided to open his house as a school for the convenience of his two sons. Although Bishop John B. Kerfoot had originally selected the Swearingen-Cook house (q.v.) for a military boarding school of the Protestant Episcopal Church, the Smith estate was chosen instead. The church later gave up the project, and Smith financed the school until his death in 1904. Ulysses S. Grant often visited the Smiths (see *Washington Town Hall*); and Smith's son, who was named for Grant, managed the school later. He made it a financial success, preparing men for Annapolis and West Point. In 1904 William McKennan Smith, Smith's other son, rented it to Charles Eckels and Finis Montgomery, and the school continued until 1907. The building was then vacant until 1913 when it was used as an armory. In 1925 it became Trinity Joint High School, later Trinity High School, said to have been the largest vocational school of its kind east of the Mississippi, with the largest agricultural department in Pennsylvania at that time. A fine rural stone gateway is in the rear, and the present gymnasium houses one of the exhibit buildings of the Buffalo World's Fair brought here by the elder Smith. *Location:* Just south of Washington, on Pa. 18 (Park Avenue).

51. Chambers Mill House (stone) was built in 1823 by William and Robert Chambers on Banes Fork of Ten Mile Creek. Their father, James Chambers, came from Downpatrick, Ireland, and took up land here between 1795 and 1797. The mill, built in 1832 on the site of a former one, is in ruins near the house. A later addition to the home has been removed. A fine stone smokehouse is in the front yard. *Location:* Chambers, 6.7 miles on l.r. 62128 off Pa. 18 (in Gabby Heights).

52. Bane House (fieldstone), built by one of the original five Bane brothers who settled in Amwell Township in 1769, is a small cottage that was later stuccoed. Located beside Bane Run, it is one of the oldest houses in the county. The crossroads where it is located was originally called Pleasant Sunset. *Location:* Baker Station, junction of l.r. 62128 and l.r. 62098.

Note: The brick house that sits across the road was the home of the stationmaster for the Waynesburg & Washington Railroad at Baker Station. It is more than a century old.

53. North Ten Mile Baptist Church (brick) is presently called Mount Hermon Baptist Church. The first services were held in the home of Enoch Enoch (*cq*) of Little Ten Mile Creek in 1773. The first pastor was James Sutton. In 1786 the first log meetinghouse was built and replaced by a larger hewn-log structure in 1794. The present building was erected in 1840, with an addition in 1975. A later brick church of the divided congregation, built in 1904, is located at Lone Pine. *Location:* About 1.5 mile south of Baker Station, junction of l.r. 62128 and l.r. 62102.

54. Bethel Cumberland Presbyterian Church (brick) has a round signature stone above the front entrance which reads, "Bethel C. P. Church, Fiftieth anniversary celebration May 20th 1883." A bell tower is in the front yard, and in the rear of the church is a ceme-

tery containing the cut-stone family vault of H. B. Lindley (see *Lindley Fort Site House*) erected in 1883. *Location:* Three miles south of Lagonda, at corner of Pa. 18 (Park Avenue) and Bethel Church Road.

55. Upper Ten Mile Presbyterian Church (brick) and Lower Ten Mile Presbyterian Church (q.v.) were organized together August 15, 1781, by Thaddeus Dodd (Dod). Dr. Dodd, who first preached in the community about 1777, continued to serve the congregation until his death in 1793. The first church building, of log, was erected in 1792 followed by two wooden structures of 1818 and 1854. The present church was built in 1860 on land donated by Demas Lindley and remodeled in 1894. *Location:* Prosperity, about 0.2 mile off Pa. 18 at Lindley Fort marker.

56. Lindley Fort Site House (brick) was built about 1840 by Isaac Connett, whose father James had bought the land in 1801 from the Lindleys. Demas Lindley had settled on this tract, known as Mill Seat, in 1773 and patented it in 1785. In 1928 the descendants of the Lindley family erected a monument on the lawn of this property at the site of the Lindley fortified blockhouse, which was built in 1774–75. *Location:* About a quarter mile south of Prosperity, on Pa. 18.

57. Old Concord, founded in 1826, has a number of noteworthy landmarks, all in view of one another.

a. Mansion House (frame) was built by Elias Day in 1837. In the 1920s, when the property was owned by the Rogers family, a group of ministers and laymen decided to establish an Institute of Practical Arts for immigrant boys here. It operated for over twenty years and was closed in 1943. The Mansion House restaurant was opened here in 1947 by the James Simpson family and features family-style dinners.

b. Concord Cumberland Presbyterian Church (frame) was organized in 1831, a year after missionaries from Cumberland College in Kentucky held meetings on the campgrounds. The picturesque country church has an interesting interior with designs painted by construction employees building the Waynesburg & Washington Railroad.

c. Old Concord Gristmill (frame) has remained in the Earnest family for years. It was run first by steam and then by a gasoline engine for the nearby farmers. A village blacksmith shop operating on the grounds from Civil War days until the 1920s has been converted into a garage.

Note: About one mile from Old Concord on Pa. 18 is a sawmill built by E. L. McCormick, who invented and patented one of the fastest wedge-shaped cap-cutting machines.

d. General Store and Post Office (frame) was once the halfway hotel between Waynesburg and Washington. Also a drovers' stand, it accommodated many cattlemen driving their stock through the village. This house, now being restored, belonged to the Parkinsons the same family that owned an 1830 yellow frame house on Pa. 18 near the north edge of town.

58. Dunn's Station (frame) was a depot on the old Waynesburg & Washington Railroad. It is presently being used for storage along the abandoned track, which carried the last train in 1965. After 1931 there had been only one run a year, to keep the franchise alive. *Location:* Dunns Station, on Pa. 221.

59. Amity was founded in 1797. The village has been most widely acclaimed as the home of Rev. Solomon Spaulding, long erroneously supposed to be the real author of the *Book of Mormon.* (His book, discovered some years ago, bears no resemblance to that work.) He is buried in the cemetery at the Lower Ten Mile Church.

a. Lower Ten Mile Presbyterian Church (brick) was organized at Jacob Cook's house in 1781 at the same time that the Upper Ten Mile Presbyterian Church (q.v.) was formed. From 1805 to 1817 Cephas Dodd served these congregations, following his father Thaddeus. This church has had four buildings: the first of log (1785), the second of brick (1832), the third of brick and frame (after 1842), and the present church (1875). Another church evolved from this one when some of the members moved away (see *Fairfield Presbyterian Church*, Mercer County).

A monument commemorating the life and service of Thaddeus Dodd, organizer of the church, is in the front yard on the exact site of the first log church. Thaddeus Dodd also established the first Latin school west of the Allegheny Mountains in 1782–85. Dodd's Classical Academy was the forerunner of Washington Academy (see *Washington and Jefferson College*). *Location:* On U.S. 19.

b. Amity Hotel (painted brick) has a large porch running full length across two of its sides. It is now a machine shop. *Location:* On U.S. 19.

Note: Across the road is an early stone house.

c. Methodist Protestant Church (frame), organized in 1832, first met in the original log church belonging to the Lower Ten Mile Presbyterian Church, which adjoined its land. The building, later moved to the location of the present church, was replaced in 1851 with a frame structure, rebuilt in 1867. *Location:* On U.S. 19.

60. Sibbits House (fieldstone) has a signature stone on the gable end which reads, "S.S 1807," the first initial standing for Solomon. A fine springhouse stands in the back yard. The property is now part of a dairy farm. *Location:* Between Lone Pine and Marianna. Go 0.3 mile south of bridge on Lone Pine–Marianna Road (l.r. 62194); turn east on t. 728 at dairy sign; thence 0.2 mile to house.

61. Ten Mile Brethren Church (brick), a Dunkard congregation said to have met as early as 1775 at the Spohn home, was organized about 1800 by a clergyman named Bruist. It was built in 1832 and, until a recent reconstruction, had a fireplace with an iron kettle and crane. On March 14, 1905, it was incorporated as the German Baptist Brethren Church. *Location:* North of Marianna. Go 1.5 mile north on Lone Pine–Marianna Road (l.r. 62194); turn east on red-dog road. Church is at top of hill (0.3 mile).

62. Martin's Mill (frame) was built before 1850. *Location:* 1.5 mile east of Ten Mile Village, on l.r. 62082.

63. Ross House (brick) has on its gable end a signature stone which reads, "Joseph S. & Elizabeth Ross, 1835." *Location:* 0.5 mile from Glyde, on Glyde–Lone Pine Road (second house on right from Glyde).

Note: On a hill, one-half mile to the south of the Ross house and on l.r. 62085, is an old log cabin behind the Bethlehem Lutheran Church. The church was founded in 1787, with the present building erected in 1906.

64. Samuel Ross House (brick) has a signature stone on the gable end that reads, "Samuel and Matilda Ross, July 1, 1859." This house, with a cut-stone foundation, has an early butchering kitchen in the basement and a brick springhouse near the back door. The original two-story porch is in the back. *Location:* East of Glyde, on l.r. 62077, twelve miles south of U.S. 40.

65. Gantz House (cut stone) has a signature stone which reads, "John & Anna Gantz 1814." The Gantz family owned the first oil well in the county. *Location:* Between Lone Pine and Marianna, 0.8 mile below bridge on Lone Pine–Marianna Road (l.r. 62194).

66. Ulery Gristmill (brick), a large structure with a stone foundation, was built in 1835 by the Ulery family on the bank of the north fork of Ten Mile Creek. Originally operated by water, the mill was later converted to steam power. After ceasing to function as a mill, it became a grocery store and is at present an antique shop. *Location:* Zollarsville, on ·Beallsville Road (l.r. 62078), 0.3 mile off l.r. 62194.

Note: Traces of an Indian site have been uncovered behind this mill.

67. Ulery House (brick) has a signature stone which reads, "This Building was erected by Jacob Ulery & Israel in the [year] of our Lord 1838." Once operated as a hotel it is now a private residence and is located near the Ulery gristmill (see above). In the past, this mill and house have erroneously been described as being constructed of stone. *Location:* Zollarsville, on Beallsville Road (l.r. 62078), 0.2 mile off l.r. 62194.

68. Ulery Homestead (fieldstone and brick) was the old Ulery farmhouse across the creek from the mill and Ulery brick house, and has always been owned by the family. At the rear of the stone section is an attached two-story brick ell. A large barn with a cut-stone foundation is on the property. *Location:* Near Zollarsville, on l.r. 62194 north of its junction with l.r. 62078 (in West Bethlehem Township).

69. Ten Mile Methodist Church (brick) has a front signature stone which reads, "Ten Mile 1842 Methodist Episcopal Church erected by Stephen Ullery [old spelling] for use of the Methodist Society." The building, which has two front entrances, is adjacent to the old cemetery. *Location:* Zollarsville, on l.r. 62194 (West Bethlehem Township).

70. Crumrine House (covered log and stone) dates back to the early 1800s. The log section was built by George Crumrine in 1801 and the stone section in 1810. George was the father of Daniel Crumrine, who was an uncle of Boyd Crumrine, the historian. Signed masonry work on the front steps reads:

Virtu, Liberty & Independence
Rebuilt by Daniel & Margaret Crumrine
June 22, 1847
Francis Fogler

Location: Near Zollarsville, on Plum Run Road, 0.2 mile off l.r. 62194.

Note: Nearby is a fine log barn built in 1805.

71. Wise House (fieldstone), an unusually constructed house with a narrow front, was built before 1815. It was almost certainly erected by Jacob Wise, an early stonemason. *Location:* Halfway between Marianna and Beallsville, at junction of l.r. 62129 and l.r. 62194.

72. Kinder Stone Gristmill, now ivy covered, was erected before 1785 by George Kinder (see below). Valentine Kinder, George's son, was killed in 1781 while operating the mill. The business later became a woolen mill, followed by a distillery run by Samuel Thompson at this location, still know as Thompsons Corners. This business, which made the well-known Sam Thompson rye whiskey, was later taken to West Brownsville (see *Sam Thompson Distillery*). *Location:* Three miles south of Beallsville on l.r. 62194.

73. George Kinder House (fieldstone), one of the earliest houses west of the Alleghenies, was built in 1783. A smaller stone section was erected even earlier. A solid, bulletproof (for that time) door was discovered in the house by the latest owners, and there are portholes in the third floor of the house. The basement ceiling is constructed of heavy beams placed within inches of one another. Sheep were raised in this house for twenty years, and at present it is being restored into a lovely home by the Charles Appel family. *Location:* Three miles south of Beallsville, on l.r. 62194.

74. Cumberland Presbyterian Church (brick), now United Presbyterian, has a signature stone which reads, "This building dedicated to the worship of God by the C.P. Church A.D. 1840." A later addition is adjacent to the church. *Location:* Millsboro, on Pa. 88.

Note: The brick Methodist church in the community was built in 1855. This river town has many old structures.

75. Bower House (stone) was built on a tract called "Apple Bottom" which was patented by David Blair on May 14, 1789. It is reputed that Blair, a gunsmith, built the small portion of the house with the large chimney. He sold the property for $1,000 on August 8, 1801, to John Bower, who built the larger part. A signature stone has an engraved flower on it and reads, "J. and E. Bower, 1806." Bower came to western Pennsylvania from York County in

1796 and married Elizabeth Rex. He was a miller, distiller, justice of the peace, school director, potter (patenting a type of clay pipe in 1814), and boat builder (among his craft the *Fancy* and the *Ariadne*). His sons Andrew and Benjamin also lived in the house. In the late 1800s it was sold but was returned to the family in 1972 when John Bower's great-great-grandson, W. Scott Bower, purchased it from the Russell Bane family. *Location:* North end of Fredericktown, on Pa. 88.

76. Old Stone Parsonage has a plaque on the front that reads, "Old Stone Parsonage, 1803." The community where this house is located was not founded until 1817. *Location:* Fredericktown, on Pa. 88 next to First Methodist Church.

Note: Three miles north of town is the Regester log house built about 1830. It is an L-shaped double log structure on l.r. 62176.

77. Dorsey House (fieldstone with dressed stone corners) was built in 1787 by James Dorsey, who migrated from Baltimore and lived here until his death. The house, with a beautiful doorway, faces the Monongahela River and Brownsville. A stone story-and-a-half addition, reputedly built by slave labor, is on the south side of this Georgian house. The woodwork in the house is cherry. *Location:* Denbo Heights, 113 Cherry Avenue, opposite Maxwell locks and near Pa. 88.

78. California State College was founded in 1852. Old Main (brick), the oldest existing building on the campus, was constructed in 1868. *Location:* California.

79. Stone House has on its signature stone:

$$\begin{matrix} & L & \\ T & X & R \\ & 1810 & \end{matrix}$$

The property also includes a stone barn, a springhouse, and a washhouse. Now owned by California State College, it is used as a dormitory for the tennis team. *Location:* California, near California State College stadium.

80. Large Stone House, with four sizable chimneys and a later addition on the left rear half, belongs to a physician. There is a stone springhouse on the property. *Location:* California, on l.r. 62095, 0.6 mile off Blaine Road.

81. The Poplars (painted stone) has an inscription over the door that reads, "The Poplars 1831–1906." The building is at present a California State College fraternity house. *Location:* North of California, just south of Coal Center on Pa. 88.

82. Speers House (brick) was built in 1806 by Henry Speers, Jr., a brother of Noah Speers who founded Belle Vernon (meaning "beautiful green"). The Speers family operated a ferry in the area for over 100 years. Joseph and Sally Pappalardo rescued this house from demolition and restored it as a restaurant, which opened as The Back Porch in 1975. *Location:* Speers, almost under bridge which spans Monongahela River between Speers and Belle Vernon.

83. Hell Stretch is a bend in the Monongahela River where riverboat captains have had to face the dangers of smog, a pier (now gone) in the middle of the river, and dangerous curves. (Donora made news in 1948 when poisonous fumes from a zinc-smelting plant caused the death of twenty-three persons.) *Location:* Donora, at Westmoreland-Washington County bridge.

84. Irwin House (brick), a four-story building, now in disrepair, reportedly was built (at least in part) in 1802, possibly as a hotel. It is said to have been the first brick house constructed in this community, which was formerly called Williamsport. *Location:* South edge of Monongahela, on Pa. 88.

85. Bethel African Methodist Episcopal Church (brick), of Norman Gothic design, was organized in 1834 by Samuel Clingman, the first pastor. The construction of the original building began in 1842. It was partly burned in 1849 and rebuilt in 1858. The present building, a handsome structure, was begun in 1871 and completed after 1882. *Location:* Monongahela, 715 Chess Street.

86. Aquatorium, the first theater of its kind in the state and one of the most unusual in Pennsylvania, was built in commemoration of the two hundredth anniversary of the Monongahela area. This 75-by-300-foot open-air stage was constructed over the Monongahela River and opened July 10, 1969, with a seating capacity of 3,500. *Location:* Monongahela, on Pa. 837.

87. Mingo Creek Church (brick) was organized by August 1786, but the congregation had no regular pastor until 1796. At this time

Samuel Ralston was installed and served until 1836. The first meetinghouse was a log structure 50 by 55 feet erected before 1794. This was the meeting place of the Mingo Society, which was active in the Whiskey Rebellion. Opposing an excise tax, about forty men gathered at this church and went to Bower Hill to bring John Neville, the internal revenue inspector, back for punishment. James McFarlane was killed at Bower Hill and is buried in this cemetery (see *Ginger Hill House*), along with other insurrectionists who outlived the troubles (one was John Holcroft; see *Holcroft-Story Home*). The present church was built in 1831. A monument near its front marks the site of the log meetinghouse. *Location:* About 1.5 mile south of Finleyville, on l.r. 62042 at its junction with Pa. 88.

88. Ginger Hill House (ruins) was the home of James McFarlane, who was killed while carrying a flag of truce to the soldiers guarding John Neville's home at Bower Hill. When McFarlane was shot, the insurrectionists burned Neville's house. McFarlane's home at Ginger Hill, a landmark for many years, was destroyed by fire in 1974. A brick smokehouse and other outbuildings, together with the house ruins, still exist on the property. *Location:* Near Mingo Creek Park, junction of Pa. 917 and Mansion Road.

Note: At Mingo Creek Park is a frame tavern built about 1840 by "Dutch" John Kammerer (on Pa. 136 at Kammerer Road).

89. Campbell House (stone) was built by Robert Campbell in 1837–39. Before it was completed, Campbell was killed by a team of horses while working on his farm. His wife had the construction finished. Campbell's father John, a native of Ireland, bought this farm and Robert was born near here in 1790. *Location:* Near Finleyville, close to Mineral Beach, on Pa. 88, 0.8 mile northwest of Hidden Valley Road.

90. Barr House (stone) was constructed by the Barr family in 1803 around a log cabin. *Location:* Two miles south of Finleyville, on Pa. 88 at Airport Road (t. 834).

91. James House (cut stone) was built in 1800 by Robert James. In 1786 his father Richard had purchased land from Gabriel Cox on a tract called Coxbury. In 1793 Richard James divided some of the land between his sons Robert and William. Robert built a log house and later this stone one, where he lived until his death in 1834. The house, with exterior native chestnut trim, was used for seven years as a meeting place for Peter's Creek Methodist Episcopal Church (later James Chapel Methodist Church, q.v.). The James family donated the land for the church. Near the house is a stone smokehouse. *Location:* Near Gastonville, on Stone Church Road.

92. James Chapel Methodist Church (stone) was organized as Peter's Creek Methodist Episcopal Church in 1810. The congregation erected this building in 1817 on land donated by the James family (see *James House*), and stones for the building were quarried on the James property. In 1876 the interior was remodeled and stained-glass windows installed. *Location:* Near Gastonville, on Stone Church Road. Go 1.5 mile northeast on l.r. 62087 from its junction in town with Elrama-Finleyville Road (l.r. 62174).

Note: Near the church is the site of Gabriel Cox's stockaded fort.

93. Gaston House (brick with cut-stone foundation) is reputed to have been built in 1800, but its architectural design denotes a later time. John Gaston came from New Jersey and purchased a tract of land called "Belmont" from John Cox in 1790. Before his death he divided the property among his four sons. An 1807 mill stood below the house where a later mill, now a residence, is located. *Location:* Gastonville, junction of McChain and Stone Church Roads.

94. Holcroft-Story Home (stone) is better known for the original owner of the land than for the man who built this early residence. A log house formerly at this site belonged to John Holcroft, one of the most active insurrectionists of the Whiskey Rebellion and reputedly known as "Tom the Tinker." He bought this property called "Liberty Hall" from Robert Henderson in 1795. Holcroft, who lived in the log house until 1818, had eight sons and eight daughters. T. Story purchased the property in 1832 and built the present house. A signature stone bears the date. *Location:* Near Finleyville, on l.r. 62174, 2.4 miles west of its junction with Pa. 837 in Elrama.

95. Wright House (brick) was built with wings on both sides of a center section about 1821. Joshua Wright and his brother James came from Cumberland and settled on Peters Creek about 1765, buying a tract of over one thousand acres. Joshua married Charity Sauns, daughter of John Harris, for whom Harrisburg was named. In 1776 he was one of

99. McMillan's Log Cabin School

the justices of the peace in Yohogania County and ex-officio judge of the court. *Location:* East edge of Venetia, on l.r. 62034.

96. Pigeon Creek Church (brick), one of the oldest congregations in the region, was the first meeting place of the Redstone Presbytery, the first organized west of the Allegheny Mountains. Both this church and the Chartiers (Hill) Church (q.v.) were organized in 1776. According to legend James Power preached to the settlers on Pigeon Creek in 1774, and documented services were held there in 1775 by Dr. John McMillan, who served the congregation from 1776 to 1794. A log and then a stone church were used until 1829 when the third and present 56-by-70-foot structure was erected. The signature stone reads, "A. D. 1829." A porch was added later. The church is near the village of Eightyfour, named for the year the post office was created, 1884. *Location:* Near Eightyfour. Go east two miles on Pa. 136 from its junction with Pa. 519; turn south on l.r. 62052 and continue about one mile; turn left on Church Road.

97. Newkirk Methodist Church (brick) was built with two front doors about 1842. It is now a storage building and woodworking shop. *Location:* Near Bentleyville, junction of Pa. 917 and Interstate 70.

98. James Scott House (brick), built in 1842 with a signature stone on the gable end, has been completely restored inside and out.

It has a two-column portico in front and H chimneys. A restored smokehouse is in the rear, and the Scott family cemetery is nearby. *Location:* North Strabane Township, 710 Waterdam Road (off U.S. 19).

99. McMillan's Log Cabin School, the oldest existing school building west of the Alleghenies and the forerunner of Jefferson College, was founded in 1785 by Dr. John McMillan. McMillan, who organized many of the churches in the region and was closely associated with Washington Academy, Washington College, Canonsburg Academy, and Jefferson College, first instructed a group of young men in Latin and Greek who had studied with Rev. Thaddeus Dodd and Rev. Joseph Smith until shortly after the academy was opened at Canonsburg. In 1895 the log cabin was moved to the grounds of the present Canonsburg Junior High School from its site at the McMillan farm, where a great oak still stands near the site of the old manse (go 0.4 mile on l.r. 62034—off U.S. 19 at Hill Church—to road leading north; thence 2.3 miles on this road to farm and McMillan oak).

The old brick Jefferson College building is gone, but the noteworthy Franklin literary social room and the library of that structure have been restored inside the junior high school building behind the log school. Jefferson College began in 1794 as the Academy and Library Company of Canonsburg; a stone school building was erected in 1796 and chartered in 1802 as Jefferson Academy. Dr. McMillan was appointed president in 1798. In 1824 the college chartered Jefferson Medical College in Philadelphia. *Location:* Canonsburg, on College Street near North Central Street.

100. John Hegarty House (fieldstone and frame) was built in 1805 with a later frame addition. *Location:* Edge of Houston, corner of East Pike Street and Fairmount Avenue.

101. Swearingen-Cook House (painted brick with H chimneys) was built on land originally purchased by Andrew Swearingen, a captain in McIntosh's campaign of 1778. It was later owned by his daughter Sally, who married John Cook. The old Cook family cemetery is near the house. The wife of Alfred Creigh, a Washington historian, is buried here. The house is now the Washington Country Clubhouse. *Location:* Near Meadow Lands, on Country Club Road (l.r. 62190) off Locust Road, at Washington Country Club (can be seen on hill from Interstate 79).

106. Arden Trolley Museum

102. Octagon Barn (frame) was built in 1888 by Robert D. Wylie. *Location:* North of Washington, at Octagon Acres on west side of U.S. 19, about one mile south of The Meadows racetrack.

Note: Next to this structure is a colonial brick house built in 1823.

103. Meadow Lands Harness Racing Museum, founded and operated by Albert and Delvin Miller, is housed in a Union Pacific business car and a Norfolk & Western caboose located on the grounds of the racetrack. Nearby is the Adios champion pacer monument (see *S. White's Sons*). *Location:* Near Washington, on Race Track Road (off U.S. 19).

104. Linn House (brick), with H chimneys and a one-story portico of Greek Revival architecture, was built in 1848. *Location:* Near Washington, on Brehm Road (t. 631) (0.7 mile off U.S. 19 on Conklin Road, almost beside racetrack).

105. William M. Quail House (brick), with an unusual two-story portico for that period, was built in 1837 with H chimneys. The Quail, Linn, and James Scott houses appear to have been designed by the same person. *Location:* Near Washington, at Quail Acres, on U.S. 19 on Race Track Road (l.r. 62092).

106. Arden Trolley Museum, located on the site of an original trolley line, was founded and is operated by the Pennsylvania Railway Museum Association. It features visual aids and conducted tours. Included in the museum is the famous trolley, the *Streetcar Named Desire* from New Orleans. *Hours:* May–October: Saturday and Sunday, and holidays, 1–6 P.M. *Admission charge* for trolley

rides. *Location:* Two miles from downtown Washington, in Arden Downs Industrial Park, on North Main Street extension.

107. Roberts House (stone and brick) was built in 1804 by John Roberts, with later brick and stone additions. The Georgian house has a fanlight and pedimented doorway with fine woodwork on the interior. *Location:* Canonsburg, 225 North Central Avenue.

108. Morganza State Training School (brick) for disturbed boys and girls between the ages of ten and twenty-one opened in Allegheny County in 1854 as a reform school and was removed to Morganza, a farm named by Col. George Morgan, in 1876. The land was patented by Alexander and Matthew McConnell.

Colonel Morgan's house, now razed, was built in 1796 by John Morgan, his oldest son, and the colonel lived here until his death in 1810. He was an Indian agent during the Revolution and later was noted for his scientific work in farming. The home site is marked by a monument made from the foundation stones and erected in 1928. The former penal institution is now a school and mental hospital. *Location:* Near Canonsburg, on Pa. 519 (0.2 mile northeast of roadside marker at east gate of industrial school).

109. Chartiers (Hill) Church (brick) dates from the time when Dr. John McMillan, on his first missionary tour of the West in 1775, preached at John McDowell's on Chartiers Creek. Dr. McMillan took charge of the Chartiers and the Pigeon Creek congregations in 1776 and served Chartiers until 1830. The first log church was built in 1778 and was used until 1800, when it was replaced by a stone structure, enlarged in 1832. The third and present church was erected in 1841 and remodeled in 1909, with a tower addition in 1912. Dr. McMillan and his wife are buried in the walled-in cemetery adjacent to the church. Woodrow Wilson's father was one of the pastors of this congregation. *Location:* Hill Church, on U.S. 19 at junction of Pa. 980 and l.r. 62173 (five miles northeast of Washington).

110. McConnell House (stone) was built by Alexander McConnell in 1805 and is still owned by the family. *Location:* Near Bishop. Take Muse Road (l.r. 62045) off Pa. 50 in Bishop for 0.4 mile; then turn left on Hickory Grade Road (t. 793) and continue 0.5 mile to house.

111. Millers Run Church (brick) was founded in 1793. The present church was built in 1835. An early cemetery is adjacent to it. The old manse is next to the church, which is only used for anniversary services. *Location:* Near Venice. At its junction with Pa. 50, go south on Pa. 980 for 0.7 mile; turn right on Swihart Dairy Road (t. 771); thence 0.4 mile and church is on right.

112. Bigger House (cut stone) was built in 1848 by the Bigger family on the Glenlock tract. Thomas Bigger was the original property owner. Oddly enough, it is still owned by a Thomas Bigger, of the same family, which has provided the only occupants of this house since its construction. The first Bigger house, a log cabin, which Thomas found half-finished upon his arrival here from Philadelphia in 1774, was located nearby on Raccoon Creek. There is a later log house still standing on the property. *Location:* 0.9 mile from edge of Murdocksville, on l.r. 62003.

Note: Matthew Dillow's fort site, built in 1779, is somewhere in the vicinity of this property, in the fork of Dillow Run off Pa. 115 just west of Murdocksville.

113. Tucker Church (stone) was built in 1824 on land owned and set aside for the church by John Tucker. Stonemasons named Minesingers constructed this building for less than ninety dollars. The congregation first met in the home of James Holmes. In 1965 an addition was built on the front from stones taken from the foundation of the old Cross Roads Church that was destroyed by fire and replaced by a brick structure. *Location:* Halfway between Paris and Florence, on old U.S. 22 two miles west of Pa. 18.

114. Tucker House (stone) reportedly was built by Wesley Tucker, son of Jonathan II. Pioneers, John and Henrietta Tucker, came to Hanover Township in 1775, raising their children on a tract called "Grace." Their first son, Jonathan, was born in Fort Vance ten miles away during an Indian raid. John Tucker was a Quaker and a leader of Methodism in the area (see *Tucker Church*). He died in 1830 at the age of one hundred. Both he and his wife are buried in the church cemetery. A depression in the ground marks the original log cabin, and the frame Mansion House built by John Tucker in 1825 (now covered with siding) is nearby. *Location:* 1.8 mile west of Florence, turn north 0.2 mile on unmarked road off old U.S. 22, east of Tucker Church.

Note: Another stone house in the area is the Black house on t. 352, 1.7 mile off U.S. 22

northwest of Tucker Church. The Hanlin–Phillips stone house is on t. 853 near its junction with t. 350. Also in this area is the King's Creek Cemetery which has been restored in recent years (on t. 867 north of Tucker Church).

115. Livingston House (stone), a long one-story structure, was built on the old James Livingston farm. This early house served as a Boy Scout cabin in later years. *Location:* 1.4 mile south of Florence. Turn off U.S. 22 on Harmon Creek Coal Road for 2.3 miles. House can be seen from Interstate 70, 1.5 mile east of Florence interchange.

116. McCabe Store (frame) was built prior to the Civil War and was operated by James C. McCabe in 1856 when he moved his business here from Florence. McCabe dealt extensively in wool and other farm items. The old ledger from this store has been preserved in the market across the street (formerly the Seceder Church, q.v.). This long building, covered with shingles, has been converted into apartments. *Location:* Paris, off old U.S. 22, across from market.

117. Seceder Church (brick) was built in 1843–44 on the Pittsburgh–Steubenville Pike. In 1858 this denomination merged with the Associate Reformed Church, and the building was used as a house of worship until 1927. In 1931 the Longs bought the church and converted it into a grocery store which they continue to operate. *Location:* Paris, across road from McCabe store.

118. Wallace House (stone and brick) was obviously a tavern, but little is remembered about this remarkable structure. It has probably been in its present form since 1830. The stone section of the house has a fine arched doorway with a fanlighted entranceway. The home was owned a century ago by J. Harper Wallace and was later purchased by Michael Pollock. *Location:* About one mile north of Florence, on Pa. 18 (junction of Pa. 18 and Purdy Road).

119. Seminary-Academy House (painted brick), built prior to 1832 on land owned by Philip Jackson, became Mrs. Lambden's Seminary in 1832. Between 1833 and 1848 the building housed an academy founded by Robert Fulton in 1832 in a log building on land that turned out to have a title defect. Fulton, a cousin of the famous steamboat builder, was a teacher in this school from 1832 to 1839. William Burton succeeded

Fulton in 1839 and continued until 1848. The house was later purchased by the Thomas Moore family. *Location:* Florence, near corner of old U.S. 22 and Pa. 18 (between gasoline station and cemetery).

Note: This community was once called Bricelands Crossroads. Next to this house is the burial site of Elisha McCurdy, first pastor of Crossroads Church across the street, where the "Great Revival" began in 1802. A new church now stands on the site.

120. Raccoon Presbyterian Church (brick) dates from Dr. John McMillan's first visit to the Raccoon Creek settlement in 1778. In his journal Dr. McMillan recorded that he preached at Raccoon also in 1779, 1780, 1782, and 1785. The first regular pastor was Joseph Patterson, who served from 1789 to 1816. The congregation's first house of worship was a rough-log meetinghouse built in 1781. This was followed by a hewn-log church of 1785, a brick church of 1830, and the present structure, built in 1872–73. The early pews and original pipe organ have been preserved inside the church. In the front churchyard, about one hundred yards southeast of the church, is the site of Beelor's blockhouse, built by Capt. Samuel Beelor, who came to this region around 1774. On his second trip to Raccoon Creek, Dr. McMillan preached at this blockhouse. *Location:* Candor, on l.r. 62021, which leads off U.S. 22 near Allegheny–Washington County line.

Note: An early log house, now covered with siding, is next to the Fort Beelor site at a spring.

121. Cross Creek Presbyterian Church (brick) was organized in June 1779 by Dr. John McMillan. James Power preached the first sermon under an oak tree at nearby Vance's Fort in 1778. Joseph Smith served as the first pastor from 1779 to 1792. There have been five churches here: the first of unhewn logs (1781), one of hewn logs (1784), the third of stone (1803), an 1830 brick structure, and the present one built in 1867. A cemetery is across the road. *Location:* Cross Creek, on Main Street (l.r. 62185).

122. Vance House (brick) was erected in 1830 by Col. Joseph Vance, builder of Vance's Fort (site on Ridge Road, one mile north of Cross Creek Presbyterian Church, q.v.). The house has always been a private residence. *Location:* Cross Creek, on Main Street (l.r. 62185) next to Cross Creek Church.

123. Wilkin-Stockton House (brick) was built in 1821 by David Wilkin, who sold the property in 1827 to John Stockton, minister of the Cross Creek Presbyterian Church. Dr. Stockton kept bachelor's hall in this house for about two years. He later married, and his five sons and one daughter were born in the home. Stockton lived here until his death in 1882. At the turn of the century, William H. Allen bought the house, which is one of the oldest in the area. At one time it was considerably larger than it is now. *Location:* Cross Creek, on Main Street (l.r. 62185) near church and across from cemetery.

124. Russell House (brick), built in 1875 by Andrew Russell, was called Mount Pleasant Valley Farm. Alexander Russell was an early settler, and William M. Russell was the last of that family to live in this house, which overlooks the reservoir. The Russells were breeders of Durham cattle, hogs, and sheep. *Location:* About 2.5 miles north of Hickory, on l.r. 62031 at Cherry Valley Reservoir.

125. Hickory Associate Presbyterian Church (brick) was founded in 1795. The present building was erected in 1868 and is now the United Presbyterian church office. *Location:* Hickory, on l.r. 62031.

126. Johnson House (log), one of the oldest houses in the area, was owned in 1876 by M. Johnson. Once covered with siding, it was recently restored by the McChesney family. *Location:* Hickory, on Pa. 50 across from post office.

127. Hickory Hotel (frame covered with siding) was the first hotel in the town, which was laid out in 1797. In 1876 it was known as the Keystone Hotel, with a Mr. Hemphill the proprietor. Later owners were Peacock and McCreary. *Location:* Hickory, on Pa. 50 (across from plumbing store).

128. Hickory Academy (frame) was built late in 1892. It was an academy for ten years and later the Hickory High School. At present it is a plumbing store. The stage of the school is still intact inside the rear part of the building. *Location:* Hickory, on Pa. 50.

129. McElroy House (frame), with large columns in the front, was the home and office of Dr. J. McElroy in 1876 and is at present an antique shop. *Location:* Hickory, on Pa. 50.

130. Kline House (brick), with a large front porch, was owned by W. H. Kline in 1876. It was later purchased by Jacob Stewart about 1900. It is at the supposed site of the hickory tree from which the town acquired its name. *Location:* Hickory, on Pa. 50 and Washington Avenue.

131. Meadowcroft Village, opened in 1969, was developed by Albert and Delvin Miller on their old farm property originally settled by their great-great-grandfather, George Miller, Sr., in 1795. The original patent dating back to the 1780s was a Virginia grant. The land, now comprising more than eight hundred acres, had been since the early 1880s a harness and racehorse farm, where many champion trotters and pacers were bred.

The name "Meadowcroft" is derived from a combination of Meadow Lands (Delvin's horse farm) and Bancroft Farm (the original Miller holdings). Operated as an educational and historical museum by the Meadowcroft Foundation, a nonprofit corporation, this early nineteenth-century village started with the Miller schoolhouse built about 1834, the Miller log house of 1795, and a 100-year-old covered bridge. It has grown to include more than thirty structures, many of which house permanent exhibits.

A University of Pittsburgh archeology team has recently uncovered at Meadowcroft Village the earliest documented evidence of inhabitants in the eastern United States dating back to about 15,000 B.C. *Hours:* May 1–December 1: Weekdays, 9 A.M.–5 P.M. Sunday, 1–6 P.M. *Admission charge. Location:* Three miles west of Avella, on Pa. 50.

132. Patterson's Mill House (painted brick) was built in 1820 by W. J. Patterson. Gen. Thomas Patterson built a mill on land purchased from his father William in 1793–94. Thomas enlarged his business in 1812 by building a fulling mill. (The mill scars can be detected along Cross Creek near this house.) He was also a member of Congress (1817–25) and a member of the electoral college (1816). Materials from the stone ancestral home of the Pattersons, built in 1794 on a hill above the mill, have been used to build another house in Ligonier (Westmoreland County). The barn was relocated at Meadowcroft Village (q.v.). *Location:* About one mile northeast of Avella, on Pa. 231 at l.r. 62024.

Note: A later brick house built in 1838 by T. M. Patterson, grandson of Gen. Thomas Patterson, is now being restored. It is on a dirt road 0.5 mile north of l.r. 62185 at the west end of Cedar Grove. Another early brick house, built by Robert Perrine, is in Cedar Grove.

131. Schoolhouse at Meadowcroft Village

133. Old Independence Hotel (brick) was built in 1803 and is the oldest building in the village, which was laid out the same year and originally called Williamsburg. *Location:* Independence, on Pa. 844.

Note: This community has many old log (covered) and brick houses.

134. Plumer House (brick) was built in 1831 by Jerome Plumer, a prosperous farmer. (The date was discovered on a locally fired brick from the house.) The DiPietro family bought the house in 1930. *Location:* Independence, on Pa. 844 near old hotel on opposite side of street.

Note: Another of Plumer's houses, a log structure built in the early 1800s, is off Pa. 844.

135. West Middletown, once active in the underground railroad, is a charming community of early historic buildings too numerous for most to be listed. Miraculously just about every dwelling on the picturesque main street has been preserved in its original exterior condition. The community is worth visiting if only to stroll along its sidewalks and see the quaint structures. Laid out in 1796, the town became a borough in 1823. (Robert Fulton, of steamboat fame, owned land in this area, on which his mother and sister lived.)

a. The McKeever Study (frame polygon) is a reconstructed copy of the original one erected at Pleasant Hill Seminary by and for Thomas Campbell McKeever during the 1860s. McKeever was a grandson of Thomas Campbell, nephew of Alexander Campbell, and son of Matthew and Jane Campbell McKeever, founders of the seminary about 1845. Thomas became the first teacher in the seminary and later took over the job of principal, which his mother had held. This building is an almost exact replica of the original study, which was patterned after the study of Alexander Campbell at Bethany, W.Va., and was moved to West Middletown following the close of the seminary. In the 1930s it was torn down. The present structure, erected under the sponsorship of the borough council, was built by Rea Dunkle and Homer Denning, among others, and now houses historical and genealogical records as well as a circulating library. The center is a good source of information about the historic buildings in West Middletown. *Location:* On West Main Street (Pa. 844).

b. McKeever House (brick) was built prior to the Civil War by Thomas Campbell McKeever, who, in addition to being a seminary teacher and principal, was a justice of the peace, associate county judge, noted abolitionist, early associate of John Brown, and a leader of the underground railroad. His home has been used as a hat factory, a store, a post office, and a community club. It is now owned by the King family. *Location:* On Main Street, across from post office and down street.

c. Old McClure Log House is believed to be the oldest log house in West Middletown. At the time of its construction people from miles around came to see a two-story house being built. James Hardy had a blacksmith shop on the property, and from 1860 to about 1876 it was the home of Robert B. McClure, who operated a machine shop (which stood next to the house) for the manufacture of threshing machines, an invention of Andrew Ralston of Hopewell Township in 1842. About five hundred machines were produced here until 1859 when many farmers went bankrupt because of a disastrous frost and McClure's business was ruined. That year he had shipped a large number of machines to Saint Louis, but they rusted on the wharf since there was no demand for them. *Location:* 61 Main Street (Pa. 844), next to Ralston Thresher historical marker.

d. First Christian Church (brick) dates back to about 1830 when members of the Disciples group began worshiping in a McKeever school at the east end of town, with formal organization taking place in 1837 at Pleasant Hill Seminary. The original Disciples church at Brush Run was organized in 1811 several miles southeast of here. The present building was erected in 1848. (The congregation sold it in 1861 and erected another church, which stands one-half mile east of this point.) The older building is presently used for commercial purposes. Alexander Campbell, founder of Bethany College in W.Va., was ordained here. *Location:* On Main Street, not far from Ralston Thresher historical marker.

e. Henderson House (brick), erected in 1798, is the oldest brick building in town. In the 1850s and 1860s it was occupied by T. Lane who had a chair factory here with a horse-driven lathe. It became the home of Milton Hemphill, who served as deputy sheriff, and later was owned by the Henderson family. *Location:* 43 East Main Street.

f. McNulty-France Hotel (frame) was built in 1804. From 1856 to 1861 W. W. McNulty conducted a hotel here. Later R. M. Garrett operated the establishment. Prior to his death in 1929 John D. France operated it. In 1903 Samuel Ferguson, a contractor for the Wabash Railroad, lived at the France Hotel. Funeral services were conducted here for him after he was murdered at the foot of Seminary Hill that same year. A brick addition to the building is believed to have been built by Samuel Urie. The building is now a residence and antique shop, presently owned by William Huston. *Location:* On Main Street.

g. Lindsey Hotel (frame), the first in town, was built by James Lindsey in 1801 and at one time was the finest tavern between Baltimore and the Ohio River. Traveling circuses at various times were on exhibit at this drovers' tavern. Here Henry Clay and Philip Doddridge debated the issue of the proposed National Road. *Location:* On Main Street, next to France Hotel antique shop.

h. African Methodist Episcopal Church (frame) was built about 1860 by a Wesleyan Methodist congregation on the former site of a blacksmith shop owned by J. W. Smith. The AME church had met in the old Doddridge chapel located about three miles west of town. When the Wesleyan Methodist congregation disbanded, the AME took over its building. *Location:* On Main Street.

i. Grove United Presbyterian Church (brick) was built in 1859. Samuel Taggart, who lived in a stone house in West Middletown, was pastor of this church for fifty years. *Location:* On Main Street.

j. Stewart House (brick), an outstanding residence, was built in 1859–60 by Galbraith Stewart. *Location:* 1 West Main Street.

k. Armour House (log covered with siding) was built in the early 1800s. It is situated on a bank next to a soldier's and sailor's monument at the west end of town. *Location:* On Main Street.

136. Plantation Plenty (brick), the ancestral home of the Manchesters, was finished in 1815 by Isaac Manchester. While he was traveling to Kentucky from his home in Newport, R.I., in 1796, he came across this land and liked it so much that he brought his family to settle here. Manchester purchased a 380-acre tract of land, originally called "Plenty," from Capt. Samuel Teeter and built a home of post-Colonial architecture, similar to houses in Newport. The interior, trimmed in native black cherry, was completed by an experienced cabinetmaker whom Manchester brought from Philadelphia. This beautiful mansion, in its original condition with a captain's walk, window shutters, and classic doorway, is the private residence of the great-great-grandson of Isaac Manchester. In the front yard of the house is the site of Samuel Teeter's fort. Teeter, a relative of John Doddridge, had come to the area after 1773 and took up this tract of land patented in 1785 and situated off the old Buffalo Trail. There are numerous outbuildings on the property including a smokehouse, a workshop, a springhouse, and a barn built in 1803. Private residence. *Location:* West of West Middleton, on Pa. 844, 0.6 mile northeast of its junction with Pa. 231.

137. Upper Buffalo Presbyterian Church (brick) was organized in 1779, with Joseph Smith the first pastor, serving from 1780 to 1792. Smith, who is buried in the cemetery, founded an academy of languages and sciences in 1785. Among those who received their training there were John Brice, James McGready, James Hughes, Samuel Porter, and Joseph Patterson. The first two churches were log, one built in 1779, which stood in the northwest corner of the present cemetery, and the other in 1798. The third and present building was constructed in 1872. *Location:* Buffalo, one square south of Pa. 844 (old Pa. 31).

138. Buffalo Associate Presbyterian Church (brick), now the North Buffalo United Presbyterian Church, was founded in 1775 with Matthew Henderson the first pastor in

136. Plantation Plenty

1782. It was one of the oldest congregations of this sect in the county. Another early minister was Thomas Campbell, father of Alexander Campbell, who founded Bethany College in W.Va. The first hewn-log church was built in 1811, at the time the members divided into the North and South Buffalo congregations. It served the North Buffalo Associate group until 1848, when the present brick church was erected. It was remodeled and enlarged in 1896. *Location:* 1.8 mile west of Wolfdale. Turn south off Pa. 844 onto l.r. 62134 for 0.6 mile to l.r. 62096; thence west 0.5 mile.

Pennsylvania Historical and Museum Commission Markers

Augusta Town   U.S. 40, 3 miles southwest of Washington

Bradford House   Washington, at property, 175 South Main Street (2 markers)

Capt. Philo McGiffin   Washington, U.S. 40, Main and Beau Streets

Col. George Morgan   Pa. 519 south of Morganza

Cross Creek Church   Cross Creek, l.r. 62185

David Reed   Venice, north of Pa. 50

Doddridge's Fort   Pa. 844, 2.5 miles west of West Middletown

Edward Acheson   Washington, southwest corner of Main and Maiden Streets

Elisha McCurdy   Florence, U.S. 22

Gantz Oil Well   Washington, West Chestnut Street at Brookside Avenue

George Washington   Venice, Pa. 50

Globe Inn   Washington, 155 South Main Street

Hill Church   U.S. 19, 5 miles northeast of Washington at Hill Church

Hill's Tavern   Scenery Hill, U.S. 40

James G. Blaine   West Brownsville, 238 Main Street

John McMillan   U.S. 19, 5 miles northeast of Washington

Le Moyne Crematory   Washington, l.r. 62131, South Main Street

Le Moyne House   Washington, 49 East Maiden Street

McGugin Gas Well   Pa. 18 northwest of Washington

Miller's Blockhouse   U.S. 40, 3.5 miles west of Claysville

Monongahela   On main highways leading into city

The Mounds   Monongahela, Memorial Park, Mound and Decker Streets

National Road   U.S. 40 southeast of Washington near Scenery Hill; U.S. 40, 3.6 miles southwest of Washington; and U.S. 40 west of Claysville

Ralston Thresher   West Middletown, Pa. 844

Rice's Fort   U.S. 40, 3.5 miles west of Claysville

S-Bridge   U.S. 40, 5 miles southwest of Washington

Washington   On main highways leading into city

Washington and Jefferson College   Washington: East Maiden Street at gateway; East Beau Street opposite gymnasium; and College Avenue at main entrance

Whiskey Point   Monongahela, Pa. 481 at Park Avenue

William McGuffey   Claysville, intersection of U.S. 40 and Pa. 231

Wolff's Fort   U.S. 40, 3.3 miles southwest of Washington

Garvers Ferry
Leechburg
ARMSTRONG
Vandergrift
New Kensington
Camp Joan
Apollo
Salina
Perryville
Saltsburg
Mamont
INDIANA
Murrysville
Slickville
Blairsville
ALLEGHENY
Export
Lockport
White Valley
Delmont
New Alexandria
Boquet
Congruity
Shieldsburg
Harrison City
Forbes Road
Crabtree
New Derry
Manor
Jeannette
Hanna's Town
Circleville
Grapeville
West Fairfield
CAMBRIA
Irwin
Adamsburg
Greensburg
Latrobe
Derry
Herminie
Kingston
Fort Allen
Youngstown
(Harrolds)
New Stanton
Waterford
Bells Mills
Darlington
Mill Grove
Trauger
Ligonier
Laughlintown
Fellsburg
Yukon
Hunker
Donora
West Newton
Lycippus
SOMERSET
Webster
Norvelt
Pleasant Grove
Rostraver
Stahlstown
Monessen
Barren Run
Mt. Pleasant
Alverton
Laurelville
Belle Vernon
Jacobs
West Overton
Donegal
Creek
Jones Mills
Scottdale
FAYETTE
WASHINGTON

Westmoreland County

Capsule History

Westmoreland, the eleventh and last county founded by the colony, was the first English-speaking one in the nation established west of the Allegheny Mountains. "Land of the western moors," named for a county in England, it was called star of the west by eastern politicians in the 1800s. More often referred to as "mother of the western counties," it embraced all the land west of Laurel Mountain. Its original area, erected from Bedford County on February 26, 1773, comprised the counties which are now Westmoreland, Greene, Fayette, and Washington together with parts of Allegheny, Armstrong, Beaver, and Indiana. Today the county has 1,024 square miles and a population of 376,935.

The military road cut by Gen. John Forbes in 1758 became a well-worn highway, following the general course of U.S. 30. Many Indian trails and trader paths traversed the county. The *Catawba Path* ran from New Florence past Fort Palmer, Ligonier, Pleasant Grove, Stahlstown, and Acme, exiting near Laurelville. The *Glades Path* ran almost along the course of Pa. 31 by Acme, Mount Pleasant, and West Newton. *Nemacolin's Path* entered east of Prittstown, passing through or near Mount Pleasant, Hunker, and Madison, and exited on a ridge near Greenock. It was followed by Braddock on most of his way through Westmoreland County. The *Raystown Path* followed approximately the course of the Lincoln Highway (U.S. 30) in this area, passing Laughlintown, Big Bottom, Saint Vincent's (College), Luxor, Hannastown, Harrison City, and Trafford. Forbes swung northward after passing present-day Forbes Road, turning south of Export, and passing along the ridge near Murrysville. The *Salt Lick Path* left the Catawba Path near Laurelville, following the Glades to Mount Pleasant and Braddock's Road to Hunker. The *Sewickley Old Town Path* joined two Indian towns of the same name, one near West Newton, the other near New Kensington. It passed Trafford, New Texas, and Logans Ferry.

In 1763 Col. Henry Bouquet and his troops defeated the Indians at Bushy Run, thus raising the siege of Fort Pitt and checking attacks on British posts and settlements during Pontiac's Rebellion. From 1777 to the end of the Revolutionary War, the militia of Westmoreland County manned a chain of many forts and blockhouses from Fort Reed on the Allegheny to Fort Ligonier at the western base of Laurel Ridge on the banks of the Loyalhanna Creek, which had been the depot for Gen. John Forbes's expedition against Fort Duquesne in 1758.

Hanna's Town (historic village not to be confused with nearby Hannastown mining town) became the first county seat in 1773. Courts were held here until Greensburg, originally called Newton (New Town) but later named for Revolutionary War hero Nathanael Greene, took the honor. On May 16, 1775, the settlers of Hanna's Town drew up resolves somewhat similar to the Declaration of Independence, which was written the following year, and formed the Westmoreland County Association and the First Battalion under Col. John Proctor, whose regiment in the Revolution carried the famous rattlesnake flag with the motto "Don't Tread on Me" (preserved in the state museum at Harrisburg). In 1782 the settlement was destroyed by the Seneca Indians.

Among the noteworthy people in the early days of the county were Gen. Arthur St. Clair, president of the Continental Congress and governor of the Northwest Territory; Henry Clay Frick, who made the manufacture of coke a large-scale industry in the county; William Freame Johnston (1808–72), eleventh governor of Pennsylvania from 1848 to 1852; John White Geary (1819–73), sixteenth governor of Pennsylvania from 1867 to 1873; Frederick Pershing, an ancestor of Gen. John J. Pershing who settled on a tract called Coventry in 1769; and Erskine Ramsey, a noted steel maker.

Flax-scutching, an early pioneer method for preparing flax for linen, has been revived at an annual festival (since 1907) at Stahlstown, first settled by Leonard Stahl. Other early products of the county included iron, bituminous coal, coke, glass, salt, and gas. Westmoreland had sixteen stone blast furnaces, with Westmoreland furnace (1792) the first in the county and the third west of the Alleghenies.

Today New Kensington, the largest city in the county, is one of the most extensive producers of aluminum in the world, while Arnold and Jeannette have large window-glass plants. Mount Pleasant and Grapeville are noted for glass manufacture, and Monessen is important for iron and steel. Latrobe is widely known in industry as the "tool steel capital," and here are manufactured some of the world's largest casting molds. It is the home of golf pro Arnie Palmer and also the site of the world's first all-pro football team of 1897.

Landmarks

1. Courthouse (stone) was erected in 1906–08 in French Renaissance style. After the county seat was moved from its location in Robert Hanna's log tavern at Hanna's Town, another log courthouse was built in Greensburg. The first court was held at the new county seat January 7, 1787. This structure was replaced by a brick building in 1798. In 1854–56 the third courthouse in Greensburg was built, a stone Roman-porticoed building that looked like a temple. The bell from the brick building of 1798, later placed in the old jail tower, has been preserved by the county historical society. *Location:* Greensburg, Main Street.

2. Firemen's Museum (brick), located in the old West Penn freight station, contains fire-fighting memorabilia from the collection of a former assistant fire chief, Al Rosetti, Sr. The museum was started largely through the efforts of two young men who at the time planned to become firemen themselves. It is operated by the Junior Firefighters. Included in the display is the first fire engine to be used west of the Alleghenies. *Hours:* Usually open during Fire Prevention Week and by appointment. *Location:* Greensburg, Pennsylvania Avenue (behind City Hall, which faces South Main Street).

3. Westmoreland Museum of Art (brick) is located in a Georgian-style building with a large columned portico. It opened in 1959, the gift of Mary Marchand Woods, the widow of Cyrus Woods, who was minister to Portugal and ambassador to Spain and Japan. The museum features American, European, and Oriental art, as well as mid-Victorian rooms containing furniture which originally belonged to the Woods family. It also includes the restored rooms from Penglyn, the summer mansion of the Scaife family which was formerly located at Ligonier. Along with its art exhibits and an extensive toy collection, the museum provides space for concerts, lectures, and films, as well as a fine-arts reference library. The Westmoreland County Historical Society has its headquarters in this building. *Hours:* Sunday, 2–6 P.M. Tuesday, 1–9 P.M. Other days, 10–5 P.M. Closed Mondays and holidays. *Location:* Greensburg, 221 North Main Street.

4. YWCA Building (brick), with a large portico, was built in 1900 for the William A. Huff family. The architect was Ralph Adams Cram. In 1970 it was donated to the YWCA by Katherine Huff Horn. Around World War I the building behind it was moved from across the street at 419 North Main Street to its present site (12 O'Hara Street) by the Huff family for their daughter as a wedding gift. It is constructed of log and was stuccoed after it was moved. Former owners were the Armstrong family. In 1975 it was sold to the YWCA for a program building. *Location:* Greensburg, North Main and O'Hara Streets.

5. Saint Clair Opera House (brick) was the site of silent movies, later-day "talkies," and other entertainment in the early 1900s. It is now an office building. *Location:* Greensburg, 218 Maple Street.

6. Strand Theater (brick) is an early theater with many of the original features retained inside the building. On the exterior is written "1879–1916 Keaggy." *Location:* Greensburg, on Otterman Street.

7. Mount Odin Park was once the estate of Dr. Frank Cowan (1844–1905), Westmoreland County's eccentric genius who was a lawyer, medical doctor, horticulturist, scientist, author, poet, scholar, printer, and editor of a journal which he called *Frank Cowan's Paper.* In addition, Cowan, an extensive world traveler, served as secretary to a U.S. Senate committee, as a private secretary to President Andrew Johnson, and as county district attorney. Interested in Norse tradition and mythology, he gave his estate and everything involved with it Norse names, such as Mount Odin. He loved trees and plants and had 2,000 different varieties planted on his property, together with over 220 kinds of grapevines. Cowan wanted to be buried in a Viking boat, burned with quicklime, but his wish was thwarted. However, one of his dreams did come true. To the citizens of Greensburg he willed Mount Odin Park "for the sole and exclusive use of the people thereof and adjacent boroughs, as a place for play, recreation and social enjoyment." Today the park is a public golf course. The log cabin on the property was erected during Cowan's time by the Ludwick Hose Company. The great stone pillars at the entrance to the park are reproductions of the original ones which Cowan had built with round tops, symbolic of the two hemispheres and in keeping with the Egyptian rules of proportion. *Location:* Greensburg, on old U.S. 30, at top of Grapeville Ridge about 1.3 mile west of center of town.

8. Frans House (stone) was built in 1796 by Jacob Frans, according to the signature stone in the gable end of the house. Although its interior has been modernized, the house still retains the original plank floors. The basement, once used for a barn, has a large double door. At present this dwelling is the home of the country club greens keeper. *Location:* Greensburg, on old Jeannette Road at Greensburg Country Club.

9. Seton Hill College was founded by the Sisters of Charity, mainly through the efforts of Mother Aloysia Lowe, who procured the 200-acre Jennings farm August 7, 1882. Seton Hill remained the Motherhouse until 1969 when nearby Ennis Hall became the novitiate and convent. (Ennis Hall on Mt. Thor Road was once the stone mansion of Henry Coulter. Another old brick mansion, once the Margaret Coulter house, is on the same road.)

On this property Saint Joseph's Academy (1883–89), Saint Mary's Preparatory School for boys (1889–1927), a conservatory of music, and an art school were located at various times. In 1889 the present administration building was erected. Seton Hill became a junior college in 1914 and was chartered in 1918 as a four-year liberal arts college. In 1975 Mother Elizabeth Seton (1774–1821), founder of the order of Sisters of Charity at Emmitsburg, Md., in 1809, became the first American-born saint.

The *Stokes House* (brick), which housed the academy and preparatory school and presently is the home economics department, was the former home of Col. William A. Stokes, chief counsel for the Pennsylvania Railroad. (This land was claimed in 1784 by Ludwig Otterman, and it remained in his family until George Otterman sold it in 1817. Stokes acquired title in 1850 and sold it to John Jennings in 1868.) In 1853, Andrew Carnegie, who at the time was a seventeen-year-old telegraph operator for the Pennsylvania Railroad, visited this home and was so impressed by Major Stokes' private library that he was inspired not only to have one of his own but to build public institutions as well. Carnegie later donated more than seven thousand libraries. (An abandoned 1911 depot is on the site where Carnegie worked at that time in Greensburg.) *Location:* Greensburg, on College Avenue.

10. Hawksworth House (brick) was built by the Hawk family a few years after receiving a 1790 land grant. This family was the sole possessor of the property until 1955 when the Barclays purchased it and renovated it in French, German, and English decor. *Location:* North side of Greensburg, on Hawksworth Drive off Main Street.

11. Coulter Mansion (stone) was built by Gen. Richard Coulter, who served in the Spanish American War and World Wars I and II. His father, Gen. Richard Coulter, Sr., was an officer in both the Mexican and Civil Wars. The elder Coulter's uncle, Richard Coulter (1788–1852), was an eloquent orator and first of three members of the Westmoreland County bar who became justices of the Supreme Court of Pennsylvania. Now owned by the Roman Catholic Diocese of Greensburg, the building is a convent, the Regina Coeli Missionary Cenacle. *Location:* Greensburg, on College Avenue near Hawksworth Drive.

12. Kepple House (brick) was built between 1799 and 1807 on the Kepple farm later owned by the Rughs. In the front yard of this property is the site of the Kepple blockhouse erected in 1774, where some of the settlers fled during the 1782 attack on Hanna's Town by the Indians and British. An account written by historian George Dallas Albert describes the incident as follows:

Across the country, at a little block-house, the remains of which are still to be seen about a mile and a half north of Greensburg on the Salem road, lived Kepple, a brother-in-law of Michael Rugh, Sr. Kepple was in the field with his team, his dog running towards him, frisking and barking with all signs of fear, and the sound of the far-off crack of the guns made him on the instant strip the gear from his horses and hasten back to the house, built for war and peace, and barricade the openings.

Some of the logs from this blockhouse were later used in the construction of a corn crib on the property. *Location:* North of Greensburg, off Pa. 66, 135 Locust Valley Road.

13. Alwine School House (painted brick), named for the Samuel Alwine family, was built in 1874 and still has the original bell in its belfry. The first classes were taught by Lawrence Strump at the Shuster home until this school was erected. Bell Young was the first teacher in the new building. In 1949 it was incorporated as the Alwine Community Civic Association. It is located on the old Forbes Road. *Location:* From Pa. 66, 3.2 miles north of Locust Valley Road (near Greensburg), turn east onto old Pa. 66 and continue 0.2 mile to right. School can be seen from new Pa. 66.

14. Bair (Bierer) House (brick) was built in 1838 by Frank Bair, who was from an old German family. Signature stones are in the gable ends of the house. A fine brick barn is also on the property. The house was later purchased by the Heinnickel family. This area has yielded an abundance of Indian artifacts. *Location:* Near old Hanna's Town, junction of U.S. 119 and l.r. 64038.

15. Steele (Steel) House (brick) was built in 1861 by William Steel. The structure retains its original woodwork and has had few alterations. A rose-glass entranceway is directly across from the stairway where seven brides of this family have descended to be married at various times. The property, still owned by the Steels, includes a brick complex consisting of a springhouse, smokehouse, and various other structures. A fine stone stile is in the front yard. *Location:* Near Hannastown, junction of l.r. 64054 and Fire Station Road.

Note: Other early Steel houses are on this road also.

16. Hanna's Town, the first county seat from 1773 to 1787, held its first court April 6, 1773, at the house of Robert Hanna, who kept a log tavern on the Forbes Road. During Dunmore's War over the Virginia-Pennsylvania boundary in 1774, Arthur St. Clair recommended the erection of a fort here. John Connolly, an agent of the governor of Virginia, who had

16. Courthouse-Tavern at Hanna's Town

stirred up trouble between the Indians and Pennsylvania settlers, was arrested and put in jail in Hanna's Town. Instead of appearing for trial after being released on bail, he became the leader of 150 Virginia militiamen and returned, barring the Pennsylvanians from entering their own courthouse.

Hanna's Town became the principal outpost for defense in 1776 when Kittanning was abandoned. On July 13, 1782, the village was attacked by a party of Seneca Indians and British rangers—one of the last border raids of the Revolution. At this time Peggy Shaw, a young girl, lost her life rescuing a child. The town was burned, all except the fort and two houses. The Indians also attacked Miller's blockhouse several miles away. Joseph Brownlee was captured at this time; and while the Indians were taking the prisoners from Miller's to Canada, he and his child were tomahawked. A lone marker on a hillside farm indicates the place where they were buried (off Pa. 119 near its junction with Luxor-Bovard Road). Some histories read "John" instead of "Joseph." Hanna's Town, which had consisted of nearly thirty dwellings, was never rebuilt.

The Steel family, which bought the land in 1826, sold 183 acres to the county in 1969, when the restoration project of the Westmoreland County Historical Society began, with archeological excavations under the direction of Jacob Grimm, curator of Fort Ligonier (q.v.). In 1973 during the county's bicentennial the log courthouse-tavern was rebuilt by contractor Carl Schultz. Construction began in 1975 on the stockaded fort at its exact site (69 by 122 feet). *Hours:* Saturday and Sunday, 1–5 P.M. Closed in winter. Tours given by costumed hostesses and hosts. A field museum is also open to the public. *Admission charge. Location:* Hanna's Town, about three miles northeast of Greensburg, junction of l.r. 64054 and l.r. 64038 (Forbes Road).

Note: A very early log house is on the county property on l.r. 64054, and another weather-boarded log structure is located near the site over the hill on l.r. 64038 from its junction with l.r. 64054.

17. Saint Walburga Wayside Chapel (glass and frame), dedicated in 1974, was designed by architect Francis Church at St. Emma's Convent. Incorporated in its walls are twelve stained-glass windows depicting the life of the Benedictine nun and missionary, Saint Walburga, patron of the order's mother house in Eichstaett, Bavaria. Over fifty years ago Saint Walburga's Roman Catholic Church (German) at the corner of Lincoln and Campania Avenues in Pittsburgh was constructed with these windows made in Munich. When the parish was dissolved, the church was sold to a Baptist congregation. At that time the windows were dismantled and sent here to be used in the walls of this star-shaped chapel as a gift of Bishop Leonard of Pittsburgh. (Saint Emma's, built in 1931 next to where the chapel now stands, was originally John Robertshaw's residence. It was bought by the Sisters in 1943 after Emma, the young daughter of this family, had died and named in her honor. The property itself dates back to a land deed of 1789 and was first owned by John Brownlee.) *Location:* Near Greensburg, on Five Points Road (Pa. 819).

18. Kepple-Rial House (log) was built about 1812. The remains of a stone barn foundation contain a cornerstone that reads, "J S 1847." Behind the home is a stone springhouse. The property, once owned by the Kepple and Rial families, was later purchased by Matthew Doyle followed by actor-director Jack Zaharias. *Location:* Northwest of Greensburg, junction of Stony Springs Road and l.r. 64038.

19. Oliver Perry Smith House (brick) was built about 1850. It has been restored by the J. H. Malkames family. *Location:* Near village of Forbes Road, on Pa. 819 near Carasea Drive.

20. Ross House (stone), built by Thomas Alexander Ross in 1832, has remained in this family for seven generations. Alexander Ross died in 1873, at age eighty-three. His wife Elizabeth died in 1846, at age fifty-four. They are buried in St. Clair Park, Greensburg. *Location:* Near old Hanna's Town, off U.S. 119,

2.3 miles on l.r. 64038 (about three miles northeast of Greensburg).

21. Sindorf-Brown House (brick) was built by George Sindorf in 1850. This L-shaped building has a double porch and original interior woodwork, and is a fine example of Asher Benjamin's architecture. At a later date William Brown, a Greensburg druggist, acquired the property, consisting of about 127 acres, from Lucinda Sindorf Ehrle. After it had changed hands several more times during the coal-mining era, George Barnhart sold the house (which had been owned by W. R. Barnhart in 1876) and much of the land to Stowell Mears, who refurbished the exterior in 1959. The restored brick springhouse is now a tack shop. *Location:* Northeast of Greensburg, on U.S. 119, 0.5 mile from l.r. 64142.

22. Blank Farmhouse (brick with shutters) was built before 1850 by the Blank family. In 1876 J. Blank, Sr., owned the property. The woodwork in this pre–Civil War home is all original. A third floor was added in 1890, and several porch additions were built in 1920. This farm was the site of the first Westmoreland Hunt Steeplechase in October 1926 (now the Rolling Rock races at Ligonier). The Weidlein family purchased this house from the McNareys in 1919. *Location:* Northeast of Greensburg, on U.S. 119 at l.r. 64142.

23. St. Clair Monument marks the site where Maj. Gen. Arthur St. Clair and his wife Phoebe Bayard are buried, having died within eighteen days of each other. St. Clair (1734–1818) was a lieutenant in the Sixtieth Royal American Regiment in 1759, commander at Fort Ligonier from 1767 to 1769, major general in the Revolution in 1777 (the only officer from Westmoreland County who attained this rank during the war), president of the Continental Congress in 1787, first governor of the Northwest Territory in 1789, and commander of the U.S. Army at the battle of the Wabash in 1791. In 1832 the Masonic Society of Greensburg erected a sandstone monument over the double grave; it was replaced with a granite one in 1913. (See also *Fort Ligonier* and *Arthur St. Clair Homes.*) In this cemetery (incorporated in 1856) is also the site of the first church organized in Greensburg in 1788 and built in 1816. A monument with an engraved picture of the church stands at the site. *Location:* Greensburg, St. Clair Park, Maple Avenue and Otterman Street.

24. Old Zion Lutheran Church (brick), the first church of this denomination organized west of the Allegheny Mountains, was erected in 1884. At first this congregation and Saint John's (below) worshiped in the same church. Balthasar Meyer, the schoolmaster, had baptized children as early as 1772, since the congregation did not have a pastor at that time. A log schoolhouse, built that year, had been its original place of worship. The Pittsburgh Synod of the Evangelical Lutheran Church erected a monument on the site of the log schoolhouse to celebrate the one hundred fiftieth anniversary of the congregation. The marker stands in the cemetery, directly across the road from this church, which is now the Hempfield Township Maintenance Building. *Location:* Harrolds area, 0.2 mile south of Pa. 136 on I.r. 64113 in Fort Allen School district (about three miles southwest of Greensburg).

25. Saint John's Evangelical and Reformed Church (brick) is one of this denomination's oldest congregations in western Pennsylvania. In 1783 Rev. John William Weber (see *Milliron Church*) organized this church and also the Brush Creek–Salem church (q.v.). Originally, this Reformed congregation and the Old Zion Lutheran congregation held joint ownership of the building, but today there are separate churches, with cemeteries, beside each other.

The first Reformed church building was erected in 1829. Its cornerstone is now located in the present structure, built in 1892, which is presently United Church of Christ. In the front churchyard stands a monument erected by the Pennsylvania Historical and Museum Commission in memory of the German settlers from Harrolds who petitioned for the erection of a fort in 1774 at the time of Indian attacks. The actual fort site is marked by another monument about 150 yards to the south of the church. *Location:* Next to Old Zion Lutheran Church.

26. Plank Road School (frame), built in 1901 on a plank road, has not been a school for years. This two-room structure has been renovated for a community center. *Location:* Acme, on Three Mile Hill in Mt. Pleasant Township.

27. Polish Catholic Church (brick) has a signature stone above the door which reads, "Kosciol Przemienienia Panskiego built in 1899" (Church of the Transfiguration). Across the street is a Polish Catholic school erected in 1906. *Location:* Mount Pleasant, at Hitchman and Smithfield Streets.

Note: Also In Mount Pleasant is the Tree of David Synagogue built in 1871 as a Presbyterian church (South Church Street and Stand Pipe Alley).

28. Smith Glass Company was founded in 1907 by L. E. Smith and features hand-crafted glass. A boarding house (brick), now used as a gift shop and visitors' center, was built at the same time for out-of-town employees. In the early days, before child-labor laws, eleven- to fourteen-year-old boys worked in factories such as this. The company had its own football team between 1911 and 1916. Henry Ford visited the plant and brought a lens as a sample of those to be made for Model T Ford headlights. It may be seen in the showcase in the visitors' center. Visitors are welcome. *Location:* Mount Pleasant, on Factory Street off Pa. 31.

29. Lobingier Stone House was built about 1804 by John Lobingier, who was a member of the 1776 Pennsylvania Constitutional Convention. He also erected a stone mill here at the same time. This mill replaced a log one built by Ralph Cherry before 1772. The Lobingier mill, operated by three generations of the same family, is no longer here. (The site is across the road from the house, where a gasoline station now stands.) Lobingier also built a tannery which was just over the Fayette County line on a site now occupied by another gasoline station.

A private cemetery, surrounded by a stone wall, is about 300 yards behind the house. The residence and a nearby stone springhouse have been completely restored. *Location:* Laurelville, on Pa. 31.

30. Pollins House (brick) was built by David S. Pollins in 1852. This farm was part of Sewickley Manor, one of the manor lands of the Penns, and was called the garden spot of Westmoreland County. The overshot of the barn, built in 1849, is supported by nine black walnut columns turned by a horse-powered lathe. Calvin E. Pollins, who resides in this house and owns the farm with his late brother John's widow, is the seventh generation of the same family to own it. His ancestor who acquired it from the Penns in 1769 was Abraham Leasure (LeSueur), who lived on this land until his death in 1805. *Location:* Turn east on Greensburg–Mount Pleasant Road at County

Fairgrounds entrance on l.r. 64136 toward Pleasant Unity; then turn right on first road (t. 830).

Note: Also on Mount Pleasant Road are the 1923 Charles McKenna Lynch mansion (brick), now Lynch Hall on the University of Pittsburgh campus at Greensburg, and the Thomas Lynch log house off this road on Airport Road.

31. Saint Paul's Reformed and Lutheran Congregations were organized in 1782 by John William Weber, first Reformed minister to serve west of the Alleghenies. Their church was first known as "Ridge Church" or "Frey's." The land for the first meetinghouse was purchased in 1796. The second log church had two stories with a balcony on three sides. A brick church was built in 1846, and it was considered unsafe in 1896, at which time the Reformed and Lutheran congregations agreed to separate. A new Reformed church (brick) was built, and the Lutherans purchased six acres on the opposite side of the road. The Lutherans' present church (brick) was dedicated in 1904. They are known as the twin churches since they are across the road from each other. The cemetery adjoins the older Reformed church. *Location:* Trauger (in Mount Pleasant Township).

32. Middle Presbyterian Church (brick) was the last of four buildings erected by this congregation. As early as 1772 David McClure preached at Jacob's Swamp or Mount Pleasant, and James Power preached there two years later. Power organized the church in 1776, one of the first established in western Pennsylvania. He became the first regular supply from 1776 to 1779, and then pastor until about 1817. He died in 1830 and is buried in the church cemetery. (See also *Sewickley Presbyterian Church* at Bells Mills.)

In 1781 the trustees purchased the church property, a tract of more than six acres. The first two houses of worship were built of logs, the last two of brick. The present church, built in 1854, replaced the one built in 1830.

The Middle Church Cemetery Association administers the cemetery, which has been the church burial plot since 1773. It is here (across the highway from the church) that Peggy Shaw, heroine of the 1782 Indian raid at Hanna's Town, is buried. *Location:* North of Mount Pleasant, at junction of Pa. 981 and l.r. 64213.

33. Henry Clay Frick Birthplace

33. Henry Clay Frick Birthplace (stuccoed stone) is a two-room springhouse on the property of Frick's Mennonite grandfather, Abraham Overholt. In 1800 Abraham's father, Henry Overholt, had acquired the land. Here Abraham established a large distillery where Old Farm pure rye whiskey was made. In 1838 he built a brick mansion next to the springhouse.

Abraham's daughter Elizabeth was Henry Clay Frick's mother. Henry was born in 1849 at the springhouse "cottage," which the family used as a temporary residence until its permanent home was constructed. Henry, a pioneer in the manufacture of coke, organized the Henry C. Frick Coke Company in 1871 and later became a partner of Andrew Carnegie, the steel magnate.

A brick flour mill erected on the estate in 1859 has been a museum since 1929 and contains local Indian artifacts and other items; it also houses the headquarters of the Westmoreland-Fayette Historical Society. The estate is owned by Helen Clay Frick, Henry's daughter, who sponsors the civic program of the historical society. (See also *Clayton* [Frick House], Allegheny County.) *Hours:* May 15–October 15: Weekdays, 10 A.M.–5 P.M. Saturday and Sunday, 2–5 P.M. *Donation. Location:* West Overton, on Pa. 819 one mile north of Scottdale.

Note: There are a number of early buildings at West Overton and numerous one-room school houses in the Scottdale area.

34. Espey Water-Powered Mill (ruins) is across from the early miller's stone house. *Location:* North of Wesley Chapel, three miles west of Scottdale-Smithton Road.

Note: Another old cut-stone house is beyond the mill site toward Reagantown.

35. Scottdale Mennonite Church (brick) was built in 1939 and is the oldest church of this sect in the county. It replaced a former church of 1893. Prior to this the Mennonite church for the area was at Alverton; it had been built in 1841. The old cemetery is on the property of East Huntingdon Township High School (q.v.). This land formerly belonged to Jacob Loucks.

The first minister of the present church was Aaron Loucks. Next to the church is a frame parsonage, built in 1895. It was first occupied by another minister, Jacob Ressler. It is possibly the first Mennonite Church manse in the United States. *Location:* Scottdale, at Grove and Market Streets.

36. East Huntingdon Township High School (brick) was the area's first high school, built in 1899. This structure, now abandoned and in disrepair, was constructed on the site of and from bricks of the old Stonerville Mennonite Church, erected in 1841. *Location:* Alverton (formerly Stonerville).

37. Loucks House (brick) was built in 1853 by Jacob S. Loucks, eldest son of Rev. Martin Loucks. The same year Jacob married Mary Saylor. Their eleven children were later born here. On the property is a brick building containing a bake oven, washhouse, springhouse, and fuel shed. Their son Aaron was a Mennonite minister at the Pennsville meetinghouse (Fayette County) in 1892. *Location:* Scottdale, near corner of Walnut and Broadway Avenues.

Note: Another brick Loucks house, at 527 North Chestnut Street, was built in the 1820s by Martin Loucks, Mennonite preacher and father of Jacob.

38. Stoner House (brick) was built in 1842 by John Stoner (1784–1865), the son of Christian Stoner who came to Westmoreland County in 1799. The lumber was prepared by "Sawmill" Joe Stoner at his mill near Hawkeye. According to legend Christian paid $1,000 and a metal plow point for nearly 600 acres. John's son, Adam, later lived here. In 1926 George Kintigh purchased the farm, which includes a springhouse, smokehouse, and bake oven. *Location:* Near Alverton, on t.

670 about 0.5 mile off Smithton Road from Mt. Nebo.

39. Olive Branch Baptist Church (brick) was built in 1857. It is situated next to a stone barn. *Location:* One mile east of Twin Coaches, on l.r. 64187 near junction of Smithton and East McClain Roads.

40. Hurst House (brick) was built in 1812 by Nathaniel Hurst, who settled in the area in the late 1700s. His name appears on a 1789 tax list and in 1780 he owned four slaves. In 1790 he had patents for 1,000 acres of land. Lydia Hurst, born in 1811, married John Irwin, of Irwin. A log house next to the main home was moved from Lone Pine, Washington County, and rebuilt as an antique shop. *Location:* Near Norvelt, vicinity of Hurst High School; off Mount Pleasant Road at corner of Hecla Road and Astor Drive.

Note: An L-shaped brick house with a double porch in the rear on the old Fisher property, called Century Farm, is nearby on Brinkerton Road.

41. Hepler's Gristmill (frame), designed by William Pollock, was built by Israel Painter in 1853. The mill, operated by the Stantons, was later run by the Heplers. With a private rail siding, it is situated on Jacks Run. *Location:* New Stanton, at bridge on U.S. 119.

42. Martin Wertz House (brick), built in 1869, was constructed with an open court in the rear of the house. A signature stone is above the front entrance. *Location:* South of New Stanton, on U.S. 119 (1.1 mile north of junction with Pa. 31).

43. Krause Farmhouse (brick), built by a Dr. Krause in 1875, has been remodeled with new brick and windows. The interior woodwork has been restored. It is on the Donald Funk farm. *Location:* South of New Stanton, on U.S. 119 (1.9 mile south of automobile assembly plant and next to Martin Wertz house).

44. Saint Paul's Reformed Church (Seanor's) (brick) was founded before 1816. The first meetinghouse of both the Lutheran and Reformed congregations was built of logs on the Seanor property. The Reformed group was part of the First Greensburg Reformed congregation from 1829 to 1867, when it became attached to the Second Greensburg charge. A brick church was built in 1837 and replaced in 1875 by the present one. Among the congregation's first ministers were John William Weber, William Weinel, Nicholas Hacke, H. E. F. Voigt, and John Love. *Location:* South of Hunker, on Seanor's Church Road toward Yukon.

Note: About one and a half miles from Seanor's Church is the old Errett cemetery on the present Miller property.

45. Milliron Church (Mühlisen) (frame) was built in the 1890s on the original foundation of a former log church. At first a Reformed church, this congregation later became the United Church of Christ (now Weber Memorial Center, Penn West Conference). John William Weber (1735–1816), one of the first Reformed missionaries in western Pennsylvania, is buried in the adjacent cemetery. A rose marble obelisk erected in 1874 marks his grave. Inside the church, now used as a chapel in the summer, is the original octagonal wineglass pulpit, which was formerly at Saint John's Evangelical and Reformed Church (q.v.) and was recently discovered under a porch. It is now located on a tree stump in the front interior of the sanctuary, next to an altar table made from early cemetery stones whose epitaphs had been obliterated. *Location:* West of Youngwood. On U.S. 119 at first traffic light in town, turn west on Depot Street; thence 1.5 mile where l.r. 64112 continues on to Whitehead Road; church is situated off road to left.

46. Plumer House (frame and brick) was built by John Campbell Plumer (1788–1873) in 1814 soon after his first marriage. In 1846 a four-bay brick addition of two-and-a-half stories was made to the gable end of the house.

Plumer was the son of Congressman George Plumer and his wife Margaret Lowrey Plumer. He acquired his name in honor of Col. John Campbell, who had rescued George Plumer when he was a boy from drowning at Fort Pitt. John bought a gristmill and sawmill near his property from his brother Alexander and William Clark. About 1820 he erected a new stone mill, which at the time was one of the largest in western Pennsylvania, and sold it in 1866.

Plumer was superintendent in the erection of the bridge across the Youghiogheny at Robbstown (West Newton's former name) and in 1819 was commissioned justice of the peace by Governor William Findley. In 1830 Plumer was elected to the state legislature and in 1839 to the state Senate, serving from 1840 to 1842. Resembling Andrew Jackson in appearance and being of the same party, he was nicknamed "Old Hickory." In addition, he

was a member of the Sewickley Presbyterian Church and burgess of West Newton in 1847–49. This house is a proposed museum. *Location:* West Newton, 131 Water and Vine Streets.

Note: West Newton is the site of Sumrill's ferry where a group of Revolutionary War veterans from New England, with their leader Gen. Rufus Putnam, arrived in 1788. Here they built a fleet of five boats and started out for Ohio, founded Marietta, and became the first permanent settlers in the Northwest Territory. This original trek was recreated in 1938 by modern-day pioneers, who built replicas of Putnam's boats for their journey.

47. Salem Regular Baptist Church (brick) was organized in 1792 and is the oldest of this denomination in the county. Land for the first church was donated by Joseph Budd, Sr. The second and present church was built in 1842. The cemetery is adjacent to the church. *Location:* West of West Newton, on l.r. 64143, 1.3 mile northeast of its junction with Pa. 51.

48. Rehoboth Presbyterian Church (brick), also known as the "Upper Meetinghouse in the Forks of the Yough," was organized in 1778. Before the first meetinghouse was built, the congregation met at the home of Col. Edward Cook (see *Cook Mansion,* Fayette County). Dr. John McMillan preached here in 1784, the same year that James Finley was installed as the first regular pastor. The congregation has built two churches: a log meetinghouse and the present brick one erected in 1899–1900. Colonel Cook (1725–95) is buried in the cemetery that adjoins the property. *Location:* Near Belle Vernon, 0.2 mile on l.r. 64137 from its junction with Pa. 981.

49. Barren Run School (brick) was held in this one-room schoolhouse built by William Crise in 1871. Nearby stood an old molasses mill, owned and operated by John Baird, which the schoolchildren used to visit at noon for samplings. The school's first teacher was W. H. McBeth and the last was Grace Hoenshel. In 1959 the school was vacated and returned to the original landowners. The school and property were sold in 1962 for $1,500 to the Evangelical United Brethren Church (now United Methodist) next door. (This frame church was built in 1883.) *Location:* Near Jacobs Creek, 1.2 mile on l.r. 64122 from its junction with l.r. 64169.

Note: There are several early log houses in this area.

51. Concord School

50. Church of Hope (Hoffman Cemetery Chapel) (brick) was built in 1813 as Hoffman's Evangelical Lutheran Church. Henry Hoffman, a settler in 1794 when the congregation was organized, donated the land and funds for this church in his will. Prior to 1842 all services were conducted in German. Services are held here once a year. *Location:* Jacobs Creek, on hillside near junction of l.r. 64122 and l.r. 64169 (Smithton area near Barren Run School).

51. Concord School (stone), built in 1830 of local materials, is the oldest stone schoolhouse still standing in the county. It was erected from the subscription of land, money, and labor, and used as a school until 1870. Later it became a dwelling, a store, a storage shed, and a stable. In 1947 it was restored by the schoolchildren of Rostraver Township. *Location:* Rostraver, on Pa. 51.

52. Fells Methodist Church (stone), organized in 1785, was known as Teal's, since worship services were held in the home of Edward Teal. Robert Ayers conducted the first services here, one of the original meetingplaces on the Redstone circuit. In 1787 Benjamin Fel (*cq*) donated land to the society, and the first meetinghouse was built between 1792 and 1804. In 1835 the original log church was replaced by the present stone one, which has log beams in the basement. *Location:* Fellsburg, junction of l.r. 64118 and Pa. 330.

53. Daily House (brick) was built in 1797 and used as a store by John Daily. The front door of this Georgian style house has a remarkable fanlight. *Location:* Near Webster, junction of Pa. 51 and Pa. 330.

54. Black Horse Tavern (brick), built by the Donaldsons about 1800, has been in the same family ever since. The house has beams in the cellar with the bark still intact and fireplaces in every room. The present living room is located where the bar was. *Location:* Two miles east of Donora, junction of Pa. 51 and l.r. 64143 (near Daily house).

55. Donner House (brick) was built by William H. Donner, who founded the tin-plate mill in Monessen (named for "Essen"—German steel center—on the Monongahela). He was a partner of Andrew Mellon in the Donner mill across the river, which gave part of its name, "Don," along with "Nora" (Mellon's wife), to the town of Donora. *Location:* Monessen, 435 McKee Avenue.

56. Dillinger's House (stucco) was a private hospital that handled minor surgery. It was founded and headed by G. A. Dillinger. At this house plans were formulated for the construction of the Charleroi-Monessen Hospital, now of major importance, serving the Monessen Valley and located in Charleroi. *Location:* Monessen, 657 McKee Avenue.

Note: Next to this house (at 653 McKee Avenue) is a frame one, the former home of Colonel Derrickson, an aide to President Lincoln.

57. Markle Plantation was settled in 1770 by Gaspard Markle who two years later founded an enterprise which continued for almost 100 years. Markle built one of the first gristmills in the area in 1772 and retired in 1799. It was here that Col. Archibald Lochry and his militia en route to join George Rogers Clark's expedition camped overnight in 1781. Mill Grove, Markle's frame mansion with an arched doorway, was built here by him before 1800. In 1811 Markle's son Gen. Joseph Markle and Simon Drum built a paper mill, the third to be established west of the Allegheny Mountains. Later the Markles established paper mills at West Newton and woodpulp mills in Somerset County.

Gaspard Markle's second home was built of stone in 1818. The mansion stands between the site of the old blockhouse and the family burial ground known as Mill Grove Cemetery. Today one may see Markle's first home, an old stone smokehouse, the stone mansion (on the H. W. Branthoover farm), the cemetery, and remnants of the millrace and the foundation of the paper mill. *Locations:* Mill Grove and ruins: near Turkeytown, along Pa. 136 at bridge over Little Sewickley Creek.

Stone mansion and cemetery: follow l.r. 64278 (also t. 449) leading northwest off Pa. 31 at Turkeytown. Turn off l.r. 64278 to no-outlet road which leads past cemetery to Branthoover farm.

58. Sewickley Presbyterian Church (stone) was organized in 1776 by James Power, who had preached in the area on his first missionary tour in 1774. During this first service it is said that the men in the congregation had to stand with rifles in their hands to guard against Indian attack. In 1782 the Redstone Presbytery was formed, but the first meeting, which was scheduled at Sewickley, was canceled due to an insufficient number of members because of threatened Indian incursions near the homes of the Washington County members.

The first log meetinghouse, built during Dr. Power's pastorate (1776–87) was built about one and one-half miles north of the present church on the road leading from Markle's mill toward Pittsburgh. The second log church was erected on the present church site. The third church, built of stone in 1831, is one of the few remaining stone churches of the area. This structure is next to the county's only remaining covered bridge (built in 1850). *Location:* Bells Mills (west of Yukon), on l.r. 64180 off Pa. 136 near covered bridge over Big Sewickley Creek.

Note: Bells Mills bridge, the only remaining covered bridge in the county, was built in 1850 by Daniel McCain.

59. Means (Mains) House (stone) was built in 1840. Along with the date on the signature stone are the initials "F. M." This home, at one time owned by Linley Means, has two hex signs carved on stones in one gable end of the house. One stone depicts an eight-shafted design and the other an eagle. The house, now in disrepair, is used as a barn. *Location:* Near Herminie, 0.2 mile from junction of l.r. 64191 and l.r. 64102.

Note: A Quaker cemetery is nearby (on l.r. 64191, 0.1 mile from its junction with l.r. 64102). Another early stone house is in this area on Main Street in Madison.

60. Long Run Church (brick) dates from a service led by missionaries David McClure and Levi Frisbie in 1772. Three years later at the same location Dr. John McMillan preached. In 1791 Rev. William Swan became the pastor, serving until 1821.

A log meetinghouse was built on property donated by William Marshall, who with his family was later massacred by the Indians in

58 (note). Bells Mills Bridge

1780. This edifice was destroyed by fire about 1782. In 1800 the first brick church was built. It was replaced in 1865 by the third church, also of brick, which is now the Christ United Presbyterian Church. Many soldiers of the Revolutionary War, War of 1812, Civil War, and other past conflicts are buried in the adjacent cemetery, as is John Scull of Brush Hill (q.v.). *Location:* Circleville, two miles west of Irwin just south of U.S. 30.

61. Larimer House (frame) was built in the 1790s by William Larimer, who died in 1838 at the age of sixty-seven. Larimer entertained William Henry Harrison and Aaron Burr at his home, known as Mansion Farm. According to tradition, Larimer sold a slave girl by mistake to Harrison before he realized that the Pennsylvania law forbade it. Larimer's son, Gen. William Larimer, Jr., became a coal baron in the area, and the town of Larimer and a county in Colorado were named for him. This house was later purchased by James Leach. *Location:* Circleville, 50 Maus Drive, at its junction with Clay Pike.

62. Jacktown (Jacksonville), between Irwin and Circleville, was laid out in 1810 by James Irwin and Humphrey Fullerton. It was notable for the following early inns:

a. McIntyre's Hotel (frame), operated by a Mrs. McIntyre, served as a stagecoach stop and voting place for the community. *Location:* Old Lincoln Highway (U.S. 30) near Southside Road.

b. Fullerton Inn (stone) was built in 1798 by William Fullerton and later purchased by J. E. White. *Location:* Corner of Old Lincoln

65. *Brush Creek–Salem Church*

a remodeled mansion about one hundred fifty years old.

65. Brush Creek–Salem Church (brick) was first jointly owned and used by the Evangelical Lutheran and Evangelical and Reformed congregations. It now belongs to the United Church of Christ. John William Weber was the first pastor, beginning in 1783, and early services were held at the Loutzenheiser and Davis homes. After obtaining their church property in 1797, the congregations built a log meetinghouse. The cornerstone of the present church was laid in 1816. This brick edifice, still in use, has a fine interior with original pews and other outstanding features. Four churches in Iowa are reputed to have begun from this congregation. *Location:* Near Adamsburg, on spur 120 off old U.S. 30.

66. Penn Methodist Church (frame) was built in 1866–67 as part of the Irwin circuit with George W. Cranage as pastor. First services were conducted in a school every other week by William F. Lauck. On December 22, 1865, organization took place in the home of Alexander Watson, a preacher who came to Penn as foreman of the coal pits. The charge was changed to Penn in 1870. *Location:* Penn (just west of Jeannette), on Emma Street.

67. Westmoreland Glass Company, founded in 1889, produces glass made by hand using the same methods employed three centuries ago. The location was chosen because of a successful gas well drilled in the area in 1885. (In 1887 President Cleveland and his bride stopped nearby at the Grapeville station, and local citizens set the gas well on fire, the flame leaping forty feet in the air.) The company has been under the management of the Brainard family for three generations on the same factory site. Visitors are welcome. *Location:* Grapeville, along Pennsylvania Railroad about 0.5 mile east of Jeannette.

68. Painter House (stone), located at Monsour Hospital, was built by John and Tobias Painter in 1783 on a tract of land called "Paintership" deeded by Gov. Thomas Mifflin. The house was constructed about sixteen years before the deed, pursuant to a warrant dated June 2, 1755. The building, once a stagecoach tavern, was later occupied by the Gordon family. In 1952 Monsour Hospital and Clinic had its beginning in this house, where the first X-ray room was located in the so-

Highway and Southside Road (opposite side of road from McIntyre's).

   c. Jacktown Stagecoach Tavern (painted brick), built in 1826, is presently the Ride and Hunt Club. In the rear is an early log building. In later years this property was purchased by John Serro. *Location:* Old Lincoln Highway, behind Jacktown Motel.

   Note: Jacktown Hotel (log) was built in 1810. Enlarged and remodeled, this landmark was a well-known inn until it burned down in 1966. A modern Jacktown Motel is on the property.

63. Walthour House (brick), with alterations to the front, was built in the early or middle 1800s by the Walthour family. Michael Walthour operated a gristmill in Manor in 1785 at the junction of Brush Creek and Bushy Run. Fort Walthour was at Strawpump, east of Irwin. *Location:* Near Manor, on Manor-Pleasant Valley Road.

   Note: There are also several early log houses on this road.

64. Taylor Plantation (brick), originally consisting of 320 acres, was owned from 1820 to 1855 by Samuel and Sarah Black Taylor, who were Irish immigrants from Virginia. Reputedly slaves helped build the house, which has a winding cherry staircase, original woodwork, and plank floors. A fine springhouse is also on the property. *Location:* North Huntingdon Township, 3210 Pine Hill, Colonial Manor Road.

   Note: Nearby on the same road is the Manor East Restaurant (next to White Barn Theater),

called Indian Room, constructed with narrow windows. By 1958 plans were made to enlarge the hospital, and it was moved to an adjacent structure. The old stone house is now the administration building. *Location:* Jeannette, junction of U.S. 30 and l.r. 64289.

Note: Another early stone house in Jeannette is at 291 Locust Street.

69. Irwin, once known as Irwin Station on the Pennsylvania Railroad, was laid out in 1853 by John Irwin and incorporated as a borough in 1864. It was the western terminus of the original Pennsylvania Turnpike. Many of the early Scotch-Irish settlers in this area during the late 1700s were active in the Whiskey Rebellion of 1794, and the town was called Tinker Run (derived from "Tom the Tinker," a name given to those who destroyed the stills of the farmers who paid the whiskey excise tax).

a. Irwin Inn (painted brick) was built at Tinker Run in 1836 by John Irwin, the nephew of Col. John Irwin of Brush Hill (q.v.). In addition to the inn, which served as a stagecoach stop for travelers on the Pittsburgh and Greensburg Pike, there originally were servants' quarters, a smokehouse, a washhouse, and a bake oven on the estate. The barroom used to be in the present living room. Irwin also ran a canal freight line between Pittsburgh and Philadelphia about 1830 with his partner, William Larimer, Jr., and was one of the first coal operators in the area. In 1834 he married Lydia Hurst (see *Hurst House*). This house, later occupied by his granddaughter Lydia Irwin Altman, has remained in the same family since its erection. *Location:* Pennsylvania Avenue and Main Street (old U.S. 30).

b. Irwin House (weatherboarded log) was built about 1783 when James Irwin, brother of Col. John Irwin, came to America from northern Ireland. He served as justice of the peace in 1810 and helped lay out the area known as Jacktown. James Irwin married Jane Fullerton. His house was later purchased by Charles McIntyre. *Location:* 141 Verdant Boulevard.

70. Brush Hill (stone) was built in 1798 and owned by Col. John Irwin, founder of Irwin. It was the third house he built on his Penglyn estate. The first was a log fur-trading post which was burned by Indians in 1782. The second house, a frame dwelling, was struck by lightning and burned to the ground. When he built his third dwelling, he was quoted as saying, "I'll build a house that neither the Indians nor the Devil can destroy." Colonel

70. Brush Hill

Irwin was an associate judge of Westmoreland and a representative in the General Assembly.

Brush Hill, as it is known today, consisted of 700 acres in 1782. Along with the house were slave quarters and a gristmill on Brush Creek. The dwelling faced the pike and originally had a beautiful tree-lined driveway leading up to it.

John Scull, founder of the *Pittsburgh Gazette* in 1786 and son-in-law of Colonel Irwin, lived here after Irwin died in 1856. (Irwin's grave is in Irwin Unity Cemetery—originally his property.) In 1972 the LaSalles restored this home. *Location:* One mile east of Irwin, 651 Brush Hill Road off Pennsylvania Avenue (Lincoln Highway).

71. Bushy Run Battlefield is the site where an army under a Swiss colonel, Henry Bouquet, defeated the Indians in a two-day action on August 5 and 6, 1763, raising the siege of Fort Pitt and marking a decisive victory for the British which ended Pontiac's Rebellion. On the first day of battle Bouquet's army was surrounded and attacked by about fifteen hundred Indians. The British quickly threw up a breastwork of flour bags and other provisions. (Bouquet had started from Carlisle on July 18 with 500 regulars and 340 horses loaded with supplies for the starving troops of Fort Pitt.) Feigning withdrawal of his advance guard on the second day, the colonel drew the enemy into the open, and ambushing troops caught the Indians in crossfire.

In 1930 Bushy Run Battlefield State Park was created and a monument erected to mark the site of the "flour-bag fort" with shrubbery outlining its limits. On the hill to the west another marker shows the approximate location of graves of fifty soldiers who died in the battle. A museum on the property is administered by the Pennsylvania Historical and Museum Commission. Visitors are welcome any time before sunset. *Admission charge* for museum. *Location:* Bushy Run State Park, on Pa. 993 (l.r. 64078) (north of Greensburg and just east of Harrison City).

72. Gongaware-Lazar House (brick) was built in 1871. Formerly owned by Lewis Gongaware, this property was later purchased by William Lazar. The first day's fighting during the battle of Bushy Run in 1763 took place on part of this farm (see *Bushy Run Battlefield*). *Location:* Near Harrison City on the road to Bushy Run Battlefield Park (Pa. 993).

73. Whiskey Bonding House (cut stone), purchased in recent years by John Beacom, was erected about 1818 as a whiskey storage plant. Later, Sanford Beck constructed a gristmill across the road from the house. *Location:* Bouquet, on l.r. 64076.

74. Denmark Manor Church (brick) was built on the tract reserved by the Penns under this name. Originally it was composed of members of the Evangelical Lutheran and Evangelical and Reformed churches. Rev. John Steck of the Lutheran congregation and Rev. John William Weber of the Reformed shared the first services. In 1811–15 the first church was built. A log school served as a meeting house until this brick structure was erected. The present church was built in 1888, and is now the United Church of Christ. *Location:* Near Harrison City, on Harrison City Road, next to Manor Valley Country Club.

75. Murrysville, formerly Franklin Township, was erected between 1785 and 1788. Named for Benjamin Franklin who signed the patent issued to Jeremiah Murry, founder of Murrysville, it became a borough in 1975 and was renamed in 1976.

a. Oldest Producing Gas Well, no. 1 of Peoples Gas Company, is the oldest well in the United States, and perhaps the world, that was drilled commercially for gas and is still producing. It was struck in the 1880s. *Location:* Murrysville, on Old William Penn Highway near its junction with North Hills Road (at Presbyterian church property).

b. Old Presbyterian Church (brick) was built in 1871. This was the location of Turtle Creek Valley Academy (later called Laird Institute), founded by Francis Laird Stewart at the home of his father, Dr. Zachariah Stewart, in 1861. From 1871 until its closing about 1900, classes were held in the basement of

this church. Principals after Stewart were Rev. G. M. Spargrove and Rev. J. I. Blackburn. *Location:* Murrysville, corner of North Hills Road and Old William Penn Highway.

c. Haymaker Gas Well was struck in 1878 by Michael and Obadiah Haymaker, grandsons of Justice Jacob Haymaker, an early settler (see *Obadiah Haymaker House, Rugh House,* and *George Haymaker House*). Gas suddenly exploded when they had drilled down 1,400 feet in search of oil. It caught on fire and burned out of control for about a year and a half, the flame seen from a distance of up to eighteen miles away. A large lamp-black works operated here for some months until its building burned in 1881.

After the Haymaker gas well riot of November 26, 1883, at which time Obadiah was murdered defending his enterprise from a Chicago promoter who tried to claim the well, it was finally bought by Joseph Newton Pew, founder of the Sun Oil Company. This well was the first in the county and one of the world's most productive. *Location:* Murrysville, on bank of Turtle Creek near community clubhouse and library at end of Carson Street on Norbatrol Avenue.

d. Obadiah Haymaker House (painted brick), built during the middle 1800s, was the home of Obadiah Haymaker who was murdered in 1883 during the Haymaker Riot. He was shot and stabbed while two factions were fighting over possession of the well, and died while being carried into this house. *Location:* Murrysville, 4146 Old William Penn Highway.

e. Rugh House (stone) was built by Michael and Phoebe Hawkins Rugh. Their first house, a log cabin (site on adjoining golf course) was burned by Indians in 1778. The family members were captured and taken to a camp near Oil City and then to Canada. They eventually returned to their property, where, it is believed, they built a second log structure in 1798 (date found on foundation stone) followed by this stone house constructed from plans which Michael brought from Philadelphia. (He served in the Pennsylvania House of Representatives and died on his farm in 1820. His father, also Michael Rugh, lived in Rughtown near Greensburg.) George, the son of Michael, Jr., died during captivity and his wife died in 1809. Michael's daughter, Mary (Polly, a common nickname for Mary at that time), married Jacob Haymaker in 1794 (see *Haymaker Gas Well*). The Haymakers lived in this house and built a mill nearby. At one time the house was called the Philadelphia Mansion. In 1916 the Meisters bought it and served Sunday dinners here from 1923 to 1947. *Location:* Murrysville, on Sardis Road near Bulltown Road at Meadowink Golf Course.

Note: The nearby brick house at the golf course on Bulltown Road was built in 1837 for Catherine (daughter of Michael Rugh, Jr.) and William Meanor, a descendant of the first settler in the area.

f. Bossart-Osterman House (brick), with a classic doorway and fanlight, was owned by V. Bossart, a manufacturer and dealer in tinware, before 1867. The home was later purchased by the William Osterman family. At present it is an office and apartment building. *Location:* Murrysville, on Old William Penn Highway near Mill Street (next to savings and loan building).

g. Glunt House (log) was built before 1818. Early owners were Jane Glendy and James Elliot. In 1826 John Heddinger purchased the property, followed by Lewis Glunt and his son Frank, who between them owned it for fifty-two years. It was later purchased by the Hay family. *Location:* Murrysville, 3752 Windover Road.

h. Dible House (log) was built between 1799 and 1820. Jacob Dible purchased the property from Jeremiah Murry in 1818. Dible, a justice of the peace, raised eleven children here. This structure will be restored in the future, possibly as a museum for the community. *Location:* Murrysville, on Crowfoot Road near its junction with Sardis Road.

i. Wallace House (cut stone) was built in 1854 by Samuel Hilty for George Wallace. A signature stone on one gable is inscribed with "G. W." and the date. George Evans and the Shields family were later owners. This house, which has interior chestnut beams, was restored in the 1930s by Stephen Ondish, and Adelaine Hunter purchased it shortly afterwards. A gas well on the property still supplies energy for the house. *Location:* Murrysville, 5011 Hunter Lane.

j. Staymates House (log), on property originally belonging to James Hoy, was owned in 1852 by William Staymates. This was the home of Staymates' granddaughter Bessie Iola Staymates, a teacher in the area for fifty years. (Nearby Girl Scout Camp Iola is named for her. She died here in 1972 and willed this house to the Boy and Girl Scouts.) *Location:* On Round Top Road at Staymates Road.

Note: About one half mile on the same road and beyond Staymates Road is another log structure, now weatherboarded. It was built by the Moore family in 1829 on property formerly belonging to Jeremiah Murry.

k. Amity Hill Farmhouse (painted brick) was built about 1820 by the Ramaley family. The owner, "Doc" Ramaley, continued to make house calls until he was in his nineties. This interesting house was remodeled and later purchased by the James Ackerman family. *Location:* On Harrison City Road near junction with Round Top Road.

l. George Haymaker House (painted brick), of late Greek Revival architecture, was built in 1860 by George Haymaker, a grandson of Stoffel Haymaker, a German immigrant. George's father was Jacob Haymaker and his two sons were Michael and Obadiah (see *Haymaker Gas Well*). This mansion, which has a cupola on top, was used by the Trinity Episcopal Cathedral of Pittsburgh for a girls' summer vacation retreat, which became Trinity Manor–Girls' Friendly Society Holiday House. It later became a duplex, and in the early 1940s George Haymaker's great-granddaughter, Mrs. Lee (Margaret) Simmons, and her husband bought the property. In 1950 the surrounding acreage was sold and it became Marlee Acres, in honor of Mr. and Mrs. Simmons. The house is still owned by this family. *Location:* On Haymaker Farm Road (Marlee Acres), off U.S. 22 just east of Murrysville.

m. McCall House (brick) was built in 1825 by John McCall, who is buried outside the kitchen door of the homestead. His gravestone reads, "John McCall, died April 30, 1836, age 67." John's son Robert built the log barn (covered with siding) near the house. The signature stone on the barn's foundation reads, "R. McCall 1826." Below the farmhouse, near a spring, is a smaller brick house with two front entrances. This was the so-called honeymoon house where John and his wife lived before 1825, when they first moved to the property. It has the original woodwork and cupboards. Behind it is a log springhouse. Both brick houses are in the process of being restored. *Location:* Haymaker Farm Road (Marlee Acres), off U.S. 22 just east of Murrysville (southeast of George Haymaker House).

n. Ryckman House (log and brick) was built in 1868 by Levi Ryckman. (At a later date the logs were completely concealed by brick.) Both Levi and his father, Alonzo, served in the Civil War. They were taken as prisoners to Andersonville, Ga., and later transferred to Florence, S.C. *Location:* Junction of Old William Penn Highway and Sunset Drive.

o. McAlister Stagecoach Tavern (frame) was built in the early 1800s. A veteran of the Civil War, Duncan McAlister, operated a post office here at one time. *Location:* 5380 Logans Ferry Road.

p. Mellon House (weatherboarded log) was built in 1825 by Andrew Mellon, who had come with his father Archibald to the United States from Ireland in 1816. Their first house in this area was near the present property, along a stream where the family had a still. The Mellons bought the farm that had belonged to John Hill and later to a man named Shaeffer. Thomas, Andrew's son, helped haul the logs for this house and the stones for the chimney. He later became judge of the Court of Common Pleas of Allegheny County, was the founder of the Mellon fortune, and was the father of Andrew W., secretary of the treasury from 1921 to 1932; Richard B.; W.L.; and James. This house was purchased by Peter Pifer after the Mellons moved to Allegheny County in 1841. It was weatherboarded about 1856 for Pifer's wife, Catherine Cline Pifer. It is still owned by a member of this family, Mrs. Edgar Martz. In 1975 the county historical society erected a marker here. A replica of the house has been constructed at the Mellon homestead in Ireland. *Location:* Corner of Cline Hollow and Hills Church Roads.

q. Hill's (Emmanuel Reformed and Lutheran) Church (brick) dates back to 1828 when Peter Hill and Philip Drum, who had served in the Revolutionary War, donated the land, at which time a log church was built. This union church (now United Church of Christ) was enlarged in 1845 by sawing out the eastern end and adding fourteen feet to its length. In 1858 it was replaced by a brick church which was rebuilt in 1884. Near this site in about 1782 white settlers were attacked by Indians, and the unmarked graves of both groups are located near the church. Before their church was erected, the members traveled to Brush Creek–Salem Church (q.v.). The first Reformed pastor was William Weinel, and the first Lutheran minister was Michael John Steck. *Location:* Hill's Church Road.

r. Toll House (log) was built on the Northern Pike, which was opened in 1818 and reached this area the next year. Simeon Clark was the last to operate the toll house, and his daughter Nancy was its final resident. It is presently owned by Emanuel Viola. This rare structure, now in disrepair, has a huge chimney with an exterior fireplace. It formerly had a balcony and a pike, or pole, for stopping travelers in order to collect the toll. *Loca-*

75.p. Mellon House

tion: Corner of Kistler Road and West Pike Street.

Note: The one-room Clark schoolhouse (brick), built in 1908, is across the road (now private).

76. Saint James Reformed Church (brick), once known as Yockey's, was founded in 1803 on land donated by Simon Hine for a Lutheran and German Reformed church. The first pastor was John William Weber. A log structure was begun sometime between 1797 and 1803. It was never finished due to a disagreement over land and a deed. Only a cemetery marks this site. About 1808 a brick church was built about three miles southwest of the first site. The present church was erected in 1838. In the adjoining cemetery is the grave of Mathias Ringle, who was a wainwright for George Washington at Valley Forge. *Location:* Near Salina, off old Pa. 380. From Perryville turn right on Church Road near Kiskiminetas River.

Note: In Perryville, 0.2 mile from the junction of Pa. 380 and Pa. 819, is the site of Adam Carnahan's blockhouse of 1774, commemorated by a stone monument.

77. Ludwick House (stone) was built before 1822 by Conrad Ludwick. The home is constructed against a hillside with the back of the second story on ground level. A spring still flows by the side of the house. In 1822 Ludwick sold the property to Samuel Ludwick, and in 1856 William Ridenour purchased it. The 1880 Ridenour frame house is next to this structure. *Location:* Camp Joan, junction of

75.r. Toll House

Pa. 366 and Pa. 380 (southeast of New Kensington).

78. Massa Harbison Log Cabin was moved to this site from Butler County, where Massa Harbison, once an Indian captive, lived briefly in later life. *Location:* Elizabeth Crawford Memorial Park, four miles east of New Kensington, off Pa. 366. Turn north on Merwin Road and take dirt road at top of hill on right; cabin sits back in woods.

Note: Nearby on the same road in sight of its junction with Pa. 366 is an 1849 stone house built by George Thompson, who operated a tannery there.

79. Parnassus Presbyterian Church (frame) was founded in 1842. The present white frame structure, with a bell tower, was built in 1889. John W. Logan donated the church property. To the right of the church is the site of Fort Crawford, built by Colonel William Crawford, whose home was near Connellsville (Fayette County). The fort is recorded as being in existence in 1777 and mentioned in official correspondence as late as 1792. *Location:* Parnassus (New Kensington), Main and Church Streets.

80. Beale House (fieldstone) was built about 1805 by John Beale, who came to this area from Juniata County. He gave the property to the Puckety Church for its house of worship and cemetery. The old church is now gone, but its foundation and a monument in the cemetery mark the site on Puckety Church Road. *Location:* East of New Kensington, in Lower Burrell on Puckety Church Road, 0.3

mile off Pa. 56. House sits out of view on dirt road off Puckety Church Road.

81. Vandergrift Methodist Church (brick) was organized September 4, 1896. The cornerstone of the present church was laid July 1, 1897, and the building was remodeled in 1958–59. This church is one of the first in Vandergrift, a model community that was laid out in 1896 by the Apollo Iron and Steel Company at a point known as Townsend Station and named in honor of Capt. J. J. Vandergrift. The Vandergrift Land and Improvement Company had offered to any church denomination sufficient ground upon which to erect church buildings and a donation of $7,500 provided the church membership would subscribe a similar amount and build a church worth at least $15,000. The First United Methodist congregation agreed to these conditions; and J. D. Allison of Pittsburgh designed the church, and Kennedy, Hamilton, and Fair of Blairsville built the structure for $17,240. The first pastor was Noble G. Miller, who served in 1896–97. *Location:* Vandergrift, between Thirteenth Street and Pa. 56.

82. Glen Karns (Cairn) Estate (River Forest Golf Course) originally belonged to Stephen Duncan Karns, one of the largest producers of oil in the Armstrong-Butler oil region. In 1866 he drilled his first well at Parkers Landing. He was the founder of Karns City, builder of a pipeline from that place to Harrisburg, builder of a railroad from Karns City to Parkers Landing, and controller of several banks. In 1880 this oil king, who owned numerous racehorses, operated a ranch in Colorado. He returned to his home in the middle 1880s, practiced law, and ended his career as manager of a Populist newspaper in Pittsburgh. When Coxey's Army came through that city, he marched at the head of the parade.

This estate, including eighteen farms, was purchased in 1902 by Andrew Carnegie, and in 1957 Allegheny Ludlum Company bought it. In 1964 it became a golf course and, a shelter was erected on the site of the $35,000 mansion built by Karns in 1873. The original cistern was restored and is in use today. *Location:* 0.7 mile south of Garvers Ferry, 0.2 mile off t. 662.

83. Zimmerman House (brick) was built in 1830 by Daniel Zimmerman, a tailor. His son, Jacob, was a Lutheran clergyman who in 1841 took charge of Klingensmith's church near Leechburg and Hill's and Hankey's in Franklin Township. This house is one of the few remaining structures that still retain the original spring in the interior of the home. The building has in recent years been converted into a furniture and gift shop. *Location:* Near Leechburg, junction of Pa. 356 and Pa. 56.

84. Fort Hand Marker (stone) was erected by The Fort Hand Chapter, DAR. According to G. D. Albert's *Frontier Forts of Pennsylvania* (1896), "Fort Hand was erected [1777] near the house of John McKibben, whose 'large log house' had been the refuge and asylum of a number of people whither they had fled at times." In 1779 "during the night the Indians were there they fired a deserted house near the fort—the old building of McKibben's." Albert continues with, "Fort Hand was located on what is now the farm owned by Jacob M. Kearns. . . . Francis Kearns, the father of Jacob M. Kearns, purchased and occupied the farm in 1835. At that time the signs of the ditch which marked the course of the palisade—the earth having been thrown up against it from the inside—were to be seen distinctly. This line included nearly an acre, and would have enclosed the ground which is now occupied by the [brick] farm house, garden and spring." Some believe that a nearby log house was built by John McKibben. *Location:* Near Apollo, on Pine Run Church at Watt Road, 0.8 mile off Pa. 66.

85. Silvis Blacksmith Shop (frame) was built about 1892 by Joseph Silvis. His father, Jacob, settled here in 1830 and opened the forerunner of this shop. *Location:* Washington Township, off Pa. 66 on Silvis Road.

86. Poke Run Presbyterian Church (brick) was organized in 1785. John McMillan was the first supply minister, and Samuel Porter was the first regular pastor from 1790 to 1798. It was originally known as "Head of Turtle Creek" and in 1780 as "Poke Run." A log structure, 70 by 30 feet, was built in 1789–90 by a spring near the present building. A brick church was erected in 1836. (According to tradition, ladies' riding skirts and saddles were stored in the basement of this structure during services. The choir sat in the back, and the pulpit was in the center. The floor was covered by a red carpet, the only one in the area at that time.) From 1835 to 1869 David Kirkpatrick served as minister here. The present building was constructed in 1881. *Location:* Near Mamont, on Pa. 66, 0.4 mile north of its junction with Pa. 366.

Note: David Kirkpatrick's home, built in 1840, is nearby just off Pa. 286 on a dirt road leading from Evans Road. This restored brick house was later purchased by the Potts and Krokosy families. Also in Mamont are the 1848 brick Metzgar house, off Pa. 66 (east of its junction with old Pa. 66), and the weatherboarded log George house, owned by the Ferdinand Garbin family on George Drive.

87. McKown House (brick) was owned by a Callen sister. Theophilus Callen fought in the Civil War with the Kiski Squad of ten farm boys who were in Company E of the 155th Pennsylvania Regiment. (All ten came from the region lying between Puckety Creek and the Kiskiminetas River, from which the group took its name.) Only one—J. King Alter—lived to return. Theophilus, age eighteen, was shot one night while on picket duty. His friend, Sgt. John M. Lancaster, wrote the Callens to tell them of their son's death. Lancaster fell in love with Callen's sister, Louisa, but she died before he had a chance to marry her. Lancaster and Mr. Callen brought back the body of Theophilus from the Shenandoah Valley in Virginia, and today his burial site is in the cemetery of Poke Run Presbyterian Church (q.v.), along with those of his sisters. A monument to Theophilus and some of the others who fought in the same squad is in the Sardis Methodist Church cemetery. *Location:* Near Mamont, on Pfeffer Road at Lover's Lane, just off U.S. 66 near Poke Run Presbyterian Church.

88. Delmont was laid out in 1814 and incorporated as a borough in 1833. Originally called Salem Crossroads or New Salem, it was a well-known stopping place, with as many as five lines of stages passing through on the Northern Pike between Pittsburgh and Philadelphia until 1853. The main street of Delmont has become a preservation area, and many early houses are being restored to the 1830–70 period.

a. Watering Trough (wooden) was restored in 1972 at the original spring where travelers stopped to refresh themselves and their horses. *Location:* On East Pittsburgh Street, near old Pa. 66.

b. Trinity Reformed Church (brick) was built about the end of the Civil War. This congregation together with a Lutheran one had worshiped in the Union Church built in 1849. The first pastor was S. H. Giesy, followed by Thomas G. Apple in 1855. In 1864 the old Union Church was in disrepair, and the Reformed congregation built its present structure in 1866–67. It is now proposed as the Salem Crossroads Christian Museum. *Location:* On East Pittsburgh Street.

Note: The Lutheran church, built in 1868–70, is also located on East Pittsburgh Street.

88.a. Watering Trough

c. Old Tannery (log covered with siding) was owned in the 1930s by John Hutton, followed by Robert Shields. *Location:* On East Pittsburgh Street next to Trinity Church.

d. Lutheran Hill Home (brick), built between 1830 and 1840, was one of the first restored buildings in the community and is owned by the Donald Sparkenbaugh family. *Location:* 100 East Pittsburgh Street.

e. Kepple House (frame) was the home of Anna Martha McQuilkin Kepple (1880–1969), daughter of Jacob and Hettie Leightner Kepple. A talented musician who later in life became an eccentric recluse, she left her entire fortune to schools in Switzerland. It was not known until her death that she was a millionaire and that she had invested in the New York stock market. Her home, on the property of one of the original lots in town, contains a museum and is the Salem Crossroads Historical Society headquarters. *Location:* 39 East Pittsburgh Street, next to Trinity Church.

f. Old Wagon Shop (brick) is now an office building owned by Frank Piper. It was built in 1830 with another section added about five years later. *Location:* 19 West Pittsburgh Street.

g. Central Hotel (brick), built in or before the 1830s as an inn, has been restored and is now a commercial building. *Location:* Corner of Pittsburgh and Greensburg Streets.

h. Thompson House (brick) was built before the Civil War. It has been restored by the Peter Muse family. *Location:* On Mark Drive.

i. Christy House (brick) was built by David Christy and later owned by his son. This family at one time owned much of the land which is presently Delmont. *Location:* On Vrbanic farm on Rock Springs Road.

Note: Beyond this house is another brick house, once owned by the Vrbanics, that has been completely restored.

j. Waugaman House (painted brick) was built about 1830. It was owned by Peter Waugaman and is reputed to have been a drovers' stand on the Northern Pike. *Location:* On Old William Penn Highway just east of White Valley (across from Valley Stream Apartments).

89. Congruity, a small village, has grown up around the church of this name.

a. Congruity Presbyterian Church (brick) was organized in 1789. On September 22, 1790, Samuel Porter and John McPherrin were ordained at a tent on James McKee's farm. Porter, the first pastor, was followed by W. K. Marshall and Edward R. Geary. The first brick church, erected in 1830, was badly damaged by wind. The second and present structure was built in 1855 and damaged by fire in 1953. *Location:* Congruity, on old U.S. 22 between Delmont and New Alexandria.

b. Congruity Tavern (stone) was built about 1820 and opened as a tavern the same year. At this time the owner planned a party for the young people of the area. However, Rev. Samuel Porter (see *Congruity Presbyterian Church*) in a sermon discouraged the congregation from attending the open house, which was then canceled. The second story has a large dormitory room where male guests stayed overnight. A small room off this one was for occasional women travelers. Early owners of this house were the David Kirkpatricks and the Stewarts. In 1976, during restoration, it was badly damaged by fire. *Location:* Congruity, near junction of U.S. 22 and l.r. 64054.

c. Stagecoach Inn (painted brick) was built in the early 1800s and has had an interesting history. First operated as an inn on the Northern Pike, this building was a recruiting station for Civil War soldiers, later a glove factory, and now contains a stained-glass studio (Silianoff's) as part of a private residence. *Location:* Congruity, at Old William Penn Highway (Northern Pike) and l.r. 64186.

90. Sloan House (log) This nearly 200-year-old house is in remarkable condition. It was built by the Sloan family at what was once known as Sloan's Crossing. *Location:* Slickville, on Pa. 819.

91. Rugh Home (brick with shutters) was built in 1860 by the Rugh family. Now on the Turner dairy farm, it overlooks several ponds. *Location:* Near Slickville, on Pa. 819.

92. Crabtree Beehive Coke Ovens are located in this mining town, which was laid out about 1890. These ovens were discontinued about 1932. The area is honeycombed by coal-mine tunnels, with the entry at Hannastown several miles west. *Location:* Turn south on Pa. 119 at Crabtree, near firehall, and go 0.8 mile; turn left across bridge and go 0.2 mile to remains of ovens.

Note: Company-owned houses and the large frame company store, now Neilson's general store, can be seen from U.S. 22 just west of New Alexandria.

93. New Alexandria, once known as Denniston's Town, was laid out by Alexander Denniston. Its first post office was established in 1804, and it became a borough in 1834. Numerous early structures are located here.

a. Old Stone Inn was the first stagecoach tavern at this village. It was built about 1800 by Samuel Reed. One early innkeeper was Samuel Parr. A fire in this building in the 1940s accounts for the flat roof. It now houses apartments. *Location:* On Main Street next to bank.

b. Gallagher Store and House (both brick) were built in the 1840s by J. E. Gallagher. His first store, which connects the long store building and the adjacent house, was erected earlier. The house has an interesting metal signature plate on its front near the roof. A bell tower, since removed, used to grace the store. Gallagher Hall, where dances, concerts, and other entertainment took place, was located on the top floor of this store. *Location:* On Main Street across from bank and old stone inn.

c. Turnbull House (frame) was the former home of Agnes Sligh Turnbull, well-known western Pennsylvania novelist who wrote, among other works, *The Day Must Dawn* and *The Rolling Years* which concern the area where she grew up. The house later became a private convalescent home. *Location:* On Church Street across from old Presbyterian Church (q.v.).

d. New Alexandria Presbyterian Church (brick) was organized in 1837 with Adam Torrance serving as first pastor until he took a fourteen-and-a-half-month leave of absence to serve as chaplain during the Civil War. The present church, now Community Presbyterian, was built in 1858. Gen. Arthur St. Clair's daughter Jane Jarvis, who lived in a log house in New Alexandria, is buried in this church cemetery. *Location:* On Church Street.

Note: Adam Torrance's brick house is on U.S. 22 just west of New Alexandria and situated on a bank overlooking the highway.

94. Craig House (brick) was built by Gen. Alexander Craig (1755–1832) who married Jane Clark. "A. Craig" is inscribed on a stone at the foot of the front steps of this home. In 1793 Craig purchased the farm on Loyalhanna Creek from Samuel Wallace, who had bought it from Loveday Allen in 1769. An early barn at this site burned in 1974. Craig was commissioned lieutenant colonel of the state militia in 1793, and brigadier general in 1807 and again in 1811. Samuel Craig, Sr., and his three eldest sons, John, Alexander, and Samuel, all served in the Revolution. (The father, Samuel, was killed while defending the Pennsylvania border. He had served with Washington in the 1777 campaign.) This family preserved the original rattlesnake flag of Col. John Proctor's battalion. In 1914 it was presented to the state and is in the museum at Harrisburg. *Location:* Near Shieldsburg, across east side of creek from New Alexandria Presbyterian Church.

95. Alter's Halfway House (log with weatherboards) was built during the 1830s as a tavern halfway between Johnstown and Pittsburgh, overlooking Spruce Run and situated on the Northern Pike. The first known proprietor was Jacob Alter of Berlin, Pa., who in 1829 also built the Henry Hotel (run by John Henry for a number of years at the corner of East Market and Brady Streets in Blairsville). "Jockey" McLaughlin also kept a tavern at this halfway house. Jacob Alter, Jr., lived in the house during the 1890s, when it became known as "Alter's Voting Precinct." *Location:* Between Blairsville and New Alexandria, on U.S. 22 on hillside (4.6 miles east of junction of U.S. 22 and Pa. 981 at New Alexandria).

96. Simpson-Giffen Stone House Tavern was built on the old Northern Pike, possibly as a stagecoach tavern, about 1820. Stage coaches operated along this road between Pittsburgh and Philadelphia as early as 1805. In 1866 Joseph Simpson purchased the property. His granddaughter Mrs. John E. Giffen operated a tearoom in this house in the early 1920s and later an antique showroom. Her ancestor Dorcas Miller was taken captive during the Hanna's Town (q.v.) raid of 1782. *Location:* Just east of New Alexandria, 1.4

mile east from junction of U.S. 22 and Pa. 981. House is situated on old U.S. 22 but can be seen from new U.S. 22.

97. Stoney Run Ferry House (painted brick) was built about 1802. It is reputed to have been a ferry hotel near the Conemaugh River at one time. In 1840 the Burkley family purchased the property. In later years, a descendant, Dr. George Burkley, owned this house and restored it. *Location:* On old U.S. 22 along Stoney Creek. Just west of U.S. 22 bridge before reaching Blairsville exit, turn northeast. House is 0.1 mile from present U.S. 22.

98. Baird House (stone), with a signature stone on the right front side, was built in 1834 by William Baird, brother of James Baird who founded the village of Bairdstown on the west side of the Conemaugh River across from Blairsville (in Indiana County). *Location:* On l.r. 64264 just west of bridge at Blairsville between Indiana County and Westmoreland County.

99. Kiskiminetas Springs School, founded in 1888, is still functioning as a private boys' school. The site had first been known as Stewart's Grove, including land where the Pennsylvania National Guard held its encampments in the 1850s and 1860s. The grove became known as Mineral Springs Grove in the latter part of the 1870s, at which time it was a hotel and health spa for the elite. In 1888 Andrew Wilson, Jr., and R. W. Fair purchased the resort property and founded the school.

Old Main (frame), which burned in 1955 and was restored, is now the admissions office. A picturesque walk from the campus along the wooded hillside below follows an old Indian trail to the springs, now dry. *Location:* On hill across Kiskiminetas River from Saltsburg (Indiana County).

100. Lockport Hotel (frame) was in business during the heyday of the Pennsylvania Canal. The canal crossed the Conemaugh River near here on a cut-stone aqueduct, most of which was removed in 1893. The remaining piers are now a part of the Pennsylvania Railroad bridge. *Location:* Go north 1.9 mile on l.r. 64061 from its junction with l.r. 64190 (l.r. 64190 leads northwest off Pa. 711 north of West Fairfield, beside railroad tracks).

101. Old Salem Presbyterian Church (brick) was founded in 1786. The first "tent"

church was located in a depression of Sugar Loaf Hill. Later a small log building was erected and given the name of Salem. Before the close of the century another log structure (70 by 40 feet) was erected and renovated in 1832. This church was destroyed by fire in 1848, the same year that the present church was built. It was remodeled in 1963. Early ministers were James Power, Robert McPherrin, and Thomas Moore. An adjoining cemetery contains graves of Revolutionary War soldiers. *Location:* North of New Derry, on Derry Road (Pa. 982), 2.2 miles south of U.S. 22.

102. Pomeroy House (brick) stands on the Fort Pomeroy property. The fort site is directly across the road from the house, which was built about 1835. At one time it was owned by the late John C. Walkinshaw. *Location:* Near New Derry, at Bergman's Dairy about 0.7 mile on l.r. 64041 (which is 0.2 mile east of Pa. 982).

Note: Nearby on the same road is the Skacel brick farmhouse, formerly owned by the Atlantic Coal Company and also built in the middle 1800s.

103. Gilson Farmhouse (brick) is a mid-nineteenth-century home at the site of Fort Barr on the old Gilson farm. In 1769 Robert Barr, one of the first settlers who came to the region, established the New Derry settlement. A barn across from this house has the name Fort Barr written on it. Old coke ovens are in view from the house and barn. *Location:* Atlantic, 0.6 mile off Pa. 982, one mile northwest of New Derry.

104. Eicher Tavern (stone) was a wagon stand kept in the early days of the old Greensburg-Stoystown Turnpike by Peter Eicher from Bedford. It is now a neurological office. *Location:* Just east of Greensburg, on old U.S. 30 at Tollhouse Apartments on right.

105. Rowe House (brick), reputed to have been a tavern, was built on the old McCausland farm and purchased in 1872 by Andrew Rowe, who came from Germany and operated a blanket mill. His granddaughter lives here presently. *Location:* About 2.3 miles east of Greensburg on old U.S. 30, 0.4 mile east from its junction with new U.S. 30 (near Greendale Drive and early brick schoolhouse).

Note: Farther east on this road, just before its junction with U.S. 30, is a small early fieldstone house which was owned formerly by Polly Hough and later by the Crissinger family.

106. Fishel (Fishell) House (log and stone) was erected by Henry Fishel, a carpenter who constructed the log section in 1817 and the first stone part in 1830. In 1936 another stone addition was erected. This home was later purchased by the Wakefield Murray family. *Location:* Near Greensburg, on Pa. 130, one mile southeast of Pa. 30 (in Hempfield Township).

107. White Stone House (stone and log) was built of log before 1782 with a later addition of stone by the White brothers. During the attack by the Indians on Hanna's Town, these men helped rescue the settlers in the fort. A group of neighbors rode their horses back and forth over a bridge to deceive the Indians into believing there were many troops arriving during the night. (See *Hanna's Town.*)

In recent years the Charles Cunningham family bought the house, which had fallen into disrepair, and has completely restored it. During the remodeling a note from an indentured servant was found concealed behind a stone in an interior wall. A door with the date 1776, under many layers of paint, was discovered during the reconstruction. *Location:* Just east of Greensburg turn off U.S. 30 onto Pa. 130 and go three miles toward Pleasant Unity (two miles beyond Fishel house).

108. Shaffer House (log) was built before 1859 with a later log addition. The parlor and two bedrooms were the original home. In 1903 Margaret Shaffer willed the property to the George Schaeffer (*cq*) family. William Haines purchased it in 1959 and restored the house. *Location:* 4.5 miles east of Greensburg, 0.5 mile off Mt. Pleasant Road on l.r. 64175.

109. Ferguson Farm includes a small stone house and a later frame house. Across from these are two early barns, one constructed of logs. The frame barn now serves as a clubhouse. All the structures are over 100 years old. The farm was at one time owned by the Fergusons and later bought by the Statlers, who operate a golf range here. *Location:* 0.7 mile west of Beatty Crossroads (l.r. 64040 and U.S. 30), on old U.S. 30 but visible from new U.S. 30.

Note: Just east of Beatty on a hillside on the north side of U.S. 30 is the early M. Keough brick tavern, presently a residence.

110. Earhart Museum (brick) is a Victorian house built in 1882. Both floors contain antiques and household furnishings and are open to the public, along with a barn in which early vehicles are on display. *Hours:* Saturday, Sunday, and holidays, opens at noon. Closing hours indefinite. *Admission charge.* *Location:* Near Latrobe (at Beatty), on l.r. 64040, 0.8 mile north from its junction with U.S. 30.

111. Saint Xavier's Academy (brick) was opened by the Sisters of Mercy in 1845. Partially burned in 1867, the school finally closed after another fire in 1972. This is the oldest Roman Catholic academy in western Pennsylvania. *Location:* Seven miles east of Greensburg, on U.S. 30.

112. Geiger Inn (brick), pictured on a map of 1820, was the third toll stop on the Greensburg-Stoystown Pike. A fire about 1880 destroyed the second floor. During remodeling the roof was built nearly flat and the windows were lowered. Sisters of Mercy at nearby Saint Xavier lived here after the Steel family. *Location:* East of Greensburg, on U.S. 30 (just west of Saint Vincent College).

113. Saint Vincent Archabbey (brick) was the first abbey in America founded by the Benedictine order of the Roman Catholic Church. In 1790 Father Theodore Brouwers, a Franciscan, bought a 350-acre tract, called "Sportsman's Hall," and built a log cabin on it. Father Brouwers died before his dream of an abbey came true, but in 1846 a monastery was founded here by Boniface Wimmer, O.S.B., a monk of St. Michael's Abbey in Metten, Bavaria. It became a priory in 1852 and an abbey in 1855. The church of St. Vincent de Paul, built in 1835, became the students' chapel in 1846, and the college was incorporated April 18, 1870. From here ten abbeys and colleges in eight states were founded. A multi-million-dollar fire destroyed many of the buildings, including the chapel, in 1963. A new monastery was completed in 1967 and a science center opened two years later. A museum in Alfred Hall and an old mill are also on the college property. *Location:* 7.7 miles east of Greensburg, on U.S. 30, near Latrobe.

114. Unity Presbyterian Church (brick) was founded in 1774, when the Penns granted the congregation seventy acres of land for a burial ground and a meetinghouse. Before the house of worship was built on this land, known as "Unity," James Power and John McMillan preached in "Proctor's Tent," so called because it was on John Proctor's property and consisted of a pulpit covered by a roof. Power was conducting a preparatory communion service in Unity Church the afternoon that Hanna's Town was raided in 1782, at which time the congregation upon hearing the news dispersed and the pastor hastened to his home near Mount Pleasant. (See *Hanna's Town.*)

The present brick church was built in 1874. Remodeling, spearheaded by the late James H. Rogers of Latrobe, began in 1937 with money provided by the Mellons and the McFeely/Rogers families. The red, white, and blue art glass in the windows at the front are Tiffany glass from the old East Liberty Presbyterian Church, previously donated by the Mellons in memory of early members of their family who worshiped here and are buried in the cemetery.

The congregation was dissolved in 1921, and the building now belongs to the Unity Church Cemetery Association. *Location:* Near Latrobe, behind Saint Vincent College, off U.S. 30. Turn west off Pa. 981 in Latrobe at Unity Street (l.r. 64152); thence 0.6 mile to its junction with l.r. 64147 and travel 1.2 mile west on that road.

115. Baldridge House (stone) was built in 1777 by Joseph Baldridge. This spacious structure was remodeled in 1933 and added on to in 1960. Baldridge erected a mill nearby on the Loyalhanna in 1804, laid out part of the village of Youngstown, and, according to historian G. D. Albert, "died in 1840, a very wealthy man for his day." *Location:* Near Youngstown, south edge of Latrobe, on Pa. 982, 0.4 mile from its junction with U.S. 30.

116. St. Clair House (log) was built in 1777 by Daniel St. Clair on property originally belonging to his father (the general). In 1959 it was moved 125 feet to its present site. *Location:* Near Youngstown, on U.S. 30 at its junction with Pa. 982.

117. Latrobe, which owes its existence to the railroad, was laid out by Oliver J. Barnes in 1851 and was incorporated as a borough in 1854. It was named for J. H. B. Latrobe, a prominent civil engineer associated with the Baltimore & Ohio Railroad. Three of the early houses are located at 401 Depot Street, 208 Lloyd Avenue at Unity Street, and corner of Ligonier and Thompson Streets (1868 Dickie house).

a. McHenry Hotel (brick), a railroad inn with a second-floor porch and iron railing, was built in 1851–53 by the Baker brothers, S. H. and Reuben, who owned the Pennsylvania Car-works. They also organized the Loyalhanna Coal and Coke Company. This hotel,

erected adjacent to the railroad tracks, is still operating. *Location:* Ligonier and Railroad Streets.

b. Sloan House (stone) was built in the late 1700s by Samuel Sloan, who was one of the county's first justices. The Daily family purchased the property at a later time, followed by the Palmers. *Location:* 1909 Raymond Avenue at Cedar Street (next to shopping center).

118. Youngstown, one of the oldest communities in the area, was a turnpike town about halfway between Ligonier and Greensburg. Named for Alexander Young, it became a borough in 1831.

a. Cunningham Barber Shop and Jewelry Store (weatherboard), the former home of John Cunningham, is one of the oldest houses in town. Construction underneath the siding is believed to be log. *Location:* On Main Street.

b. Youngstown Borough School (frame), built in 1873, was the third school in the area. Plans are being made to convert it into a community center. *Location:* Latrobe Street.

c. Washington House (painted brick) was once an inn along the Forbes Road, later the Pittsburgh-Philadelphia Turnpike. This tavern, built in the late 1700s, later became the Barrett Hotel and continues to operate as a tavern. *Location:* On Main Street.

119. Fisher Mansion House (log and stone), originally known by this name, was at one time used for shelter from Indians. It was built in 1773 by Abel Fisher on the Forbes Road. It is believed that this house at one time served as an inn. The stone addition is over 100 years old. *Location:* Ligonier Township, on l.r. 64071 (road to Graham's antique barn), about 1.4 mile south of U.S. 30 along Two Mile Run. House sits at junction with unmarked road, 0.5 mile from Ross Road.

Note: Nearby on the same road is another log house which was a former school, moved to this location at an uncertain date. A smaller, earlier log house in the area of these two structures was reconstructed at Fort Ligonier.

120. Saint Boniface Catholic Church (brick) was built in 1847. Next to the church a stone and brick structure, originally a farmhouse for the monks, now serves as a retreat building. *Location:* Between Stahlstown and Lycippus, turn north on private road off Pa. 130 (a quarter mile west of new Saint Boniface Church).

Note: A weatherboarded log building, a

former post office, is located across the road.

121. Small House (log) was built about 1812. In 1835 it was owned by David Small. *Location:* On a ridge 0.5 mile from Youngstown, on Forbes Road leading to Darlington.

122. Kingston House (stone) was built by Alexander Johnston in 1815 and named after his tract of land patented under the name Kingston. Johnston, who came to this country from Ireland, settled in western Pennsylvania and became engaged in a Pittsburgh business. Later he bought Kingston and built a forge (which proved unsuccessful) on Loyalhanna Creek in 1811. About the same time he began keeping a tavern in his home. His son William was governor of Pennsylvania from 1848 to 1852. The stone mansion is now a private residence, still owned by the original family. *Location:* Kingston, on U.S. 30 across from Kingston Dam.

123. Idlewild Park, part of a 410-acre recreational complex, includes an amusement park dating back to 1878 with an early merry-go-round, Story Book Forest, a general store, historic village, and the Ligonier Valley Railroad station dating from the early 1900s. *Hours:* Mid-May–Labor Day. Closed Mondays, except for holidays. *Admission charge. Location:* 2.5 miles west of Ligonier, on U.S. 30.

124. Ligonier is located in a picturesque valley along the Loyalhanna Creek. It became a borough in 1834. The historic Ligonier Diamond, with a newly constructed bandstand at the same location as an 1894 one, is the site of a corral where stagecoaches and horses on the Philadelphia-Pittsburgh Turnpike used to stop. This area has many interesting buildings.

   a. Fort Ligonier (restoration), "Key to the West," was constructed, on Col. Henry Bouquet's recommendation, near the site of Loyalhanning Indian Town. In the fall of 1758 the fort served as a staging area for Gen. John Forbes. The structure was but partially finished when the men, under Col. James Burd, withstood an attack by the French and Indians a month before Forbes took Fort Duquesne. (This battle is reenacted every year.) This fort also withstood a siege during Pontiac's Rebellion in 1763. Following the Indian wars, it was abandoned in 1765. During the Revolution, since the old fort had fallen into decay, another stockade called Fort Preservation was built on property below the first.

124.a. Fort Ligonier

In 1949 the Fort Ligonier Memorial Foundation began a fund-raising campaign for the reconstruction of the original fort, and ground was broken in 1954. Excavations have yielded many artifacts from the French and Indian War which may be viewed in the museum on the property. Authentically dressed mannequins depict scenes in the restored buildings. The main or inner fort was a 200-foot square with four bastions. There are four outlying redoubts, a hospital, and a blacksmith's forge.

The administration building and museum (stone) contains an annex furnished in Georgian style. It includes the Lord Ligonier room, which has an original painting of Ligonier by Joshua Reynolds, and an original room from Maj. Gen. Arthur St. Clair's home, Hermitage (see *Arthur St. Clair Homes*). *Hours:* June–November: Daily, 9 A.M.–dusk. *Admission charge. Location:* Junction of Pa. 711 and U.S. 30.

   b. Arthur St. Clair Homes include "Hermitage," built in 1802 when Major General St. Clair (1734–1818) retired as governor of the Northwest Territory. The house was dismantled in 1962 and one room moved to Fort Ligonier where it was rebuilt as an annex to the museum. Only the chimney of this house remains on the original property. A historical plaque marks the site. *Location:* 1.8 mile north of Ligonier, on Pa. 711.

St. Clair's "Cottage" site still has an early springhouse on it. This property was the last home of Arthur St. Clair and his wife Phoebe Bayard St. Clair (1743–1818). They operated an inn here, after they had unfortunate financial losses. *Location:* Chestnut Ridge, on l.r. 64254 (old Forbes Road) 2.3 miles from Youngstown. Pennsylvania Historical and Museum Commission marker is directly over ridge from house site and is on U.S. 30 near Sleepy Hollow Restaurant.

c. Town House (frame) was built as an inn in 1870 by Jacob and Nancy Frank. For years it was a small hotel and boarding house. In 1915 it was acquired by Mrs. Agnes Frye, mother of the present owner, Mrs. June Millison, and was reopened as the Town House restaurant in 1951. A fine collection of antiques are on display here. *Location:* 201 South Fairfield Street.

d. McFarland House (brick) was built in 1830 by Col. John McFarland, a contractor for the West Penn Railroad and a state senator. This property was purchased by John H. Frank in 1886. At this time a front bay window was added, together with side porches and an iron fence. It was later purchased by the Fairfield family. *Location:* South Fairfield and Loyalhanna Streets.

Note: A cottage in the rear was the ticket office for the Ligonier Valley Railroad about 1900 and at one time was an ice cream parlor.

e. Ivy Manor (brick) was built in 1850 as a home by Noah M. Marker, "prominent merchant, legislator and civic leader." This building, with much of the original woodwork, is presently a restaurant owned by the Brant family. *Location:* Corner of East Main and South St. Clair Streets.

Note: Marker built another brick house, for his son, on 108 South Market Street.

f. Shaw House (brick) was built before 1830 by Bales McColly, who operated a harness shop next to his home. *Location:* 204 East Main Street.

g. Clark House (frame) was built about 1796 by William Ashcom. The building was originally a cobbler's shop. *Location:* 230 East Main Street.

h. Robb Shop (frame), known as the "crooked house," is over 150 years old. It was a cabinet- and coffin-makers shop. *Location:* 243 East Main Street.

i. Graham House (brick) was built before 1860, probably by Robert Graham. Later owners were William Houston, Edmond Kibble, Reuben Wilt, and the Menoher family. *Location:* 131 West Main Street.

j. Miller House (frame) was built by the Miller family about 1850 and was later occupied by C. F. Cairns. An outdoor bake oven, smokeshop, and workshop are also on the property. *Location:* 216 East Church Street.

k. Stitt Jewelry Store (brick) was built in the 1840s and at one time belonged to the Stecks. Conrad George, a cabinet maker, also lived here. *Location:* 111 South Market Street.

l. Cook Insurance Office (brick) was built in the 1830s, probably by the Steck family, descendants of John Michael Steck, first Lutheran minister west of the Alleghenies. The Noah Marker family also lived here at one time. *Location:* 115 South Market Street.

m. Bunger Spring, originally known as Bonjour Spring, was named for Andrew Bonjour, a wagoner with Gen. John Forbes's army and a tavern keeper in 1771. Andrew's wife, Barbara, owned this land, which was later purchased by Arthur St. Clair. The saying about this spring, which is still in use, is, "Once you drink from Bunger Spring, you will always return to Ligonier Valley." *Location:* Near Bunger Street, northwest section of town.

125. Speedwell Carding Mill (stone) was operated by Abraham Brant and produced yarn, blankets, and cloth until 1896. The mill, originally built of logs and rebuilt with stone quarried nearby, was closed after Abraham's death, and his son John A. Brant sold the property to Edward S. Carne in 1906. It was restored in 1917 and used as a gristmill. The mill, part of the Rolling Rock property, functions today as a pumping station, sending water from McGinnis Run to Rolling Rock Club at the top of the hill. Stones from the millrace were used to build the small bridge nearby. The brick house next to the mill was erected before 1800. *Location:* Five miles southeast of Ligonier, off Pa. 381 near Rolling Rock Racetrack on private road (wildlife preserve) at Rector.

126. Powdermill Nature Reserve Museum, a gift of Alan Scaife and Gen. Richard K. Mellon, is a field station of Carnegie Museum in Pittsburgh. It contains displays of mounted birds and mammals, wax flowers, and models of amphibians and reptiles at an 1,800-acre sanctuary devoted to the study of the flora and fauna of the Ligonier Valley. At one time the property included an early powder mill on the nearby run. Although the sanctuary is closed to the public in order to maintain undisturbed environmental conditions, the small roadside museum and a bird-banding laboratory are open. *Hours:* April–October: Saturday and Sunday, 9 A.M.–5 P.M. *Location:* Southeast of Ligonier, on Pa. 381, about three miles south of Rector.

127. Robbins House (log) was built before 1800. William (Billey) Robbins had a shoe shop in this house in the early 1800s. The

132. *Compass Inn*

second story was added early in the nineteenth century by a soldier who was later killed in the Civil War. *Location:* South of Ligonier on Pa. 381, near Rolling Rock Club.

128. Boucher-Beebe House (brick) is believed to have been built by the family of historian John Newton Boucher. This home at one time had a veranda and white pillars. It was later owned by Mrs. Amanda Smith. *Location:* Near Ligonier, on Pa. 711 about 0.5 mile south of its junction with U.S. 30.

Note: Across the road is another brick house built in 1830 by the Boucher family. It was later owned by Gen. John Ramsey, who laid out the town of Ligonier.

129. Forbes Road Gun Museum (brick) contains a wide collection of more than 500 firearms dating from the year 1450 to models of the present day. The museum is operated by Russell Payne, third in a line of gunsmiths who have worked in the area for more than 100 years. *Hours:* 9 A.M.–dusk. *Admission charge.* Special group rates. *Location:* Four miles north of Ligonier, on Pa. 711.

130. Pleasant Grove Presbyterian Church (stone), formerly called Old Donegal, was organized in April 1785. George Hill became the first pastor in 1792. The name of the church was changed from Old Donegal to Pleasant Grove between 1856 and 1859. The first two meetinghouses, which stood south of the present church, were built of logs. The present church was built in 1832 and rebuilt in 1892. *Location:* 4.2 miles north on Pa. 711 from its junction with Pa. 130 in Stahlstown; thence 0.3 mile on private road from "church arrow" on Pa. 711.

Note: At this location are two early one-room structures: a schoolhouse and an 1857 Evangelical United Brethren church (later Methodist).

131. Warden House (fieldstone), possibly built before 1789, has chestnut beams and hand-forged iron hinges. This restored structure at one time was a store. *Location:* Stahlstown, on Pa. 711.

132. Compass Inn (stone and log) was built in 1799 by Philip Freeman, whose license is preserved in the inn. Frederick Meyers operated it until it was taken over by the Armor family in 1813. Seven generations of Armors occupied the building until the Ligonier Valley Historical Society acquired it in 1968.

The inn accommodated drovers and travelers coming over the Philadelphia-Pittsburgh Turnpike (now U.S. 30). Among its early guests were Daniel Webster, Henry

Clay, Andrew Jackson, William Henry Harrison, and Zachary Taylor—who held a political reception here in 1849. One guest, Sally Hastings, wrote in her diary in 1808 that the inn had "one large, unfinished and unfurnished room, with a Kitchen of equal dimensions."

The building is now completely furnished with authentic nineteenth-century items. A newly constructed log barn behind the inn contains other interesting exhibits. *Hours:* May–November: Tuesday–Saturday, 10 A.M.– 5 P.M. Sunday, 1–5 P.M. Candlelight tours are arranged on weekends during November until December 14. *Admission charge. Location:* Laughlintown, on U.S. 30 east of Ligonier.

Note: Across the road is an old-time general store open daily, except Sunday, from 8 A.M. to 6 P.M.

133. Naugle Inn (weatherboard), sometimes called "the Yellow House," was built near the end of the eighteenth century by William Curry. It was later purchased by Joseph Naugle and is still owned by descendants of this family. The structure, with a double balcony or drovers' porch and a special wine cellar, was the only tavern in the area in continuous use from 1830 to 1885. *Location:* Laughlintown, on U.S. 30, east end of town.

134. Jacob Kinsey Memorial Museum (log), authentically furnished, consists of four early buildings that have been moved to the site from other locations. The largest is a log house of mortise and tenon construction which had been the earliest schoolhouse in Juniata County. The washhouse was formerly used by a third-generation Kinsey family and contains a beehive oven. Another structure contains a collection of primitive tools, and the fourth is a small smokehouse. The museum is a nonprofit organization operated by a family whose ancestors, Jacob and Eliza Kemp Kintzy, migrated from Germany to Bedford County in 1795. *Hours:* Memorial Day– Labor Day: Saturday, Sunday, and holidays, 2–7 P.M. *Admission charge.* Special group rates. *Location:* Waterford, on Pa. 271 northeast of Ligonier.

135. McKelvey House (brick) was built in 1851 by Reuben McKinley McKelvey. This property in 1777 belonged to Capt. Robert Knox, commander of Fort Preservation. Known as the Reliance Tract, it was originally owned by Gen. Arthur St. Clair. A later owner

134. *Jacob Kinsey Memorial Museum*

was Rev. Scroggs. *Location:* Between Oak Grove and Waterford, on Pa. 271.

136. Jones Mill (frame), for which the town was named, was built before 1800 and was originally powered by water. The present mill has the name of Matthews on it. *Location:* Jones Mills, on Pa. 31 about three miles north of Champion.

Pennsylvania Historical and Museum Commission Markers

Arthur St. Clair   U.S. 30, 6.5 miles northwest of Ligonier

Bushy Run   U.S. 30 at Jeannette; Adamsburg, U.S. 30 at l.r. 64096; Delmont, old U.S. 22 and Pa. 66; and at property on Pa. 993, 1 mile east of Harrison City

Dagworthy's Camp   U.S. 30, 8.3 miles east of Greensburg

Forbes Road   U.S. 22, 1.2 mile east of Murrysville; and U.S. 22 east of Murrysville

Fort Allen   Pa. 136 southwest of Greensburg

Fort Ligonier   Ligonier, Main and Marker Streets

Hanna's Town   Pa. 819 north of Greensburg

Henry Clay Frick   U.S. 119 north of Scottdale

John W. Geary   Pa. 31 east of Mount Pleasant

Johnston House   U.S. 30, 7 miles northwest of Ligonier

Loyalhanning   U.S. 30 southeast of Ligonier

Murrysville Gas Well   Murrysville, U.S. 22

Saint Vincent   U.S. 30, 6.6 miles east of Greensburg at entrance to college

Saint Xavier's   U.S. 30, 6 miles east of Greensburg at Saint Xavier

Toll House   Greensburg, at Mount Odin Park

Toll House   Greensburg, East Pittsburgh Street east of Stark Street

Twelve Mile Camp   U.S. 30, 7.1 miles east of Greensburg

West Newton   Pa. 136 at bridge

Bibliography

No attempt will be made to list manuscript collections, theses, monographs, and other specialty items applicable to one or two sites. These are more in the realm of the researcher than the historical pilgrim to whom this book is addressed. (A fair listing of these—at least for the early period—may be found in Mulkearn and Pugh's *A Traveler's Guide to Historic Western Pennsylvania,* available in most libraries. For a fuller listing of published works up to 1957 the reader may consult Norman B. Wilkinson's *Bibliography of Pennsylvania History* [Harrisburg: Pennsylvania Historical and Museum Commission, 1957]). For the same reason, we are not including maps or atlases, although helpful material may be found by the researcher in atlases published for various counties and in the warrantee atlas maps of original land grants, available in Harrisburg and in some county courthouses and large libraries. Much material, especially for Allegheny County, is to be found in the *Western Pennsylvania Historical Magazine* and in publications of several other county and regional historical groups. The titles listed here are limited to those most likely to be available and helpful to the person seeking more information on some of the sites in this work.

General Works

Agnew, Daniel. *A History of the Region of Pennsylvania North of the Ohio and West of the Allegheny River.* Philadelphia, 1887.

Albert, George Dallas. *Report of the Commission to Locate the Site of the Frontier Forts of Pennsylvania.* Vol. 2. Harrisburg, 1896.

Day, Sherman. *Historical Collections of the State of Pennsylvania.* Philadelphia, 1843.

Egle, W. H. *An Illustrated History of the Commonwealth of Pennsylvania.* Harrisburg, 1876.

Esbenshade, A. H. *Pennsylvania Place Names.* State College, Pa., 1925.

Godcharles, Frederic A. *Daily Stories of Pennsylvania.* Milton, Pa., 1924.

———. *Pennsylvania, Political, Governmental, Military and Civil.* New York, 1933.

Guidebook to Historic Places in Western Pennsylvania. Pittsburgh, 1938.

Haas, Henry A. *Guide to the Historical Markers of Pennsylvania.* Harrisburg, 1975.

Jenkins, H. M., ed. *Pennsylvania, Colonial and Federal* . . . . Philadelphia, 1903.

McKnight, W. J. *A Pioneer Outline History of Northwestern Pennsylvania.* Philadelphia, 1905.

Montgomery, Thomas L., ed. *Report of the Commission to Locate the Site of the Frontier Forts of Pennsylvania.* Vol. 1. Harrisburg, 1896.

Mulkearn, Lois, and Pugh, Edwin V. *A Traveler's Guide to Historic Western Pennsylvania.* Pittsburgh, 1954.

Pates, Mrs. William S., ed. *Historia.* Tarentum, Pa., 1972.

Pennsylvania Historical Commission. *Marking the Historic Sites of Early Pennsylvania.* Harrisburg, 1926.

Pennsylvania Writers Project. *Pennsylvania Cavalcade.* Philadelphia, 1942.

———. *Pennsylvania, A Guide to the Keystone State.* New York, 1940.

Ray, J. W. *A History of Western Pennsylvania.* Erie, Pa., 1941.

Rieseman, Joseph. *History of Northwestern Pennsylvania.* New York, 1943.

Rupp, I. D. *Early History of Western Pennsylvania.* Pittsburgh, 1846.

Searight, T. B. *The Old Pike.* Uniontown, 1894.

Sharp, Myron, and Thomas, William H. *Guide to Old Stone Blast Furnaces in Western Pennsylvania.* Pittsburgh, 1966.

Stevens, S. K. *Pennsylvania, Birthplace of a Nation.* New York, 1964.

Stotz, Charles Morse. *The Architectural Heritage of Early Western Pennsylvania*. 1936. Reprint, Pittsburgh, 1966.

Swank, J. M. *Progressive Pennsylvania*. Philadelphia, 1908.

Swetnam, George. *Pennsylvania Transportation*. 2d ed. Gettysburg, Pa., 1968.

———. *Pittsylvania Country*. New York, 1951.

Van Atta, Robert B. *Guide to Allegheny Power System Service Area Communities' Cultural, Historic, and Recreation Attractions*. Greensburg, Pa., 1970.

Walkinshaw, L. C. *Annals of Southwestern Pennsylvania*. New York, 1939.

Wallace, Paul A. W. *Indian Paths of Pennsylvania*. Harrisburg, 1965.

Allegheny County

Baldwin, L. D. *Pittsburgh: The Story of a City*. Pittsburgh, 1937. Reprinted in paperback, Pittsburgh, 1970.

Borkowski, Joseph A. *Historical Highlights and Sites of Lawrenceville Area*. Pittsburgh, 1969.

Botset, Elizabeth K., and Waldrop, George B. *Fox Chapel: The Story of a District*. Pittsburgh, 1954.

Boucher, J. N. *A Century and a Half of Pittsburg and Her People*. New York, 1908.

Cushing, Thomas, ed. *History of Allegheny County, Pa.* Chicago, 1889.

Fleming, G. T. *History of Pittsburgh and Environs*. New York, 1922.

Group for Historical Research. *Annals of Old Wilkinsburg and Vicinity*. Wilkinsburg, Pa., 1940.

Harper, F. C. *Pittsburgh of Today: Its Resources and People*. New York, 1931.

Johnston, W. G. *Life and Reminiscences*. Pittsburgh, 1901.

Lambing, A. A., and White, J. W. F. *Allegheny County: Its Early History and Subsequent Development*. Pittsburgh, 1888.

Lorant, Stefan. *Pittsburgh: The Story of an American City*. New York, 1964. Reprint, Lenox, Mass., 1975.

Parke, J. E. *Recollections of Seventy Years*. Boston, 1886.

Swetnam, George. *Where Else but Pittsburgh!* Pittsburgh, 1958.

Thompson, Noah. *Early History of the Peters Creek Valley and the Early Settlers*. N.p., 1974.

Thurston, G. H. *Allegheny County's Hundred Years*. Pittsburgh, 1888.

Van Trump, James D., and Ziegler, Arthur P., Jr. *Landmark Architecture of Allegheny County, Pennsylvania*. Pittsburgh, 1967.

Wilson, Erasmus, ed. *Standard History of Pittsburg*. Chicago, 1898.

Armstrong County

Armstrong County, Pennsylvania . . . . Chicago, 1914.

Smith, R. W. *History of Armstrong County*. Chicago, 1883.

Wiley, S. T. *Biographical and Historical Cyclopedia of Indiana and ₊Armstrong Counties, Pennsylvania*. Philadelphia, 1891.

Beaver County

Bausman, J. H. *History of Beaver County, Pennsylvania*. New York, 1904.

History of Monaca. Monaca, Pa., [1940].

Hoover, G. L. *Historic Stone Houses on the South Side of Beaver County*. N.p., 1969.

Richard, J. F. *History of Beaver County, Pennsylvania* . . . . Chicago, 1888.

Bedford County

Blackburn, E. H., and Welfley, William H. *History of Bedford and Somerset Counties, Pennsylvania*. Vol. 1. New York, 1906.

Garbrick, Winona, ed. *The Kernel of Greatness*. State College, Pa., 1971.

Hall, William M. *Reminiscences and Sketches*. Harrisburg, 1890.

History of Bedford, Somerset and Fulton Counties, Pennsylvania. Chicago, 1884.

Jordan, William, ed. *Bedford County Pennsylvania, Historical Background*. Bedford, Pa., 1973.

Rupp, I. D. *History of Bedford, Somerset, Cambria and Indiana Counties*. Lancaster, Pa., 1848.

Schell, W. P. *The Annals of Bedford County*. Bedford, Pa., 1907.

Blair County

Adams, P. G. *History of Hollidaysburg, 1790–1870*. State College, Pa., 1939.

Africa, J. S. *History of Huntingdon and Blair Counties*. Philadelphia, 1883.

Clark, C. B. *A History of Blair County, Pennsylvania, 1846–1896*. Altoona, Pa., 1896.

Davis, T. S., ed. *A History of Blair County, Pennsylvania*. Harrisburg, 1931.

Ewing, J. H. *A History of the City of Altoona and Blair County*. Altoona, Pa., 1880.

Sell, J. C. *Twentieth Century History of Altoona and Blair County, Pennsylvania*. Chicago, 1911.

Wolf, G. A., ed. *Blair County's First Hundred Years*. Altoona, Pa., 1945.

Butler County

Brown, R. C., ed. *History of Butler County, Pennsylvania*. Chicago, 1895.

Butler County Pennsylvania . . . . Butler, Pa., 1950.

History of Butler County, Pennsylvania. Chicago, 1883.

McKee, J. A., ed. *20th Century History of Butler and Butler County, Pennsylvania*. Chicago, 1909.

Sipe, C. H. *History of Butler County, Pennsylvania*. Indianapolis, 1927.

Cambria County

Connelly, Frank, and Jenks, G. C. *Official History of the Johnstown Flood*. Pittsburgh, 1889.

McLaurin, J. J. *The Story of Johnstown* . . . . Harrisburg, 1890.

Rupp, I. D. *History of Bedford, Somerset, Cambria and Indiana Counties*. Lancaster, Pa., 1848.

Storey, H. W. *History of Cambria County, Pennsylvania*. New York, 1907.

Swank, J. M. *Cambria County Pioneers* . . . . Philadelphia, 1910.

Cameron County

Leeson, M. A., ed. *History of the Counties of McKean, Elk, Forest, Cameron and Potter, Pennsylvania*. Chicago, 1890.

Clarion County

Caldwell, J. A. *Caldwell's Illustrated Historical Combination Atlas of Clarion County Pennsylvania* . . . . Condit, Ohio, 1877. Reprint, with supplemental data, Rimersburg, Pa., 1964.

Clarion County Centennial. [Clarion, Pa.], 1940.

Davis, A. J. *History of Clarion County, Pennsylvania*. Syracuse, N.Y., 1887. Reprint, with historical supplement, Rimersburg, Pa., 1968.

Niece, B. F., ed. *Souvenir Book of Clarion, Pa.* N.p., n.d.

Clearfield County

Aldrich, L. C. *History of Clearfield County, Pennsylvania*. Syracuse, N.Y., 1887.

Barrett, H. G. *History of Clearfield County, Pennsylvania*. Altoona, Pa., 1896.

McCreight, M. I. *Memory Sketches of Du Bois, Pennsylvania*. Du Bois, Pa., 1938.

Pentz, W. C. *The City of Du Bois*. Du Bois, Pa., 1932.

Swoope, R. D. *Twentieth Century History of Clearfield County, Pennsylvania*. Chicago, [1911].

Wall, T. L. *Clearfield County, Present and Past*. Clearfield, Pa., [1925?].

Crawford County

Bates, S. P. *Our County and Its People*. N.p., 1899.

Brown, R. C., et al. *History of Crawford County, Pennsylvania*. Chicago, 1885.

Huidekoper, Alfred. *Incidents in the Early History of Crawford County*. Philadelphia, 1850.

Miller, F. G. *Our Own Pioneers*. Meadville, Pa., 1929.

Reynolds, J. E. *In French Creek Valley*. Meadville, Pa., 1938.

Elk County

Leeson, M. A., ed. *History of the Counties of McKean, Elk, Forest, Cameron and Potter, Pennsylvania*. Chicago, 1890.

Schout, C. J. *Early St. Marys and Some of Its People*. Clearfield, Pa., 1952.

Erie County

Federal Writers Project. *Erie: A Guide to the City and County*. Philadelphia, 1938.

Miller, John. *A Twentieth Century History of Erie County, Pennsylvania*. Chicago, 1909.

Reed, J. E. *History of Erie County, Pennsylvania*. Indianapolis, 1925.

Robbins, D. P. *Popular History of Erie County, Pennsylvania*. Erie, Pa., 1895.

Sanford, L. G. *The History of Erie County, Pennsylvania*. Philadelphia, 1894.

Spencer, Herbert R., and Jack, Walter. *Roaming Erie County*. Erie, Pa., 1958.

BIBLIOGRAPHY

Whitman, Benjamin, and Russell, N. W. *History of Erie County, Pennsylvania.* Chicago, 1884.

Fayette County

Ellis, Franklin. *History of Fayette County, Pennsylvania.* Philadelphia, 1882.
Hadden, James. *A History of Uniontown* . . . . Akron, Ohio, 1913.
Hart, J. P., ed. *Hart's History and Directory of . . . Brownsville, Bridgeport and West Brownsville.* Cadwallader, Pa., 1904.
McClenathan, J. C. *Centennial History of the Borough of Connellsville, Pennsylvania, 1806–1906.* Columbus, Ohio, 1906.
Nelson, S. B. *Nelson's Biographical Dictionary and Historical Reference Book of Fayette County, Pennsylvania.* Uniontown, Pa., 1900.
Wiley, S. T. *Biographical and Portrait Cyclopedia of Fayette County, Pennsylvania.* Chicago, 1889.

Forest County

Irwin, S. D. *History of Forest County.* Tionesta, Pa., 1876.
Leeson, M. A., ed. *History of the Counties of McKean, Elk, Forest, Cameron and Potter, Pennsylvania.* Chicago, 1890.

Greene County

Bates, S. P. *History of Greene County, Pennsylvania.* Chicago, 1888.
Evans, L. K. *Pioneer History of Greene County, Pennsylvania.* Waynesburg, Pa., 1941.
Hanna, William. *History of Greene County, Pennsylvania* . . . . N.p., 1882.
High, Fred. *Waynesburg, Prosperous and Beautiful.* Waynesburg, Pa., 1905.

Indiana County

Caldwell, J. A. *History of Indiana County, Pennsylvania.* Newark, Ohio, 1880.
Rupp, I. D. *History of Bedford, Somerset, Cambria and Indiana Counties.* Lancaster, Pa., 1848.
Stewart, J. T., ed. *Indiana County Pennsylvania* . . . . Chicago, 1913.
Trexler, R. O. *History of Armagh, Pennsylvania.* N.p., 1950.
Wiley, S. T. *Biographical and Historical Cyclopedia of Indiana and Armstrong Counties, Pennsylvania.* Philadelphia, 1891.

Jefferson County

Elliott, W. C. *History of Reynoldsville and Vicinity.* Punxsutawney, Pa., 1922.
McKnight, W. J. *Jefferson County, Pennsylvania* . . . . Chicago, 1917.
———. *Pioneer History of Jefferson County, Pennsylvania.* Philadelphia, 1898.
Scott, K. M., ed. *History of Jefferson County, Pennsylvania.* Syracuse, N.Y., 1888.
Smith, W. O. *Punxsutawney, 1772–1909.* Punxsutawney, Pa., 1909.

Lawrence County

Book of Biographies: Sketches of Leading Citizens of Lawrence County, Pennsylvania. Buffalo, N.Y., 1897.
Durant, S. W. *History of Lawrence County, Pennsylvania.* Philadelphia, 1877.
Hazen, A. L., ed. *20th Century History of New Castle and Lawrence County, Pennsylvania.* Chicago, 1908.
Wood, W. W. *Historical Review of the Towns and Business Houses . . . of Lawrence County.* New Castle, Pa., 1887.

McKean County

Hatch, V. A., ed. *Illustrated History of Bradford, McKean County, Pennsylvania.* Bradford, Pa., 1901.
Henretta, J. E. *Kane and the Upper Allegheny.* Philadelphia, 1929.
Leeson, M. A., ed. *History of the Counties of McKean, Elk, Forest, Cameron and Potter, Pennsylvania.* Chicago, 1890.
McDonnell, F. M., ed. *The Book of Bradford* . . . . Bradford, Pa., 1897.
Stone, R. B. *McKean, the Governor's County.* New York, 1926.

Mercer County

Dayton, David M. *'Mid the Pines.* Grove City, Pa., 1971.
Durant, S. W. *History of Mercer County, Pennsylvania.* Philadelphia, 1877.
History of Mercer County, Pennsylvania . . . . Chicago, 1888.
History of Sharpsville, Pennsylvania. Sharpsville, 1949.

White, J. G., ed. *A 20th Century History of Mercer County, Pennsylvania.* New York, 1909.

Somerset County

Blackburn, E. H., and Welfley, William H. *History of Bedford and Somerset Counties, Pennsylvania.* Vol. 2. New York, 1906.

Cassaday, J. C. *The Somerset County Outline.* Scottdale, Pa., 1932.

Doyle, Frederic. *Early Somerset County.* Somerset, Pa., 1945.

Hause, Mary. *A Somerset County Historical Notebook.* Somerset, Pa., 1945.

Rupp, I. D. *History of Bedford, Somerset, Cambria and Indiana Counties.* Lancaster, Pa., 1948.

Venango County

Babcock, C. A. *Venango County, Pennsylvania: Her Pioneers and Her People.* Chicago, 1919.

Bell, H. C., ed. *History of Venango County, Pennsylvania.* Chicago, 1890.

The Historical Album. Franklin, Pa., 1968.

Newton, J. H., ed. *History of Venango County, Pennsylvania . . . .* Columbus, Ohio, 1879.

Warren County

Bristow, Arch. *Old Time Tales of Warren County.* Meadville, Pa., 1932.

Putnam, Mary, and Putnam, Chase, eds. *Historic Buildings in Warren County.* 3 vols. Warren, Pa., 1971–74.

Schenck, J. S., ed. *History of Warren County, Pennsylvania.* Syracuse, N.Y., 1887.

Smith, B. A., ed. *Historical Collections of Sheffield Township, Warren County, Pennsylvania.* Warren, Pa., 1943.

Warren Library Association. *Warren Centennial.* Warren, Pa., 1897.

Washington County

Baker, W. A., Jr., ed. *Canonsburg, Pennsylvania, 1773–1936.* Canonsburg, Pa., 1936.

Campbell, June, and Slasor, Kathryn, comps. *So Firm a Foundation: A History of the Tucker Methodist Church.* N.p., 1965.

Commemorative Biographical Record of Washington County, Pennsylvania. Chicago, 1893.

Creigh, Alfred. *History of Washington County . . . .* Washington, Pa., 1870.

Crumrine, Boyd. *History of Washington County, Pennsylvania.* Philadelphia, 1882.

Forrest, E. R. *History of Washington County, Pennsylvania.* Chicago, 1926.

"Historical Stops in Washington County." Typescript, Washington Area Community Resources Workshop. Washington, Pa., 1959.

McFarland, J. F. *20th Century History of the City of Washington and Washington County . . . .* Chicago, 1910.

Preserving Our Past. Washington, Pa., 1975.

Reader, F. S. *Some Pioneers of Washington County, Pennsylvania.* New Brighton, Pa., 1902.

Thompson, Noah. *Early History of the Peters Creek Valley and the Early Settlers.* N.p., 1974.

Westmoreland County

Albert, G. D. *History of the County of Westmoreland, Pennsylvania.* Philadelphia, 1882.

Altman, G. P., and Agnew, Thomas. *Tales from Tinker Run.* Irwin, Pa., 1972.

Biographical and Historical Cyclopedia of Westmoreland County, Pennsylvania. Philadelphia, 1890.

Bomberger, C. M. *Brush Creek Tales.* Jeannette, Pa., 1950.

———. *A Short History of Westmoreland County . . . .* Jeannette, Pa., 1941.

Boucher, J. N. *History of Westmoreland County, Pennsylvania.* New York, 1906.

———. *Old and New Westmoreland.* New York, 1918.

City of Greensburg: A History. Greensburg, Pa., 1949.

Foley, Helene M., and Berger, Marion L. *This Is Murrysville.* Murrysville, Pa., 1959.

History of Greensburg . . . . Greensburg, Pa., 1899.

History of Our City, Monessen, Pennsylvania. Columbus, Ohio, 1902.

Laughlintown, Pennsylvania, 1797–1947. Laughlintown, Pa., 1947.

Pollins, John W. *Dr. Frank Cowan: A Biographical Sketch.* Greensburg, Pa., 1950.

Studer, Gerald C., ed. *Over the Alleghenies.* Scottdale, Pa., 1965.

Woman's Club of Ligonier. *Our Heritage in Ligonier Valley.* Ligonier, Pa., 1963, 1965, 1976.

Index of Sites and Proper Names

Italicized page numbers indicate illustrations. The index beginning on page 287 lists the towns and cities where the sites are located. The index beginning on page 290 breaks down the sites according to category and then by county.

278

279

INDEX OF SITES AND PROPER NAMES

Index of Site Locations

Classified Index

Each of the categories in this index is broken down according to county. The numbers refer to sites, not to pages. Allegheny County areas are abbreviated as follows:

P(GT):   Pittsburgh—The Golden Triangle (pp. 6–9)
P(L):   Pittsburgh—Lawrenceville (pp. 9–11)
P(U,O,H):   Pittsburgh—Uptown, Oakland, Hazelwood (pp. 11–15)
P(EE):   Pittsburgh—East End (pp. 15–18)
P(NS):   Pittsburgh—North Side (pp. 18–19)
P(SS,WE):   Pittsburgh—South Side and West End (pp. 19–20)
E: Suburban—East (pp. 21–23)
W,NW: Suburban—West and Northwest (pp. 23–26)
N: Suburban—North (pp. 26–29)
S: Suburban—South (pp. 29–33)

Auditoriums. See Theaters, auditoriums, and arenas

Barns: Allegheny: E, 14, 18; W,NW, 17, 20; N, 19; S, 9; Beaver, 20; Bedford, 24; Blair, 30; Clearfield, 11; Crawford, 23; Erie, 33; Jefferson, 18; Mercer, 14, 46; Somerset, 7, 10; Washington, 37, 44, 46, 68, 79, 102, 132, 136; Westmoreland, 30, 39, 75m, 103, 109

Botanical gardens and nature preserves: Allegheny: P(U,O,H), 10; P(NS), 6; Beaver, 51; Butler, 32; Cambria, 17; Westmoreland, 126

Bridges: Allegheny: P(GT), 29, 34; E, 7, 20; Armstrong, 22; Beaver, 14; Bedford, 23, 27; Blair, 9; Butler, 13a, 39a; Cambria, 9c, 13; Clarion, 7; Clearfield, 14; Fayette, 31, 69; Greene, 11; Indiana, 18; Lawrence, 7; McKean, 12; Mercer, 21; Somerset, 4, 14, 15; Washington, 26, 131; Westmoreland, 58

Businesses and office buildings: Allegheny: P(GT), 3–6, 9–12, 14–17, 19–23, 27, 29–33; P(L), 1, 3, 5, 7, 14; P(U,O,H), 7d, 19, 20; P(EE), 8; P(NS), 13; E, 6, 19; W, NW, 5; S, 20
   Bedford, 2, 9, 55; Blair, 30, 34; Butler, 8, 24d, 26c, 39a, 39d, 40; Cameron, 8; Crawford, 19–21, 28; Elk, 13; Erie, 14, 29, 43; Fayette, 41, 89a, 89d, 89e, 89i; Indiana, 2; Jefferson, 20; Lawrence, 9; McKean, 10, 16; Mercer, 42; Washington, 17, 23, 34, 47, 57d, 116; Westmoreland, 85, 88c, 88f, 93b, 118a, 124h, 124k, 124l

Canals and locks: Beaver, 12; Crawford, 10, 13; Mercer, 31

Cemeteries and graves: Allegheny: P(GT), 13; P(L), 15; P(SS,WE), 6; E, 5, 8, 10; W,NW, 3, 11; N, 17, 21; S, 5, 13
   Armstrong, 11; Beaver, 30, 50, 55, 56, 62; Bedford, 4, 6, 41; Butler, 22, 24k, 24l, 27, 31, 32, 39c; Cambria, 9d, 19, 23; Clearfield, 2; Crawford, 24; Elk, 10; Erie, 18, 24, 42; Fayette, 11, 26, 33, 42–44, 46, 56, 80, 89f,

93; Forest, 4, 7; Greene, 5, 21, 28; Indiana, 6, 15, 16, 37, 39; Jefferson, 21c; McKean, 15; Mercer, 24, 26–28, 47, 50; Somerset, 9; Venango, 5; Washington, 15, 41–43, 54, 59, 69, 87, 98, 101, 109, 114, 119, 121, 137; Westmoreland, 16, 23, 24, 29, 32, 35, 44, 45, 47, 48, 57, 59, 60, 70, 71, 75m, 75q, 76, 80, 87, 93d, 101, 114

Churches, chapels, and cathedrals: Allegheny: P(GT), 13, 18, 24, 26; P(L), 6, 8; P(U,O,H), 2, 5, 7c, 8, 13, 15–17; P(EE), 3, 4, 9, 11, 16; P(NS), 8, 10, 11, 15, 16; P(SS,WE), 4, 6, 9; E, 3, 5, 8, 16; W,NW, 3, 6, 11, 15, 21; N, 1, 9, 13, 18, 19, 28; S, 5, 10, 21, 22, 25
   Armstrong, 5, 11, 16, 18, 23; Beaver, 7, 22, 23, 36, 39f, 41, 42, 49, 50, 53, 55, 56; Bedford, 4, 6, 30, 31, 52; Blair, 3, 13, 17, 27, 28, 35; Butler, 5, 7, 13c, 15, 22, 24j, 24l, 26b, 27, 28, 31, 32, 36; Cambria, 15, 19, 20, 23; Cameron, 6; Clarion, 5, 8b, 10, 11; Clearfield, 2; Crawford, 5–7, 12, 18; Elk, 10, 12; Erie, 3, 11, 44, 52; Fayette, 11, 26, 27, 33, 37, 39, 42, 44, 47, 80b, 89f; Greene, 2, 3, 9, 13, 21; Indiana, 15, 16, 20, 30, 34, 39, 40; Jefferson, 25; Lawrence, 3, 5, 15; McKean, 8, 15; Mercer, 6, 8, 44, 51, 54; Somerset, 14, 24a, 24b, 25, 27; Venango, 2, 15, 16; Warren, 14, 20, 26; Washington, 4, 15, 19, 24, 41, 49, 53–55, 57b, 59a, 59c, 61, 69, 74, 85, 87, 91, 92, 96, 97, 109, 111, 113, 117, 120, 121, 125, 135d, 135h, 135i, 135i, 137, 138; Westmoreland, 17, 24–27, 31, 32, 35, 36, 39, 44, 45, 47, 48, 50, 52, 58, 60, 65, 66, 74, 75b, 75q, 76, 79, 80, 81, 83, 86, 88b, 89a, 93d, 101, 113, 114, 120, 130

Clocks: Allegheny: P(GT), 4; E, 19; Beaver, 39f; Butler, 1, 24a, 24j; Erie, 11; Warren, 1

Colleges and universities: P(GT), 11, 28; P(L), 8; P(U,O,H), 3, 6, 7, 12; P(EE), 6; P(NS), 4; Beaver, 6, 17; Butler, 7, 34; Cambria, 16, 17; Clarion, 3; Crawford, 8; Erie, 5, 23, 50; Greene, 2, 9; Indiana, 7; Lawrence, 10; Mercer, 23, 43; Washington, 3, 78, 99; Westmoreland, 9, 113